DATE DUE

DEMCO 38-296

CONTEMPORARY MUSICIANS

CONTEMPORARY MUSICALS

ISSN 1044-2197

CONTEMPORARY MUSICIANS

PROFILES OF THE PEOPLE IN MUSIC

MICHAEL L. LaBLANC,
Editor

VOLUME 4

Includes Cumulated Indexes

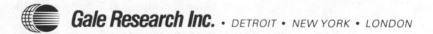 **Gale Research Inc.** · DETROIT · NEW YORK · LONDON

While every effort has been made to ensure the reliability of the information presented in this publication, Gale Research Inc. does not guarantee the accuracy of the data contained herein. Gale accepts no payment for listing; and inclusion in the publication of any organization, agency, institution, publication, service, or individual does not imply endorsement of the editors or publisher. Errors brought to the attention of the publisher and verified to the satisfaction of the publisher will be corrected in future editions.

The paper used in this publication meets the minimum requirements
of American National Standard for Information Sciences—Permanence
Paper for Printed Library Materials, ANSI Z39.48-1984.

Library of Congress Catalog Card Number 90-656201
ISBN 0-8103-2214-5
ISSN 1044-2197

Printed in the United States of America

Published simultaneously in the United Kingdom
by Gale Research International Limited
(An affiliated company of Gale Research Inc.)

Computerized photocomposition by
Roberts/Churcher
Derby Line, Vermont

Contents

Introduction ix

Photo Credits xi

Cumulative Subject Index 265

Cumulative Musicians Index 275

Introduction

Fills the Information Gap on Today's Musicians

Contemporary Musicians profiles the colorful personalities in the music industry who create or influence the music we hear today. Prior to *Contemporary Musicians*, no quality reference series provided comprehensive information on such a wide range of artists despite keen and ongoing public interest. To find biographical and critical coverage, an information seeker had little choice but to wade through the offerings of the popular press, scan television "infotainment" programs, and search for the occasional published biography or expose. *Contemporary Musicians* is designed to serve that information seeker, providing in one ongoing source in-depth coverage of the important figures on the modern music scene in a format that is both informative and entertaining. Students, researchers, and casual browsers alike can use *Contemporary Musicians* to fill their needs for personal information about the artists, find a selected discography of the musician's recordings, and read an insightful essay offering biographical and critical information.

Provides Broad Coverage

Single-volume biographical sources on musicians are limited in scope, focusing on a handful of performers from a specific musical genre or era. In contrast, *Contemporary Musicians* offers researchers and music devotees a comprehensive, informative, and entertaining alternative. *Contemporary Musicians* is published twice yearly, with each volume providing information on 80 to 100 musical artists from all the genres that form the broad spectrum of contemporary music—pop, rock, jazz, blues, country, new wave, New Age, blues, folk, rhythm and blues, gospel, bluegrass, and reggae, to name a few, as well as selected classical artists who have achieved "crossover" success with the general public. *Contemporary Musicians* will occasionally include profiles of influential nonperforming members of the music industry, including producers, promoters, and record company executives.

Includes Popular Features

In *Contemporary Musicians* you'll find popular features that users value:

- **Easy-to-locate data sections**—Vital personal statistics, chronological career summaries, listings of major awards, and mailing addresses, when available, are prominently displayed in a clearly marked box on the second page of each entry.

- **Biographical/critical essays**—Colorful and informative essays trace each personality's personal and professional life, offer representative examples of critical response to each artist's work, and provide entertaining personal sidelights.

- **Selected discographies**—Each entry provides a comprehensive listing of the artist's major recorded works.

- **Photographs**—Most entries include portraits of the artists.

- **Sources for additional information**—This invaluable feature directs the user to selected books, magazines, and newspapers where more information on listees can be obtained.

Helpful Indexes Make It Easy to Find the Information You Need

Contemporary Musicians features a Musicians Index, listing names of individual performers and musical groups, and a Subject Index that provides the user with a breakdown by primary musical instruments played and by musical genre.

We Welcome Your Suggestions

The editors welcome your comments and suggestions for enhancing and improving *Contemporary Musicians*. If you would like to suggest musicians or composers to be covered in the future, please submit these names to the editors. Mail comments or suggestions to:

The Editor
Contemporary Musicians
Gale Research Inc.
835 Penobscot Bldg.
Detroit, MI 48226-4094
Phone : (800) 521-0707
Fax: (313) 961-6241

Photo Credits

AC/DC

Heavy metal band

"**A** heavy metal band must have a vocalist who can imitate a man having an impacted wisdom tooth removed without anesthesia, a rhythm section that can pummel an innocent riff into submission, a lead guitarist/showoff, and lyrics that deal with sexism, satanism, and militarism. AC/DC scores high in each of the categories, and it has been rewarded accordingly," declared a *High Fidelity* reviewer. Songs such as "Hell's Bells," "Big Balls," and "Highway to Hell," have assured the Australian group of an enduring reign at what an *Audio* contributor called "the zenith of simple headbanger heavy metal." Protests by conservative organizations associating AC/DC with Satanism have probably only increased the group's popularity.

Angus and Malcolm Young, who form the nucleus of AC/DC, had emigrated from Scotland along with the rest of their family in the 1960s. Their eldest brother, George, was a member of The Easybeats, known for their hit "Friday on My Mind." George gave Angus and Malcolm their grounding in guitar work and also helped arrange a contract for them with Albert Records, an

For the Record. . .

Band formed 1973, in Sydney, Australia; original members included **Angus Young** (born March 31, 1951, in Glasgow, Scotland), guitar; **Malcolm Young** (born January 6, 1953, in Glasgow), guitar; **Ronald Belford "Bon" Scott** (born July 9, 1946, in Kirriemur, Scotland; died of acute alcohol poisoning February 19, 1980, in London, England), vocalist.

In 1974, **Phillip Rudd** (born May 19, 1946, in Melbourne, Australia) and **Mark Evans** (born 1957, in Melbourne) joined AC/DC on drums and bass. In 1977, Evans was replaced by **Cliff Williams** (born December 14, 1949, in Rumford, England). In 1980, **Brian Johnson** (born October 5, 1947, in North Shields, England) replaced deceased vocalist Scott. In 1982, Rudd was replaced by **Simon Wright** (born 1963).

Australian company, after AC/DC had built up a local following. The band's early days of constant touring on the rowdy Australian bar circuit certainly influenced their no-holds-barred, attention-grabbing style. Angus Young explained to *Newsweek*'s Jim Miller, "An Australian audience likes to drink a lot. . . . So I used to jump on tables—anything to get them to stop drinking for ten seconds." Angus further riveted his audience by dressing in knickers and a beanie, in the manner of an English schoolboy. Onstage he jerked his head up and down savagely, thereby developing a hugely muscled neck. He charged up and down the stage like an enraged bull, pausing occasionally to drop his pants and moon the audience. The more outrageous and raunchy his antics became, the more AC/DC's Australian fans liked it. Both albums on the Albert label were number-one sellers in Australia.

A compilation of those two albums, released in the United States and England in 1976 as *High Voltage,* introduced AC/DC to an international audience. Supporting their albums with constant touring, the band gradually built up a loyal following. By the time of their 1978 world tour, they were drawing roaring crowds of over 15,000. Tapes from these concerts were edited into AC/DC's first live album, *If You Want Blood— You've Got It. Highway to Hell* followed. Its domination of the U.S. charts signalled that AC/DC had indeed become a major heavy metal presence.

Tragedy struck the band just as sales of *Highway to Hell* peaked. Leader singer Bon Scott choked on his own vomit and died after a marathon drinking session. His presence had been considerable within the group,

yet the surviving members decided almost immediately to replace him and continue on. Brian Johnson, formerly of the group Geordie, seemed to click immediately with the other band members when he joined AC/DC shortly after Scott's death. He even co-wrote the music on *Back in Black,* the group's tribute album for Scott. Released in mid-1980, the album was certified platinum by the year's end. *Rolling Stone* named *Back in Black* "one of the milestone hard-rock albums of the decade," and commended its "brute force and raunchy humor."

For Those about to Rock, We Salute You is considered by some critics to be AC/DC's most effective album, epitomizing the crushing guitar attack on which they'd built their success and from which they seldom varied. It was released in 1981 and swiftly became the top-selling album in the United States. The band seemed to lose momentum after that, however; *'74 Jailbreak* and *Flick of the Switch* were only moderately successful, and by 1984 AC/DC was playing to less than full houses for the first time in years. Controversy swirled around the group in 1985 after the "Night Stalker," Los Angeles mass murderer Richard Ramirez, cited the album *Fly on the Wall* as a source of Satanic inspiration for him.

Conservative groups called for a boycott of AC/DC's albums and concerts, but their efforts only rekindled interest in the group. As heavy-metal groups became increasingly acceptable to the music establishment, AC/DC began to be respectfully referred to as one of the foundation bands of the genre. Reviewing their 1988 release, *Blow up Your Video,* Jim Farber wrote in *Rolling Stone:* "It's time the world stopped thinking of AC/DC as just a heavy-metal band. For thirteen albums now, Angus and Malcolm Young have been crafting the kind of guitar riffs any Who-style rock & roll band would kill for. Yet, the members of AC/DC have allowed no production compromises whatsoever: They've carved every one of these irresistible guitar hooks out of pure stone. . . . Perhaps *Blow Up Your Video* will finally convince those who have doubted the truth about AC/DC: it's the metal band that plays solid-gold rock & roll."

Selected discography

High Voltage, Albert, 1974.
T.N.T., Albert, 1975.
High Voltage (compilation of tracks from the previous *High Voltage* and *T.N.T.*), Atlantic, 1976.
Dirty Deeds Done Dirt Cheap, Atlantic, 1976.
Let There Be Rock, Atlantic, 1977.
Powerage, Atlantic, 1978.

If You Want Blood, You've Got It, Atlantic, 1978.
Highway to Hell, Atlantic, 1979.
Back in Black, Atlantic, 1980.
For Those About to Rock, We Salute You, Atlantic, 1981.
Flick of the Switch, Atlantic, 1983.
'74 Jailbreak, Atlantic, 1984.
Fly on the Wall, Atlantic, 1984.
Who Made Who (soundtrack from the film *Maximum Overdrive*),
   Atlantic, 1986.
Blow Up Your Video, Atlantic, 1988.

Sources

Audio, December 1983.
High Fidelity, March 1982.
Newsweek, April 19, 1982.
Rolling Stone, April 7, 1988; November 16, 1989.
Stereo Review, May 1982.

—Joan Goldsworthy

Julie Andrews

Vocalist of Broadway and film musicals

Singer and actress Julie Andrews has long been famed for her perfect pitch and impressive vocal range. From her 1954 Broadway debut as Polly in "The Boy Friend," she has received rave reviews from critics and lasting devotion from music fans. Best known for her roles in stage and film musicals, including "My Fair Lady," *The Sound of Music,* and *Mary Poppins,* Andrews has concentrated in later years on acting on the screen rather than singing, appearing in husband Blake Edwards's films, including *S.O.B.* and *That's Life.*

Andrews had a somewhat unusual childhood. Born Julia Elizabeth Wells on October 1, 1935, at Walton-on-Thames, England, her parents divorced when she was very young. Her mother, a pianist, married Edward Andrews, who sang in music halls, and the child took her stepfather's last name. The newly made family traveled throughout England, Mr. and Mrs. Andrews performing for a living. Julie, as they called her, first began displaying her own considerable vocal talents during World War II, when she was about eight years old. While hiding in community air-raid shelters, Mr. Andrews led the frightened citizens in singing to keep spirits up. Mrs. Andrews began to notice that her daughter's voice often rose far above those of even the men and women; when examined by a doctor, Julie's vocal chords proved to have already developed to an adult level. As soon as they were able, the Andrewses provided their prodigy with professional singing lessons by Madame Stiles-Allen.

By the time Andrews was twelve, she was performing in the same venues as her mother and stepfather; she made her professional singing debut with the "Starlight Roof" revue at the Hippodrome Theatre on London's West End. But she was destined to go further than her parents. After performing in several other pantomimes, Andrews played the featured role in a pantomime of "Cinderella" in 1953, and in this capacity she caught the attention of director Vida Hope, who was working on the London production of Sandy Wilson's musical about the 1920s, "The Boy Friend." Hope brought this discovery to the United States to shine on Broadway, where she won rave reviews portraying Polly Brown, an earnest young British flapper. Critic John Beaufort asserted in the *Christian Science Monitor* that the young singer's interpretation of the part was both "comic and adorable" and that "her solemnly pretty ingenue-ness" was "a triumph of controlled exaggeration"; Wolcott Gibbs agreed, calling Andrews "the season's dramatic highlight" in the *New Yorker.* The New York version of "The Boy Friend" ran for four hundred and eighty-five performances.

Andrews moved to an even bigger triumph in 1956, when she became the youngest actress ever to play the part of Eliza Doolittle professionally. She starred in the musical version of George Bernard Shaw's *Pygmalion*—"My Fair Lady"—and in it warbled songs such as "Wouldn't It Be Loverly" and "Just You Wait, Henry Higgins." In this capacity Andrews garnered a nomination for an Antoinette Perry (Tony) Award and the New York Drama Critics Award for best actress in a musical. Despite her critically acclaimed performance, however, she was passed over for the film version in favor of

actress Audrey Hepburn. Andrews received another Tony nomination in 1961 for her portrayal of Queen Guinevere in the smash Arthurian musical, "Camelot."

Though Andrews was again passed over for the film version of "Camelot"—this time in favor of actress Vanessa Redgrave—her time in films was not long in coming. She made her screen debut in 1964 in *Mary Poppins.* Her appearance as the magical nanny won her both an Academy Award and a Golden Globe Award for best actress. This film and the following year's *The Sound of Music,* in which she played a children's governess who wins the love of her charges' father, began to establish Andrews as a specialist in wholesome family entertainment. As Clive Hirschhorn put it in his 1981 book, *The Hollywood Musical, The Sound of Music* was accused of "mawkish sentimentality" by many critics, but "it was Andrews's extraordinarily assured and appealing central performance . . . that was largely responsible for the film's enormous success." Her featured songs in the film included the title theme, "I Have Confidence in Me," and "My Favorite Things."

Another musical film featuring Andrews was 1967's *Thoroughly Modern Millie,* which Hirschhorn hailed as "an irresistible mixture of brashness, charm, and nostalgia put together with expertise." Like her first major stage play, *Millie* had Andrews portraying a young woman during the 1920s—a young woman who goes to New York City as a secretary in search of a rich husband and becomes involved in a white slavery ring. During what Hirschhorn describes as a "thoroughly captivating star performance," Andrews sang ditties such as "Jimmy" and "Poor Butterfly."

Not long after filming *Millie,* Andrews divorced her first husband, theatrical designer Tony Walton, and married motion-picture producer and director Blake Edwards, famed for his "Pink Panther" films. She began working in Edwards's efforts, including 1970's *Darling Lili.* Andrews was also featured as actor Dudley Moore's long-suffering girlfriend in Edwards's *10.* In 1981's *S.O.B.,* Edwards spoofed his wife's wholesome image by making a big production of her character, Sally Miles, baring her breasts for the camera. Andrews perhaps moved even further from her former reputation when she portrayed a singing transvestite in Edwards's 1982 motion picture, *Victor/Victoria.* The critics especially took her seriously in the latter role, and she received nominations for both an Academy Award and a Golden Globe for her part in the film.

During the late 1980s, Andrews concentrated on more serious film roles, ones that did not utilize her talent for singing. Though Edwards's 1986 effort *That's Life* is a comedy, Andrews's portrayal of Gillian Fairchild is a serious one—Gillian is waiting for the results of a biopsy. Andrews "is the movie's strong, quiet heart," declared reviewer David Ansen in *Newsweek*, "and it is she who devastates us when she finally unleashes her pent-up emotions." Despite some negative comments about the film in general, critics tended to agree favorably about Andrews's performance in *Duet for One.* Playing a famed violinist dying of multiple sclerosis, "Andrews doesn't tear a passion to tatters; she uses it to stitch a coherent soul," according to Richard Corliss of *Time*. And *Maclean's* critic Lawrence O'Toole asserted that "Andrews gives what may be the performance of her life in *Duet for One*."

But Andrews continues entertaining fans with her voice. In 1988 she released the album *Love, Julie,* which featured her renditions of songs like "Tea for Two," "Come Rain or Come Shine." Though *People* reviewer David Hiltbrand considered the disc a mixed effort, he had praise for the "sensuousness to her tone," and said that her voice was "sweet and clear, often frosted with an appreciable sparkle."

Selected discography

Albums

(With cast) *My Fair Lady,* Columbia, 1956.

(With cast) *Camelot,* Columbia, 1960.
Love, Julie, U.S.A., 1988.

Also recorded *Christmas with Julie Andrews,* Columbia; *Tell It Again, Broadway's Fair Julie, Lion's Cage,* and, with Carol Burnett, *Julie Andrews and Carol Burnett at Carnegie Hall.*

Sources

Books

Hirschhorn, Clive, *The Hollywood Musical,* Crown, 1981.

Periodicals

Christian Science Monitor, October 9, 1954.
Maclean's, March 2, 1987.
McCall's, November 1986.
Newsweek, October 6, 1986.
New Yorker, October 9, 1954.
People, January 25, 1988.
Time, September 29, 1986; March 2, 1987.

—Elizabeth Thomas

Joan Armatrading

Pop singer, songwriter

In the late 1980s the pop music world enjoyed a refreshing change of pace when several gifted young female singer/songwriters—among them Tracy Chapman, Suzanne Vega, and Sinead O'Connor—emerged to give a powerful voice to the struggles of contemporary women. Their songs were substantive, urgent, and yet strangely simple and direct. Invariably these women will point to a particular artist as one of their earliest inspirations, a woman who has been writing soulful, personal songs since 1973. And Joan Armatrading has endured as an international pop star through the lean years of the late 1970s and early 1980s, when being a "woman folk singer" was not "in."

A self-described loner with an introspective disposition, the shy, reclusive Armatrading would seem the unlikeliest of pop stars. But her powerful, emotional songs, brought forth from the rich, smoky confines of a voice that seems to emanate directly from her soul, quickly convert any skeptics who might expect a flashier, more self-conscious performer. "Armatrading's heroic songs are an irresistable brew of jazz, rock, soul, and West Indian influences, performed in a dusky, Odetta-like voice and accompanied by sinewy chordal attacks on acoustic rhythm guitar," wrote *Newsweek*'s Barbara Graustark. "As an interpreter, she is the fastest change-of-pace artist in the business today: from rich chest tones of silky smoothness, her voice will suddenly take off into a light scat with the ease of a Porsche negotiating a hairpin turn."

It is this sort of critical response which has helped Armatrading on her way and established her with a small but intensely devoted following—and it is help she dearly needed, mainly due to her reserved nature and the fact that quiet, ordinary-looking, West Indian-British black women do not ordinarily become pop stars. Even today, despite her success, Armatrading lives a hermitic existence at her little home outside London, rarely associating with paparazzi, record industry people, or even other musicians. "I haven't picked up lots of friends along the way," Armatrading told *Rolling Stone*. "I'm not going out to dinner and parties. I don't need a million acquaintances; one or two friends are plenty for me."

Born on the Caribbean island of St. Kitts in 1950, Armatrading was one of six children who moved with their father and mother to the English industrial city of Birmingham. It was a disruptive move for a delicate child of seven, and Armatrading's childhood was spent mostly at a distance from other children, where she lived vicariously through the play of others and practiced on her guitar. As a teenager she began writing songs and performing with a boyfriend in a Jamaican group that played clubs in black sections of Birmingham. But Armatrading quickly tired of the Jamaican sound, and so it was mostly luck that launched her early career. She was working as an office girl when she accompanied a friend to an audition for the English production of *Hair;* though her friend was turned away, Armatrading landed a role in the chorus and spent the next eighteen months touring Great Britain with the troupe—and distinguished herself as the only member of the cast who refused to disrobe onstage during a particular scene in the musical.

Armatrading spent the next couple of years writing songs and trying to find someone to produce them. Her first album, *Whatever Is for Us,* was released in 1973 with the help of lyricist Pam Nestor. The album drew critical acclaim but sold very few copies. Armatrading went solo on her second LP, *Back to the Night* (1975), but it was not until her third record, *Joan Armatrading* (1976), that she received enough publicity from her record company, at the time A & M Records, to ensure a wider audience. The result was more excellent reviews, extensive radio play, and Armatrading's first Top 10 U.K. single, "Love and Affection." Over the next few years Armatrading continued to build a loyal following of sophisticated adult listeners.

The story of the ensuing few years is a testament to Armatrading's determination to keep evolving as a musician. Rather than rely on a tried-and-true format, she consistently broke new ground with each record by working with different producers, musicians, and record companies, which lent new flavors to her music and also served to keep any outsiders from getting to close to her fiercely independent creative niche. Her peak period seemed to arrive in the early 1980s, when her

LPs *Me, Myself, I* (1980), *Walk under Ladders* (1981), and *The Key* (1983) all were very popular in the U.K. and even had some success in the United States, a market that had never really warmed to Armatrading's music.

But her music is such a distinctive blend of a wide variety of musical styles from around the world, Armatrading could truly be called an international pop star, and more than twenty gold records in seven countries can surely testify to that. Though she has always insisted that nothing, especially money, can influence her creative world, Armatrading admitted to trying to lure a larger audience. "To talk about making more 'commercial' music is misleading," Armatrading told *Rolling Stone.* "It makes it sound as if you're just making records for the sake of selling them . . . But I would like millions of people to buy what I do rather than ten people. And it is your living, you know? You've got to be realistic; it's what buys your food, pays to get your clothes cleaned and puts petrol in the car. I can't say it's art for art's sake."

Selected discography

Whatever Is for Us, Cube, 1973.
Back to the Night, A & M, 1975.
Joan Armatrading, A & M, 1976.
Show Some Emotion, A & M, 1977.
To the Limit, A & M, 1978.
How Cruel, A & M, 1979.
Me, Myself, I, A & M, 1980.
Walk Under Ladders, A & M, 1981.
The Key, A & M, 1983.
Secret Secrets, A & M, 1985.
The Shouting Stage, A & M, 1988.
Hearts and Flowers, A & M, 1990.

Sources

Books

Hardy, Phil, and Dave Laing, *Encyclopedia of Rock,* Schirmer, 1988.

Periodicals

Esquire, September 1982.
Newsweek, February 11, 1980.
Rolling Stone, March 18, 1982; December 1, 1988.

—*David Collins*

Louis Armstrong

Jazz trumpet player, singer

Louis Armstrong was generally acclaimed by critics as the greatest jazz performer ever. Both with his trumpet and with his rich, gravelly voice, he made famous such jazz and pop classics as "West End Blues," "When It's Sleepy Time Down South," "Hello, Dolly," and "What a Wonderful World." Armstrong's influence on the jazz artists that followed him was immense and far-reaching; for instance, according to George T. Simon in his book *The Best of the Music Makers,* fellow trumpet player Dizzie Gillespie has affirmed that "if it weren't for Armstrong there would be no Dizzie Gillespie." Reviewer Whitney Balliett declared in the *New Yorker* that Armstrong "created the sort of super, almost celestial art that few men master; transcending both its means and its materials, it attained a disembodied beauty." Apparently, fans all over the world agreed with this assessment, for during his lifetime Armstrong made extremely successful tours to several countries, including some in Africa and behind the Iron Curtain.

Armstrong was born July 4, 1900, in a poor black

For the Record. . .

Full name, Daniel Louis Armstrong; nickname, "Satchmo"; born July 4, 1900, in New Orleans, Louisiana; died July 6, 1971, in Long Island, New York; son of Willie (a turpentine worker) and Mary Ann (a domestic servant) Armstrong; married Daisy Parker (divorced, 1917); married Lilian Hardin (a jazz pianist), February 5, 1924 (divorced, 1932); married Lucille Wilson (a singer), 1942.

Worked odd jobs as a boy, including delivering milk and coal and selling newspapers and bananas; played the cornet with various bands in the New Orleans area, c. 1917-22; played with King Oliver's Original Creole Jazz Band, c. 1922-24; played trumpet with Fletcher Henderson in New York City, 1924; played trumpet independently and fronted his own bands, including the Hot Five and the Hot Seven, 1925-71; recording artist beginning in the early 1920s.

Appeared in Broadway shows, including "Hot Chocolates" and "Swingin' the Dream"; appeared in motion pictures, including *Pennies from Heaven,* Columbia, 1936, *Every Day's a Holiday,* Paramount, 1937, *Going Places,* Warner, 1938, *Dr. Rhythm,* Paramount, 1938, *Cabin in the Sky,* MGM, 1943, *Jam Session,* Columbia, 1944, *New Orleans,* United Artists, 1947, *The Strip,* MGM, 1951, *Glory Alley,* MGM, 1952, *The Glenn Miller Story,* United Artists, 1954, *High Society,* MGM, 1957, *The Five Pennies,* Paramount, 1959, *A Man Called Adam,* Embassy, 1966, and *Hello, Dolly,* 1969.

Awards: "West End Blues" was one of the first five records elected to the Recording Academy's Hall of Fame; won several periodical jazz polls, including *Esquire* and *down beat;* honored by the American Guild of Variety Artists.

neighborhood in New Orleans, Louisiana. He had a deprived childhood; his parents separated when he was five years old. His poverty was perhaps a motivating factor in discovering his affinity for music, however, for he sang in the streets for pennies as a child. When Armstrong was thirteen years old, he fired a pistol into the air to celebrate New Year's Eve and was punished by the authorities by being sent to the Negro Waif's Home. Actually, this proved somewhat providential: the home had a bandmaster who took an interest in the youth and taught him to play the bugle. By the time of his release from the facility, Armstrong had graduated to the cornet and knew how to read music. Working odd jobs, he scrounged up the money to continue lessons with one of his musical idols, Joe "King" Oliver.

From 1917 to 1922, Armstrong played cornet for local New Orleans Dixieland jazz bands. He also tried his hand at writing songs, but was only partially rewarded—he saw his composition "I Wish I Could Shimmy Like My Sister Kate" published, but the company cheated him out of both payment and byline. Then Oliver, who lead a successful band in Chicago, sent for Armstrong. As second cornetist for Oliver, the young jazzman made his first recordings. In 1924, Armstrong enjoyed a brief stint with bandleader and arranger Fletcher Henderson in New York City. By the time jazz pianist Lilian Hardin, who would become the second of his three wives, persuaded Armstrong to work independently around 1925, he had switched from the cornet to the trumpet. During the next few years he made recordings fronting his own musicians; depending on the number assembled, they were known as the Hot Five or the Hot Seven. Around the same time, Armstrong is credited with the invention of the jazz technique of scat singing—legend has it that Armstrong dropped his sheet music during a recording session and had to substitute vocal improvisations until someone picked up the sheets for him. Also during this period, his experimentations led him to break free of the more rigid Dixieland style of jazz to pave the way for a more modern jazz genre.

But in 1930, Armstrong began taking yet a different direction with his career, performing with larger bands and recording more pop-sounding songs. Jazz purists fault him for this move, but others point out that he helped inspire the later swing sound. Nevertheless, Armstrong was still identified with jazz by the public, and on his extensive European tours was considered an "ambassador" of the genre. When he gave a concert in Ghana, he was considered a hero by its natives; he also performed a few times before the British royal family. It was in England that he won the nickname "Satchmo," a distortion of "satchelmouth," which described the extent to which his cheeks puffed out when he played the trumpet.

Armstrong also helped spread jazz's popularity throughout the 1930s, 1940s, 1950s, and 1960s by appearing in musical roles in several films, from 1936's *Pennies from Heaven* to 1969's *Hello, Dolly.* He was probably included in the latter because his recording of the title song in 1964 sold over two million copies and momentarily displaced the then-phenomenal Beatles from the pop charts. Armstrong also made successful recordings of popular songs such as "Mack the Knife" and "Blueberry Hill" and, as late as 1968, scored a chart hit with the single "What a Wonderful World."

But Armstrong filmed his guest appearance in *Hello, Dolly* in between visits to the hospital. For a brief period during 1970, he was forbidden to play his trumpet by his concerned doctor. Undaunted, he made a couple of purely vocal albums. Later in the year, Armstrong's physician lifted the ban on his instrument; he did a Las Vegas show with singer Pearl Bailey and played a benefit in London. After a few appearances in 1971, Armstrong suffered a heart attack in March and was hospitalized once again. He recovered sufficiently to be allowed to return to his home in May, but he died in his sleep July 6, 1971.

Armstrong's fame and popularity, however, have continued long after his death. In 1975, a program dedicated to the jazz great's music by the New York Jazz Repertory Orchestra toured the Soviet Union as part of official cultural exchange between that country and the United States. A bust of Armstrong has been placed on the site of the Nice Jazz Festival in France. One of his hit records even became a hit again during the late 1980s—"What a Wonderful World" was included on the soundtrack of the Robin Williams film *Good Morning, Vietnam,* received a great deal of airplay, and introduced Armstrong's music to a new generation of fans.

Selected discography

Hello, Dolly, MCA.
At the Crescendo, MCA.
Best of Louis Armstrong, Audiofidelity.
Definitive Album, Audiofidelity.
Louis Armstrong with the Dukes of Dixieland, Audiofidelity.
Disney Songs the Satchmo Way, Buena.

I Will Wait for You, Brunswick.
Louis "Satchmo" Armstrong, Archive of Folk & Jazz.
Mame, Pickwick.
Satchmo: A Musical Autobiography (four-album set), Decca, 1957.
Verve's Best Choice, Verve.
What a Wonderful World, ABC, 1968.
Louis Armstrong with His Friends, Amsterdam.
July 4, 1900/July 6, 1971, RCA.
The Genius of Louis Armstrong, Columbia.
Louis Armstrong in the Thirties, RCA.
Louis Armstrong in the Forties, RCA.

Sources

Books

Collier, James Lincoln, *Louis Armstrong: An American Genius,* Oxford University Press, 1985.
Jones, Max, and John Chilton, *Louis: The Louis Armstrong Story,* Little, Brown, & Co., 1971.
Simon, George T., *The Best of the Music Makers,* Doubleday, 1979.

Periodicals

Ebony, November, 1964.
New Yorker, January 15, 1966.

—Elizabeth Thomas

Mike Auldridge

Dobro player

Mike Auldridge is the country's best-known master of the dobro, a modified guitar much in demand in bluegrass and country music. In fact, the modest Auldridge helped to rescue the dobro from certain extinction—at the time he began to play the instrument in the 1950s it was not being manufactured anymore. Today Auldridge's dobro is an essential component of the Seldom Scene bluegrass band and is heard backing up such artists as Dolly Parton, Linda Ronstadt, and Jonathon Edwards on their albums. Additionally, Auldridge has released a number of solo albums that have sold extremely well, at least by the standards set for bluegrass music.

The dobro is a twentieth-century invention of John Dopyera and his brothers (hence the name *do-bro*). It is essentially a guitar, usually made of laminated maple, with a raised bridge and a resonator cone placed in the traditional sounding hole. The musician plays the instrument by sliding a bar up and down the neck while picking the strings with the other hand, for a sound reminiscent of the pedal steel guitar but with a greater range of fluidity. The dobro was created to provide amplified guitar music to country bands before the era of sophisticated electronics. Its usefulness therefore took a dive in the 1940s and 1950s when technicians perfected the pedal steel guitar.

Auldridge is the rare younger musician who was exposed to dobro music as a youth. He was born in Washington, D.C., in 1938 and moved to the suburb of Kensington, Maryland, while he was still a child. He was not born into a musical family, but his uncle, Ellsworth Cousins, had played dobro with Jimmie Rodgers in the 1920s. Auldridge heard his uncle play at family gatherings, and gradually he too became a disciple of old-time country music.

By the time he was in his teens, Auldridge could play guitar and banjo. His first love was still dobro, however, and he spent many hours trying to find one to buy. The artist told *Pickin'* magazine that in the early 1950s "it was impossible to find a Dobro. I used to go around to pawn shops and music stores asking if any of them had one." Eventually Auldridge made his own instrument, which he used until 1961, when the Dopyera brothers began manufacturing dobros again.

Auldridge's hero as a youth was Josh Graves, a dobro player who worked with Flatt & Scruggs during the 1950s. Through many painful years of trial-and-error practice, Auldridge taught himself to play the dobro, principally by slowing Flatt & Scruggs records down and imitating Graves's licks. Auldridge has estimated that he spent eight years perfecting his basic technique and many, many more years developing the unique bell-like tones associated with his work. Although he minored in music theory while a student at the University of Maryland, he taught himself dobro by ear and only rarely applied the college lessons to his craft.

Auldridge began playing bluegrass professionally as a teenager, but he simply could not envision himself performing for a living. Instead he took a day job as a commercial artist for the *Washington Star* newspaper and worked there for more than a decade. In the meantime he spent weekends playing dobro with Cliff Waldron and the New Shades of Grass, quitting that band when it began to impinge on his regular job. In 1971 he joined a small group of ex-professional and amateur bluegrass musicians in the Washington area for informal picking sessions. The group members decided to call themselves the Seldom Scene because, like Auldridge, they all had day jobs.

"It was going to be our weekly card game," Auldridge joked of his early days with the Seldom Scene. Instead the group—which also contains tenor John Duffey, banjo player Ben Eldridge, bassist Tom Gray, and guitarist Phil Rosenthal—became one of the most sought-after bluegrass acts in the country. In the early 1970s dobro was still a relative rarity in bluegrass

For the Record. . .

Born in 1938 in Washington, D.C.; married; children: two. *Education:* Attended University of Maryland; majored in commercial art.

Artist for the *Washington Star* newspaper, 1960-76; full time dobro player and singer, 1976—. Member of the New Shades of Grass (bluegrass band), 1969-71, and the Seldom Scene (bluegrass band), 1971—. Solo dobro player and studio musician, 1976—; has performed on numerous albums for Linda Ronstadt, Emmylou Harris, Jonathon Edwards, J. D. Crowe, and the Country Gentlemen. Columnist for *Frets* magazine, 1979-80.

Awards: Named best dobro player of the year by *Muleskinner News,* 1974-80; Grammy Award nomination for best male vocalist in country music, 1975.

Addresses: *Record company*—Sugar Hill, Box 4040, Duke Station, Durham, NC 27706.

bands; part of the Seldom Scene's success can certainly be traced to Auldridge, who wowed audiences with his virtuoso licks. Auldridge became so popular with bluegrass fans, and so revered for his playing, that his fellow Scene members called him "Larry the Legend." Before long most Seldom Scene albums featured an Auldridge solo.

Still Auldridge held on to his steady job with the *Star,* but finally fate intervened. The newspaper folded in 1976, and Auldridge found himself out of work. Free for the first time to devote himself entirely to music, the artist blossomed. He began to cut solo albums and made numerous trips to California and Nashville to work as a session musician for some of the top country entertainers. Among his new "customers" were Dolly Parton, Emmylou Harris, Linda Ronstadt, and the Country Gentlemen. Auldridge also continued his work with the Seldom Scene and prepared dobro lessons in a variety of formats for the many musicians who had become interested in the instrument.

"I always thought it would be nice but never dreamed it would be possible to make a living off of music," Auldridge told *Pickin'.* "In those [early] days it was a really limited audience compared to what it is now." Auldridge's career has indeed prospered in tandem with bluegrass music in general, but he is more than just another bluegrass musician. The dobro is a demanding instrument, and few if any pickers have mastered it like Auldridge has. The artist notes that he has

been lucky to have chosen to learn dobro at a time when it was almost obsolete, but he has assured his fame by working hard every day to be the best dobro player alive.

"I get up in the morning, and half an hour after I'm out of bed, I'm playing," Auldridge told *The Big Book of Bluegrass.* "That's all I do. I probably play ten hours a day. I hope it doesn't go away some day. I worked for a long time at a day job, wishing I could play music and have the time for it. Now I'm like a guy who was poor all his life, and all of a sudden came into a lot of money. I've got this time, and I just can't learn enough about music. I can't develop my technique enough. . . . I'm always working on it. I love playing music."

Mike Auldridge is probably one of the most approachable musicians in the business. At bluegrass festivals he is often found surrounded by a cluster of would-be dobro players who are eager to glean information from a master. Auldridge's special brand of acoustic guitar—bluegrass with blends of country, jazz, and even big band—is likely to remain popular in years to come, especially since country music is moving back to its roots. Despite his success, however, the idea that he is the country's best dobro player does not sit well with Auldridge. He once told *Pickin':* "I just don't like to live up to anything. I just want to pick and have a good time."

Selected discography

Solo albums

Mike Auldridge and Old Dog, Flying Fish, 1978.
Mike Auldridge, Flying Fish.
Eight-String Swing, Sugar Hill.
Dobro, Takoma.
Blues & Bluegrass, Takoma.

With the Seldom Scene

Act One, Rebel, 1972.
Act Two, Rebel, 1973.
Act Three, Rebel, 1973.
Old Train, Rebel, 1974.
The Seldom Scene Live at the Cellar Door, Rebel, 1975.
The New Seldom Scene Album, Rebel, 1976.
Baptizing, Rebel, 1978.
Act Four, Sugar Hill, 1979.
After Midnight, Sugar Hill, 1981.
At the Scene, Sugar Hill, 1983.
A Change of Scenery, Sugar Hill, 1988.
Seldom Scene and Special Guests, Sugar Hill, 1988.
Best of the Seldom Scene, Rebel, 1989.

Sources

Books

Kochman, Marilyn, editor, *The Big Book of Bluegrass*, Morrow, 1984.
Malone, Bill C., *Country Music U.S.A.,* revised edition, University of Texas Press, 1985.

Periodicals

Bluegrass Unlimited, July 1980.
Pickin', April 1978, November 1978.

—*Anne Janette Johnson*

B-52's

New wave band

The B-52's have been a presence on the new wave music scene since 1979, when their hit "Rock Lobster" started people jumping on dance floors all over the United States and Great Britain. The band, composed of Cindy and Ricky Wilson, Kate Pierson, Fred Schneider III, and Keith Strickland, quickly became known for their wacky lyrics and bouncy music. They followed "Lobster" with a string of popular 1980s dance tunes, including "Planet Claire," "Private Idaho," and "Quiche Lorraine." After a three-year dry spell and the loss of Ricky Wilson to AIDS in 1985, the B-52's re-emerged with the 1989 album *Cosmic Thing* and its smash hit single, "Love Shack."

The Wilsons, who were brother and sister, and Strickland grew up in Athens, Georgia. Schneider and Pierson also lived in Athens for a long time, but are natives of New Jersey. The five became friends in Athens during the mid-1970s and, after an outing together at a Chinese restaurant late in 1976, decided to form a band. Though all had instrumental talent, they had varied levels of experience: the Wilsons had never

For the Record. . .

Band members include **Cindy Wilson** (lead vocals, percussion, guitar), born c. 1957, in Athens, Ga., daughter of a fireman and a factory worker, married Keith Bennett (an advertising executive); **Ricky Wilson** (guitar), born c. 1953, in Athens, Ga., brother of Cindy Wilson, died 1985 (one source says 1986) of AIDS (one source says an AIDS-related illness); **Kate Pierson** (vocals, keyboards, guitar), born c. 1948, in Weehawken, N.J.; **Fred Schneider III** (vocals, keyboards, guitar), born c. 1952, in Belleville, N.J.; **Keith Strickland** (drums, percussion), born c. 1954, in Athens, Ga., son of bus station managers.

Formed group in 1976; recording artists and concert performers, 1979—.

Addresses: *Record company*—Warner Bros. Records, Inc., 3300 Warner Blvd., Burbank, CA 91505.

played with a band before, Strickland had been in a high school rock group, Pierson had worked with a folk group called the Sun Donuts and played classical piano, and Schneider had been in bands with whimsical names like Bridge Mix and Night Soil. Taking their name not from the military airplane but rather from Southern slang for outrageous bouffant hairdos—which the women in the group wore during performances—the B-52's premiered at a friend's Valentine's Day party in 1977. They played for free at this gig and many others in and around Athens, not having the money to buy equipment for professional stints at the time. Until the group felt confident about their ability, they recorded their music before a performance and played it back on tape, miming their instruments—the only live part being the vocals. Apparently this worked all right except for the time someone accidentally pulled the plug on the tape player in the middle of a show.

Eventually the B-52's improved to the point where they decided to press a few of their own records, notably the song that would later become their first big hit, "Rock Lobster." They distributed the disc to reviewers and sold them to the fans at local appearances. The band received sufficient praise for "Lobster" to convince them to try their act in New York City. Late in 1977 they performed at audition night at Max's Kansas City, a Manhattan club where singers such as Patti Smith and Blondie had made their debuts. Schneider recalled for Michael Small in *People:* "There were only 17 people. We made 17 bucks."

By 1979 the B-52's were making more lucrative club appearances in New York, and had landed a contract with Warner Bros. Records. In that year, they released their first album, titled simply *The B-52's*. On the disc, they re-recorded "Rock Lobster," and the song received wide exposure for the first time. Another cut from the album that became popular in dance clubs was "Planet Claire." As Parke Puterbaugh in *Rolling Stone* put it, the B-52's had "unleashed" these "kitschy classics on a world that had no idea how badly it wanted to have some danceable, unselfconscious fun." The band followed their debut with 1980's *Wild Planet*. Though the singles from that album, "Private Idaho" and "Quiche Lorraine" did not match the success of "Rock Lobster," they were still featured numbers in discotheques.

But even with "Rock Lobster," the B-52's had not received much airplay on mainstream radio stations. As Small explained, "the . . . quintet had an eccentric musical style that only the underground truly appreciated." He elaborated in a different *People* article that the group sounds "as if they might be the illegitimate offspring of [futuristic cartoon character] George Jetson and [early 1960s pop group] the Shirelles." Schneider had a different response: "Radio stations wouldn't play us," he told Small, "because the people who listened to us didn't buy $30,000 cars."

When Michael Tearson reviewed *Bouncing Off the Satellites* in *Audio*, the B-52's 1986 album, he noted that it seemed "subdued." If it was, it might have been because while the group was recording it, Ricky Wilson was dying of AIDS. Shortly after the studio sessions for *Bouncing* were completed in 1985, the band's lead guitarist passed away. As Puterbaugh reported, "his death devastated the members of the band," and the remaining B-52's did not work together again for about three years.

But, as Pierson confided to Puterbaugh, "it was really a healing thing to get together and be creative again." In 1988, they decided to compose and record a new album. Pierson talked of their composition techniques to Small: "We go into a creative netherworld where you don't monitor yourself. In jam sessions, we're all singing at the same time, bouncing off each other." Further, Strickland explained to Puterbaugh that the album that was released as *Cosmic Thing* in 1989 was a low-pressure activity: "We unanimously agreed that we wanted to have fun with this record and not worry about what was on the radio or what was current." As Puterbaugh pointed out, however, "ironically, radio has been extremely receptive to *Cosmic Thing*," and Schneider believes it is due to the fact that the professional disc jockeys of the late 1980s were working in the college stations that used to play the B-52's music when they first became popular, and still like the band. At any rate, "Love Shack," a single from the album, has proved the B-52's most mainstream, and therefore best-selling hit so far. The title track was featured in the motion picture "Earth Girls Are Easy," and another single, "Roam," has received a great deal of airplay on pop stations.

Selected discography

Albums; on Warner Bros./Reprise

The B-52's (includes "Rock Lobster" and "Planet Claire"), 1979.
Wild Planet (includes "Private Idaho" and "Quiche Lorraine"), 1980.

Bouncing Off the Satellites, 1986.
Cosmic Thing (includes "Cosmic Thing," "Love Shack," and "Roam"), 1989.

Also released the albums *Whammy* and *Mesopotamia.*

Sources

Periodicals

Audio, January 1987.
People, August 21, 1989; December 11, 1989.
Rolling Stone, July 13, 1989; November 30, 1989.
Stereo Review, January 1987.

—Elizabeth Thomas

Jeff Beck

Guitarist

In 1980 Mikal Gilmore wrote in *Rolling Stone* that Jeff Beck "was an archetypal figure: a resourceful, iconoclastic guitarist who helped mold and inform many of the rock-related movements in the last fifteen years, including psychedelia, heavy metal, art rock, fusion and—yes—punk."

Beck's road to stardom began with the unenviable chore of replacing Eric Clapton in the Yardbirds band in the mid-1960s. Beck quit the band Trident and took over the role by moving beyond Clapton's blues-based licks and creating a whole new style that relied on feedback, distortion, volume swells, slide guitar, and sitar simulations based on modal scales.

"The Beck-Yardbirds represented the group at their highest peak of creativity, unpredictable and generally miles beyond the activities of their contemporaries," as stated in *Rock 100*. Jimmy Page joined the band on second guitar and kicked their energy level up another notch until Beck's ego reportedly led to his departure. Although he was only with the Yardbirds for twenty months, Beck's manic playing fueled their biggest hits: "Over Under Sideways Down," "Heart Full Of Soul," "I'm A Man," and "Shapes Of Things."

Beck left in 1966 and soon released the singles "Hi Ho Silver Lining," "Tallyman," "Love Is Blue," and "Beck's Bolero," with the latter featuring Page, Keith Moon, and John Paul Jones. He then formed the first Jeff Beck Group with Rod Stewart on vocals, Ron Wood on bass, Micky Waller on drums, and Nicky Hopkins on piano. Their first release, *Truth,* was "truly a showcase album for a guitar hero," wrote Gene Santoro in *The Guitar: The Music, The History, The Players*. "Beck's unpredictable pyrotechnics are at their wildest, wooliest, and most off-the-wall imagination here." On cuts like Howlin' Wolf's "I Ain't Superstitious," Beck's playing overwhelms Stewart's vocals and stretched rock's roots to their furthest yet. "That's my whole thing," said Beck in *Rolling Stone,* "trying to explore the blues to the maximum, really. It's in the blood." As wild as Beck got, he still felt second to the most exciting electric guitarist ever, Jimi Hendrix. "I was embarrassed because I thought, God, that should be me up there—I just hadn't had the guts to come out and do it so flamboyantly," he told *Guitar World*.

The first version of the Jeff Beck Group, which provided a blueprint for heavy metal groups like Led Zeppelin and Deep Purple, lasted for one more LP, *Beck-Ola,* before the leader canned Waller, prompting Stewart and Wood to leave for the Faces. Beck's reputation for being a moody egomaniac who couldn't hold a band together was showing. "My problem is that I'm not very professional," stated Beck in *Rolling Stone*. "I get bored very quickly, then I get irritable." In the fall of 1969 Beck suffered a fractured skull in an auto accident and was out of commission for the next eighteen months. The 1971 incarnation of the Jeff Beck Group included Cozy Powell on drums, Max Middleton on piano, Clive Chaman on bass and Robert Tench on vocals. Middleton added a jazzy flavor to tunes like "Situation" and their two LPs, *Rough and Ready* and *Jeff Beck Group,* represent a musical shift that Beck would fully embrace on his first solo album in 1975.

In the meantime, however, Beck would join forces with Tim Bogert and Carmine Appice for one album, *Beck, Bogert & Appice,* in the tradition of Cream's power trio. "We were just three maniacs, complete and utter maniacs," said Beck in *Guitar For The Practicing Musician.* "It went on all day, off stage and on stage." After that fling of insanity, Beck produced his most creative and passionate work ever, *Blow by Blow.* As Beck described to Lowell Cauffiel in *The Guitar Player Book,* "It crosses the gap between white rock and Mahavishnu or jazz-rock. It bridges a lot of gaps. It's more digestible, the rhythms are easier to understand than Mahavishnu. It's more on the fringe."

One of the main reasons for Beck's change in style was keyboardist Jan Hammer's influence. "He plays the Moog a lot like a guitar and his sounds went straight into me," continued Beck. "So I started playing like him. I mean, I didn't sound like him, but his phrases influenced me immensely." Beck had combined jazz, rock, funk and even classical themes to create a masterpiece. *Blow by Blow* was eventually listed by the Guitar Institute of Technology in Hollywood, California, as "essential listening," including such songs as: "Freeway Jam," "Diamond Dust," "Cause We've Ended As Lovers," "Scatterbrain," the Beatles' "She's A Woman," "You Know What I Mean," "Constipated Duck," "Air Blower," and "Thelonius." *Blow by Blow* "was a major change in my life," Beck told *Guitar Player,* "but that was an accident. The album was sort of put together naturally. You couldn't force out another album like that, so it's difficult to make a follow up."

He may not have topped *Blow by Blow,* but he came very close to equaling it with *Wired* in 1976. Beck used songs by Charlie Mingus, Narada Michael Walden, Jan Hammer, and Max Middleton to win the Best Guitar LP of the year in *Guitar Player* and chart out at Number 6 in the U.S. market. Songs like "Goodbye Pork Pie Hat," "Led Boots," "Sophie," and "Blue Wind" were similar to those of *Blow by Blow,* due in part to the same producer, George Martin (knob fiddler for the Beatles), but with a slightly funkier edge.

Jan Hammer played on *Wired* also and the two teamed up for a tour later released as a surprisingly flat live LP. Beck's next studio project, *There And Back,* did not really break the new ground his fans had come to expect, and it relied too much on Hammer's rock and roll side. "On the album I just didn't play as good as I know I can," Beck said in *Guitar Player.* "It's just when you're looking for something, you have to take what's best at that time." It would take another five years for Beck's next solo album. In the meantime he spent much of his time doodling with his hot rod collection and working occasionally on other people's musical projects. His playing on the Honeydrippers' *Rockin' At Midnight* gave Beck the chance to emulate some of his earliest musical influences, Cliff Gallup of Gene Vincent's band and Paul Burlison of the Rock 'N' Roll Trio.

On September 20, 1983, at London's Royal Albert Hall, Beck reunited with the two other former Yardbirds' guitarists, Clapton and Page, in a benefit show for Action and Research into Multiple Sclerosis (ARMS). Pleased with the results, he continued on to play ten dates on the ARMS tour of 1984.

Beck also teamed with his former lead singer, Rod Stewart, on two separate occasions in 1984-85. *Flash* featured Stewart's stirring vocals on "People Get Ready" as Beck furthered his distance from jazz and began to turn up some hard rock heat on his wildest, wang bar-infected solo yet on "Ambitious." "A guitar can take you wherever you want it to go," Beck said in *Guitar For The Practicing Musician.* "I could do a country and western album if I wanted to, heaven forbid."

Beck returned Stewart's favor by adding his six-string to *Camouflage* and even agreed to tour with the singer.

But the deal would only allow Beck about fifteen minutes of stage time, which the guitarist figured to be unacceptable. "Musical suicide is what it would have been," he continued. "My career would have been in shreds. I'd have been a millionaire—not a very good trade off." Beck went on a blues-metal binge in 1989 with *Guitar Shop*, "the work of a player who has integrated technique, emotion, spontaneity, and attitude so completely that you can't begin to separate them," wrote Joe Gore in *Guitar Player*. "It's a superb rock instrumental record, one of the best ever."

The tour to support the record was his first North American venture in almost 10 years and included band members Terry Bozzio and Tony Hymas only. The fact that Beck was going to be playing live was enough to make any guitar nut drool. But, to top it off, he co-billed the tour with another blues-rocker, the late Stevie Ray Vaughan, and "The Fire and The Fury" tour of 1989 was an indication that Jeff Beck has no intentions of putting his axe away for quite some time to come.

Selected discography

With the Yardbirds

Having A Rave Up, Epic, 1965.
Over Under Sideways Down, Epic, 1966.
Great Hits, Epic, 1967.

With the Jeff Beck Group

Truth, Epic, 1968.
Beck-Ola, Epic, 1975.
Rough and Ready, Jeff Beck Group, issued as a double album by Epic.

With Donovan

Barabajagal, Epic, 1968.

With Girls Together Outrageously

Permanent Damage, Straight, 1969.

With Stevie Wonder

Talking Book, Motown, 1972.

With Beck, Bogert and Appice

Beck, Bogert & Appice, Epic, 1973.

Solo LPs

Blow by Blow, Epic, 1975.
Wired, Epic, 1976.
There and Back, Epic, 1980.
Flash, Epic, 1985.

Guitar Shop, Epic, 1989.

With Stanley Clarke

Journey to Love, Columbia, 1975.
School Days, Columbia, 1976.
Modern Man, Epic, 1978.
I Wanna Play For You, Epic, 1979.
Time Exposure, Epic, 1984.

With Billy Preston

Billy Preston, A&M, 1976.

With the Jan Hammer Group

Live, Epic, 1977.

With Narada Michael Walden

Garden of Love Light, Atlantic, 1977.

With Box of Frogs

Box of Frogs, Epic, 1984.

With Rod Stewart

Camouflage, Warner Bros., 1984.

With Tina Turner

Private Dancer, Capitol, 1984.

With Vanilla Fudge

Mystery, Atco, 1984.

With the Honeydrippers

The Honeydrippers, Volume 1, Atlantic, 1985.

With Mick Jagger

She's the Boss, Columbia, 1985.

Sources

Books

Dalton, David and Lenny Kaye, *Rock 100*, Grosset & Dunlap, 1977.
Kozinn, Allan, Pete Welding, Dan Forte, and Gene Santoro, *The Guitar—The History, The Music, The Players*, Quill, 1984.
The Illustrated Encyclopedia of Rock, compiled by Nick Logan and Bob Woffinden, Harmony, 1977.
The Rolling Stone Record Guide, edited by Dave Marsh with John Swenson, Random House/Rolling Stone Press, 1979.

Periodicals

Guitar For The Practicing Musician, January 1986.
Guitar Player, August 1975; November 1975; September 1976;
October 1980; December 1980; January 1984; September
1985; November 1985; May 1986; January 1987; October
1989.
Guitar World, January 1985; March 1985.
Rolling Stone, July 29, 1976; September 4, 1980; October 16,
1980; March 5, 1981; November 30, 1989.

—*Calen D. Stone*

Michael Bolton

Singer, songwriter

Michael Bolton is a young singer and songwriter on the rise. With Laura Branigan's hit recording of his "That's What Love Is All About," he became a sought-after songwriter for artists such as Barbra Streisand, Cher, Kenny Rogers, and Kiss. Branigan was the first artist to record his popular single (written with Doug James) "How Am I Supposed to Live Without You," in 1983. Bolton's own recording of the song became a hit and won him the 1989 Best Male Vocalist Grammy. His 1987 solo album, *The Hunger,* occupied the charts for the better part of the year. But it was Bolton's 1989 album *Soul Provider* that went platinum. Performing an eclectic mix of rock and roll, sentimental ballads, and soulful rhythm and blues—both his own compositions and classics—Bolton has captivated audiences with the power of his raspy, four-octave voice and with the emotional intensity he conveys in his music. Tall and well-built, with chiseled features and shoulder-length brown curls, Bolton has engaged a young female audience with his appearance as well.

Reviewing *Michael Bolton,* the singer's 1983 album, for the *Wilson Library Bulletin,* Bruce Pollock called it "the classic, leather-lunged Mister Macho sound of high-power rock . . . honed to a glistening agony." Noting Bolton's kinship to singers Bob Seger and Bruce Springsteen, the critic nonetheless judged the young artist's "agony . . . truly his own,. . . his dramatic, at times overly bombastic, but always convincing vocals crashing like breakers against the rocks." *Stereo Review* writer Alanna Nash, assessing another album— *Soul-Provider*—reported that "Bolton's four-octave range can be powerful and spellbinding . . . [as] he soars through some truly amazing flights of melody." But "his bigger gift is songwriting," decided the critic. "The songs here are all uncommonly soulful . . . [and] reach an affecting level of angst."

Turning to music early, Bolton was eight when his parents rented a saxophone for him. Sitting in front of a mirror, he only pretended to play—but sang with abandon—indicating that "even then the voice was the main instrument for me," related Bolton in an interview with *Seventeen*. While lacking formal musical training, Bolton could always retain melodies and create harmonies when he performed at home or at school; most important of all, he was passionate about music, stirred by the possibility to communicate emotion. Thus soul performers like Ray Charles and Marvin Gaye were favorites: "They sing with feeling. . . . They're not inhibited about expressing emotion," Bolton explained. The young singer/songwriter penned his first composition—a love song—at the tender age of thirteen, and by fifteen had landed a record contract for the single (though its release, unfortunately, fell flat). Around 1982 Bolton finally tasted real success as a composer of rhythm and blues pieces for himself and other vocalists—his lyrics exploring "compelling things . . . that hit hard and mean a lot." Bolton's performing career has

mirrored the same steady progress. "Music is the air I breathe, how I express myself," he told *Seventeen.* "I want to move women to tears—and men—with my vocal ability and strength."

Selected discography

Michael Bolton, Columbia, 1983.
The Hunger, Columbia, 1987.
Soul Provider, Columbia, 1989.

Sources

People, June 3, 1985.
Seventeen, September 1988.
Stereo Review, October 1989.
Wilson Library Bulletin, June 1983.

—Nancy Pear

Bobby Brown

Pop singer, songwriter

"When Bobby Brown moves, fans swoon," writes Steve Dougherty in *People*. "And critics shift into hyperpraise. Even the far-from-funky *New York Times* cheered a 'bravado [Brown] performance that harks back to the glory days' of 60s music." Brown is the latest in an impressive string of pop superstars who danced their way to the top of the music world in the 1980s. Such 1980s music phenoms as Michael Jackson, Madonna, Prince, and Paula Abdul all infused their pounding rhythms and up-tempo lyrics with plenty of acrobatic dance steps in their performances. Indeed, in these days of elaborate tour productions and slick music videos, a performer's ability to dance, set new fashion standards, and make a good appearance on camera are nearly as essential as the actual music in determining their success in the increasingly competitive pop market.

And all of this has certainly not been lost on Brown, who, though still in his early twenties, has already discovered what he believes to be the key to a lasting show-business career—diversification. "I'm not just a singer, or a dancer, or a performer," Brown told *Rolling Stone*'s Rob Tannenbaum. "I want to be a lot of different things. People don't know what Bobby Brown is. I want to be mysterious. I don't want people to be able to label me. I just wanna be Bobby, the Man Who Does Everything." Brown took one large step in attaining that status with his second solo album, *Don't Be Cruel,* a 1988 release that has sold more than six million copies and spawned the Top 5 singles "My Prerogative," "Roni," and "Don't Be Cruel." The album reached Number 1 on the Billboard charts in 1989, making Brown, then just nineteen, the first teenager to record a Number 1 album since Ricky Nelson in 1957 and Stevie Wonder in 1963. The key to Brown's music, says *Rolling Stone*'s Tannenbaum, lies in Brown's ability to adapt "the traditional techniques of soul to the coarser language of rap . . . it's obvious that Brown has displaced his elders on the pop charts not just because his songs adapt hip-hop beats but also because he has revived the aggressive sexuality that rap drew from James Brown."

This hybrid sound, which has been called "the new funk," or "new jack swing," was developed simultaneously in the late 1980s by New York producer Teddy Riley and the L.A. team of Antonio Reid and Kenny "Babyface" Edmonds. The purpose of the new sound was to make the hard edges of rap a little softer for a wider teen audience. And the smooth, charismatic Brown has proven to be the perfect vehicle for the dawn of the new funk.

When Brown became a bona fide superstar with the success of *Don't Be Cruel,* he was already considered a veteran performer despite his youth. Many music fans would recognize him as a member of the early 1980s teen group New Edition, but Brown's career had its informal debut when he was just three years old. It was then that his mother set him down onstage during a James Brown concert at Boston's Sugar Shack—and his two-minute, impromptu boogie brought down the house. "I just strutted around to the music," Brown told *People.* "Ever since, I liked being onstage."

Brown grew up in Roxbury, a rough section of Boston, and though he admits his mischief in those days sometimes placed him on the wrong side of the law, he insists that his main weakness was for expensive clothes and jewelry that would set him apart. "There were two kinds of fellas at my school—the stoners and the kind who liked women and wore sharp clothes and put lotion on their hands and said nice things to the ladies," Brown told *People.* "I was the second kind. I lo-o-o-ove women . . . They've got so much more to offer emotionally."

But a tragic incident helped transform Brown from a petty thief and pretty-boy to the serious young musician he has become. When he was just eleven, Brown watched as his best friend was fatally stabbed in a knife fight. It was then that he made the determination to get out of the life he was leading. Together with several friends, Brown formed a singing group that started out doing harmony covers of Larry Graham and Donny Hathaway records. By 1980, when Brown was just twelve, the group became formally known as New Edition, and the boys had their first major break when the producer Maurice Starr heard them performing in a talent competition.

In 1981 the band signed a recording contract with MCA and, under Starr's direction, began producing singles that sounded strangely similar to such successful teen groups as the Jackson Five and the Osmonds. Starr has even admitted that New Edition's first hit single, "Candy Girl," was modeled after the Jackson Five

songs "ABC" and "I Want You Back." Regardless, Starr and MCA both knew they had a hot act on their hands, and for the next five years New Edition performed before throngs of screaming teenage girls across America.

The New Edition experience was for Brown, in progression, a dream, an experience, a business, and finally a hassle. He quit the group in 1986 when infighting among the band members had grown intense, and when Brown grew suspicious that he was being swindled by MCA and Starr. There were also rumors that the band was using drugs, rumors which Brown claims were fanned by the rejected managers. "People at MCA thought we was into drugs," Brown told *Rolling Stone.* "That wasn't us. We were a bunch of brats, but we wasn't into drugs, we wasn't into liquor. We was into girls."

Embarking on his solo career, Brown decided that he wanted to keep his career closer to home, so he put his affairs into the hands of his brother, Tommy, and his mother. Starr, on the other hand, told *Rolling Stone,* "I was gonna make New Edition the biggest group in the world. When we parted, I said, 'Let me show them how smart I am—I'm coming back with a *white* teen group.'" Sure enough, Starr did return with the immensely successful, all-white group New Kids on the Block in the late 1980s.

But Brown knows he has moved beyond the teenybopper circuit. His heroes have always been the greats— like Michael Jackson, Elvis, and James Brown—and for good measure he would like to develop himself as an actor, a la Madonna, Prince, and Eddie Murphy. When the producers of the film *Ghostbusters II* came knocking on the door of MCA records in search of a distributor for the film's soundtrack album, Brown was MCA's hottest act. MCA was awarded the contract on the stipulation that Brown appear prominently on the album, a project the singer was only too happy to undertake. There was some risk, however, in that the record would have to stand up to comparison with the first *Ghostbusters* soundtrack, which featured Ray Parker's gigantic single "Ghostbusters." Realizing that his participation was the key to the deal, Brown shrewdly agreed to sing on the album on the condition that he be given a role in the film. The result was Brown's surprisingly effective cameo appearance in the film as the obnoxious butler of the mayor of New York. "Acting is just a frame of mind," Brown told *Rolling Stone* with a characteristic shrug. "If you know how to block the camera off from being there, it's easy to act like another person. It's very easy." And for now, Brown is acting like the new edition of the ultimate pop superstar.

Selected discography

King of Stage, MCA, 1987.
Don't Be Cruel, MCA, 1988.
Ghostbusters II Motion Picture Soundtrack, 1990.

Sources

Rolling Stone, September 7, 1989.

—David Collins

Jimmy Buffett

Singer, songwriter, guitarist

The grandson of a sea captain and son of a Navy shipbuilder, singer/songwriter Jimmy Buffett has also embraced the seagoing life in his singular way, celebrating its easy charms in his songs. A lifetime resident of the Gulf Coast and frequent Caribbean traveler in his fifty-foot ketch, *Euphoria II,* Buffett affectionately and humorously chronicles his adventures on land and sea, his vivid portraits of people and places—and his own genial drunken-sailor persona—taking him from local cult figure to international pop and country star. The once-starving artist (who recalls his secret supermarket raids in the early song "Peanut Butter Conspiracy") scored his first big success with the 1977 gold record "Margaritaville," introducing the nation to his fine songwriting and unique folk-country-rock-Caribbean sound. From that point on, Buffett has enjoyed steady success as a performing and recording artist. "His music, like his life-style, is a gentle blend of folksy Southern rock and infatuation with the Caribbean," observed one critic in *Time* magazine. "Buffett writes, often puckishly, of Gulf Stream idyls, Latin crimes of passion, and tequila-filled days. His themes, presented in simple rhythms and sung in an engaging baritone, have the languorous appeal of a fishnet hammock." "A bit of reggae here. A little Beach Boys there. A dash of country and a pinch of rock," detailed *People* reviewer Ralph Novak. "That is the basic Buffett recipe, which is cooked up . . . to good effect."

Raised in Mobile, Alabama, and educated in Catholic schools, Buffett felt the need "to bust out" after high school graduation. The pleasures of New Orleans beckoned, distracting him from his journalism studies at a nearby university; a decent guitarist with a good voice, Buffett began to perform folk music in local clubs, and to compose original folk songs. In the late 1960s he moved to Nashville, intent on entering the music business. While writing for *Billboard* magazine Buffett performed on the side, eventually obtaining a recording contract with Barnaby Records. His *Down to Earth,* a country-oriented album, appeared in 1972 and sold poorly; in another bad break, Barnaby Records misplaced the master tape to his second album before its release. Discouraged—and stricken by the familiar wanderlust—Buffett moved to Los Angeles to pursue other music opportunities, but succumbed to life in the fast lane once again. He finally settled near Key West, Florida, living for a time aboard his ketch, island-hopping and smuggling marijuana to support himself. Feeling at home around the Caribbean, the singer explained in *Time:* "There are a lot of incredible characters down there, as migratory and gypsy-souled as I am."

Buffett performed his folk-rock-country songs at local shrimpers' bars as he struggled to obtain new recording contracts. Dunhill released his moderately successful third album, *A White Sport Coat and a Pink Crustacean,* in 1973. *Living and Dying in 3/4 Time* added to the singer's small circle of fans, as well as earning him the chance to score and appear in the motion picture *Rancho Deluxe.* His first platinum album, *Changes in Attitudes, Changes in Latitudes* (with its runaway hit single "Margaritaville") appeared in 1977, and illustrated Buffett's crossover appeal as it climbed both pop and country charts. More gold and platinum recordings followed; the performer's infrequent tours and concerts were also successful. In 1975 Buffett had formed his own backup group, the Coral Reefer Band, with Roger Bartlett on guitar, Greg "Fingers" Taylor on harmonica, Harry Dailey on bass, and Phillip Fajardo on drums (Tim Krekel and Keith Sykes later replaced Bartlett and Fajardo; Jay Spell joined on keyboard). While a handful of critics have frowned on Buffett's preoccupation with strong drink and American camp (with tunes like "My Head Hurts, My Feet Stink and I Don't Love Jesus" and "Cheeseburger in Paradise"), he is generally regarded as a superior songwriter, his albums distinguished by exceptional moments. "Buffett is predictable," concluded Novak in a review of *Riddles in the Sand,* "but he's predictably entertaining too."

Writings

(With Savannah Jane Buffett and illustrator Lambert Davis) *The Jolly Mon* (juvenile), Harcourt, 1988.
Tales From Margaritaville: Fictional Facts and Factual Fictions (short story and autobiographical sketch collection), Harcourt, 1989.

Compositions

Has written and co-written numerous songs, including "Peanut Butter Conspiracy," "Havana Daydreamin'," "Margaritaville," "Cheeseburger in Paradise," and "Who's the Blonde Stranger?" Scored motion picture *Rancho Deluxe;* contributed to soundtrack of motion picture *Going West.*

Selected discography

Dawn to Earth, Barnaby, 1972.
A White Sport Coat and a Pink Crustacean, Dunhill, 1973.
Living and Dying in 3/4 Time, Dunhill, 1974.
A-1-A, Dunhill, 1974.
Rancho Deluxe (soundtrack), United Artists, 1975.
High Cumberland Jamboree, Barnaby, 1976.
Havana Daydreamin', ABC, 1976.
Changes in Latitudes, Changes in Attitudes, ABC, 1977.
Son of a Son of a Sailor, ABC, 1978.
Jimmy Buffett Live, ABC, 1978.
You Had to Be There, MCA, 1978.
Volcano, MCA, 1979.
Somewhere Over China, MCA, 1981.
Coconut Telegraph, MCA, 1981.
One Particular Harbor, MCA, 1983.
Riddles in the Sand, MCA, 1984.
Last Mango in Paris, MCA, 1985.
Songs You Know by Heart: Jimmy Buffett's Greatest Hits, MCA, 1986.
Floridays, MCA, 1986.
Hot Water, MCA, 1988.

Sources

Books

The New Rolling Stone Record Guide, edited by Dave Marsh and John Swenson, Random House, 1983.
The Rolling Stone Encyclopedia of Rock 'n' Roll, edited by Jon Pareles and Patricia Romanowski, Summit Books, 1983.
The Encyclopedia of Folk, Country, and Western Music, St. Martin's, 1983.

Periodicals

Library Journal, October 1, 1989.
People, November 5, 1984; April 15, 1985.
Publishers Weekly, February 12, 1988.
Time, April 18, 1977.

—Nancy Pear

Kate Bush

Singer, songwriter

Much like her British compatriot, Peter Gabriel, to whom she is often compared, Kate Bush is a cult pop-star in the truest sense of the term. With each successive album, her followers become more convincingly hooked, and a handful of new devotees join the growing ranks of her audience. Dark, mysterious, and otherworldly, her highly theatrical musical arrangements are as disturbing as they are beautiful. "In one or two of the American reviews of *The Dreaming*," writes Peter Swales in *Musician*, referring to Bush's 1982 LP, "[her] music was described as schizophrenic—and it seems to me that, in a manner of speaking, [it] does represent a virtual compendium of psychopathology, alternately hysterical, melancholic, psychotic, paranoid, obsessional, and so on." It is an assessment that Bush is not altogether uncomfortable with. "I think that is the most fascinating thing to write about," she told Swales, "the way people distort their attitudes."

But at the heart of this intense, exploratory music is a woman who is very much in control of her art and her life. Since her impressive debut at the age of nineteen with the album *The Kick Inside,* Bush has shown a maturity far beyond her years, especially in maintaining a firm guard over her private life. "I try very hard to keep privacy in my life," she told *Rolling Stone.* "I don't see what my private life has got to do with my music. Although obviously there's a lot of me in my music. It's my music I feel I want to give to the world, and not myself."

This distancing of herself from her music may be the most fascinating aspect of Bush's stage performances, which are highly contrived, visual presentations of the stories her songs are telling. Trained in classical dance and mime, Bush is, on stage and in her elaborate videos, more like an opera diva than a pop star. Her costumes and makeup are masks that Bush hides behind as she enters the world of her music. "I don't want to be up there on the stage being *me,*" she told Swales. "I don't think I'm that interesting. What I want to do is to be the person that's in the song. If I can be the character in the song, then suddenly there's all this strength and energy in me which I wouldn't normally have."

In recent years, Bush has abandoned live performing, however. It is a policy she adheres to despite the objections of her record company, fans, and the music press. "I go straight from an album into making videos, and it's a total involvement for me," Bush told Sheila Rogers of *Rolling Stone.* "By the time the video and promotion are done for an album, I'm absolutely exhausted; there's nothing left of me. . . . What matters to me now is spending as much time in the studio as I can, trying to make a good album."

For the Record. . .

Born c. 1959 in Great Britain; daughter of a surgeon; single. *Education:* Attended school in Kent, England.

Studied piano and violin during childhood; performed informally with brothers, Paddy and John, during childhood and early teens; after a family friend played several of Bush's original compositions for Pink Floyd's David Gilmour, c. 1975, Gilmour arranged and paid for a demo record, which led to a recording contract; released first album, *The Kick Inside,* 1977; professional singer-songwriter, 1977—.

Addresses: *Record company*—EMI America, c/o CEMA, 1750 N. Vine St., Hollywood, CA 90028.

In the studio is where Kate Bush the artist feels most at home; there, she is able to retreat from the circuslike media attention that surrounded her when she burst onto the British music scene in the late 1970s. The first single from *The Kick Inside,* the fiery "Wuthering Heights," went to Number 1 on the U.K. charts, and Bush was soon overwhelmed by the strange way in which her public persona was manipulated. One sophomoric British tabloid even went so far as to cast Bush in the role of a cute pinup girl. "It became one big promotional public exercise," she told *Rolling Stone*'s Rogers. "I had no control over the situation. . . . It was exactly not what I wanted." It was not until she acquired her own studio and put up walls around her private life that Bush found her stride again.

But Bush had not entered the music world as a total innocent. Raised in a highly musical family, she was blessed from the outset of her career with a tightly knit support center that helped pave her way to success. Though her father was a surgeon, he also played piano, and Bush's mother was an accomplished Irish dancer. But it was her two brothers, Paddy and John, who probably had the most to do with shaping Bush's musical tastes and bringing her songs to the attention of producers. The brothers, both accomplished musicians and lovers of traditional English and Irish music, gave to their younger sister an appreciation of storytelling in music, as well as exposure to a wide variety of traditional instruments, such as the mandolin, bouzouki, and Celtic harp.

It was Paddy who first introduced Bush to her longtime companion, bassist and engineer Del Palmer. "I'd heard about Kate," Palmer told *Musician,* "but I'd had this impression that she was older, more mature. At our first rehearsal I felt an emotional involvement right from the word go . . . Her songs all started off in a familiar way, but then suddenly they'd leap somewhere completely different and you'd think, 'How could you think of going *there?* ' It was a phenomenon completely different from what anyone else was doing. I've never had any desire to work with anyone else since." Around that time a friend played a couple of Bush's songs for Pink Floyd's David Gilmour, who was impressed to the point that he paid to have three of the songs professionally recorded. The demos led to a recording contract with EMI. "He gave me a pathway through," Bush said of Gilmour in *Rolling Stone.* The two worked together again in 1989, when Gilmour appeared on Bush's album *The Sensual World.*

Though Bush's records have sold steadily in England, her cultlike following in America has probably been due as much to her distaste for self-promotion as to the eccentricity of her music. Still, her 1985 album *The Hounds of Love* did produce a Top 30 hit single, "Running Up That Hill," which was accompanied by an extremely popular video. But Bush is hardly concerned that she is not seen as a superstar in the U.S.; rather, she is glad for a little anonymity. "It's really nice for me to feel that I'm being seen almost as a new artist by America," she told *Rolling Stone.* "I like the idea . . . of being able to start from a musical base. That's what I've always wanted."

Selected discography

The Kick Inside, EMI, 1977.
Lionheart, EMI.
Never For Ever, EMI.
The Dreaming, EMI, 1982.
The Hounds of Love, EMI, 1985.
The Whole Story, EMI, 1987.
The Sensual World, Columbia, 1989.

Sources

Musician, January 1986.
People, November 13, 1989.
Rolling Stone, February 13, 1986; February 8, 1990.
Stereo Review, January 1986.

—Dave Collins

The Canadian Brass

Brass quintet

S ince their appearance on the music scene in the 1970s, the Toronto-based Canadian Brass have established themselves as the first self-supporting professional brass quintet. With a popular blend of virtuosity, spontaneity, and humor the Canadian Brass has played to sold-out crowds worldwide. They have appeared on many popular television shows and are recording favorites. According to Arnold Jacobs, a founding member of one of the world's first brass quintets, the Canadian Brass has revolutionized brass music. "They are both splendid performers and a musically aggressive group," Jacobs declared to Ed Haag of the *Canadian.* "If it wasn't for them, brass music would not have the major audience appeal it enjoys today."

While the members of the quintet have varied over the years, its founders, Eugene Watts and Charles Daellenbach, remain. Although they both held respected positions with various organizations, they were dissatisfied with the performance opportunities available to them. To create the opportunities they wanted, Watts

For the Record. . .

Members of quintet include **Charles Daellenbach** (tuba); *Education:* graduated (at 25) from the Eastman School of Music, Ph.D. in music education; **Fred Mills** (trumpet); *Education:* Juilliard School of Music; **David Ohanian** (French horn); *Education:* New England Conservatory of Music; **Ronald Romm** (trumpet); *Education:* Juilliard School of Music; **Eugene Watts** (trombone), born and raised in Sedalia, Mo.; *Education:* University of Missouri.

Before joining the Canadian Brass: Daellenbach was head of the brass division at the University of Toronto; dean of apprenticeship program called the Hamilton Philharmonic Institute, 1974. Mills was principal trumpet in the American and Houston symphony orchestras; performed at the Casals Festival in Puerto Rico, and the Marlboro Music Festival; principal trumpet of New York City Opera Orchestra, six years; principal trumpet of National Arts Center Orchestra, Ottawa, Ontario. Ohanian's career began in Fountainbleu, France, where at sixteen he was awarded a scholarship to study with Nadia Boulanger; performed more than ten years with the Boston Symphony and Boston Pops; founding member of Empire Brass Quintet. Romm became a trumpet soloist at age ten; member of the Romm-Antics at twelve (his family's band); by age eighteen he performed regularly with the Los Angeles Philharmonic; freelance trumpeter while in college with the New York Philharmonic and the Radio City Music Hall Symphony Orchestra; joined the Canadian Brass in 1971. Watts played trombone in various taverns and nightclubs; formed a Dixieland band while at college called the "Missouri Mudcats"; held positions with the North Carolina, the San Antonio, and the Milwaukee symphonies; principal trombone of the Toronto Symphony.

Addresses: *Office*—Canadian Brass Management Office, 40 Alexander St., PH 1, Toronto, Ontario, Canada, M4Y 1B5. *Manager*—Gurtman and Murtha Associates, Inc., 162 W. 56th St., New York, NY 10019. *Publicist*—Avril Helbig, Canadian Brass Music Producing, 6 Wychwood Park, Toronto, Ontario, Canada, M6G 2V5. *Other*—Columbia Artists Festivals, 165 W. 57th St., New York, NY 10019.

and Daellenbach founded a brass quintet with French-horn player Graeme Page (who was replaced by David Ohanian in 1983) and several temporary trumpeters before current trumpeters Fred Mills and Ronald Romm joined the ensemble. In order to draw financial support during the developmental period, the group rehearsed with the Philharmonic Orchestra of Hamilton, Ontario, once a week, and spent the rest of the time performing in local schools. In one year they gave as many as 300 concerts. The exposure was important and helped them develop their distinctive style. When children in their audiences would become distracted, one of the group would crack a joke to attract the children's attention.

Since then a desire to show the audience that classical music can be fun has become a central goal of the Canadian Brass. The comical onstage antics that have led to their being called "The Marx Brothers of Brass" and "The Court Jesters of Chamber Music" are their trademark—that and sterling musicianship. "Rather than approaching music with the idea of simply faithfully reproducing something Beethoven wrote," Watts told *Ovation*'s Jeanne Quill, "we present ourselves as people who talk, think, have feelings and relate to our audiences as people. Just as ballet is a combination of music and dance, and opera is a combination of music, theater and art, what we are doing is combining everything that we can do. It's not just a concert or a recital—it's really a very special presentation of our talents." Sometimes that presentation includes dancing across the stage as they play music from Tchaikovsky's ballet *Swan Lake* or strolling into the concert hall as if in a New Orleans jazz funeral procession. Tubist Daellenbach often prefaces pieces with a humorous, but informative, introduction. The group's repertoire includes music that spans four centuries, from Bach and Mozart to Gershwin and Dixieland. They have also commissioned numerous arrangements and works, such as *Hornesmoke,* "the first horse opera written for brass quintet," by musical satirist Peter Schickele (also known as P.D.Q. Bach), and avant-garde works by Lukas Foss and Michael Colgrass.

Touring widely, the Canadian Brass gives more than 150 concerts annually, with 100 of those in the United States alone. It was the first musical ensemble to tour the People's Republic of China in 1977 as part of a cultural exchange program arranged by the Canadian government. Since then the group has performed to packed houses in Europe, the Middle East, the Soviet Union, Australia, and Japan. The Canadian Brass has also been seen often on commercial television in such shows as "Entertainment Tonight," "The Today Show," "The Tonight Show" with Johnny Carson, and "Sesame Street." The Canadian Brass has been the subject of a one-hour special on Public Broadcasting Service, "Canadian Brass Live," and appeared as guest artists with the Boston Pops and in "Music around the World," hosted by the celebrated soprano Beverly Sills.

With more than twenty albums to their credit, the Canadian Brass's discography reflects the group members' far-ranging musical tastes. *Brass in Berlin* features music of sixteenth- through eighteenth-century Europe, *Basin Street* is a Dixieland jazz recording with actor George Segal singing and playing the banjo, and *A Canadian Brass Christmas* presents holiday favorites. The classical release *The Art of the Fugue*, which marks the first complete recording of Johann Sebastian Bach's fugues by a brass quintet, was on the Billboard Classical Music Chart for fourteen weeks, peaking at the Number 9 spot. The *Basin Street* recording was even more successful: it was on the Billboard Crossover Chart for forty-two weeks, peaking at the Number 4 spot. The group's success in the record stores has given its members greater freedom to pursue projects that most record producers would not consider lucrative.

The players' interest in education is also reflected in many activities: brass workshops, video tapes, and music publishing under the corporate names of *Brass Works Music* and *Dr. Brass*. Despite a hectic performance schedule, the group has conducted many workshops and master classes with students of varying ages, encouraging excellence in ensemble playing throughout North America. An hour-long educational program on video, *A Canadian Brass Master Class*, shows the group working with students on specific topics of performing: posture and breathing, tonguing and embouchure, and playing with an ensemble. Because their music has become so popular, the Canadian Brass has published as sheet music many of the works from their recordings in *The Canadian Brass Ensemble Series* as well as pieces for early and intermediate performers in *The Canadian Brass Educational Series* and for more advanced soloists in *The Canadian Brass Solo Performing Editions*. With the sheet music in these educational series are recordings of the works which include insightful introductions and comments by the players.

The Canadian Brass performs exclusively on Yamaha instruments, a perfectly matched set of horns plated with 24-carat gold.

Selected discography

Canadian Brass, Vanguard Records.
Canadian Brass Encore, CBC.
Ain't Misbehavin' (music of Fats Waller), RCA Red Seal.
Pachelbel Canon and Other Great Baroque Hits, RCA Red Seal.
The Village Band, RCA Red Seal.
Christmas with the Canadian Brass, RCA Red Seal.
High Bright, Light and Clear, RCA Red Seal.
Canadian Brass—Greatest Hits (from *The Village Band* and *Strike Up the Band*), RCA Red Seal.
Strike up the Band, RCA Red Seal.
Canadian Brass—More Greatest Hits, RCA Red Seal.
Champions, CBS Masterworks.
Brass in Berlin, CBS Masterworks.
Canadian Brass Live, CBS Masterworks.
A Canadian Brass Christmas, CBS Masterworks.
Vivaldi: The Four Seasons, CBS Masterworks.
Basin Street (featuring George Segal), CBS Masterworks.
Bach: The Art of the Fugue, CBS Masterworks.
The Mozart Album, CBS Masterworks.
Gabrieli/Monteverdi: Antiphonal Music, CBS Masterworks.
Elizabethan Renaissance Album, CBS Masterworks.
Beethoven Album, Philips Classics.

Selected video tapes (distributed by Hal Leonard Publishing)

The Canadian Brass Master Class, Recording Special Video Productions, Fairfield, Iowa.
The Canadian Brass SPECTACULAR.
Canadian Brass Live, Gurtman and Murtha Associates, New York.

Sources

Canadian, April 1988.
Fairfield Ledger (Iowa), February 16, 1989.
Maclean's, August 21, 1989.
Ovation, July 1987.
Toronto Star, June 10, 1989.

—Jeanne M. Lesinski

Kim Carnes

Singer, songwriter

In 1981 Kim Carnes released the year's hit single, "Bette Davis Eyes." The provocative song about a *femme fatale* who "snows you off your feet with the crumbs that she throws you," "Eyes" seemed the perfect vehicle for Carnes and her distinctively raspy voice, a voice once described by Karen Stabiner in *Rolling Stone* as having "a fault line running through it." In a singing career of more than a decade "Eyes" was Carnes's first runaway top seller, its rock beat and insouciant feel a departure from the soulful ballads she had favored in prior recordings—and in her successful songwriting partnership with husband Dave Ellingson. Calling "Bette Davis Eyes" "the most seductive pop single in years," *Newsweek*'s Jim Miller wrote that "its lyric has an offbeat after-hours allure that is given shape and texture by Carnes's husky voice—a hoarse shrug of pleasure." Jay Cocks similarly observed in *Time:* "She does not try to camp it, or torch it. Carnes just glides through it, getting inside its slinky rhythm as if it were a cocktail dress cut on the bias. . . . She has, simply, a good solid way with a ballad. . . . Despite what she calls her 'perpetual frog,' she sings as if she has a gardenia behind her ear." The *Time* writer added that, despite its rock leanings, "Eyes" shows "the kind of straight-on pop craftsmanship that distinguished some of [Carnes's] previous albums, an unashamed hovering right above the middle of the road."

The only child of a lawyer and a hospital administrator, Carnes grew up in San Marino, California—a conservative, affluent suburb of Los Angeles. Her enthusiasm for show business was not encouraged, save for the acceptable classical piano lessons; nonetheless, Carnes pursued her interest in pop and rock music, sang at school functions and with local bands, and tried her hand at songwriting. After high school she wrote and performed commercials and made demonstration records. A successful audition with the folk-oriented New Christy Minstrels had Carnes "singing about slavery with eight other kids with these big smiles pasted on our faces" for a year—an admitted embarrassment mitigated by her romance with fellow minstrel and future husband Ellingson. With Ellingson as her songwriting collaborator and personal adviser, Carnes embarked on a solo career, occasionally working as an opening act for touring performers, then obtaining a recording contract with Amos/Bell Records. Her first album, *Rest on Me,* quietly came and went in 1972, but its original Carnes-Ellingson numbers piqued the interest of other recording artists. While Carnes continued to struggle in her singing career (A&M released two more critically-approved, poorly-selling albums in 1975 and 1976), things were heating up for the songwriting duo—music executives were frequently engaged by the new compositions the singer introduced in her demos, often suggesting that big-name clients record them.

For the Record. . .

Born in 1948 in Los Angeles, Calif.; raised in San Marino, Calif.; daughter of an attorney and a hospital administrator; married Dave Ellingson (a singer and songwriter) in late 1960s; children: Collin. *Education:* Attended Pasadena City College.

Singer, songwriter, mid-1960s—; vocalist with New Christy Minstrels, late-1960s; songwriter with husband Ellingson, late-1960s—; solo recording artist, 1972—. Writes and performs themes for commercials.

Awards: "Love Comes From Unexpected Places," written with Ellingson, won American and Tokyo Song Festivals in 1977; Grammy Award for record of the year, 1981, for "Bette Davis Eyes"; co-recipient of Grammy for best album of an original score written for a motion picture, 1983, for *Flashdance.*

Addresses: *Home*—Sherman Oaks, Calif. *Record company*—CEMA/EMI, 1750 N. Vine St., Hollywood, Calif. 90028

In 1977 Barbra Streisand recorded the Carnes-Ellingson ballad "Love Comes From Unexpected Places" (released a year earlier by Carnes) and the cut went platinum. Frank Sinatra recorded the duo's "You Turned My World Around," and other clients included Anne Murray and Rita Coolidge. The pair collaborated on Kenny Rogers's top-selling 1978 album *Gideon:* Carnes and Rogers dueted in "Don't Fall in Love With a Dreamer," a cut that climbed to Number 5 on the country charts. With success begetting success, Carnes followed with a popular single of her own, a remake of Smokey Robinson's 1967 hit "More Love" on her briskly-selling fifth album *Romance Dance.* With a mix of rhythm and blues, country tunes, rock and roll, and the soft ballads that dominated Carnes's earlier recordings, the album showed a clear effort to broaden the singer's appeal. Especially interested in capturing the album-oriented rock listener, Carnes concentrated more on rock and roll in subsequent recordings, with the platinum album *Mistaken Identity* and its Grammy-winning "Eyes" one happy result. Ironically, the song was co-written and recorded by pop singer Jackie DeShannon in 1975, and was a sleeper given new life by Carnes's throaty delivery and Bill Cuomo's high-tech arrangement. Carnes explored hard rock in the album *Voyeur,* which appeared the following year.

Carnes continued to release charted singles throughout the 1980s, although none quite duplicated the success of "Bette Davis Eyes." To some fans of the "old" Carnes, the singer—trading her tennis shoes and overalls for a sexy black jacket and recording less of her own compositions in favor of more commercial songs—seemed to be selling out, an assessment Carnes dismisses as misinformed and simplistic. "I want to keep a variety of styles because they all reflect different sides of me," the singer explained to *Time.* "I've always loved rock 'n' roll. I'm not a manufactured product. I've made a point of changing." After too many years with an idling performing career, Carnes is enjoying her late arrival thoroughly.

Selected discography

Rest on Me, Amos, 1970.
Kim Carnes, A&M, 1975.
Sailin', A&M, 1976.
St. Vincent's Court, EMI America, 1979.
Romance Dance, EMI America, 1980.
Mistaken Identity, EMI America, 1981.
Voyeur, EMI America, 1982.
The Best of Kim Carnes, A&M, 1982.
Cafe Racers, EMI America, 1983.
Barking at Airplanes, EMI America, 1985.
Lighthouse, EMI America, 1986.
View From the House, MCA, 1988.

Recorded single "She Dances With Meat" under pseudonym Connie Con Carne, 1979.

Scored, with Ellingson and Jimmy Bowen, motion picture *Vanishing Point;* contributor to score of motion picture *Flashdance.*

Sources

Books

Stambler, Irwin, *The Encyclopedia of Pop, Rock and Soul,* revised edition, St. Martin's, 1989.

Periodicals

Newsweek, September 21, 1981.
Rolling Stone, September 18, 1980; July 9, 1981.
Stereo Review, December, 1988.
Time, July 27, 1981.

—Nancy Pear

Tracy Chapman

Singer, songwriter, guitarist

In an era when the label folksinger-songwriter does little to guarantee success, Tracy Chapman has seen her dreams come true. When Chapman takes the stage sporting short dreadlocks, blue jeans, and a turtleneck sweater, accompanied only by her acoustic guitar, listeners lean forward to hear her husky contralto pour forth poignant reflections on contemporary urban life. As Steve Pond of *Rolling Stone* noted, Chapman's voice "is the sound of a smart black woman growing up in the city with her eyes wide open."

Though she is a relative newcomer to the folk music circuit, Chapman has always made music an important part of her life. Chapman's parents divorced when she was four years old, and she grew up with her mother and older sister in a largely black middle-class neighborhood in Cleveland, Ohio. At an early age she learned to sing, play the clarinet and organ, and compose simple songs that she sang with her sister, Aneta. While still in grade school Chapman began to teach herself how to play the guitar. She told *Washington Post* writer Richard Harrington: "I've been singing ever since I was a child. My mother has a beautiful voice, as does my sister. At that point I wasn't really listening to that much music at all, except what my parents were listening to, or my sister. I think I just picked up a guitar because my mother had played it at some point—started teaching myself things and writing my own songs."

Wanting to make a better life for herself than those she witnessed about her, Chapman worked hard to earn A Better Chance (ABC) minority placement scholarship to the Wooster School, a small, progressive, private high school in Danbury, Connecticut. In contrast to the metal-detector-equipped public high school she had attended, at Wooster she was thoroughly immersed in an atmosphere of social and political discussion. At times she had difficulties with her sheltered classmates; she told *Time* that "students there just said very stupid things. They had never met a poor person before. In some ways they were curious, but in ways that were just insulting." The school was a haven for musicians, however. She met other guitar players who introduced her to a variety of popular music, including the early protest works of Bob Dylan. Chapman's teachers recognized her talent and gave her ample opportunities to perform. In a gesture of support, the school chaplain took up a collection among the faculty and students and bought the young singer a new guitar to replace her battered one.

Despite the strong support for her musical talent, Chapman did not seriously consider music as a career. When she enrolled at Tufts University, near Boston, she aspired to become a veterinarian. However, a short while later she changed her major to anthropology with

For the Record. . .

B orn 1964, in Cleveland, Ohio. *Education:* Tufts University, B.A. in anthropology, 1986.

Played ukelele, organ, and clarinet as a young child; began playing guitar and singing original songs at the age of ten; during high school, performed at school functions and at local coffee houses in Connecticut; while in college, performed at church services, on street corners, and in coffee houses in Boston, Mass.; signed a recording contract, 1986; live performer at clubs, festivals, and in U.S. and international concerts, 1986—.

Awards: Grammy Award for best new artist, for best female pop vocal performance, and for best contemporary folk performance, all 1989.

Addresses: *Home*—Boston, Mass. *Office*—c/o Elektra Records, 75 Rockefeller Plaza, New York, N.Y. 10019.

an emphasis on West African cultures, the field in which she eventually earned her bachelor's degree. In college Chapman continued to perform her own compositions in coffee houses, on street corners, and at folk-oriented church services. She was offered a recording contract with an independent label but turned it down, not wanting to interrupt her education. Chapman's decision proved to be fortuitous. One of her classmates, Brian Koppelman, approached her after hearing her play to suggest that his father might be able to help her singing career. The father in question was Charles Koppelman, the K in SBK, one of the world's largest music publishing companies. At Brian's suggestion, Charles Koppelman came to hear Chapman perform, and later he told *Newsweek:* "Her songs were wonderful melodies with important lyrics. That was enough. But when I saw her in front of an audience! When she smiled, everyone smiled. When she was serious, you could hear a pin drop."

Chapman had considered working toward a master's degree in ethnomusicology, the study of chiefly non-European music, especially in relation to the culture that produces it. But after graduating in 1986, she signed a management agreement with SBK, to be represented by Elliott Roberts, who also manages singers Joni Mitchell and Neil Young. A demonstration cassette taped by Chapman at the SBK studios eventually led to a recording contract with Elektra Records.

Chapman settled on producer David Kershenbaum and hired a backup band to contribute to the record

for Elektra. Describing Chapman's voice to *Time,* Kershenbaum said, "The timbre of it is rare to find. It instantly disarms you." Because she is a prolific songwriter, there was no lack of music from which to select the pieces that make up her self-titled debut album. *Tracy Chapman* breaks all of the rules of popular music marketing. The melodies wander and are oddly phrased, and many of the songs explore serious subjects—racism, domestic violence, the failed American dream, material and emotional self-determination—and do not fit the format of commercial radio. The background instrumentals are limited, focusing attention on Chapman's percussive use of the acoustic guitar, and one selection is even sung a cappella. In seeming defiance to trends, Chapman's album rose to the number one position on *Billboard*'s best-seller chart without discernible airplay and engendered a music video, which alternates segments of Chapman singing in her usual concert attire and still photographs of gritty real-life scenes.

For just this sort of blunt realism, reviewers describe *Tracy Chapman* as downbeat, particularly the cuts "Talkin' 'bout a Revolution" and "Why?" Yet Chapman remains hopeful that her music can reach a wide audience *and* deliver a message. As she told the *New York Times:* "On a certain level, I think something positive is going to happen, though I don't think it's necessarily going to be an actual revolution. Even though I'm a cynic, there's still a part of me that believes people will get to a certain point where they can't stand the way things are and have to change the way they think."

The power of Chapman's songs to motivate change lies in their psychological realism, their universal poignancy. With an eye for detail, Chapman uses just enough specifics to suggest events or situations known to listeners regardless of where they live. She chronicles in song the human condition. When asked about her songwriting ability, Chapman told *Musician* writer Kristine McKenna: "I don't have structured writing habits. I've written hundreds of songs and have enough material for three albums so I don't see writing as a problem. I play my guitar every day and always have fragments of ideas floating around my head, but I never force a song into being. My songs aren't autobiographical, but they usually combine a variety of things I've seen, heard or read about. Occasionally it will be something that happened to me, but I'll combine that with other things."

Chapman has frequently been compared to folksingers Joan Armatrading, Joni Mitchell, and Phoebe Snow. Some reviewers see her as "a bridge between the folk music revival of the eighties and the socially conscious folk movement of the sixties," a bridge girded by the efforts of another female folksinger—Suzanne Vega. Chapman balks at being labeled, whether the label is folksinger or black woman artist. As she told a *Chicago Tribune* writer: "I don't just think of what I do as folk music, which I define as music rooted in an Anglo-European tradition, but as music that also reflects Afro-American black music. Personally, it wasn't a matter of being drawn to a particular music; in a sense, the instrument you play defines what you play."

Chapman's performance schedule has no doubt been influenced by her social conscience: the Sisterfire festival in Washington, D.C.; Amnesty International's worldwide Human Rights Now! tour; and a march to commemorate Dr. Martin Luther King. Chapman takes to the stage with more ease than she wears her star status, however. Even as a young dreamer, Chapman never expected to sign with a major label, and when she did she didn't foresee the popularity of Tracy Chapman, albums and person.

Her second record, *Crossroads,* was tremendously popular, selling 4 million copies in the first five months of its release. Because of her repeat success many critics believe that a resurgence in protest music is likely in the 1990s, thanks in part to Chapman. Not altogether comfortable with her celebrity, she admitted to McKenna, of *Musician:* "The idea of being famous doesn't appeal to me because I hate parties and it seems like it might be one big party. I value my privacy and I'm not used to dealing with lots of people. The prospect of wealth is scary too. When you're poor your first responsibility is to yourself, but when you have money you have to think about other people—and other people are definitely thinking about you!"

Selected discography

Tracy Chapman (includes "Fast Car," "Baby Can I Hold You," "Talkin' 'bout a Revolution," "She's Got Her Ticket," "Behind the Wall," "For My Lover," "If Not Now. . .," "Why?" "Across the Lines," "Mountains o' Things," and "For You"), Elektra, 1988.
Crossroads, Elektra, 1989.

Sources

Chicago Tribune, August 14, 1988.
Detroit News, September 4, 1988.
Musician, June 1988.
Newsweek, June 20, 1988.
New York Times, September 4, 1988.
Rolling Stone, June 2, 1988; June 30, 1988.
Time, August 15, 1988; March 12, 1990.

—*Jeanne M. Lesinski*

Neneh Cherry

Singer

At first, critics identified her as the step-daughter of Don Cherry, the noted jazz trumpeter. But as her debut album began to catch on, Neneh Cherry stepped out of that shadow and found herself with an impressive following of her own. Her first single, "Buffalo Stance," shot to the top of the charts in both England and the U.S., earning praise in *Rolling Stone* as 1989's "best and boldest hit single." Then, following the release of her album *Raw Like Sushi, Rolling Stone* commented that while "many musicians have built retirement funds by imitating the musical and sexual paths of Prince and Madonna . . . [Cherry] may be the first newcomer inspired by them who also poses a threat to their preeminence." The reason was clear: *Raw Like Sushi* delivered not only great music but the hope that America's pop-goddess icon might be reinvented in a more positive form. Cherry, to be sure, has beauty and sex appeal to spare. But unlike the vast numbers of MTV glam queens, she also exudes power, confidence, creativity, intelligence, and, having given birth to her second daughter during the making of the album, an uncommon level of maturity.

Cherry's songs are a groovacious blend of rap, pop, and jars; their content, as the *New York Times* noted, amounts to "streetwise pep talks urging self-respect." Her style is to alternate between rap and melody, which allows her to sound eloquent and tough in a single song. "People are beginning to use the power of melody in combination with the power of blatant aggression," the singer told *Pulse!,* "and I don't mean aggression as in violence, but as in reality, honesty, raw edge." That edge is part and parcel of her music: as *Musician* noted, "There's no coy nonsense or pouting in her spitfire vocals." But unlike the militancy and bravado that's so common among rappers, Cherry's rapping is also playful. "Using rap is fun," she told *Rolling Stone,* "because rap means that you can have a *song* song— a song with a melodic chorus that gives it the soul, and then with the rap you can hammer the blatant facts and truths down. And in a rap you can use phrases like *cornflake packets.* You can say things that really matter, in a fun way." As the *New York Times Magazine* pointed out, Cherry's "particular knack is for combining the socially uplifting message—the responsibilities of motherhood, the need for self-knowledge—with a sexuality that could safely be described as up-front."

Her song "Outre Risque Locomotive" is a good example of this two-sided message. "Baby," she sings, "you're an outre risque locomotive . . . driving me crazy," and then elaborates on how attracted she is to her man. "I think the [girl] in the song is, before giving herself up to this person, questioning whether she really wants to," Cherry explained to *Pulse!* "She's telling the guy to slow down. . . . The thing is, she's not saying no be-

For the Record. . .

Born August 10, 1964, in Stockholm, Sweden; daughter of Swedish artist Moki Cherry; father, West African percussionist Ahmadu Jah; children: Naima, Tyson Cherry Kwewanda McVey. *Education:* Attended country school in the south of Sweden and a state school in New York; dropped out at age 14.

Background singer and sometimes-percussionist for underground cult bands The Slits, Rip Rig & Panic, Float Up C.P., all in the mid-1980s; solo performer, 1989—.

Awards: Grammy nomination for Best New Artist, 1989.

Addresses: *Home*—London, England. *Record company*—Virgin Records, 30 West 21st Street, 11th floor, New York, NY 10010.

cause she doesn't want to do it; she's saying no because she's got self-respect and she wants to make sure it's something she wants to do before she gives him too much.

"Sex is probably one of the most important things in our society," she continued, "but unfortunately, it's been turned into this incredibly big deal . . . It's almost been removed from us as something that's natural. . . . You see videos and things on TV and it's completely like manufactured sex, which makes it very unsexy, because it's not real. The things that are really sexy are the things that a person might be completely unaware of—a twinkle in your eye, or the way you do something. It's not the length of your skirt, necessarily. . . . A lot of people use sexuality and end up abusing themselves whilst using it. To respect yourself and to be proud of who you are and what you're doing, you have to have some dignity; and then whatever it is, you're gonna do with grace.

"The reason my album is so sexual is that sex is what obsesses so many people," she told the *New York Times.* "I once read about a study that discovered people have sexual thoughts at least once every eight seconds. I think it's accurate, even if that thought isn't direct. If there's a message in the album, it's that in order to survive you have to take control of your destiny and keep from being brainwashed by opening your eyes and seeing yourself clearly."

Neneh Cherry was born in 1964 in Stockholm to Swedish artist Moki and West African percussionist Ahmadu Jah. From infancy, however, she was nurtured by Don Cherry, who met Moki during a European tour with saxophonist Sonny Rollins. Because of Moki and Don's respective careers, Cherry and her younger step-brother, Eagle-Eye Cherry, spent their childhood years being shuttled between Sweden and New York, where Don was based, and when Don went on tour, Neneh and Eagle-Eye often went with him. "It's the sort of life that could have become very confusing," she told *Rolling Stone.* "But most of the time we were traveling between two environments that we knew really well. And when we changed places, it was very natural. When we were on tour, it was in a bus with beds in the back, and the whole home went. And when we stayed in a hotel, we'd set up house. There's a classic story of my mother smuggling a portable camping kitchen into a hotel under her cape and dropping it in the lobby." For Don, who told the *New York Times Magazine* that he would not have toured without his children, those years left fond memories. "When we were on the road, it was always important for me to have the time to read the kids a story or relax with them before they went to sleep."

Don Cherry has been a pivotal figure of jazz's American avant-garde since his groundbreaking work in the 1950s with saxophonist Ornette Coleman. During the 1970s, not only did he share with his children his love for African, Indian, Chinese, and other musical traditions, he also introduced them to the vital scene that he belonged to. "I knew that it was different," Cherry told *Rolling Stone,* "and that it was about something else. But I think I appreciate it a lot more now. When I was about nine, my brother and I would be falling asleep next to the stage, thinking, 'God, not another twenty-minute solo.'" Nevertheless, Don's music made a deep impression on his young step-daughter. "Don used to take us with him to rehearsals at Ornette's place on Prince Street, in Manhattan," she told the *New York Times Magazine.* "And I can remember Denardo Coleman being, like, eleven, playing the drums and [my] being very fascinated by him. It was like 'Hmmm . . . that *boy* is playing the drums.'" At the same time, Cherry was cultivating other tastes in music—the Jackson 5, Sly and the Family Stone, Earth Wind & Fire, and Chaka Khan, a singer she has always revered, she told the *New York Times,* "for her aura of strength and fearlessness."

At the age of 14, Cherry dropped out of school. That move, she told *Rolling Stone,* is "not something that I'm particularly proud of, and I think it's because of a weakness that I didn't survive." The next year she went with her biological father to Sierra Leone, in Africa, to meet his family, and received an education of a whole other nature. "The first night there," she told *Rolling Stone,* "I cried the whole night, because it was so real. There was this overwhelming vibe of, like, 'You're in

Africa': the smell, the heat, the way people looked. It was more real and more African than I thought anything could ever be, and I was convinced that I would never get out of there. But the weirdest thing was that it was very familiar. I think that's what people mean when they say 'going back to your roots.'. . . And I saw a security there in people that I'd never seen anywhere else, probably because they hadn't been taken away from there.''

One source of Cherry's strength as a performer and lyricist seems to be her experience in Africa. That trip, she told *Musician,* exposed her to "a different side of female strength. The way African women relate to each other is so straightforward. I had a sense of belonging that was pretty mind-blowing." How, *Musician* asked her, would that kind of female strength go over "on the Brooklyn sidewalks, where even schoolboys think of themselves as God's gift to females?" "Most women find that kind of male behavior pretty boring," she answered. "I guess the message in my music is, 'Please don't give me this, 'cause I'm smarter than that.'"

Returning to New York, Cherry spent the next couple of years looking for her niche in the job world—"looking after kids," she told *Virgin Records,* "working in a couple of offices, cleaning whatever I could get my hands on." Nothing held her interest, though, and so in 1980, she went with Don to England. There, in London's arty, late-punk scene, she found her calling. First she joined the all-female proto-punk band the Slits, playing a bit of percussion and singing background vocals; from there she went on to sing for Rip Rig and Panic—a jazz-funk-punk outfit—and its offshoot, Float Up C.P. "It wasn't until I was thrown into music that the passion surfaced," she told *Rolling Stone,* "and all of a sudden it was, 'Oh, yeah, this is what I love.'" But more than the music itself, it was the spirit of the punk scene that drew her in. "It was a real identity that I could cover myself with," she explained in the *New York Times Magazine,* "that would give me an excuse to be more fearless." During that period, when she was 17 or 18, she gave birth to her first daughter, Naima.

While singing with Float Up C.P., Cherry ventured into rap music. She began hanging out at a London club that paid five pounds to anyone who would rap onstage. "I used to go there every week to get a fiver," she told *Rolling Stone.* Attracting the interest of an A & R man (a talent scout), she was asked to record her first single.

"Stop the War" was the result, a song protesting England's war in the Falkland Islands; on the B side, "Give Sheep a Chance" pleaded for the island's majority population group.

Following the single, Cherry and her boyfriend, London musician/producer Cameron McVey (who goes by the name Booga Bear on her album), began writing the songs that would comprise *Raw Like Sushi.* They blocked out a demo recording in their small pink bedroom (which they dubbed Cherry-Bear Studios), and then brought in outside producers to polish each track. In the midst of recording the album, Cherry gave birth to her second daughter, Tyson Cherry Kwewanda McVey. (Tyson, she told *Musician,* "as in Mike. As in Cicely. She was born on International Women's Day, so we figured we'd better give her a heavyweight name, you know?") Tyson's arrival sparked a new song—"The Next Generation," a powerful and tuneful rap song that spells out Cherry's view of parenting. "I'm not saying that having kids is what everyone should do," she told *Rolling Stone.* "The song is saying, 'Yes, I've had a baby, and I'm really happy,' but it's also saying that children are our future and it's up to us to give them a fair break, so they can do something about our mistakes."

Selected discography

Raw Like Sushi, (includes "Buffalo Stance," "Manchild," "Kisses on the Wind," "Inna City Mamma," "The Next Generation," "Love Ghetto," "Heart," "Phoney Ladies," "Outre Risque Locomotive," and "So Here I Come"), Virgin, 1989.

Sources

Musician, June 1989; August 1989.
New York Times, June 28, 1989; July 9, 1989.
New York Times Magazine, December 10, 1989.
Newsday, January 7, 1990.
Pulse!, August 1989.
Rolling Stone, August 10, 1989.

Other

Virgin Records, publicity information, May 1989.

—*Kyle Kevorkian*

The Clash

Punk group

A new musical movement began to rear its head in England in the latter part of the 1970s as a revolt against the establishment and high unemployment rate more than as an artistic statement. "Punk" rock was not a pretty sight but its emotion and power gave pop music a long overdue and much needed kick in the head.

Punk bands like the Sex Pistols and Generation X burned with an incredible intensity that was unique at first, but their energy also caused them to burn out much sooner than they expected. One band, however, was able to rise above the punk death wish, to go beyond the limited musical range of their contemporaries, to survive and create important statements and well-crafted songs: the Clash. "They may well be the greater rock band [compared to the Sex Pistols], as that judgment is conventionally understood," wrote Greil Marcus in the *Rolling Stone Illustrated History of Rock & Roll.* "That they were not the greater punk band has been their salvation." The Clash formed in 1976 with Joe Strummer, Mick Jones, Paul Simonon, Terry

For the Record. . .

Band formed in 1976 with guitarist and vocalist **Joe Strummer** (name originally John Mellor; born 1953, in Ankara, Turkey); **Keith Levene** (left the band after first tour); guitarist and vocalist **Mick Jones** (born 1956; from Brixton, England); bass player **Paul Simonon**; drummer on first and last LP, **Terry Chimes** (a.k.a. Tory Crimes); drummer who replaced Chimes, **Topper Headon** (real name, Nicky Headon; from Dover, England).

Band first toured the U.K. and the U.S. with the Sex Pistols in 1976; first recording contract granted by CBS records in February of 1977, first album released soon after; first solo tour in 1977; LP *Combat Rock* went platinum in 1982.

Awards: Selected band of the year, 1980, in *Rolling Stone* Critics Poll; *London Calling* named 25th best guitar LP of the 1980s by *Guitar World,* and named album of the year, 1980, and best LP of the 1980s by *Rolling Stone.*

Chimes, and Keith Levene. Guitarists Strummer and Jones had both been in other bands (the 101ers and London SS, respectively) but bassist Simonon had never even played an instrument before. Levene soon left the group and later joined Johnny Rotten's band, Public Image Ltd.

The Clash, managed by punk guru Malcolm McLaren's friend, Bernie Rhodes, earned immediate recognition with their political viewpoints. Singles like "White Riot," "London Burning," and "Career Opportunities" told the British youth to stand up and take a look at the blight of their nation. In live settings, like their billing on the Sex Pistol's "Anarchy in the U.K." tour, the Clash created energetic dance rhythms that drove crowds into a frenzy. "Their music is primitive and aggressive," reported the *Illustrated Encyclopedia of Rock,* "but the chemistry is combustible—on stage they are a complete audiovisual experience, driven forward on a wave of passion and pure energy."

The band signed with CBS Records for $200,000, and their first LP, *Clash,* was released in the United Kingdom in 1977. The record company considered the album too crude for U.S. release, however. It wasn't until 1979 that a compilation LP of ten album cuts and seven later British singles would be released as *The Clash* in America. Even though this version was weaker than the English one because the songs were out of order and out of context, American listeners were impressed to say the least. "Here was a record that

defined rock's risks and pleasures, and told us, once again that this was music worth fighting for," wrote Tom Carson in *Rolling Stone.* In Robert Christgau's *Record Guide,* the author gave the album an "A" and wrote: "Cut for cut, this may be the greatest rock and roll album ever manufactured in the U.S." When the Clash finally toured the States, audiences were blown away by the band's energy and stance. They "arrive in America not simply to make themselves know but precisely to make a difference, as rock and roll politicians out to create a new rock version of the public space," said Greil Marcus in the *Rolling Stone Illustrated History of Rock & Roll.*

When the Sex Pistols disintegrated, the Clash carried on the punk flag with the 1977 "Complete Control," a rocking reggae attack on record companies which was produced by Jamaican Lee Perry. "The force of character and the sense of epic in the band's songs, for all their topical urgency, have a grandeur that's almost Shakespearean," wrote Tom Carson in *Rolling Stone.*

When their second LP, *Give 'Em Enough Rope,* came out on Epic in 1978 and entered the U.K. charts at Number 2, the band immediately was criticized by the press for their strong political views and seeming advocation of violent terrorism. "Our music's violent. We're not," said Strummer in *Rolling Stone.* "If anything, songs like 'Guns on the Roof' and 'Last Gang in Town' are supposed to take the piss out of violence. It's just that sometimes you have to put yourself in the place of the guy with the machine gun. I couldn't go to his extreme, but at the same time it's no good ignoring what he's doing."

The band had replaced Chimes with Topper Headon on drums and also recruited rock band Blue Oyster Cult's producer, Sandy Pearlman, for the album. "The Clash see the merit in reaching a wider audience," said Pearlman in *Rolling Stone,* "but they also like the idea of grand suicidal gestures. We need more bands like this as models for tomorrow's parasites." The band fired and sued their financial manager, Rhodes, as his ineptitude had threatened the band with extinction. Caroline Coon took over the books in an effort to straighten matters out as the band worked on *London Calling* with producer Guy Stevens. The Clash took an unprecedented risk by releasing the 19-song, double LP at an extremely low price. "I remember that things were so up in the air, and there was quite a good feeling of us against the world," said Strummer in *Rolling Stone.* "We felt that we were struggling, about to slide down a slope or something, grasping with our fingernails. And that there was nobody to help us."

Critics went crazy over the hastily released album in which the hit "Train In Vain" was thrown on so quickly that it didn't even make it onto the cover label. The Clash had drawn on rock, reggae, and rockabilly to create a diversified effort that *Rolling Stone* picked as the best LP of the 1980s (it had reached Number 27 on the charts). It was also voted "25th Best Guitar LP of the 1980s" by *Guitar World,* a publication that usually caters to pyrotechnics, proving that Mick Jones was more than a three-chord basher. A critic in that magazine wrote: "He moves nimbly from subtlety to excess, wielding the scalpel and the wrecking ball with equal facility."

By now the band had dumped their third management group, Blackhill Enterprises, and bassist Paul Simonon took over the band's business affairs. Still wanting to flex their musical muscle for more accessibility, the Clash began working on their angry three-record set, named *Sandinista!* in honor of the Nicaraguan revolution. "The music—just bang, bang, bang—was getting to be like a nagging wife," Jones said to James Henke in *Rolling Stone.* The new albums featured an updated studio sound, extra musicians, women and children on vocals and a more varied musical style than its predecessor. "An everywhere-you-turn guerrilla raid of vision and virtuosity," wrote John Piccarella in his *Rolling Stone* 5-star review. If *London Calling* shocked the music industry's conception of marketing, *Sandinista!* gave them a heart attack. The three-record set was priced at $14.95 for kids who listened, not for the pockets of executives. "We believe what we're doing is right," said Simonon in *Rolling Stone.* "If we had to be dictated by what other people say, it wouldn't be The Clash."

In 1982, the year of the band's biggest album, *Combat Rock,* Topper Headon left the band, citing "political differences," and was quickly replaced by former member Terry Chimes. The LP (which went platinum) yielded a Top 50 single, the college party anthem "Should I Stay or Should I Go," and a Top 10 single, "Rock the Casbah." The success would not keep them together; it wasn't long before the group followed the path of most punk bands and broke up after an album's release. In what may best describe the movement and the band's demise, Paul Simonon said in *Rolling Stone,* "People don't understand. Punk was about change—and rule number one was: there are no rules."

Selected discography

Clash, CBS Records, 1977.
Give 'Em Enough Rope, Epic, 1978.
The Clash, Epic, 1979.
London Calling, Epic, 1979.
Sandinista! Epic, 1980.
Combat Rock, Epic, 1982.
The Story of The Clash, Vol. 1, Epic, 1988.

Sources

Books

Christgau, Robert, *Christgau's Record Guide,* Ticknor & Fields, 1981.
The Illustrated Encyclopedia of Rock, compiled by Nick Logan and Bob Woffinden, Salamander, 1977.
The Rolling Stone Record Guide, edited by Dave Marsh with John Swenson, Random House/Rolling Stone Press, 1979.
The Rolling Stone Illustrated History of Rock & Roll, edited by Jim Miller, Random House/Rolling Stone Press, 1976.

Periodicals

Guitar Player, September 1988.
Guitar World, February 1990.
Rolling Stone, January 25, 1979; March 8, 1979; April 5, 1979; October 18, 1979; April 17, 1980; March 5, 1981; April 16, 1981; August 19, 1982; November 16, 1989.

—*Calen D. Stone*

Joe Cocker

Vocalist

Powerful, raw, and full of anguish, Joe Cocker's voice is perfectly suited to sing the blues, and it was by doing so that he became well known in the late 1960s and early 1970s. Personal and professional problems rivalling those described in any blues song have plagued him since then, and at times it seemed that his career was finished. In recent years, however, Cocker has not only returned to music, he has expanded his range and established a presence as a romantic balladeer as well as a blues shouter.

Born into a working-class family, Cocker studied plumbing at a trade school and worked at that profession for several years before his musical efforts began to pay off. As a teen, he was heavily influenced by the music of Ray Charles, which led him to begin playing harmonica in a local group, The Cavaliers. When The Cavaliers reorganized and became Vance Arnold and The Avengers, Cocker was transformed into the lead vocalist. In this role, he made his first recording, a 1963 version of The Beatles' "I'll Cry Instead." Soon afterwards he was offered a solo contract with British Decca, but this venture led nowhere; before long, Cocker was back to plumbing.

In 1966, he resurfaced as the leader of The Grease Band, which included Chris Stainton on keyboards, Alan Spenner on bass, Henry McCullough on Guitar, and Bruce Rowlands on drums. Producer Denny Cordell signed The Grease Band to the Regal Zenophone label. Their first single, "Marjorine," was a moderate success in the United Kingdom and gave Cocker's powerful voice its first notable exposure. The Grease Band followed "Marjorine" with a slow version of the Beatle's "With a Little Help from My Friends"; it went to Number 1 in Britain, and was a hit in the United States as well as in many other countries. An album of the same name was recorded, featuring the likes of Jimmy Page, Albert Lee, and Steve Winwood.

The Grease Band played the United States in 1969, winding up their tour with an appearance at Woodstock. Cocker met musician and songwriter Leon Russell at the festival, where the two became fast friends. Russell penned Cocker's next hit, "Delta Lady," and supervised the recording of the album *Joe Cocker!* When The Grease Band dropped out as Cocker's backup band, Russell organized a forty-day tour of the United States for his friend. Over twenty musicians were involved, including the Delanie and Bonnie Band. The "Mad Dogs and Englishmen" tour was a terrific success, leading to a live album that went gold and a film that made Cocker's strange, spastic stage presence as familiar as his rasping voice. Russell was propelled to major star status as a result of "Mad Dogs and Englishmen." Ironically, the only major casualty of the tour was its star, Joe Cocker. By some accounts, he made only $800 from the entire event. Physically, mentally, and emotionally drained, he recorded one more song—"High Time We Went"—before returning to England and retiring from performing.

By 1972, Cocker was attempting a comeback, but legal disputes, drinking, health problems, and a noticeable deterioration in his vocal prowess all plagued his efforts. He toured the United States and then Australia, where repeated arrests finally caused him to be deported. He jumped from one record company to another and put himself in the hands of many different producers and writers, resulting in a catalog of recordings that is now considered wildly uneven. Despite all his difficulties, he persisted in recording and touring, and by 1975 he had climbed back into the U.S. Top 10 charts with the uncharacteristic ballad "You Are So Beautiful." The rest of the decade was rocky, with albums such as *Stingray* and *Luxury You Can Afford* being largely overlooked despite some good performances.

It wasn't until 1982 that Cocker had another significant hit. Again, it was a ballad—"Up Where We Belong," a duet with Jennifer Warnes, which gained wide exposure through its use in the popular film *An Officer and a Gentleman.* Thereafter, Cocker's managers seemed determined to change his image from that of a boozy bluesman into that of a gentle crooner. The change led to some moderately successful recordings, but proved puzzling and disappointing to some, such as the *Stereo Review* writer who complained about the "cautious and polite" renditions of "mild love songs, sung with only a trace of Cocker's famous rasp and guttural fury" that are found on the 1982 release *Sheffield Steel.* Other commentators were less critical, believing that a mellower

style was an appropriate indication Cocker's maturation. "A certain world-weary calm seems to have settled into his music," noted Ralph Novak in his *People* review of *Civilized Man,* "and it combines with the raggedy-edged blues that made him famous to produce a uniquely affecting sound."

Cocker's voice has improved markedly since its low point in the 1970s, and today he continues to exercise his greatest gift: that of reading meaning into others' words. "At his most inspired, Cocker is truly a masterful interpreter," stated *High Fidelity* writer Steven X. Rea. "He has transformed material like the Beatles' cutesy-poo 'With a Little Help from My Friends' and the schmaltzy 'You Are So Beautiful' into ragged, soulful numbers of his own creation. . . . Few singers are as readily identifiable; fewer interpreters are as adept at making outside material sound like their own creation. It's good to hear Cocker in fine form again."

Selected discography

With a Little Help from My Friends, Regal Zenophone, 1969.
Joe Cocker, Regal Zenophone, 1969.
Mad Dogs & Englishmen, A&M, 1971.
Cocker Happy, Fly, 1971.
Something to Say, Cube, 1973.
I Can Stand a Little Rain, A&M, 1974.
Jamaica Say You Will, A&M, 1975.
Stingray, A&M, 1976.
Live in L.A., Cube, 1976.
Luxury You Can Afford, Asylum, 1978.
Platinum Collection, Dakota, 1981.
Joe Cocker, Dakota, 1982.
Space Captain, Cube, 1982.
Sheffield Steel, Island, 1982.
Civilized Man, Capitol, 1984.
Off the Record, Sierra, 1984.
Cocker, Capitol, 1986.
Unchain My Heart, Capitol, 1988.
Joe Cocker Live!, Capitol, 1990.

Sources

High Fidelity, September 1982.
People, June 14, 1984; May 19, 1986.
Rolling Stone, June 19, 1986.
Stereo Review, October 1982; September 1984.

—Joan Goldsworthy

David Allan Coe

Songwriter and vocalist

Country performer David Allan Coe is "a bold and inventive artist," according to Alanna Nash of *Stereo Review*. Yet it is debatable whether he has had greater success as a singer or writing songs for other country stars. Tanya Tucker's "Would You Lay with Me" and Johnny Paycheck's "Take This Job and Shove It" are both Coe's compositions. As for his own recordings, Coe is perhaps best known for the humorous "You Never Even Called Me by My Name" and "Long-Haired Redneck." Those two hit the tops of the country charts during the mid-1970s, but his later work has also received much critical acclaim.

Coe's path to country stardom was more difficult than most. Born September 6, 1939, in Akron, Ohio, he came from a broken home. Because of his early antisocial attitude, he was sent to a reform school in Michigan when he was nine years old. Coe spent most of his youth in similar facilities; every time he was released, he managed to do something to get incarcerated again. His early crimes included possession of burglary tools and car theft.

Eventually, at the age of twenty, Coe began a series of prison terms in the Ohio State Penitentiary. During one of these, he killed a fellow inmate who made homosexual advances towards him. Despite a possible self-defense motive in the incident, Coe was sentenced to death. While on death row, he was reunited with his foster father, who had also been convicted of murder. Coe had found the time during his various prison terms to learn to play the guitar, and he and his foster father occupied themselves by writing songs.

Before their sentences could be carried out, Ohio repealed the death penalty, and Coe's term was commuted to life. Thus reprieved, he began to take an even greater interest in his music, and was allowed to perform for his fellow inmates. This constructive activity made the parole board look favorably upon Coe, and they freed him in 1967. He headed straight for Nashville, Tennessee. He slept in his old car, and sang and played for food. Coe tried to sell the songs he had written in prison; his lyrics reflected his experiences, and were often seen as too raw and harshly realistic for country music. Even so, he was soon signed to the small SSS label and released his debut album, the aptly titled *Penitentiary Blues*. It was not a popular success, but it received favorable notice from many music critics. Two singles from *Penitentiary Blues* got a fair amount of airplay—"Tobacco Road" and "Two Tone Brown."

Coe switched to the Plantation label during the early 1970s, recording a spoof called "How High's the Watergate, Martha?" and a minor hit, "Keep Those Big Wheels Running." But his first major attention came

For the Record. . .

Born David Allan Coe, September 6, 1939, in Akron, Ohio; married twice; has a daughter from his second marriage.

Was in and out of juvenile correctional facilities from age nine to age eighteen; in and out of prisons, including the Ohio State Penitentiary and Marion Correctional Institution until 1967; singer and songwriter, 1967—. Cofounder of Captive Music Publishing Company.

Awards: "Take This Job and Shove It" (a song he wrote) was nominated for a Grammy for Best Country and Western Song of the Year, 1978.

Addresses: *Record company*—Columbia Records, 51 W. 52nd St., New York, NY 10019.

through other artists recording his compositions. More famous country singers had gradually begun adding Coe's songs to their albums or performing them in concerts, when his "Would You Lay with Me (In a Field of Stone)" was selected for one of Tanya Tucker's albums. The tune became a huge hit for the young woman in 1973, and it made major record companies notice its composer.

One such company was Columbia Records, which asked Coe for some demonstration tapes. Satisfied with what he provided, Columbia signed him, and Coe released his first major album, *The Mysterious Rhinestone Cowboy,* quickly followed by *The Mysterious Rhinestone Cowboy Rides Again.* Ironically, his first smash hit, 1975's "You Never Even Called Me by My Name," was not one of his own compositions, but rather Steve Goodman's. Something of a novelty, the song featured Coe's imitations of various famous country singers, including Merle Haggard and Charlie Pride. But it might not have fared as well with the fans without the last verse that Coe added. Apparently Goodman had told him that "You Never" was the perfect country song; Coe allegedly replied that Goodman had left out several elements essential for making that claim—getting drunk, rain, prison, trains, trucks, and Mama. So Coe threw them all into his last verse, which describes being drunk while driving his pickup truck through the rain to get his mother, who had just gotten out of prison. Unfortunately, he arrives to find that she has just been run over by a train.

Coe's follow-up hit was 1976's "Long-Haired Redneck," which satirizes the trials of a performer whose

image does not fit the public expectation of what a country singer should be. Though he released other singles during the late 1970s, such as "Willie, Waylon, and Me" and "If This Is Just a Game," perhaps one of his greatest triumphs was when Johnny Paycheck recorded his composition "Take This Job and Shove It." The tune struck a chord with many fans, and received a Grammy nomination for Best Country and Western Song of 1978.

Son of the South, Coe's 1986 album, prompted Nash to exclaim: "It's startling just how good . . . Coe can be when he cools his King of the Weirdies act and gets down to the business of music." She went on to praise the songs "Love Is a Never Ending War" and "Cold Turkey." But apparently Coe was back to his usual eccentricities with the following year's *A Matter of Life . . . and Death;* the album cover featured a photograph of his dead father in his coffin, wearing a shirt advertising one of his son's concert tours. Nevertheless, Nash was pleased with this album, too, citing especially the song "Child of God."

Despite his success, Coe has not forgotten his less fortunate days. He still performs for prison audiences, and is the founder of a music publishing company called Captive Music that seeks to gain exposure for imprisoned songwriters. He has also written his autobiography, *Just for the Record.*

Selected discography

Singles

"Tobacco Road," SSS, c. 1968.
"Two Tone Brown," SSS, c. 1968.
"How High's the Watergate, Martha," Plantation, c. 1973.
"Keep Those Big Wheels Running," Plantation, c. 1973.
"If I Could Climb the Walls of a Bottle," Columbia, 1974.
"Sad Country Song," Columbia, 1974.
"You Never Even Called Me by My Name," Columbia, 1975.
"Would You Be My Lady?" Columbia, 1975.
"Long-Haired Redneck," Columbia, 1976.
"When She's Got Me," Columbia, 1976.
"Willie, Waylon, and Me," Columbia, 1976.
"Lately I've Been Thinkin' Too Much," Columbia, 1977.
"Face to Face," Columbia, 1977.
"Just to Prove My Love for You," Columbia, 1977.
"Divers Do It Deeper," Columbia, 1978.
"You Can Count on Me," Columbia, 1978.
"If This Is Just a Game," Columbia, 1978.
(With Bill Anderson) "Get a Little Dirt on Your Hands," Columbia, 1980.
"Stand by Your Man," Columbia, 1981.

Albums

Penitentiary Blues, SSS, c. 1968.
The Mysterious Rhinestone Cowboy, Columbia, 1974.
The Mysterious Rhinestone Cowboy Rides Again, Columbia, 1974.
Long-Haired Redneck, Columbia, 1976.
Once Upon a Rhyme, Columbia, 1976.
David Allan Coe Rides Again, Columbia, 1977.
Tattoo, Columbia, 1977.
Family Album, Columbia, 1978.
Human Emotions, Columbia, 1978.
Son of the South, Columbia, 1986.
A Matter of Life . . . and Death, Columbia, 1987.

Sources

Books

Coe, David Allan, *Just for the Record,* Dream Enterprises, 1978.

Periodicals

Country Music, September/October, 1986.
People, August 25, 1986.
Stereo Review, October 1986; September 1987.

—*Elizabeth Thomas*

Albert Collins

Guitarist and songwriter

Albert Collins was born on a Texas farm and moved to Houston when he was 9. Although he is known as one of the most ferocious guitarists in contemporary blues, Collins started out on piano and actually wanted to become a professional organist. It wasn't until high school, after his keyboard was stolen, that he started to play guitar. But by age 16 he had formed a trio and began working the local scene. From 1949 to 1951 he fronted the Rhythm Rockers, an eight-piece unit fashioned after those of his idols. "I was listenin' to the big bands: Jimmie Lunceford, Tommy Dorsey, Jimmy Dorsey," he told Larry Birnbaum in *down beat*. "I used to love the big band sound. And I had some jazz musicians playin' with me. I was playin' blues, but they taught me my timin'."

Collins went on to tour the south with Piney Brown in the mid-1950s and played weekend gigs with another infamous Texas guitarist, Gatemouth Brown. He returned to Houston to work outside of the music world while continuing to play on weekends through the mid-1960s. In 1958 he jumped on the instrumental wave, brought on by Booker T., Duane Eddy, and Link Wray, and released "The Freeze"/"Collins Shuffle" on the Kangaroo label. "Sold about 150,000 copies in three weeks' time," he recalled to Dan Forte in *Guitar Player*. "That's what started getting my name halfway out there. But when my name really started to spread was when I cut 'Frosty.' I didn't follow it up until then because I had a good day job. I was playing at night and driving a truck in the daytime. And I mixed paint for automobiles for six years."

"Frosty" became a million seller for Collins and the Hall label in 1962. It also established Collins's trademark, the "cool sound." He explained to Ellen Griffith in *Guitar Player*, "One night a friend of mine and I were driving through a town called Corpus Christi, Texas, and it started raining and the windshield fogged up. My friend said, 'Why don't you turn on the defroster?' I didn't think too much about it at the time, and then the next day I thought to myself, 'I ought to put me out a tune called "Defrost."' I looked at my dashboard and it said 'freeze,' too, so I put out the tunes 'Defrost' and 'The Freeze,' and then went on to do 'Frosty.' After that my producer said he was going to keep me in the icebox, and we recorded more tunes with names like that." The motif continued through a long line of tunes with names like "Sno-Cone," "Deep Freeze," "Don't Lose Your Cool," "Hot 'n' Cold," "Shiver and Shake," and "Thaw Out." Each contained the ice pick sound of Collins's Fender Telecaster guitar blasting out a storm of high-powered licks.

The impossible-to-duplicate tone can be attributed to many factors. The main ingredient being Collins's unique tunings of either E minor (E B E G B E) or D minor (D A D

F A D) taught to him by his cousin, Willow Young. He also straps a capo (a moveable bar that attaches to the fretwork of the guitar) halfway up the neck in order to change the pitch. "I met up with Gatemouth Brown, and that's where I got the capo from: that gives me that special tone that I have, 'cause I don't play with no pick," he told Gene Santoro in *Guitar World.* "I always wanted my own thing, didn't want to play like anybody else." Collins snaps the strings off the neck (as opposed to picking them) of his Telecaster which is strapped over his right shoulder "like the old gunslingers wore their pistols: low at the hip, ready to fire," as *Guitar Player's* Jas Obrecht described it. The guitar is connected to a 100-foot cord, which enables Collins to stalk his crowd freely, and then into a 300-watt Fender Quad Reverb amp cranked up to 10. In a small club setting this setup produces a sound which is similar to having a jet land on your temple.

Collins is able to coax a barrage of special effects out of this simple arrangement. For example, the cut "Snowed In" (from the *Frostbite* LP) contains simulated car horns, an engine turning over, footsteps in the snow, and the obligatory flurry of notes. Using just his bare thumb and fingers, Collins relies on unpredictable shifts in volume and attack to separate his sound from that of his colleagues.

His influences include guitarists Lightnin' Hopkins, T-Bone Walker, Gatemouth Brown, and B.B. King, but horn players and organ sounds are vital elements also. "You know, Jimmy McGriff has been my idol since 1965—that's when I first met him, in Kansas City, Missouri," Collins said in *Guitar World.* "I sat in with him and Wes Montgomery—that was some fun, man. See, I always wanted to be an organ player: when I started out, I started on piano. I wanted to be like Jimmy McGriff or Jimmy Smith." After establishing his cool sound, Collins recorded a string of regional hits for a variety of small labels from 1958 to 1971 (Kangaroo, Great Scott, Hall, Fox, Imperial, and Tumbleweed). He even re-

placed Jimi Hendrix for a brief spell after the rock innovator quit Little Richard's band. After 20th Century-Fox released a compilation album, *The Cool Sound of Albert Collins,* he quit his paint job and moved to Kansas City in 1966 where me met and married his wife, Gwendolyn.

A year later Bob Hite of the group Canned Heat saw Collins performing and persuaded Imperial Records of Los Angeles to sign the guitarist. Hite brought him to California to record an album which led to constant touring of psychedelic ballrooms in the latter part of the decade. Collins continued recording a few albums, mainly instrumentals, while playing the better part of the 1970s up and down the west coast with various pickup bands. "I learned a lot playing with those young kids: power, for instance, I like power when I play, man," he told *Guitar World.* "I've heard so many blues players just playing, stop to take a drink play a little again—that ain't my type of blues, man. I go to sleep like that."

It would take six years, however, after his last Tumbleweed LP in 1972 before Collins would find another interested label. In 1978 he released *Ice Pickin'* on a small, young Chicago label run by Bruce Igualer called Alligator. It was one of the hottest blues records in recent memory and launched a career on Alligator that has seen six more albums since, including *Showdown!,* a collaboration with two other guitarists, Johnny Copeland and Robert Cray. "Their compatibility can be attributed to Collins' influence on both . . . and it is Collins who dominates the session, setting the tone with his stinging guitar work and nearly managing to hold his own as a singer," wrote Larry Birnbaum in *down beat.* The album went on to win a Grammy award.

Collins cut back on his ten-month yearly touring schedule during the late 1980s and is now in semi-retirement. He stole the show at Live-Aid with George Thorogood; appeared in the movie *Adventures in Babysitting;* played in a Seagram's Wine Cooler commercial with actor Bruce Willis; and was the focus of a PBS television documentary, *Ain't Nothin' But The Blues.* "One thing about the blues, you've got to keep moving," he told *Guitar Player.* "I've been touring as long as I've been playing, but I enjoy traveling . . . I play the blues because I've lived it . . . I don't want to play any of this other stuff; it may sound good, but it's just not my style."

Selected discography

Love Can Be Found Anywhere (Even In A Guitar), Imperial, 1968.
Trash Talkin', Imperial, 1969.
There's Gotta be a Change, Tumbleweed, 1971.
Ice Pickin', Alligator, 1978.

Alive & Cool, Red Lightnin', 197?.
Frostbite, Alligator, 1980.
Frozen Alive, Alligator, 1981.
Don't Lose Your Cool, Alligator, 1983.
Live in Japan, Sonet, 1984.

Sources

Books

Christgau, Robert, *Christgau's Record Guide,* Ticknor & Fields, 1981.
Harris, Sheldon, *Blues Who's Who,* Da Capo, 1979.
Kozinn, Allan, Pete Welding, Dan Forte, and Gene Santoro, *The Guitar: The History, The Music, The Players,* Quill, 1984.

Periodicals

down beat, May 1984; July 1984; September 1986; May 1987.
Guitar Player, April 1979; August 1979; July 1980; February 1981; March 1981; July 1983; May 1984; August 1986; February 1987; June 1987; May 1988.
Guitar World, April 1987; November 1987; April 1988; September 1988.

—*Calen D. Stone*

Judy Collins

Singer, songwriter, pianist, guitarist

For the past three decades, Judy Collins's clear, sweet soprano and meticulous phrasing have lent a classical elegance to the varied songs of her expansive repertoire. A major figure in the folk song revival of the 1960s, Collins began her vocal career singing traditional Anglo-American ballads, giving way to the urban protest songs that captured the era's idealism and unrest. As American folk music moved away from social protest themes, and gained more sophisticated musical arrangements (often combined with rock), the singer expanded her own repertoire, delivering folk-rock, pop, show, and cabaret tunes in addition to folk classics. Ignoring the criticisms of folk purists, the individualistic Collins's eclectic choices included the caustic theatre songs of *Marat/Sade* and *Three Penny Opera,* the introspective art-songs of Leonard Cohen, the bittersweet perceptions of composer Jacques Brel, and her own poetic, autobiographical ballads. Once observing that the search for material was her greatest challenge, the folksinger reflected: "I think there is a music coming out of this culture, a real kind of tradition being written. What I'm trying to do is find songs that are the key points of our civilization."

Growing up in Denver, Colorado, Collins enjoyed a close relationship with her father, a blind radio personality and bandleader. With his encouragement she began to take piano lessons at the age of 5; her prodigious talent led to years of discipline and solitude as she prepared for a career as a concert pianist (for much of that time she studied with conductor Antonia Brico, a former pupil of Jan Sibelius). In high school Collins rebelled against the rigors of her classical training, however, abandoning the piano, and picking out the folk tunes she had grown to love on an old guitar.

At 17 she made her singing debut before an international Kiwanis Club convention, having won the Denver chapter's "Star of Tomorrow" contest. Despite her lack of formal voice training, Collins began to sing traditional folk music in local clubs in 1959. Her success led to frequent appearances on the national "coffeehouse circuit," with regular performances in Chicago, Boston, and New York; while singing at the Village Gate in New York City she was approached by an Elektra Records executive, who soon signed her to a recording contract. Collins's first two albums, *A Maid of Constant Sorrow* and *Golden Apples of the Sun,* consisted of Anglo-American folk classics, but by the LP *Judy Collins #3* the vocalist had turned to the work of contemporary songwriters addressing social issues, like Bob Dylan, Tom Paxton, and Phil Ochs.

Her political consciousness stirred by friendships with such urban folksingers/songwriters (and heightened by concerts on restless college campuses), Collins

For the Record. . .

Full name, Judy Marjorie Collins; born May 1, 1939, in Seattle, Wash.; daughter of Charles (a radio master of ceremonies and bandleader) and Marjorie (Byrd) Collins; married Peter A. Taylor (a university lecturer) in 1958 (divorced, 1966); children: Clark Collin Taylor. *Education:* Studied classical piano with musical conductor Antonia Brico; attended MacMurray College and University of Colorado.

Began classical piano training at age 5, made public debut at 13 with Denver Symphony; began playing guitar and singing folk music while in high school; folk performer in Denver coffee-houses and clubs, 1959; regular performer on national coffeehouse circuit and at colleges, universities, and political rallies throughout 1960s; recording artist, 1961—; songwriter, late 1960s—. Performances have included international tours, folk festivals, television specials, and annual Christmas concerts at Carnegie Hall. Made acting debut as Solveig in New York Shakespeare Festival production of Henrik Ibsen's *Peer Gynt,* 1969. Has served on Newport Folk Festival's board of directors.

Awards: Grammy Award for recording "Both Sides Now," 1968; Academy Award nomination for documentary *Antonia: A Portrait of a Woman* (as writer and co-director), 1974; silver medal from Atlanta International Film Festival; blue ribbon from American Film Festival in New York City.

Addresses: *Office*—c/o Charles R. Rothschild Productions, Inc., 330 East 48th St., New York, N.Y. 10010.

became a regular performer at political rallies throughout the decade, protesting racial inequality and the Vietnam War. (Her political causes have since included ecology, endangered species, and abortion rights.) Still, despite her critical and popular acclaim, Collins felt limited by the conventions of folk music, and her 1966 album *In My Life* showed the singer's burgeoning sense of artistic adventure. A Beatle ballad, a medley of theatre songs with orchestra and full chorus, two idiosyncratic Cohen pieces (one an operatic monologue of a potential suicide) were among its offerings—an eclectic mix that Collins pursued in subsequent albums. She advanced the careers of unknown songwriters like Joni Mitchell, Randy Newman, Sandy Denny, and Robin Williamson along the way.

Beginning to write songs of her own by the end of the decade, Collins also resumed playing the piano, in accompaniment, as an alternative to her six- and twelve-string guitars. The vocalist's first gold album,

Wildflowers, was released in 1967, and contained the Grammy-winning cut "Both Sides Now" (written by Mitchell). A succession of top-selling LPs followed, with *Whales and Nightingales* introducing Collins's next surprising big hit—an a cappella rendition of the spiritual "Amazing Grace."

Through the seventies, eighties, and beyond, Collins has continued to forge her personal style and repertoire, tending towards pop, art-songs, and show tunes; in 1975 she had another hit single with Stephen Sondheim's "Send in the Clowns." Her increased sophistication has brought with it charges of inaccessibility, however: already known for her careful diction and sense of emotional control, Collins began to be perceived as too stately and chilly. "Collins distances herself from the material and her audience," wrote Alanna Nash in a *Stereo Review* critique of the 1984 album *Home Again,* "as if she's more concerned with delivering a recital than doing any kind of real communication." Others have found Collins's idiosyncratic selection of material offputting—a complaint turned on its head by admirers, who see the performer's independence as one of her greatest virtues. A *People* music reviewer suggested that when Collins effects the right balance of the popular and the experimental, as in the album *The Times of Our Lives,* her recordings are as warm and affecting as ever. "Collins' voice sounds as sweet, clear, and lovely as it did on 1961's *A Maid of Constant Sorrow,*" determined *People* critic Ralph Novak in his review of *Home Again.* "She also still seems to be an extraordinarily adventuresome singer and one who never coasts; there's a lot to be said for such musical integrity."

Writings

Trust Your Heart (autobiography), Houghton, 1987. (With illustrator Jane Dyer)
My Father (children's picture book), Little, Brown, 1989.

Compostitons

Has written, arranged, and adapted numerous songs, including "Since You've Asked," "My Father," "Secret Gardens," "Born to the Breed," "Wedding Song," and "Shoot First."

Selected discography

A Maid of Constant Sorrow, Elektra, 1961.
Golden Apples of the Sun, Elektra, 1962.
Judy Collins #3, Elektra, 1963.

The Judy Collins Concert, Elektra, 1964.
Judy Collins' Fifth Album, Elektra, 1965.
In My Life, Elektra, 1966.
Wildflowers, Elektra, 1967.
Who Knows Where the Time Goes, Elektra, 1968.
Recollections: The Best of Judy Collins, Elektra, 1969.
Whales and Nightingales, Elektra, 1970.
Living, Elektra, 1971.
Colors of the Day: The Best of Judy Collins, Elektra, 1972.
True Stories and Other Dreams, Elektra, 1973.
Judith, Elektra, 1975.
Bread and Roses, Elektra, 1976.
So Early in the Spring: The First Fifteen Years, Elektra, 1977.
Hard Time for Lovers, Elektra, 1979.
Running for Life, Elektra, 1980.
The Times of Our Lives, Elektra, 1982.
Home Again, Elektra, 1984.
Trust Your Heart, Gold Castle, 1987.
Sanity and Grace (live album), Gold Castle, 1989.

Sources

Books

The New Rolling Stone Record Guide, edited by Dave Marsh and John Swenson, Random House, 1983.
The Rolling Stone Encyclopedia of Rock and Roll, edited by Jon Pareles and Patricia Romanowski, Summit Books, 1983.
Simon, George T., and others, *The Best of the Music Makers*, Doubleday, 1979.

Periodicals

New York Times Book Review, November 29, 1987.
People, June 9, 1980; April, 19, 1982; November 12, 1984; December 11, 1989.
Stereo Review, August 1980; April 1985.

—*Nancy Pear*

John Coltrane

Jazz saxophonist

The legendary saxophone virtuoso John Coltrane continues to influence modern jazz even from the grave. Coltrane's death more than two decades ago only enhanced his reputation as an artist who brought whole new dimensions to a constantly innovative musical form. The "sheets of sound" and other bizarre stylistic elements that characterize Coltrane's jazz sparked heated debate at the time of their composition. Today his work is still either hailed as the very pinnacle of genius or dismissed as flights of monotonous self-indulgence. In an *Atlantic* retrospective, Edward Strickland calls Coltrane "the lone voice crying not in the wilderness but from some primordial chaos" whose music "evokes not only the jungle but all that existed before the jungle." The critic adds: "Coltrane was attempting to raise jazz from the saloons to the heavens. No jazzman had attempted so overtly to offer his work as a form of religious expression. . . . In his use of jazz as prayer and meditation Coltrane was beyond all doubt the principal spiritual force in music."

Andrew White, himself a musician and transcriber of many of Coltrane's extended solos, told *down beat* magazine that the jazz industry "has been faltering artistically and financially ever since the death of John Coltrane. . . . Besides being one of our greatest saxophonists, improvisors, innovative and creative contributors, Coltrane *was* our last great leader. As a matter of fact, he was the *only* leader we've had in jazz who successfully maintained an evolutionary creative output as well as building a 'jazz star' image. *He merged the art and the money.*"

John William Coltrane, Jr., was born on the autumn equinox, September 23, 1926. He was raised in rural North Carolina, where he was exposed to the charismatic music of the black Southern church—both of his grandfathers were ministers. Coltrane's father also played several instruments as a hobby, so the young boy grew up in a musical environment. Quite on his own, he discovered jazz through the recordings of Count Basie and Lester Young. He persuaded his mother to buy him a saxophone, settling for an alto instead of a tenor because the alto was supposedly easier to handle.

Coltrane showed a proficiency on the saxophone almost immediately. After briefly studying at the Granoff Studios and at the Ornstein School of Music in Philadelphia, he joined a typical cocktail lounge band. Then he played for a year with a Navy band in Hawaii before landing a spot in the Eddie Vinson ensemble in 1947. He was twenty-one at the time. For Vinson's band Coltrane performed on the tenor sax, but his ears were open to jazz greats on both alto and tenor, including Charlie Parker, Ben Webster, Coleman Hawkins, Lester

Young, and Tab Smith. After a year with Vinson, Coltrane joined Dizzy Gillespie's group for one of his longest stints—four years. By that time he had "paid his dues" and was experimenting with composition and technical innovation.

The 1950s saw a great flowering of modern jazz with the advent of artists such as Miles Davis and Thelonious Monk. Coltrane played horn for both Davis and Monk; the latter showed him tricks of phrasing and harmony that deepened his control of his instrument. Coltrane can be heard playing tenor sax on Davis's famous Columbia album *Kind of Blue,* a work that hints of the direction Coltrane would ultimately follow. Strickland writes of the period: "Coltrane's attempt 'to explore all the avenues' made him the perfect stylistic complement to Davis, with his cooler style, which featured sustained blue notes and brief cascades of sixteenths almost willfully retreating into silence, and also Monk, with his spare and unpredictable chords and clusters. Davis, characteristically, paid the tersest homage, when, on being told that his music was so complex that it required five saxophonists, he replied that he'd once had Coltrane."

What Coltrane called "exploring all the avenues" was essentially the quest to exhaust every possibility for his horn in the course of a song. He devoted himself to rapid runs in which individual notes were virtually indis-tinguishable, a style quickly labeled "sheets of sound." As Martin Williams puts it in *Saturday Review,* Coltrane "seemed prepared to gush out every conceivable note, run his way a step at a time through every complex chord, every extension, and every substitution, and go beyond that by reaching for sounds that no tenor saxophone had ever uttered before him." Needless to say, this music was not easily understood—critics were quick to find fault with its length and monotony—but it represented an evolution that was welcomed not only by jazz performers, but by composers and even rock musicians as well.

In 1960 Coltrane formed his own quartet in the saxophone-plus-rhythm mode. He was joined by McCoy Tyner on piano, Elvin Jones on drums, and Jimmy Garrison on bass, all of whom were as eager as Coltrane to explore an increasingly free idiom. Finally Coltrane was free to expand his music at will, and his solos took on unprecedented lengths as he experimented with modal foundations, pentatonic scales, and triple meter.

> *"Coltrane was attempting to raise jazz from the saloons to the heavens."*

His best-known work was recorded during this period, including "My Favorite Things," a surprising theme-and-variations piece based on the saccharine Richard Rogers tune from "The Sound of Music." In "My Favorite Things," writes Williams, Coltrane "encountered a popular song which had the same sort of structure he was interested in, a folk-like simplicity and incantiveness, and very little harmonic motion. . . . It became a best seller."

By 1965 Coltrane was one of the most famous jazz artists alive, acclaimed alike in Europe, Japan, and the United States. Critics who had once dismissed his work "all but waved banners to show their devotion to him," to quote Strickland. Not surprisingly, the musician continued to experiment, even at the risk of alienating his growing audience. His work grew ever more complex, ametric, and improvisatorial. Coltrane explained his personal vision in *Newsweek.* "I have to feel that I'm after something," he said. "If I make money, fine. But I'd rather be striving. It's the striving, man, it's that I want."

Coltrane continued to perform and record even as advancing liver cancer left him racked with pain. He died at forty, only months after he cut his album *Expression.* The subsequent years have revealed the extent of his legacy to jazz, a legacy based on the spiritual quest for meaning and involvement between man, his soul, and the universe. Strickland concludes: "Those who criticize Coltrane's virtuosic profusion are of the same party as those who found Van Gogh's canvases 'too full of paint.' . . . In Coltrane, sound—often discordant, chaotic, almost unbearable—became the spiritual form of the man, an identification perhaps possible only with a wind instrument, with which the player is of necessity fused more intimately than with strings or percussion. . . . The whole spectrum of Coltrane's music—the world-weary melancholy and transcendental yearning that ultimately recall Bach more than Parker, the jungle calls and glossolalic shrieks, the whirlwind runs and spare elegies for murdered children and a murderous planet—is at root merely a suffering man's breath. The quality of that music reminds us that the root of the word *inspiration* is 'breathing upon.' This country has not produced a greater musician."

Selected discography

(With Miles Davis and others) *Kind of Blue,* Columbia.
(With Davis) *'Round Midnight,* Columbia.
(With Davis) *Straight, No Chaser,* Columbia.
(With Thelonious Monk) *Trinkle Tinkle,* Riverside.
(With Monk) *Ruby My Dear,* Riverside.
Blue Train, Blue Note, 1957.
Bahia, Prestige, 1958.
Coltrane Jazz, Atlantic, 1959.
Giant Steps, Atlantic, 1959.
Ballads, Impulse, 1962.
My Favorite Things, Atlantic.
Impressions, Impulse, 1963, reissued, 1987.
A Love Supreme, Impulse, 1964, reissued, 1986.
Crescent, Impulse, 1964.
Ascension, Impulse, 1965.
Transition, Impulse, 1965.
Sun Ship, RCA, 1965.
Meditations, Impulse.
Expression, Impulse, 1967.

The Best of John Coltrane: His Greatest Years, Impulse.
John Coltrane and the Jazz Giants, Prestige.
The Coltrane Legacy, Atlantic.
The European Tour, Pablo.
John Coltrane from the Original Master Tapes, Impulse.
The Gentle Side of John Coltrane, MCA.
Last Trane, Prestige.
The Master, Prestige.
More Lasting Than Bronze, Prestige.
On a Misty Night, Prestige.
John Coltrane Plays for Lovers, Prestige.
John Coltrane Plays the Blues, Atlantic.
Rain or Shine, Prestige.
Soultrane, Fantasy.
Stardust, Prestige.
Dial Africa, Savoy Jazz.
Gold Coast, Savoy Jazz.
Traneing In, Fantasy, 1985.
John Coltrane & Johnny Hartman, Impulse, 1986.
Countdown, Atlantic, 1986.
Coltrane, Impulse, 1987.
Standard Coltrane, Fantasy, 1987.
Africa/Brass, MCA, 1988.
Lush Life, Fantasy, 1988.

Sources

Books

Cole, Bill, *John Coltrane,* Schirmer, 1977.
Terkel, Studs, *Giants of Jazz,* Crowell, 1975.

Periodicals

Atlantic, December 1987.
down beat, July 12, 1979; September 1986.
New Republic, February 12, 1977.
Newsweek, July 31, 1967.
New York Times, July 18, 1967.
Saturday Review, September 16, 1987.

—*Anne Janette Johnson*

Harry Connick, Jr.

Jazz pianist and singer

If jazz pianist and singer Harry Connick, Jr., has a problem, it is that he is too young, too good, and his music is too old. The New Orleans-born Connick, who has literally burst onto the American jazz scene at the age of twenty-two, has been compared to such stars of the golden era of American standards as Duke Ellington, Tony Bennett, and Frank Sinatra. But while his piano virtuosity is unquestioned, and his youth is obvious, Connick has caused some controversy by relying on a repertoire of great sounds from the past to make his musical statement. He is a throwback to another era, and yet that time is so long gone that Connick has been received by many jazz fans as a breath of fresh air.

And while some jazz sophisticates take a cool, wait-and-see attitude toward this upstart, those music lovers lucky enough to get a ticket to one of Connick's performances get something a little unexpected—an evening of genuine, old-time saloon jazz with a Bourbon Street accent. "At first blush," writes *Newsweek*'s Cathleen McGuigan, "[Connick] looks too fresh-faced to have done so much growing up in saloons. But when he starts to sing, he assumes a grown-up golden glow. With his fast fingers and slow drawl, his slicked-back hair and laid-back glamour, the New Orleans pianist has been astonishing Yankee audiences with a jazz virtuosity far beyond his years."

Right down to his snakeskin shoes, Connick is already a polished showman. Tall, smooth, and handsome in his baggy suits and pomade hairstyle, he jokes, trades places with his drummer or bassist, does imitations, taps on his piano and occasionally performs an impromptu soft-shoe. Again, this is against the grain of modern jazz standards, which tend to call for a more sedate, laid-back style of performing. "What ever happened to a show, man?" Connick asked *Rolling Stone*'s Rob Tannenbaum. "You go to hear Louis Armstrong, and they were jitterbugging. Armstrong was a bigger goof-off than I am onstage. It's so staid now."

And behind this obvious glamour, which has already won him a film role and promises of still more, Connick is a very serious musician. In fact, his musical upbringing reads like a pure jazz pedigree. His parents, both music lovers, put themselves through law school by running a record store in New Orleans, where Connick's late mother eventually became a judge. Connick was a piano prodigy who started playing the family piano at age three. By the time he was five he was accomplished enough to play "The Star Spangled Banner" at his father's inauguration as the New Orleans district attorney.

It was his father's position as D.A. that got young Harry into many of the smokey saloons of Bourbon Street on weekends, where he learned to love the sounds of

For the Record. . .

Born Harry Connick, Jr., in 1967, in New Orleans, La.; son of Harry, Sr. (a New Orleans district attorney), and Anita Connick (deceased). *Education:* Attended New Orleans Center for the Creative Arts and Manhattan School of Music.

Began playing with professional musicians on Bourbon Street, New Orleans, at age 6; studied under jazz pianist James Booker as a teen; studied under Ellis Marsalis at New Orleans Center for the Creative Arts; moved to New York at age 18 and studied briefly at Manhattan School of Music; performed at clubs and churches in N.Y.C.; signed recording contract with Columbia Records, 1986; performed music for film *When Harry Met Sally . . . ,* 1989; actor in film *Memphis Belle,* 1990.

Addresses: *Home*—New York City. *Record company*—Columbia Records, Inc., 51 W. 52nd St., New York, NY 10019.

Dixieland, bebop, and rhythm and blues in their natural element. Many of the performers, including the legendary ragtime pianist Eubie Blake, even invited the boy wonder onstage. "Eubie was ninety-six at the time, and I was nine," Connick explained to Howard Reich in the *Chicago Tribune.* "To be able to play with a man who was born in 1883. My Lord—I still can hardly believe I touched him." Another strong influence was the talented pianist James Booker. Many believed that Booker was bound for greatness himself, but drugs destroyed his talent and Booker eventually died in 1983. Booker became so fond of Connick that he often came around the house to tutor the boy. Booker was "the only genius I ever met," Connick told *Rolling Stone.* But "he'd play a tune and throw up in the middle of the song. I didn't know what was wrong. I wasn't thinking about dope when I was eight."

But Connick's most complete musical education came at the New Orleans Center for the Creative Arts. There he was taught by Ellis Marsalis, a now-legendary jazz instructor who, more importantly, is also the father of current jazz stars Branford and Wynton Marsalis. By the time Connick was in high school, Wynton Marsalis had already become a star with his horn, and Connick idolized him. "I wanted to be Wynton," Connick told *Time.* "I wanted to be in his band. I dressed like him. I talked like him." Marsalis, too, made his mark by playing the music of the past and has also been roundly criticized for it. But Connick feels that a tip of the hat to the great masters is essential for young musicians. "It's

a shame they criticize people like Wynton and me for going back, because all we're trying to do is develop our own style, and the only way you can do that is by understanding the music of your predecessors," he told the *Chicago Tribune.* "Everyone imitates when they start out. I'm not forty, I'm twenty-two."

Connick's dream was to follow the footsteps of his friend Marsalis to stardom, and the sooner the better. He went to New York at the age of eighteen, telling his father that he wanted to study at the Manhattan School of Music. His real aim, however, was to sign a record deal with Marsalis' label, Columbia. After a couple of courses at the music school, Connick dropped out and began playing at churches, on street corners, and at small jazz clubs, anywhere he could play. "I'm a New Orleans performer," Connick told the *Chicago Tribune,* "and that means you'll do just about anything anywhere for the chance to perform, even if you have to tap dance out on the street. I simply have to perform all the time."

Eventually, the talent scouts at Columbia did take notice, and Connick's first major-label album, a self-titled jazz collection, was followed by a second record titled *20* for Connick's age at the time. This second record featured Connick's Sinatra-style vocals, which he refers to as "swing." Connick's third collection was the immensely successful soundtrack to the 1989 hit film *When Harry Met Sally . . . ,* which featured Connick on vocals, solo piano, and performing with a big band.

Despite his early success, Connick has no illusions about either the reasons for it or his place among the jazz elite. Referring to his record deal with Columbia, about which he expresses some guilt due to the lack of attention some of his friends in the industry have been getting, Connick knows that part of his appeal is his novelty. "I sing, and I'm young, and I wear baggy suits, and I play jazz, and I'm white," he told *Rolling Stone*'s Tannenbaum. "The sounds that come out of me shouldn't be coming out of someone so young. That's why I got signed." And when jazz critics begin to point out that Connick's playing is derivative of such legends as Ellington, Thelonius Monk, and Erroll Garner, Connick is quick to agree. "Shoot man, I'm twenty-one years old. Of course, I don't have a style." But he's got plenty of time.

Selected discography

Harry Connick, Jr., Columbia, 1987.
20, CBS, 1987.
When Harry Met Sally . . . (film soundtrack), Columbia, 1989.
We Are in Love (includes "A Nightingale Sang in Berkeley Square" and "It's All Right with Me"), Columbia, 1990.

Lofty's Roach Souffle, Columbia, 1990.

Sources

Chicago Tribune, January 14, 1990.
New York, January 2, 1989.
Newsweek, February 20, 1989.
Rolling Stone, March 23, 1989.
Time, January 15, 1990.

—David Collins

Cowboy Junkies

Country/blues group

The Cowboy Junkies were described as "country music subversives" in *People* after their album *The Trinity Session* began to attract widespread attention. The Canada-based band is composed of Michael, Peter, and Margo Timmins (who are siblings), and Alan Anton. Their stark, slow, haunting brand of country and blues has proved popular with fans and mystified critics. After asserting that "mystery" had long been missing from country music, *Time* reviewer Jay Cocks proclaimed that "that is precisely what the Cowboy Junkies offer." *The Trinity Session* spawned the hit "Misguided Angel," and also contained re-workings of country classics such as "I'm So Lonesome I Could Cry" and "Walking After Midnight."

The roots of the Cowboy Junkies as a band lie in the experiences of Michael Timmins, the eldest of the siblings, and Alan Anton. Friends since their early childhood in Toronto, Ontario, Canada, the two formed their first band in high school. When they became adults, they moved with a band called The Hunger Project to New York City to try their musical skills. At this

For the Record...

Members include siblings **Michael, Margo,** and **Peter Timmins** (spelled Timmons in some sources), and **Alan Anton;** Michael (guitarist), born c. 1960; Margo (vocalist), born c. 1961, married; Peter (drummer), born c. 1966; Alan (bass player), born c. 1960, married.

Recording artists and concert performers, c. 1985—.

The Trinity Session voted top recording of 1988 by the *Los Angeles Times* critics' poll.

Addresses: *Home*—Toronto, Ontario, Canada. *Record company*—RCA Records, 1133 Ave. of the Americas, New York, NY 10036.

time, Timmins and Anton were primarily interested in performing punk; as Cocks reported, "they tried, mostly unsuccessfully, to make a living playing adaptations of the kind of fierce rock that was then coming out of England." Undaunted, the duo decided to offer their wares in England itself, forming with others in a band called Germinal in which all the members played whatever they wished on their instruments at the same time. As the pair told Cocks: "It was the ultimate release for us. But for the audience, it was quite a chore." Eventually, however, Timmins and Anton came to feel that the English were not receptive to their work, and returned to Toronto.

There, Michael Timmins began working on new music with his brother Peter. Anton joined them, and Margo Timmins—who had worked previously as a social worker—was invited to provide vocals. Around the same time, the newly formed group toured the southern United States, and were inspired by the country music they heard there. In 1986 they independently recorded an album entitled *Whites Off Earth Now!* Despite having to distribute it themselves, the Cowboy Junkies sold four thousand copies of the disc, and began to establish something of a cult following in Toronto. But, of course, the band's big break came when they signed with RCA Records and released *The Trinity Session* in 1988.

That album takes its name from the fact that it was recorded in Toronto's Church of the Holy Trinity for a very low cost using only one microphone. This spare recording style plays a large part in the acclaimed starkness of *The Trinity Session,* but so do Margo Timmins's "soft, haunting vocals," which *People* claimed "lend a distinctive dash of angst to the Junkies' country

sound." Some critics, however, were uncomfortable with the band's low-key approach to the material on *Trinity Session,* and even found it dull; Alanna Nash of *Stereo Review* lamented that "when I listened attentively, the hour seemed to stretch into weeks, the weeks into months." But Anthony DeCurtis in *Rolling Stone* declared that "'The Trinity Session' is in the great tradition of albums that establish a mood and sustain it so consistently that the entire record seems like one continuously unfolding song." One of the cuts from *Trinity Session,* "Misguided Angel," received a great deal of airplay on the music video channels, and helped boost sales, but critics tended to single out other songs for praise, such as the remake of Lou Reed's "Sweet Jane." Cocks revealed that "I'm So Lonesome I Could Cry" "hasn't sounded so desolate since [country pioneer] Hank Williams" recorded it. And, after first citing the soulfulness of the late Patsy Cline's rendition of "Walking After Midnight," Cocks conjectured that "in the false lull of Margo Timmins' lovely voice and measured phrasing there is the suggestion that whoever's up after midnight may be not only walking, but stalking." But on the subject of the dark tone of their musical interpretation, Michael Timmins reassured *People:* "No, we are *not* depressed, or melancholy or any of those things. We don't consider the music sad, just heartfelt. To us, it's very strange when people come up to us and say, 'You must be so depressed.'"

In 1990 the Cowboy Junkies released the follow-up to *The Trinity Session* entitled *The Caution Horses.* The latter album was originally to be called *Sharon,* but according to *Rolling Stone* the band became bored with some of the songs, decided to abandon them for other cuts, and re-recorded the disc under a new name. The first single from *The Caution Horses* is "Sun Comes Up, It's Tuesday Morning."

Selected discography

Albums

The Trinity Session (includes "Misguided Angel," "I'm So Lonesome I Could Cry," "Sweet Jane," "Walking After Midnight," "Mining for Gold," and "Blue Moon Revisited"), RCA, 1988.
The Caution Horses (includes "Sun Comes Up, It's Tuesday Morning"), RCA, 1990.

Also released the album *Whites Off Earth Now!* on an independent label in 1986.

Sources

Periodicals

Audio, May 1989.
Maclean's, April 17, 1989.
People, December 19, 1988; May 8, 1989.
Rolling Stone, February 9, 1989; December 14, 1989; February
   22, 1990.
Stereo Review, April 1989.
Time, December 5, 1988.

—Elizabeth Thomas

Michael Crawford

Theatrical singer and actor

For years an accomplished British actor in films, television, and stage musicals, Michael Crawford blossomed into full theater legend in the late 1980s with his impassioned performance as the Phantom in composer Andrew Lloyd Webber's production of *The Phantom of the Opera.* Though still enjoying a steady string of sold-out performances, *The Phantom of the Opera* is already one of the most popular musicals in stage history and would surely have done quite well even without Crawford. But audiences and critics alike seem to agree that Crawford is tailor-made for the role, as though he were born and trained to someday play the Phantom.

In the words of the *Chicago Tribune*'s Michael Kilian, Crawford "seems as married to his part as was Hal Holbrook in *Mark Twain Tonight* or Rex Harrison as Professor Henry Higgins in *My Fair Lady,"* or, one might add, as Yul Brenner in *The King and I* or Zero Mostel as Tevye in *Fiddler on the Roof.* And after more than 600 performances in the exhausting role and a triumphant Broadway opening that brought promises of sold-out performances far into the future, Crawford couldn't even begin to think about winding down his career as the Phantom. To the contrary, he felt he was just warming to the part. "I don't want to leave it yet," the actor told Kilian. "I'm still in love with doing it. I'm eating it up. I've done it now for a year and three-quarters and I'm not a bit tired of it."

A recluse as a child, Crawford grew up as Michael Dumbell-Smith in difficult circumstances in the areas around London and Kent. His father was an RAF pilot who was killed in World War II before Michael was born, and his mother, remarried to a grocery-store owner, died when Crawford was twenty-one. The boy nonetheless had a happy home life that sustained him until he was swept away with a passion for singing and performing. He was just a twelve-year-old choir boy when he won a role with a touring company in a performance of Benjamin Britten's *Let's Make an Opera,* and by age fifteen he had changed his surname to Crawford and dropped out of school altogether to perform radio plays for the BBC.

In 1962 Crawford made his West End stage debut in a production of Neil Simon's *Come Blow Your Horn,* but in the following years he made his mark primarily in films and television. He appeared in such films as *The Knack* and John Lennon's black comedy *How I Won the War,* as well as the popular British television series *Some Mothers Do 'ave 'em.* His 1967 Broadway debut in *Black Comedy* brought Crawford to the attention of Gene Kelly, who was casting the film version of *Hello, Dolly.* To impress Kelly, one of the greatest dancers in film and stage history, Crawford began practicing his

For the Record. . .

Name originally Michael Dumbell-Smith, born in Salisbury, Wiltshire, England; son of an RAF pilot and housewife; married Gabrielle Lewis, 1965 (divorced); children: Lucy and Emma.

Attended choir school as a child; won role in musical "Let's Make an Opera" at age 12; dropped out of school at 15 to perform in radio plays for the BBC; made stage debut at age 20 in "Come Blow Your Horn"; appeared in films *The Knack, How I Won the War, A Funny Thing Happened on the Way to the Forum, Hello, Dolly,* and *No Sex, Please—We're British;* appeared in British television program "Some Mothers Do 'ave 'em"; appeared in British version of stage musical "Barnum"; won lead role in original cast of *The Phantom of the Opera,* 1986—.

Awards: All for the *The Phantom of the Opera*—Tony Award, 1988; Drama Desk Award, 1988; Outer Critics Award, 1988; Circle Award, 1988; Drama League Award, 1988; Olivier Award, 1988. Also named to the Order of the British Empire.

Addresses: *Office*—c/o Chatto & Linnit, Ltd. Prince of Wales Theatre, Coventry St., London WC2, England.

was unwittingly auditioning for the choice role in *The Phantom of the Opera.* Andrew Lloyd Webber, the London theater mogul who has penned the scores of some of the stage's most elaborate and successful productions, such as *Jesus Christ Superstar, Evita,* and *Cats,* had heard Crawford and was impressed with his vocal range, a quality that made him a candidate for the Phantom role, which calls for oscillations from baritone to falsetto. Lloyd Webber invited Crawford over to hear some of the *Phantom* score, and the composer immediately liked the actor as much as the actor liked the part.

It took a little convincing to get producer Cameron Mackintosh to accept Crawford in the lead, but once he did, Crawford began intensive training for the role. He took vocal lessons to give more breadth to his range, and he began an examination of the character to find out how best to convey the tormented inner soul beneath the mask of the Phantom. In the story, which is based on Gaston Leroux's 1911 novel of the same name, the Phantom is an incredibly gifted composer and conductor who, because of his grotesquely disfig-

> *Crawford "must express the most painful emotions with his face hidden beneath a partial mask and three layers of latex . . ."*

ured face and body, is forced to live a lonely and sullen life in the shadows of the Paris Opera. His rage against the injustice of his life is taken out on the members of the opera company who perform there, but the Phantom eventually falls in love with the beautiful young ingenue Christine Daae, who helps bring the story to its chilling conclusion.

The role of the mysterious and horrifying Phantom presented Crawford with a unique acting challenge. Normally, an actor's most expressive instrument is his face, but since the Phantom's face is covered with a mask Crawford must find other ways to express the character. As the *Chicago Tribune's* Kilian writes, Crawford "must express the most painful emotions with his face hidden beneath a partial mask and three layers of latex, his eyes clouded with eerily colored contact lenses. To accomplish this, he makes artful use of his body, employing the arch of his back, the strong set of his stance and dramatic gestures of hands and fingers to express the tormented character within." To make this imposing figure visually authentic, Crawford under-

soft-shoe with his customary obsessiveness—and it paid off. He won the role of a goofy shop assistant opposite Barbara Streisand. He also had parts in the musical *A Funny Thing Happened on the Way to the Forum* and the British farce *No Sex Please—We're British.*

But the intensity with which Crawford approached his burgeoning acting career were also placing a strain on his personal life. Crawford and his wife, Gabrielle, were married in 1965 and had two children, daughters Lucy and Emma. But a series of financial setbacks, brought on mostly by Crawford's overly ambitious business manager, placed a strain on their marriage. Crawford found solace in his work, to the neglect of his family. "I went into the theater at 12:30 in the afternoon," he told *People's* Andrea Chambers. "I *needed* the feeling of being there, but Gabrielle wanted me home . . . The breakup was so painful I'm not sure I'd marry again." The Crawfords were divorced in 1975, but they remain close friends, and both daughters are following their father into show business.

While Crawford was enjoying a four-year run with the English production of *Barnum* in the early 1980s, he goes a rigorous daily regimen in the makeup room, where, for two hours, a team of handlers applies the ghastly facial textures and cloaks him in the Phantom costume. Then, practically blinded by the contact lenses, he must make his way around the elaborate set, which includes trapdoors, narrow ramps, falling chandeliers, and smoky caverns. Though the Phantom is only onstage for about thirty minutes of the production, by the end of the show Crawford is drained to exhaustion.

The dream role of the Phantom has brought Crawford unexpected dividends in addition to the obvious. He recorded an album with Columbia, entitled *Michael Crawford: Songs from the Stage and Screen,* which has been a platinum seller, and he appears to be the likely candidate to play the Phantom in the film version of the play. He also has been considered to take over the role of Jean Valjean in *Les Miserables,* another immensely successful 1980s stage musical. But whatever he moves onto next, Crawford seems to realize that in the Phantom he has found the fulfillment of his career, something he can always hang his hat on. "Someday someone else will do it," he told Kilian, "someone else will go on in your clothes and your positions and do the things that you do. But we did it from the beginning. And I know where it came from, in my soul and in my heart. That's a lovely feeling."

Selected discography

Stage musical soundtracks

Billy, CBS, 1974.
Barnum, 1981.
The Phantom of the Opera, 1987.

Solo recordings

Michael Crawford: Songs from the Stage and Screen, Columbia, 1988.

Sources

Chicago Tribune, August 21, 1988.
New York, April 18, 1988.
People, March 14, 1988.

—*David Collins*

Bobby Darin

Singer, songwriter, actor

Singer Bobby Darin began his career during the heyday of rock and roll in the late 1950s, with his smash hit "Splish, Splash." But he quickly branched out into other genres, including folk and country, and is now best known for his classic 1959 recording of "Mack the Knife," which earned him two Grammy Awards. A popular nightclub entertainer, Darin was compared to singing great Frank Sinatra, and like Sinatra, also appeared in several films. Shortly before he died during heart surgery in 1973, Darin hosted his own television variety series on the NBC.

Darin, who was born Walden Robert Cassotto on May 14, 1936, in New York City, had a harsh childhood. His father, a cabinetmaker, died a few months before he was born. Darin and his mother lived with his sister and her husband, and the family's impoverished state was deepened by Darin's severe childhood bouts with rheumatic fever, which produced high medical bills. He was such a sickly child that he did not attend school regularly until his early teens. He did, however, manage to read a lot and also learned to play the drums, piano, and guitar.

But Darin's strongest ambition was not to succeed in music but rather to become an actor. In pursuit of this goal, he attended drama classes at Hunter College, but he became impatient when instructors gave other students chances to practice in leading roles even though they admitted his talent exceeded theirs. So Darin struck out on his own, getting jobs in Catskill resorts that ranged from bussing tables to filling in for absent singers. As he told *Seventeen,* he did not stay long in any of these positions: "I would work for a month or two, then quit and make the rounds, trying to get something in the theater. But nothing happened."

Gradually Darin began to concentrate more on his singing than his acting. He was working writing and singing radio commercials when he was signed to a contract with Decca Records in 1956. Accounts vary as to how he selected his stage name; one says he picked it from a phone book, another that he got it from a malfunctioning restaurant sign advertising Mandarin Chinese food. The young crooner cut a few singles and secured an appearance on bandleader Tommy Dorsey's television show, but his vocal stylings did not capture the public imagination, and Decca dropped him after a year. Darin was then signed by Atlantic Records, and recorded on their subsidiary label, Atco. Again, his first few records caused no sensations, but in 1958 Darin released one of his own compositions, "Splish, Splash." A whimsical number about characters from other rock and roll songs showing up and starting a party at the singer's house while he was in the bathtub, it proved a hit, selling 100,000 copies in only three weeks.

Though Darin quickly followed "Splish, Splash" with another rock and roll ditty, "Queen of the Hop," he did not wish to rely on the burgeoning genre for his livelihood. He was unsure that rock and roll would last, and felt that teenagers—its primary consumers—were fickle in their affections for performers. So, hoping to attract more mature fans, Darin took the money he made from his first hit and financed an album of standards, titled *That's All*. Included on *That's All* was a revision of composer Kurt Weill's song from playwright Bertolt Brecht's *Threepenny Opera*—"Mack the Knife." Released in 1959, "Mack the Knife" did for Darin all that he could have wished, selling over two million copies, and catapulting him to the pinnacle of the nightclub circuit. He became a featured attraction at the most prestigious Las Vegas showcases, such as the Sahara and the Sands, and by 1960 had played the famed Copacabana in New York City.

Meanwhile, Darin was also getting his film career underway. Though he signed a film contract in 1959, he waited through many offers until he found the kind of parts he wanted to play. He made his screen debut playing an American in Italy in the 1961 film *Come September*. Darin also composed the title song, and met his wife, actress Sandra Dee, on the set. Faring better than most singers who venture into acting, Darin won praise for many of his film performances, including his portrayal of a young American flirting with Nazism during the 1940s in 1962's *Pressure Point,* and he received an Academy Award nomination for best supporting actor for his work in 1963's *Captain Newman, M.D.*

Darin had other hit records throughout the early 1960s, including "Beyond the Sea," "You Must Have Been a Beautiful Baby," and the country-flavored "Things." And, unlike many other artists who began their careers with the advent of rock and roll, he managed to maintain his success into the late 1960s, scoring in 1967 with the folk song, "If I Were a Carpenter." Darin also had political concerns at this time, and according to Steve Hochman in the *Los Angeles Times,* "worked on Robert Kennedy's presidential campaign in 1968." Hochman further noted that the singer was "devastated by Kennedy's assassination" later that year, and after this event sold many of his possessions, moved to California, and recorded two albums of protest songs on his own label, Direction. Though Darin's long-time manager Steve Blowner told Hochman: "I was stunned at how good he was, singing [folk songwriters Laura] Nyro and Tim Hardin and [Bob] Dylan," Darin's career began to languish somewhat. In the early 1970s, he recorded for the Motown label.

Darin had again tasted success, doing a summer replacement variety show for NBC in 1972 which was picked up again in 1973, when the heart problems that resulted from his childhood rheumatic fever caught up with him. Entering the hospital to have previously implanted artificial heart valves repaired, he died on the operating table on December 20, 1973. On the occasion of his posthumous induction to the Rock and Roll Hall of Fame in January 1990, Blowner was quoted in the *Los Angeles Times* as saying: "He could sing it all."

Selected discography

Singles

"Splish, Splash," Atco, 1958.
"Queen of the Hop," Atco, c. 1958.
"Dream Lover," Atco, 1959.
"Mack the Knife," Atco, 1959.
"Things," Atco, 1962.
"You're the Reason I'm Living," Capitol, 1963.
"If I Were a Carpenter," Capitol, 1967.

Also released singles during the 1960s: "Beyond the Sea," "Clementine," "Won't You Come Home, Bill Bailey," "Artificial Flowers," "You Must Have Been a Beautiful Baby," and "Irresistible You."

Albums

Bobby Darin, Atco, 1958.
That's All, Atco, 1959.
At the Copa, Atco, 1960.
For Teenagers Only, Atco, 1960.
This Is Darin, Atco, 1960.
(With Johnny Mercer) *Two of a Kind*, Atco, 1961.
The Bobby Darin Story, Atco, 1961.
Love Swings, Atco, 1961.
Bobby Darin Sings Ray Charles, Atco, 1962.
Oh! Look at Me Now! Capitol, 1962.
Things and Other Things, Atco, 1962.
Twist with Bobby Darin, Atco, 1962.
Earthy, Capitol, 1963.
Eighteen Yellow Roses, Capitol, 1963.
You're the Reason I'm Living, Capitol, 1963.
From Hello Dolly to Goodbye Charlie, Capitol, 1964.
Golden Folk Hits, Capitol, 1964.
Venice Blue, Capitol, 1965.
The Best of Bobby Darin, Capitol, 1966.

The Shadow of Your Smile, Atlantic, 1966.
Doctor Dolittle, Atlantic, 1967.
If I Were a Carpenter, Atlantic, 1967.
Inside Out, Atlantic, 1967.
Bobby Darin, Direction, 1968.
Commitment, Direction, 1969.
Bobby Darin, Motown, 1972.
1936—1973, Motown, 1974.

Sources

Books

DiOrio, Al, *Borrowed Time: The Thirty-Seven Years of Bobby Darin*, Running Press, 1981.

Periodicals

Life, January 11, 1960.
Los Angeles Times, January 17, 1990.
Newsweek, April 9, 1962.
Seventeen, July 1961.
Time, March 10, 1961.

—Elizabeth Thomas

Chip Davis

Composer, keyboardist, drummer, record company executive

T he only child of Louis and Betty Davis, Louis Jr.—or Chip, as his mother called him—grew up in Toledo, Ohio, where his father taught high school music and his mother played the trombone. At age five, Chip took piano lessons from his grandmother and he later learned to sing and play the oboe and bassoon. Due to a blood disorder, Davis's physical activities were restricted. So he focused his energy on music, and by the time Davis attended high school, music was his sole interest. Davis attended the University of Michigan, from which he graduated in 1969 with a music degree.

Davis went on tour with the Norman Luboff Choir for a time, during which he met Jackson Berkey, a noted pianist and keyboard player, who became a close friend and later part of Mannheim Steamroller. Davis also played with the Toledo Symphony, taught high school music, and learned to play rock and roll drums for gigs with local groups. Much of what eventually became the album *Fresh Aire I* were pieces that Davis composed to interest his high school students in classical music by giving it a jazzy cast.

By 1972 Davis was earning a living writing advertising

jingles for an Omaha advertising agency, while unsuccessfully trying to interest record companies in a demonstration tape of his works. Davis teamed up with advertiser Bill Fries to record the highly successful Old Home Bread commercials. The commercials, which related the saga of the colorful Old Home Bread delivery truck driver C. W. McCall, evolved into the hit country and western song "Convoy" that sold more than seven million copies and engendered the major motion picture *Convoy,* starring Kris Kristofferson, Ali McGraw, and Ernest Borgnine, for which Davis composed the soundtrack. One hit led to another and then a string of gold records and international recognition. Davis is not fond of country and western music, yet he paradoxically earned the title Country Music Writer of the Year in 1976. "Sometimes the irony of it gets to me," Davis told T. L. Henion of the *Omaha World Herald.* "Everything that I'm able to accomplish now came about largely because of the success of a country and western song."

The financial success of "Convoy" allowed Davis to concentrate more intensely on his own work. While working as a musical director at the recording studio Sound Recorders, Inc. in Omaha, Davis heard his music come alive. Davis loosely gathered together musicians and called them Mannheim Steamroller, after an eighteenth-century musical style called Mannheim Roller, to play his style of music, a blend of classical and pop. In 1974 he founded American Gramaphone to record, produce, and market *Fresh Aire,* "aire" meaning "song."

Davis combines authentic period instruments, such as harpsichords, clavichords, recorders with synthesizers. While his music has been solidly placed in the vanguard of New Age music—characterized by the use of synthesizers, computers, exotic instruments, multiple overdubbing, and is often amelodic—Davis's style is obviously rooted in the tradition of classical music. Each representing a different season, *Fresh Aire* (spring) is baroque in tone, *Fresh Aire II* (fall) reflects medieval influences, and *Fresh Aire III* (summer) is characterized by renaissance and contemporary sounds. *Fresh Aire IV* (winter) focuses on twentieth-century avant-garde repertoire. According to Davis, later albums reflect his interest in intellectual themes: *Fresh Aire V* explored outer space with French Impressionist overtones and *Fresh Aire VI* interprets the music and mythology of ancient Greece.

The American Gramaphone label is known for the very high quality of its recordings and packaging. Davis uses state-of-the-art equipment and innovative techniques, which include using a separate microphone for each acoustic instrument in an ensemble. Because of the very high quality of these recordings, they have been used often in stereo stores to demonstrate equipment and were initially distributed through such stores. It was one of the first labels to commit strongly to the compact disc. The sales success of Davis's recordings has been largely by word of mouth, for the Fresh Aire recordings have received little radio play and though they are frequently used by the ABC television network, Davis is not credited.

The holiday-inspired albums *Mannheim Steamroller Christmas* and *A Fresh Aire Christmas* introduced many listeners to the Mannheim Steamroller sound for the first time. These contemporary holiday classics, which numbered Number 2 and Number 1, respectively, on *Billboard*'s 1989 "Christmas Hits" list, have gone platinum, and *Mannheim Steamroller Christmas* was nominated for a Grammy. *A Fresh Aire Christmas* is unique both in its recording process and in that eleven of the carols on it were chosen by vote among thousands of fans on the American Gramaphone mailing list. The twelfth carol is an original composition by Davis. An additional Christmas album is tentatively planned to appear in the mid-nineties.

Since 1978 Davis has lead Mannheim Steamroller on an annual tour, which by 1988 had drawn large, responsive, and loyal crowds. The performing ensemble includes Davis on drums; Jackson and Almeda Berkey on keyboards; Rick Swanson on percussion; and Eric Hansen on bass, dulcimer, cello, and other stringed instruments. Several local musicians are usually hired in each city to supplement the core group's synthesizers, computers, and other special sound equipment. The shows are multimedia events, featuring slides, dances, film animation, and computerized lighting. Davis has also moved into the realm of videotapes. The video samplers feature clips that had previously been presented in Mannheim Steamroller's live concert performances, as well as those seen on network and cable television.

Davis takes on many responsibilities with American Gramaphone, yet he finds his greatest satisfaction in composing. He told Henion, "I do a lot of different things, but I consider myself a composer. That is what I do best; make music from experiences in my life and hope somebody who listens to it can grab those feelings."

Selected discography

All on the American Gramaphone label; recordings on compact disc and magnetic tape

Fresh Aire I.
Fresh Aire II.
Fresh Aire III, 1979.
Fresh Aire IV, 1981.
Fresh Aire V (with the London Symphony and Cambridge Singers), 1983.
Fresh Aire VI (with the London Symphony and Cambridge Singers).
Mannheim Steamroller Christmas, 1984.
A Fresh Aire Christmas, 1988.
Saving the Wildlife.
Fresh Aire Interludes, (interludes from *Fresh Aire I-IV*).
Yellowstone: The Music of Nature, 1989.
A Fresh Aire Motivator.
Classical Gas (Mason Williams and the Mannheim Steamroller).

Recordings on videotape

The Video Sampler I (includes "Come Home to the Sea" from *Fresh Aire VI,* "Africa" from *Saving the Wildlife,* "Crystal" from *Fresh Aire IV,* and "Deck the Halls" and "Stille Nacht" from *Mannheim Steamroller Christmas*).
The Video Sampler II (includes "Interlude I" from *Fresh Aire I,* "Door IV" from *Fresh Aire II,* "Mere Image" from *Fresh Aire III,* and "Escape from the Atmosphere" from *Fresh Aire V*).
A Fresh Aire Christmas Video (includes "Little Drummer Boy" from *A Fresh Aire Christmas,* "Deck the Halls" from *Mannheim Steamroller Christmas,* as well as Grammy nominated "Silent Night" and "Bring a Torch Jennette Isabella").

Sources

Chicago Sun-Times, August 8, 1989.
Los Angeles Herald Examiner, November 20, 1986.
Omaha World-Herald, April 23, 1989.
San Francisco Examiner, November 7, 1986.

—*Jeanne M. Lesinski*

Sammy Davis, Jr.

Singer, dancer, actor

Sammy Davis, Jr.'s death in 1990 robbed American audiences of a favorite entertainer, a star showman in the oldest vaudeville tradition. Davis was a well-rounded performer of the sort found only rarely these days: he could sing, he could act, he could dance, and he could make people laugh with clowning and impersonations. Davis's long career in show business was even more remarkable because he managed to break color barriers in an era of integration and racism. His many honors and awards—including a prestigious Kennedy Center medal for career achievement—serve as reflections of the affection his fans felt for him.

Davis was a complete variety performer. With a microphone and a backup ensemble he could entertain solo for two hours at a time. He was one of the first blacks to be accepted as a headliner in the larger Las Vegas casinos and one of the very few stars, black or white, to receive Emmy, Tony, *and* Grammy Award nominations. *People* magazine contributor Marjorie Rosen notes that Davis "made beautiful music . . . and blacks and whites alike heard him and were touched by him. He was loved. And that, of course, is what he wanted most of all."

Sammy Davis, Jr. began performing almost as soon as he could walk. Both of his parents were vaudevillians who danced with the Will Mastin Troupe. In 1928, when he was only three, Davis joined the Mastin Troupe as its youngest member. He became a regular in 1930 and travelled with his father on the dwindling vaudeville circuit. The demanding schedule of train rides, practice, and performances left little time for formal education, and Davis was always just one step ahead of the truant officer. His unconventional childhood did provide him with important lessons, however. Young Sammy learned how to please an audience, how to tap dance like a master, and how to move people with a smile and a song.

The motion picture industry all but forced most vaudeville entertainers out of business. Few acts survived the competition from the silver screen. The Mastin Troupe felt the strain, dwindling gradually until it became a trio—Sammy Davis, Sr., Will Mastin, and Sammy Davis, Jr. By 1940 Sammy, Jr. had become the star attraction of the trio, with his father and friend providing soft shoe in the background. The act was popular enough to receive billings in larger clubs, and in that environment Davis met other performers such as Bill "Bojangles" Robinson, Frank Sinatra, and various big band leaders.

Davis was drafted into the United States Army when he turned eighteen and was sent to basic training in Cheyenne, Wyoming. The boot camp experience was

Born December 8, 1925, in New York, N.Y.; died of cancer May 16, 1990, in Los Angeles, Calif.; son of Sammy (a dancer) and Elvira (a dancer; maiden name Sanchez) Davis; married Loray White (a singer), 1958 (divorced, 1959); married May Britt (an actress), November 13, 1960 (divorced, 1968); married Altovise Gore (a dancer), May 11, 1970; children: (second marriage) Tracey, Mark (adopted), Jeff (adopted); (third marriage) Manny (adopted). *Religion:* Jewish. *Military service:* U.S. Army, Special Services, 1943-45; writer, producer, director, and performer in camp shows.

Singer, dancer, and actor, 1928-90. Entertainer with Will Mastin Troupe, 1930; with Will Mastin Trio, 1930-46; and with Will Mastin Trio, Starring Sammy Davis, Jr., 1946-50. Solo performer, ca. 1950-90, with numerous appearances in concerts, cabarets, and nightclubs. Signed with Decca Records, 1955; moved to the Reprise label, ca. 1960; moved to MGM label, 1972. Had pop hits with singles "What Kind of Fool Am I," 1962, "The Candy Man," 1972, and "Mr. Bojangles," ca. 1975. Performed for soldiers stationed in South Vietnam, 1972, and in a special concert at the White House, 1973.

Actor in motion pictures, including *Rufus Jones for President,* 1929, *The Benny Goodman Story,* 1956, *Porgy and Bess,* 1959, *Three Penny Opera,* 1963, *Sweet Charity,* 1969, *Sammy Stops the World,* 1979, *Cannonball Run,* 1981, and *Tap,* 1989. Actor in plays and theatrical productions, including "Mr. Wonderful," 1956, "Golden Boy," 1964, "Sammy on Broadway," 1974, and "Stop the World—I Want To Get Off," 1978. Star of numerous television series, including "Sammy Davis and Friends," "The Sammy Davis, Jr. Show," 1964, "The Swinging World of Sammy Davis, Jr.," 1965, and "GE Presents Sammy," 1975. Guest star on numerous television programs, including "The Ed Sullivan Show," "The Jackie Gleason Show," "Laugh In," and "All in the Family."

Awards: Antoinette Perry Award nomination, 1965, for performance in "Golden Boy"; named man of the year by B'nai B'rith, 1965; Emmy Award nominations, 1965, for "The Sammy Davis, Jr. Show," and 1966, for "the Swinging World of Sammy Davis, Jr."; Springarn Medal from National Association for the Advancement of Colored People (NAACP); Grammy Award nomination for best pop vocal, 1973, for "The Candy Man"; L.H.D. from Wilberforce University, 1973; recipient of Cultural Achievement Award of State of Israel; recipient of Kennedy Center Award for career achievement.

devastating for Davis. Although he was befriended by a black sergeant who gave him reading lessons, he was mistreated relentlessly by the white troops. Transferred to an entertainment regiment, Davis eventually found himself performing in front of some of the same soldiers who had painted "coon" on his forehead. He discovered that his energetic dancing and singing could "neutralize" the bigots and make them acknowledge his humanity. This era may have marked the beginning of Davis's dogged pursuit of his audience's love, a pursuit that would sometimes earn him scorn in years to come.

After the war the Mastin Trio re-formed, playing on bills with Davis's friends like Sinatra, Mel Torme, and Mickey Rooney. Davis went solo after signing a recording contract with Decca Records. His first album, *Starring*

> *"Sammy Davis, Jr. was a true pioneer who traveled a dirt road so others, later, could follow on the freeway. He helped remove the limitations on black entertainers. He made it possible for the Bill Cosbys, the Michael Jacksons and the Eddie Murphys to achieve their dreams."—Quincy Jones*

Sammy Davis, Jr., contained songs and comedy, but another work, *Just for Lovers,* was composed entirely of music. Both sold well, and soon Davis was a headliner in Las Vegas and New York, as well as a guest star on numerous television shows.

On November 19, 1954, Davis nearly lost his life in an automobile accident in the California desert. The accident shattered his face and cost him his left eye. While recuperating, he spent hours discussing philosophy with a rabbi on staff at the hospital, and shortly thereafter he converted to Judaism. Rather than end his career, the accident provided a burst of publicity for Davis. Upon his return to the stage he sold out every performance and received thunderous ovations. Even his well-publicized conversion failed to dampen his popularity. While some critics suggested that he might have had ulterior motives, others—especially blacks—

applauded his thoughtful observations about Jews, blacks, and oppression.

Davis began the 1960s as a certified superstar of stage and screen. He had turned an average musical comedy, "Mr. Wonderful," into a successful Broadway show, and he earned critical raves for his performance in the film *Porgy and Bess.* As a member of the high-profile "Rat Pack," he hobnobbed with Frank Sinatra, Dean Martin, Tony Curtis, and Joey Bishop at fashionable bistros in Las Vegas and Los Angeles. In 1965 he starred in another Broadway play, "Golden Boy," in which he played a struggling boxer, and then he turned in creditable film performances in *A Man Called Adam* and *Sweet Charity.* Somehow he was also able to star in two television shows during the same years, "The Sammy Davis, Jr. Show" and "The Swinging World of Sammy Davis, Jr."

Davis's "swinging world" had its pitfalls, however. His marriage to Swedish actress May Britt earned him the vitriol of the Ku Klux Klan. His "Rat Pack" habits of drinking and drug-taking threatened his health, and his ostentatious displays of wealth nearly bankrupted him even as he earned more than a million dollars a year. Throughout the 1960s Davis was a vocal supporter of the Black Power movement and other left-wing causes, but in the early 1970s he alienated blacks and liberals by embracing Richard Nixon and performing in Vietnam. By that time Davis was in the throes of drug and alcohol addiction. He developed liver and kidney trouble and spent some months in the hospital early in 1974.

The last fifteen years of Davis's life were conducted at the performer's usual hectic pace. In 1978 he appeared in another Broadway musical, "Stop the World—I Want To Get Off." He occasionally served as a stand-in host on the popular "Tonight Show," and he returned in earnest to the casino and show-hall stages. Even hip surgery failed to stop Davis from performing. His best-known act in the 1980s was a musical review with his friends Sinatra and Liza Minnelli, which played to capacity crowds in the United States and Europe just a year before Davis's death.

Doctors discovered a tumor in Davis's throat in August of 1989. The performer underwent painful radiation therapy that at first seemed successful. Then, early in 1990, an even larger cancerous growth was discovered. Davis died on May 16, 1990, as a result of this cancer—only some eight weeks after his friends of a lifetime feted him with a television special in his honor.

During his lifetime, Sammy Davis, Jr. was not universally adored. Some observers—including some blacks— accused him of grovelling to his audiences, of shame-lessly toadying for admiration. Those sentiments were forgotten, however, when Davis died at the relatively young age of sixty-four. In eulogies across the country, other black entertainers cited Davis as a mentor and as a pioneer who reached mainstream audiences even though he hailed from minority groups in both race and religion. Record producer Quincy Jones told *People:* "Sammy Davis, Jr. was a true pioneer who traveled a dirt road so others, later, could follow on the freeway. He helped remove the limitations on black entertainers. He made it possible for the Bill Cosbys, the Michael Jacksons and the Eddie Murphys to achieve their dreams."

Davis, the quintessential song-and-dance man, recorded albums throughout his career and performed a number of signature songs. Chief among these were his tribute to Bill Robinson, "Mr. Bojangles," the ballads "What Kind of Fool Am I" and "I've Gotta Be Me," and his biggest hit, the spritely "Candy Man." Davis's singing was like everything else in his performance—energetic, spirited, and played to maximum effect. Rosen sees Davis as "a personal link to a vibrant mainstream of American entertainment" who "poured his jittery energy into virtuoso performances with all the intimacy of a saloon singer."

In an interview for *Contemporary Authors,* Davis analyzed his position in show business. "Nobody likes me but the people," he said. "Though I have been treated extremely well overall by the critics, I have never been a critic's favorite. But the people always had faith in me, and they were supportive of me. . . . They laugh. They have good times, and they come backstage. It's a joy."

Writings

(With Burt Broyar and Jane Broyar) *Yes I Can: The Story of Sammy Davis, Jr.,* Farrar, Straus, 1965.
Hollywood in a Suitcase, Morrow, 1980.
(With Broyar and Broyar) *Why Me? The Sammy Davis, Jr. Story,* Farrar, Straus, 1989.

Selected discography

Albums

Starring Sammy Davis, Jr., Decca, 1955.
Just for Lovers, Decca, 1955.
What Kind of Fool Am I and Other Show Stoppers, Reprise, 1962.
Sammy Davis, Jr., at the Cocoanut Grove, Reprise, 1963.
As Long as She Needs Me, Reprise, 1963.
Forget-Me-Nots, Decca, 1964.
Sammy Davis, Jr. Salutes the Stars of the London Palladium, Reprise, 1964.

The Shelter of Your Arms, Reprise, 1964.
If I Ruled the World, Reprise, 1965.
(With Count Basie) *Our Shining Hour*, Verve, 1965.
Nat Cole Song Book, Reprise, 1965.
Sammy's Back on Broadway, Reprise, 1965.
Try a Little Tenderness, Decca, 1965.
The Best of Sammy Davis, Jr., Decca, 1966.
The Sounds of '66, Reprise, 1966.
Laurinda Almeida Plays, Sammy Davis Sings, Reprise, 1966.
That's All, Reprise, 1967.
Dr. Doolittle, Reprise, 1967.
I've Gotta Be Me, Reprise, 1969.
Lonely Is the Name, Reprise, 1969.
Goin's Great, Reprise, 1969.
Sammy Davis, Jr. Steps Out, Reprise, 1970.
Let There Be Love, Harmony, 1970.
What Kind of Fool Am I, Harmony, 1971.
Now, MGM, 1972.
Portrait of Sammy Davis, Jr., MGM, 1978.
Hey There! It's Sammy Davis, Jr. at His Dynamite Greatest, MCA.
The Great Sammy Davis, Jr., Columbia, 1988.

Also recorded *Sammy Davis, Jr. Belts the Best of Broadway*, *Sammy Davis, Jr. at Town Hall*, Decca, *Porgy and Bess*, Decca, and *Mr. Entertainment*, Decca.

Singles

"Hey, There," Decca, 1954.
"Something's Gotta Give," Decca, 1955.
"Love Me or Leave Me," Decca, 1955.
"That Old Black Magic," Decca, 1955.
"I'll Know," Decca, 1955.
"Five," Decca, 1956.

"Earthbound," Decca, 1956.
"New York's My Home," Decca, 1956.
"What Kind of Fool Am I," Reprise, 1962.
(With Frank Sinatra) "Me and My Shadow," Reprise, 1962.
(With Dean Martin) "Sam's Song," Reprise, 1962.
"As Long as She Needs Me," Reprise, 1963.
"The Shelter of Your Arms," Reprise, 1963.
"Don't Blame the Children," Reprise, 1967.
"Lonely Is the Name," Reprise, 1968.
"I've Gotta Be Me," Reprise, 1968.
"Candy Man," MGM, 1972.
"The People Tree," MGM, 1972.

Sources

Books

Contemporary Authors, Volume 108, Gale, 1984.
Davis, Sammy, Burt Broyar and Jane Broyar, *Yes I Can: The Story of Sammy Davis, Jr.*, Farrar, Straus, 1965.
Davis, Sammy, Burt Broyar and Jane Broyar, *Why Me? The Sammy Davis, Jr. Story*, Farrar, Straus, 1989.
Dobrin, Arnold, *Voices of Joy, Voices of Freedom*, Coward, 1972.
Stambler, Irwin, *Encyclopedia of Pop, Rock & Soul*, St. Martin's, 1974.

Periodicals

New York Times, May 17, 1990.
People, May 28, 1990.

—Anne Janette Johnson

Taylor Dayne

Singer, songwriter

Pop vocalist Taylor Dayne first came to many music fans' attention with her 1988 debut album on Arista, *Tell It to My Heart.* The title track rocketed to Top 10 status, and the album garnered her four New York Music Award nominations. Follow-up songs "Prove Your Love" and "I'll Always Love You" also received a fair amount of radio airplay, but Dayne's second album, *Can't Fight Fate,* has brought her another smash hit with the single, "With Every Beat of My Heart." Edwin Miller summed up the singer's powerful vocal style thus in *Seventeen:* "Personality she's got."

Born Lesley Wunderman on March 7, 1963, Dayne grew up in Long Island, New York. Her earliest ambition was to be a singer, and she was active in her elementary school choruses, often performing solos. She began listening to rock music when she was in junior high, and when she reached high school, Dayne sang with her boyfriend's band. She confided to Miller: "The other boys [in the band] didn't like me. They were intimidated because I sang better than they rocked." The group entertained at school dances, and performed songs made famous by the Allman Brothers, Joni Mitchell, and Joe Walsh.

When Dayne went to Nassau Community College to study philosophy, she hooked up with a band called Felony, where she sang duets with a male vocalist. Felony played its own compositions, and Dayne told Miller that she "loved getting away from singing somebody else's music. . . . That was my introduction to original music, learning how to write and interpret." Around the same time, she began taking classical vocal lessons. Though Dayne has made her mark in the pop genre, she offered this advice for aspiring singers, as quoted by Miller: "Never study with somebody who says they can teach you how to sing pop correctly. What's pop? Get to the fundamentals. Do the basics!"

After Felony broke up, Dayne had a stint with a pop group called the Next, and eventually decided to forsake philosophy, fearing that the only thing she could do in the field was teach. She started working harder on her music career, cutting a demo tape in Los Angeles, California, and sang in New York in front of record-company talent scouts, but with few results. Somewhere along the line she recorded two singles under the name Leslee; these also went nowhere. Dayne was performing in a Russian-American nightclub in Brighton Beach, New York, "belting bawdy Russian songs," in the words of *People* magazine, when she came to the attention of Arista Records. Anxious to distance herself from her previous unsuccessful recordings, she was aided in her search for a new stage name by friend Dee Snider of the rock group Twisted Sister, who suggested she use a male-sounding one and helped her come up with Taylor. Dayne found the last name in a baby book, according to Miller.

Once Dayne was under contract with Arista, things moved quickly. *Tell It to My Heart* was recorded in six weeks; as Miller reported, "songs were picked to spotlight [Dayne's] range and power, with its strong rhythm and blues influences." The title cut was described in *People* as a "catchy dance tune," and "Prove Your Love" is in a similar vein. "I'll Always Love You," according to *People,* "is an R & B-flavored ballad that Dayne hopes . . . will establish her as the white soul singer she longs to be." Aside from the hit, "With Every Beat of My Heart," *Can't Fight Fate* also includes the ballad "Love Will Lead You Back."

Selected discography

Albums

Tell It to My Heart (includes "Tell It to My Heart," "Prove Your Love," and "I'll Always Love You"), Arista, 1988.
Can't Fight Fate (includes "With Every Beat of My Heart" and "Love Will Lead You Back"), Arista, 1989.

Also released two singles on another label under the name Leslee.

Sources

People, May 23, 1988.
Seventeen, August 1988.

—*Elizabeth Thomas*

Desert Rose Band

Country/rock group

The resurgent interest in rowdy, foot-stomping country music has proven a boon for the Desert Rose Band, a group of veteran performers in the honky tonk vein. The band's personnel roster reads like a "Who's Who" of country-rock—some of its members come from watershed groups like the Byrds and the Flying Burrito Brothers, while others have backed up entertainers as varied as Buck Owens, Fats Domino, Clint Eastwood, and Linda Ronstadt. Desert Rose owes its growing popularity to the vibrant Bakersfield brand of country music, the same California-based sound that spawned Owens, Merle Haggard, and Dwight Yoakam. "I'm not necessarily breaking in new ground," says bandleader Chris Hillman, "but I feel I am doing it better."

The Desert Rose Band presents a more or less natural evolution from the earliest country-rock acts of the late 1960s. This is not surprising, since band founder Hillman and steel guitar player J. D. Maness both played pioneering roles in the movement. Hillman grew up in California—miles from bluegrass country—but even

For the Record. . .

Members include **Chris Hillman** (acoustic guitar and vocals); **Herb Pedersen** (guitar and vocals); **John Jorgenson** (lead guitar); **Steve Duncan** (drums); **Bill Bryson** (bass); and **J. D. Maness** (steel guitar).

Band formed in Los Angeles, Calif., in 1985, signed with the Curb label, 1986. Released first album, *The Desert Rose Band*, 1987; had two country Top 40 singles, "Ashes of Love" and "Love Reunited."

Addresses: *Agent*—Chuck Morris Entertainment Agency, 4155 E. Jewel, Suite 412, Denver, CO 80222.

as a young teen he loved hillbilly music. In 1963 he took his first professional job, playing mandolin in a bluegrass band. Maness played a traditional country instrument, steel guitar, but in the mid-1960s he joined a quasi-rock band led by Gram Parsons, the International Submarine Band. That group made its first recordings in 1967 and was heralded as one of the first outfits to merge country and rock influences.

Gram Parsons was the charismatic leader of the country-rock fusion. He joined the rock group the Byrds in 1968. Hillman was also a member of the Byrds at the time, and together he and Parsons urged the group to infuse its work with more country sound. In 1969 the Byrds released *Sweetheart of the Rodeo,* widely considered *the* seminal country-rock album (*Rolling Stone* magazine lists it as one of the best 100 albums of the last twenty years). The Byrds were the first rock group to be invited to perform on the Grand Ole Opry. Soon after that performance Parsons and Hillman left to form their own band, the Flying Burrito Brothers.

Hillman was an associate not only of Parsons but of David Crosby and Steven Stills, among others. The times were wild and wooly in that musical environment, so even as the Flying Burrito Brothers were cutting an album that would garner praise for years, the members were taking drugs and living life at high speed. Parsons succumbed to the lifestyle in 1973, dying of a drug-related heart attack while still in his mid-twenties. Hillman was left without a band, but only briefly. His talent afforded him session work with a number of other country artists—like Maness, he was never unemployed.

"I look at the Desert Rose Band as a highly evolved version of the Flying Burrito Brothers," Hillman told the *Lexington Herald-Leader.* "By 'highly evolved,' I mean I've got some really good players and singers to work with." The band formed inauspiciously in 1985 from a nucleus of session musicians who had secured work with Dan Fogelberg. After touring with Fogelberg—and helping him with a bluegrass-influenced album—Hillman, guitarist John Jorgenson and guitarist-vocalist Herb Pedersen found work at the Palomino Club in Los Angeles. There they were discovered by an executive for Curb Records and offered a recording contract. Once the record company signed them, Hillman, Jorgenson, and Pedersen were able to recruit other top-quality session musicians to round out the ensemble. Billed as the Desert Rose Band, the group incorporated Maness on steel guitar, Bill Bryson on bass, and Steve Duncan on drums. They cut their debut album in 1987.

Because Hillman and Maness were relatively well known in the country music industry, the Desert Rose Band might have received more publicity than other fledgling groups. Quality counts, however, and the band's work inched into the country Top 40 on its own strength. *Arizona Republic* contributor Andrew Means calls the Desert Rose Band sound "essentially a familiar format—crisp vignettes from the pedal steel and lead guitar, balanced vocal harmonies and starched tempos." While there is indeed little innovation in the Desert Rose work to date, the musicians are of such high professional calibre, and their enthusiasm for the project is so high, that the band has drawn a following almost overnight. *Akron Beacon Journal* critic Pam Parrish put it succinctly when she noted that the music of the Desert Rose Band "makes you want to pull your car to the side of the highway, jump out and dance on the roof."

California is giving Nashville a run for its money music-wise, thanks to groups like the Desert Rose Band. Hillman, the group's spokesman, claims that his band is "at the pinnacle. . . . The best thing is to watch us in person." Having placed two singles—"Ashes of Love" and "Love Reunited"—in the country Top 40 in 1987, the Desert Rose Band seems poised to blossom as a 1990s supergroup. Hillman told the *Houston Post:* "I'm overjoyed to be out here again, playing music. It's a good time, because some great things are happening in country music—we've got great lyrics, great songs again, and real country is coming back. . . . For me, it's an exciting time and I think you're gonna hear a lot more out of this band."

Selected discography

The Desert Rose Band, Curb, 1987.
Running, Curb, 1988.
Pages of Life, Curb, 1990.

Sources

Books

Malone, Bill C., *Country Music U.S.A.,* revised edition, University
of Texas Press, 1985.

Periodicals

Akron Beacon Journal, March 29, 1987.
Arizona Republic, September 2, 1987.
Fresno Bee, August 16, 1987; August 21, 1987.
Houston Post, August 8, 1987.
Lexington Herald-Leader, May 24, 1987.

—*Anne Janette Johnson*

Dion

Singer, guitarist, songwriter

It is notoriously difficult for teen singing idols to maintain popularity as they mature—often they drift into total anonymity or appear only in "oldies" revues. These avenues have never appealed to Dion DiMucci, the Italian heartthrob of rock 'n' roll's formative years. Dion—with and without his group the Belmonts—scored a long string of pop hits in the late 1950s and early 1960s, earning millions before the British Invasion changed the face of the rock world. Once dismissed as a mere pop entertainer, Dion has earned the respect of critics for his musicianship, his honest lyrics, and his ability to sustain an audience well into middle age. Now in his 50s, he is still producing, writing, and singing new material.

In a *Los Angeles Times* review, Kathy Orloff finds much to praise in Dion's work. The critic writes: "His style is immediately identifiable and unique, his voice is strong and rich and profoundly pure. The sound is sensitive, tangible, full. His songs . . . show him to be open, vulnerable, and yet somehow steady." The vulnerability in Dion's music stems from his years of struggle with drug addiction and his subsequent satisfaction at having kicked a heroin habit. The star who has always called himself "the Wanderer" told *People* magazine that in his teen-star years he was "Mr. Macho, yeah, but . . . lost in a way. . . . Now [I'm] home."

Dion was born and raised in the Bronx, son of an itinerant puppeteer who was often unemployed. *People* reporter Steve Dougherty notes that the singer's father "was a disaster. He taught Dion to shop-lift and filled him with a lifelong sense of fear and insecurity." Dion grew up on the Bronx's mean streets, running with a gang and shooting heroin from his early teens. He hardly seemed a candidate for show business stardom, but he had two valuable assets that he learned to use: a beautiful singing voice and a cool, macho image that somehow suited rock 'n' roll music.

"The day I heard Hank Williams for the first time, my life changed," Dion told *People*. "Before that, music was boring. . . . Rock and roll didn't exist in my neighborhood before that. Hank was the dawn of creation for me." Dion was one of the millions of teens who embraced rock 'n' roll and its black counterpart, rhythm and blues. He began to spend evenings on street corners, singing a capella with several buddies. Dion was the first of the group to find his way into a recording studio, and with a group called the Tamberlanes he cut the single "The Chosen Few." When that song did well, he brought in his friends to back him up on his second single, "I Wonder Why." Soon they were traveling to-

For the Record. . .

Full name Dion DiMucci; born July 18, 1939, in Bronx, N.Y.; son of Pasquale DiMucci (a puppeteer); married, wife's name Susan; children: Tane, August, Lark.

Singer, guitarist, songwriter, 1957—. Formed group Dion and the Tamberlanes, 1957; with Fred Milano, Carlo Mastangelo, and Angelo D'Aleo, formed group Dion and the Belmonts, 1957-60; solo performer, 1960—; record labels include: Laurie Records, Columbia Records, ABC Records, Warner Bros. Records, Word Records, and Arista Records.

Awards: Elected to Rock 'n' Roll Hall of Fame, January, 1989.

Addresses: *Record company*—Arista Records, Inc., 6 W. 57th St., New York, N.Y. 10019.

gether as Dion and the Belmonts—named after Belmont Avenue in the Bronx.

While other groups of the period specialized in flashy dance routines, Dion and the Belmonts preferred to keep their stage show simple, almost a version of their street-corner doo-wopping. The group had a number of Top 40 hits between 1957 and 1960, including "No One Knows," "Don't Pity Me," "A Teenager in Love," and "A Lover's Prayer." Their most fateful appearance was certainly February 2, 1959, when they appeared in Clear Lake, Iowa on a program with Buddy Holly, Ritchie Valens, and the Big Bopper. At the show's conclusion, Dion was asked to pitch in thirty-five dollars to charter a plane to the next concert site. He chose to travel in the bus instead, and thus was spared when the plane carrying Holly and Valens crashed in a cornfield.

Dion and the Belmonts parted ways with no animosity in 1960. Dion began a solo career and soon could lay claim to a number of Top 10 hits. After several modest successes he produced the multimillion seller "Runaround Sue" in 1961 and the equally successful "The Wanderer" the following year. Between 1962 and 1964 the singer placed numerous songs on the charts, including "Lovers Who Wander," "Born To Cry," "Little Diane," "Sandy," and "Come Go with Me." Then the Beatles and the Rolling Stones arrived in America, and the music of entertainers like Dion began to seem simplistic and old-fashioned.

"A lot of people thought the British thing [the Beatles, Stones, etc.] blew a lot of people away," Dion said in *Where Have They Gone? Rock 'n' Roll Stars.* "I don't remember it that way. It didn't knock me on the roadside. I remember stopping. It was a very conscious decision. It wasn't like anything overtook me." In fact, the singer was simply ready to explore new kinds of music, especially folk and blues. He disappeared from the concert scene and began performing at small halls in the Bronx again, practicing acoustic guitar until he became a master of the instrument. He also began to face the facts about his drug use, finally quitting heroin and alcohol in 1968.

That same year a new Dion emerged on the pop scene. The singer recorded a Dick Holler song, "Abraham, Martin and John," a folk tribute to three of the nation's slain leaders. The piece was an enormous success commercially, but more important, it accorded Dion more respect among critics. In the *Rolling Stone Record Guide,* Dave Marsh suggests that "Abraham, Martin and John" is "perhaps the best, and certainly the best received, protest song of all," adding that the album from which the single came "revealed enormous artistic growth." Dion followed this success with a powerful anti-drug song, "Clean up Your Own Back Yard."

Some critics feel that Dion's work in the 1970s was hampered by lack of vision on the part of his producers. As Marsh puts it, the singer was "trapped in the company's pop-rock production mill," with shoddy backup and lackluster promotion burying his albums. Dion found a new audience in the 1980s and early 1990s, however. A religious experience in 1979 gave him the incentive to apply his brand of soft rock to gospel music. "I used to think God only liked organ music," he told *People,* "but religion puts God in a box. From what I read in the Bible, God doesn't like religion. God talks about having a personal relationship with Him. I feel comfortable with that."

From his home base in Boca Raton, Florida, Dion continues to write and record soft-rock inspirational music. "There's a real enjoyment I get out of life today that I never had before," he told *People.* Dion is not a regular on the oldies revue circuit by any means. When he performs live, it is more likely to be fresh material from recent albums rather than just another tired rendition of "Runaround Sue." Still, the singer has not forgotten his roots, the excitement of rock 'n' roll that made him a music fan in the first place. He concluded in *People:* "I show rock and rollers how to grow old gracefully. I want to rock till I drop. I love rock and roll music. It keeps you young."

Selected discography

Solo singles

"Lonely Teenager," 1960.
"Havin' Fun," 1961.
"Kissin' Game," 1961.
"Runaround Sue," 1961.
"The Wanderer," 1961.
"Lovers Who Wander," 1962.
"Little Diane," 1962.
"Love Came to Me," 1962.
"Ruby Baby," 1962.
"Sandy," 1963.
"This Little Girl," 1963.
"Come Go with Me," 1963.
"Be Careful of Stones that You Throw," 1963.
"Donna the Prima Donna," 1963.
"Drip Drop," 1963.
"Johnny B. Goode," 1964.
"Abraham, Martin and John," 1968.
"Purple Haze," 1968.
"Both Sides Now," 1969.
"If We Only Have Love," 1969.
"Clean up Your Own Back Yard," 1970.
"Sunniland," 1971.
"Sanctuary," 1971.
"New York City Song," 1974.
"Hey, My Love," 1976.
"Queen of '59," 1976.
"Young Virgin Eyes," 1977.

LPs; with the Belmonts

Presenting Dion and the Belmonts, Laurie, 1960.
Dion and the Belmonts, Laurie, 1960.
When You Wish Upon a Star, Laurie, 1960.
Together with the Belmonts, ABC, 1967.
Sixteen Greatest of Dion and the Belmonts, Laurie, 1971.
Everything You Always Wanted To Hear by Dion and the Belmonts, Laurie, 1973.
Dion and the Belmonts Reunion, Laurie, 1973.
So Why Didn't You Do That the First Time? (previously unissued recordings), Ace, 1987.

Solo LPs

Dion Alone, Laurie, 1961.

Runaround Sue, Laurie, 1961.
Lovers Who Wander, Laurie, 1962.
Dion Sings His Greatest Hits, Laurie, 1962.
Ruby Baby, Columbia, 1963.
Dion Sings to Sandy, Laurie, 1963.
Dion's Greatest Hits, Volume 1, Laurie, 1966.
Dion's Greatest Hits, Volume 2, Laurie, 1966.
15 Million Sellers, Laurie, 1966.
Dion, Laurie, 1968.
I Wonder Where I'm Bound, Laurie, 1968.
Sit Down, Old Friend, Laurie, 1970.
You're Not Alone, Laurie, 1971.
Sanctuary, Laurie, 1971.
Suite for Late Summer, Laurie, 1972.
Dion's Greatest Hits, Columbia, 1973.
Ruby Baby, Columbia, 1973.
Streetheart, Warner Bros., 1976.
Return of the Wanderer, Lifesong, 1978.
Kingdom in the Streets, Word, 1985.
Abraham, Martin and John, Ace, 1987.
Alone with Dion, Ace, 1987.
Velvet and Steel, Word, 1987.
Yo Frankie, Arista, 1989.

Sources

Books

DiMucci, Dion and Davin Seay, *The Wanderer: Dion's Story*, Beech Tree Books, 1988.
Lillian Roxon's Rock Encyclopedia, Grosset, 1978.
McColm, Bruce and Doug Payne, *Where Have They Gone? Rock 'N' Roll Stars*, Tempo, 1979.
The Rolling Stone Record Guide, Rolling Stone Press, 1979.
Stambler, Irwin, *Encyclopedia of Pop, Rock & Soul*, revised edition, St. Martin's, 1989.

Periodicals

Los Angeles Times, March 28, 1971.
People, November 21, 1988.

—*Anne Janette Johnson*

The Doors

Rock group

Though they were an immensely popular band in their time, perhaps the greatest significance of the Doors can be most appreciated in the larger context of rock and roll history, for this was the first group to bring the dark side of the rock mind-set to a mass following. Emerging from the seamy Los Angeles club scene in 1967 as a cult/underground favorite of the more sophisticated rock cognoscenti, the Doors shocked their own early followers, the numerous record companies and producers that had passed them up, and then the entire nation by bringing their unique, violent, harrowing sound to the candyland world of Top 40 AM radio and overwhelming national popularity. "The Doors seeped in through the underground early in 1967," writes Lillian Roxon in *The Rock Encyclopedia,* "a time when no one could possibly have predicted that a group that sang about the evil and the reptilian and the bloody was about to become not just the number one group in America, but the number one teenybopper group in America, which just shows what secret dreams of mayhem and vengeance and violent sexuality all

those dear little suburban nymphets were harboring in the infant hearts beating under all those preteen bras."

The heart and soul of the Doors was the enigmatic, charismatic poet/lyricist and vocalist Jim Morrison, the legendary "Lizard King," whose flame burned high and bright for a few years in the late 1960s before being snuffed out by a heart attack, probably brought on by Morrison's excessive use of drugs and alcohol, in Paris in 1971. Morrison has since become a cult hero, held with the same reverance by generations of rock fans as such other rock martyrs as Buddy Holly, Janis Joplin, Jimi Hendrix, and John Lennon.

Morrison's father, a career naval officer from a family with a long history of military service, moved his family from place to place around the country, and it was this man that young James Douglas Morrison took to represent the authority that he would rebel against for the rest of his life. As a teenager he began taking an interest in poetry and philosophy, along with film and rock music, as potential paths toward the renewal and self-recreation he sought upon his break from the authoritarian world.

Morrison's travels took him first to UCLA in 1964, where he initially entered the Theater Arts Department, but where he also began to read the poetry of William Blake and the writings of Friedrich Nietzsche. At this time he also met Ray Manzarek, a classically trained musician from Chicago who had lately begun experimenting with the blues in a group called Rich and the Ravens. Morrison told Manzarek that he had been writing some song lyrics and began to sing a few bars from "Moonlight Drive," which would later become a Doors classic.

"I said 'That's it,'" said Manzarek in *The Encyclopedia of Pop, Rock, and Soul.* "I'd never heard lyrics to a rock song like that before. We talked together for awhile before we decided to get a group together and make a million dollars."

Manzarek, a keyboardist (principally organ) and Morrison, a smokey-voiced baritone vocalist, then discovered drummer John Densmore and guitarist Robby Krieger playing in a band called the Psychedelic Rangers and the band was complete. The name of the group was decided by Morrison, who was enamored with a quote from Blake that appeared on the flyleaf to Aldous Huxley's book *The Doors of Perception* (a discussion of experimentations with the drug mescaline): "If the doors of perception were cleansed, everything would appear to man as it is, infinite."

The Doors struggled for a time in 1965-66, playing mostly as a warm-up act to more popular groups in clubs along the Sunset Strip. It was at one of these

---

"Light My Fire," lit millions of fires across the country"

---

clubs, the Whiskey A Go Go, that Jac Holzman, president of Elektra records, first saw the Doors perform as an opening act for the group Love. Holzman signed the band in late 1966, and by 1967 their first album, *The Doors,* was released along with the single "Break on Through," which did not have much success. The second single, however, entitled "Light My Fire," lit millions of fires across the country, eventually rising to Number 1 on the charts in the summer of 1967. At seven minutes, "Light My Fire" was nearly twice as long as the typical pop song, and most of the body of the tune was filled with a long, hypnotic, penetrating organ solo by Manzarek. Organ solos in a rock song? No one had ever heard of such a thing. This was not the Monkees, or even the Beatles. This was something new, and clearly the Doors had touched a nerve in the growing angst among American teenagers in the turbulent atmosphere of the late 1960s.

Even darker and more elaborate was the final cut of the first album, a work that spoke to the more hardened Doors fans and clearly had no place on Top 40 radio. "The End" is, if not the Doors most memorable song, certainly the most representative of the group's tight, eerie control of the music, along with Morrison's core personality, which comes through in this eleven-minute, brooding Oedipal rage as he symbolically kills his father.

For the next two years the Doors were the hottest group in America, somehow managing to draw the raves of sophisticated rock fans and teenyboppers, and by selling gold record after gold record while maintaining a sold-out tour circuit. And despite appearances on such all-American television shows as *Ed Sullivan* and *The Jonathan Winters Show,* Morrison conceded nothing in his stage act. He was still the Lizard King, writhing seductively on stage in a half-trance, ad-libbing poetry from the top of his head as the band continued to play. More hit LPs followed, including *Strange Days, Waiting for the Sun, Morrison Hotel,* and *Soft Parade.*

But Morrison's antics soon began to catch up with him. In New Haven before a show, Morrison was maced by police when he was discovered with a female fan in his dressing room; later that night Morrison began telling the audience of the incident and he was pulled off the stage, accused of trying to incite a riot. With his strange, manic intensity, Morrison loved to play with a crowd, to see just how far he could take them, just how close to violent, sexual frenzy he could whip them. The big blow came in Miami in 1969 when, after performing a concert, Morrison was arrested on charges that he had allegedly exposed himself to the audience during the show. *The Encyclopedia of Pop, Rock, and Soul* quotes writer Alexandra Tacht's impression of the incident: "Morrison finally did it. He culminated his career as a sex symbol of the decade by dropping his pants in front of umpteen screaming teens in Miami. Exit Morrison, who hopped the country and left in his wake 35,000 teens turning on a Decency Rally behind Jackie Gleason and Anita Bryant to show that Miami is really a straight town."

Morrison's arrest became prime tabloid fodder, and the band was forced out of the remaining dates on that particular tour. But record sales were still strong. *L.A. Woman* and *The Doors Greatest Hits* were immensely popular in 1970, and "Love Her Madly," the single from the former, rose to Number 1 on the charts in early 1971. But the constant harrassment by the police be-gan to wear on Morrison, who, in a fit of depression, left the band in 1971 for an extended hiatus in Paris, where he planned to rest and write poetry. The rest of the band remained in California, rehearsing and recording with the hopes that Morrison would return. But on July 3, 1971, Morrison suffered a heart attack in France and died. To this day there are some faithful fans who believe that Morrison's death was staged, and that the Lizard King still lives. Those dwindling few can be assured, however, that Morrison rests under the big, graffiti-covered stone in the Poet's Corner of the Pere Lachaise Cemetery in Paris.

Selected discography

The Doors, Elektra, 1967.
Strange Days, Elektra, 1967.
Waiting for the Sun, Elektra, 1968.
The Soft Parade, Elektra, 1969.
Absolutely Live, Elektra, 1970.
The Doors Greatest Hits, Elektra, 1970.
Morrison Hotel, Elektra, 1970.
L.A. Woman, Elektra, 1971.
Other Voices, Elektra, 1971.
Full Circle, Elektra, 1972.
Weird Scenes Inside the Gold Mine, Elektra, 1972.
The Best of the Doors, Elektra, 1973.

Sources

Bane, Michael, *Who's Who in Rock,* Facts on File, 1981.
Hardy, Phil, and Dave Laing, *The Encyclopedia of Rock,* Schirmer, 1988.
Lillian Roxon's Rock Encyclopedia, compiled by Ed Naha, Grosset and Dunlap, 1978.
Nite, Norm, *Rock On, Vol. II,* Harper & Row, 1984.
Roxon, Lillian, *The Rock Encyclopedia,* Workman, 1969.
Stambler, Irwin, *The Encyclopedia of Pop, Rock, and Soul,* St. Martin's, 1977.

—*David Collins*

Duran Duran

Rock group

When MTV, the 24-hour music video network, dawned in the early 1980s, it changed the face of popular music forever, and the British rock group Duran Duran was the first act to take full advantage of its possibilities. The five-member band of young, sculpted faces often adorned with make-up and frilly, expensive clothes, saw in the music video the perfect vehicle for propelling them beyond obscurity and their musical abilities to fame, fortune, and good times. Combining the sounds of 1970s British punk and the more upbeat, danceable rhythms of disco, Duran Duran began producing clean, sparkling (if not critically acclaimed), pop tunes. But what set them apart immediately were their videos: somewhat surreal escapist fantasies that took the self-styled playboys to such far-flung locales as Sri Lanka and Antigua. Screaming, record-buying, television-watching teen-age girls everywhere ate it up—and nobody could have predicted it better than the band members themselves. "Video to us is like stereo was to Pink Floyd," said Duran Duran keyboardist Nick Rhodes. "It was new, it was just happening. And we saw we could do a lot with it."

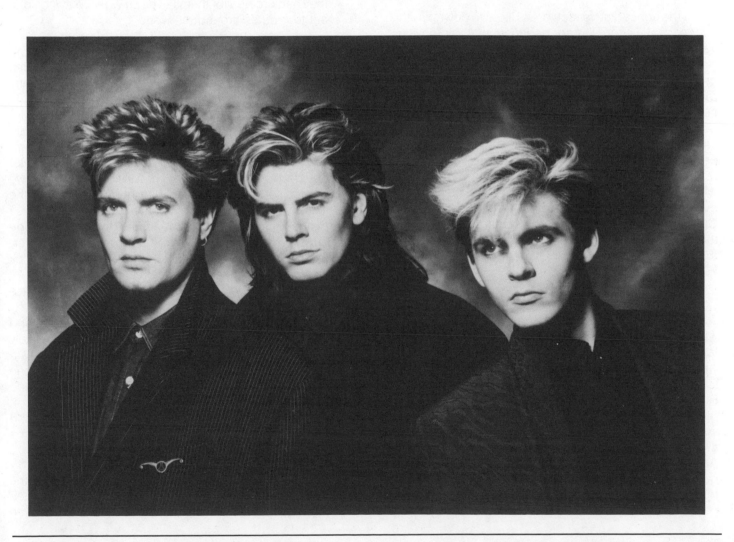

For the Record. . .

Band formed in 1978, in Birmingham, England; members include vocalist **Simon Le Bon** (born October 27, 1958, in Bushey, England); guitarist and keyboards player **Andy Taylor** (born February 16, 1961, in Dolver-Hampton, England); keyboards player **Nick Rhodes** (born June 8, 1962, in England); bassist **John Taylor** (born June 20, 1960, in Birmingham, England); drummer **Roger Taylor** (born April 26, 1960, in Birmingham, England).

Performed in the Birmingham area, 1980-84; toured the U.K., 1980—; toured internationally beginning in 1984; Number 1 album, *Seven and the Ragged Tiger*, in 1984; split into two groups: Power Station and Arcadia in 1985; reformed, 1986—.

Addresses: *Record company*—Capitol Records, 1750 North Vine St., Hollywood, CA 90028.

While the conservative rock press liked to downplay the success of Duran Duran because of their obvious vanity and lack of attention to "serious" music, it should be noted that some of rock and roll's most time-honored heroes, such as Elvis Presley and even a few members of the Beatles, were never accused of being serious musicians. Success in pop music has always depended upon image at least as much as the music itself. And "serious music" is not necessarily for everyone as *Rolling Stone*'s James Henke realized when he referred to Duran Duran's eager fans as "young girls who were glued to their television sets watching MTV every waking hour. These girls had little use for the Clash's left-wing politics, or the ranting and raving of that weird-looking Elvis Costello. But Duran Duran, now they were something else. Five extremely good-looking young men. Dream dates."

Duran Duran began coming together in 1978 (some sources say 1977) in the Midlands city of Birmingham, where Rhodes and guitarist John Taylor started performing with a variety of bandmates. The current group, which takes its name from a character in the 1968 film *Barbarella*, became complete in 1980 when Simon Le Bon, a drop-out drama student, showed up one day in pink, leopard-skin leotards and said he wanted to sing in the band. Le Bon joined Rhodes, John Taylor (who switched to bass), drummer Roger Taylor, and guitarist Andy Taylor (none of the Taylors are related), and the quintet began performing in Birmingham, most frequently at a club called Rum Runners which had become established as the home of England's burgeoning New Romantic scene. "Donning the foppish clothes of the movement and playing a slick, if superficial, brand of dance-pop, the band was tailor-made for the style obsessed New Romantics," says the *Encyclopedia of Rock.*

Duran Duran quickly became the headliners of that movement, playing at large clubs and festivals throughout England, and in early 1981 they released their first single, "Planet Earth," which went to Number 12 on the U.K. charts. Later that year their first album, *Duran Duran,* went to Number 3 on the album charts and spawned two more hit singles, including "Girls on Film." They had already been shunned by the serious music press at this point, but newer, teen-oriented, image-conscious magazines like *Smash Hits* and *The Face* were more than happy to circulate glossy photos of "The Boys," as they had become known. The lavish videos helped transfer this new-found fame to the U.S., where "Hungry Like the Wolf" reached Number 3. By 1984 Duran Duran was an international phenomenon—their third album, *Seven and a Ragged Tiger,* debuted at Number 1 and suddenly the boys were living the lives they had created for themselves on video, playing sold-out tour dates around the world.

They were dandies, playboys, and their profiles became plastered on teen magazines everywhere. First there is Rhodes (his name was originally Nicholas Bates), the man who probably most personifies the band's gaudy image. Rhodes grew up with John Taylor and both found that they liked the music of glittery stars like T. Rex. "We wouldn't buy records by ugly groups," Rhodes told *People,* adding that when he and Taylor decided to start a band they "had vivid ideas of what we wanted to look and sound like, but we looked at the instruments and said, 'Do we have to learn to *play* these things?'" John Taylor is the ladies' man and a huge target for the gossipy Fleet Street press. His wanderings have been well-chronicled there. "Being a rock star is like putting a huge sign in a window, 'For Sale,'" Taylor told *People.* "I did an interview with Penthouse and they said, 'What's your idea of a great woman?' I said, 'Someone who could tie me up and whip me and make great bacon sandwiches.'" Le Bon is an unlikely pop star in that he still opens doors for women, has a pensive streak that makes him yearn for sailing alone on the sea, and because his bandmates once tagged him with the nickname "Lardo" because of his pudginess. Roger and Andy Taylor round out the band and are more known for staying in the shadows while the others bait the screaming girls at center stage.

By 1985 Duran Duran had started suffering from the personality conflicts that hamper many bands. Their production slacked off as the players spent more time apart, getting together only occasionally for certain projects, such as the immensely successful single and video for the James Bond movie *A View To a Kill*. John and Andy Taylor began work on an outside project with Robert Palmer in 1985 and formed a band called Power Station, which recorded an album of the same name (which was Number 30 that year, according to *Rolling Stone*) and played at the Live Aid benefit concert. In the meantime the remaining "thoughtful" members of the group briefly performed and recorded as Arcadia, spawning the LP *So Red the Rose*. It, too, climbed the charts; *Rolling Stone* found it harmless and bland: "Egan's lubricated bass line contrasts nicely with Simon's hog-calling tenor. . . . like the Power Station's record, it's proficient, serviceable pop without any unifying drive or purpose. And no matter how obnoxious (or not) you may have found them, personality is one thing Duran Duran never lacked." By 1986 Duran Duran was back intact and recording again, although they would never regain the success of the early 1980s.

Their 1987 effort, *Notorious,* received the usual chilly reception from critics, but the videos were popular on MTV. *Rolling Stone* actually went so far as to call *Notorious* Duran Duran's "most consistently listenable work," but felt the band had lost personality in the search for musical maturity. *Big Thing!* of 1988 had none of the MTV audience and none of the backhanded compliments of earlier reviews. *People* panned the album; "As 'mature' musicians, they're marooned." *The Encyclopedia of Rock* summed up Duran Duran's impact on the music world in this way: "Musically, Duran Duran are no more than accomplished studio stylists, skillful welders of a host of disparate elements—hard rock, electro, white soul and, latterly, scratch and hip-hop—into an eminently commercial sound. Far more important was their marketing success, whereby they capitalized on their obvious visual attractions through the media (video and the glossy pop magazines), a technique that became increasingly important in the music industry in the Eighties."

Selected discography

Duran Duran, Harvest, 1981.
Rio, Capitol, 1982.
Seven and the Ragged Tiger, Capitol, 1983.
Arena, Capitol, 1984.
Notorious, Capitol, 1987.
Big Thing!, Capitol, 1988.

Sources

Books

Hardy, Phil, and Dave Laing, *Encyclopedia of Rock,* Schirmer, 1988.

Periodicals

People, July 22, 1985, November 7, 1988.
Rolling Stone, February 2, 1984, January 16, 1986, January 29, 1987.

—*David Collins*

Melissa Etheridge

Singer, guitarist, songwriter

Melissa Etheridge's "talents and tastes may well help define the music of her generation," according to Ralph Novak of *People.* With her hard-rocking but melodic style, she has been compared to singers as various and celebrated as Bruce Springsteen and Janis Joplin, and, as *People* reported in another article, the reviews of her self-titled debut album "could have been written by a doting relative." Etheridge has attracted even more attention with her second effort, *Brave and Crazy,* and Elizabeth Wurtzel in *New York* was moved to declare: "If you buy only one album between now and the end of the decade, make sure it's by Melissa Etheridge."

Born in Leavenworth, Kansas, during the early 1960s, Etheridge began to display her inclination towards music in childhood. "She got her first guitar at age eight," explained Michael Segell in *Cosmopolitan,* "and was writing confessional songs by the time she was ten." Etheridge also learned to play drums, saxophone, piano, and clarinet and was performing in a country band when she was only twelve. According to *People,* the group played in rough bars, and Etheridge was witness to so many fights that she lost all fear of audiences. When she turned eighteen, she left home to attend Berklee College of Music in Boston.

After Etheridge left Berklee, she decided to take her twelve-string and go to Los Angeles, California, to play a blend of country and rock. But she told *People:* "I got here, and it was all heavy metal and glitter. I thought, 'Oh, no, there's no room for a girl and her acoustic guitar.'" Thus Etheridge struggled somewhat, playing in small clubs in the area. She explained to Segell: "I made a decision not to have a day job, which meant I had to sing other people's music four or five nights a week. And I'm glad I made that decision. I learned a lot about performing." She elaborated further in *People* that she gradually added her own compositions to her act. "When no one noticed, I figured, okay, they're pretty good songs."

One evening in 1987 Etheridge was playing in a club in Long Beach, California, when she attracted the attention of Chris Blackwell, the founder of Island Records. After hearing her perform for twenty minutes, he signed her to a contract. Before making her first album, however, Etheridge was given the opportunity to write four songs for the film *Weeds;* her contract also brought her the chance to entertain in small clubs throughout the United States.

But the release of her debut album, *Melissa Etheridge,* was a far more momentous occurrence. Though it started slowly, both sales and critical acclaim steadily mounted. Segell praised it as "a ten-song primer on the dark side of love"; Wurtzel noted that "nothing [has]

For the Record. . .

Born Melissa Etheridge, c. 1962, in Leavenworth, Kan.; her father is a teacher. *Education:* Attended Berklee College of Music, Boston, Mass.

Has played in bands since the age of 12; played in clubs in the Los Angeles, Calif., area during the 1980s; recording artist and concert performer, 1987—.

Awards: Grammy nomination for song "Bring Me Some Water."

Addresses: *Home*—Los Angeles, Calif. *Record company*—Island, 14 E. 4th St., New York, NY 10012.

---

album, summed Novak, "as hard as she rocks and as angry as many of her songs get," Etheridge "always keeps a strong melodic presence in her singing."

Though she has worked hard and long to attain the status she has reached, Etheridge feels fortunate. She confessed to Segell that her "whole career has been a series of breaks." She also feels little sympathy for her female peers who complain against discrimination in their field, adding: "I refuse to buy the idea that it's harder for women to make it in rock than men. It's all how you handle yourself. I was signed because of my ability as a musician, not because of, or in spite of, my gender."

sounded this raw and real since Janis Joplin"; and Novak lauded Etheridge's "throaty, aggressively emotional, born-to-compete voice." The songs on *Melissa Etheridge* center on pain and jealousy, including "Like the Way I Do" and "The Late September Dogs." The young singer-songwriter confided to Segell: "I didn't realize it was so much about the same feelings. I just tried to put together my best, most passionate songs, and it turned out that my conflicts with jealousy and pain are the most powerful emotions."

Etheridge diversified more with *Brave and Crazy;* as Wurtzel put it, "not all of the album's songs are about love and lust." "You Can Sleep While I Drive" concerns the urge to escape the drudgery of small-town life; "My Back Door" mourns the loss of innocence. But *Brave and Crazy* has also spawned a hit single, "No Souvenirs," which Wurtzel described as "the catchiest song" that Etheridge "has yet recorded." Throughout the

Selected discography

Albums

Melissa Etheridge (includes "Like the Way I Do" and "The Late September Dogs"), Island, 1988.
Brave and Crazy (includes "Brave and Crazy," "No Souvenirs," "Royal Station 4/16," "You Can Sleep While I Drive," and "My Back Door"), Island, 1989.

Sources

Cosmopolitan, March 1989.
New York, November 13, 1989.
People, August 8, 1988; May 15, 1989; November 13, 1989.
Savvy, July 1989.

—Elizabeth Thomas

Exposé

Pop vocal group

Pop group Exposé made a stunning entrance on the music scene with their 1986 debut album, *Exposure.* The trio, composed of singers Ann Curless, Gioia Bruno (who uses only her first name professionally), and Jeanette Jurado, broke a record previously held by rock superstars the Beatles for most Top 10 singles from a first album with four hits—"Come Go with Me," "Point of No Return," "Exposed to Love," and "Seasons Change." They followed this impressive start with 1989's *What You Don't Know,* scoring smashes with the title track and with the ballad, "When I Looked at Him."

The members of Exposé did not come together in the usual way—friends deciding to form a band. Instead, Miami, Florida-based music producer Lewis Martinee wanted to create a group, and he continues to write most of the songs for the trio. Initially he had chosen three other women to become Exposé, and had already made some recordings for an album, but, as *People* magazine reported, "one original member quit and two were fired."

Curless, Gioia, and Jurado were all singing lead for different local club bands when Martinee recruited them as replacements. Jurado recounted for *People:* "It still strikes me like a dream. When you're working in clubs, you always think, 'Someone will walk in, like me and make me a star.' And that's what happened." Though brought together somewhat artificially, according to *People* the three women, who share lead vocal responsibilities, claim to be the best of friends now that they have found fame.

Being based in Miami, much of Exposé's music has a Latin flavor to it. They have been compared to salsa-spiced pop star Gloria Estefan and her Miami Sound Machine, but also to singers like Madonna and Deborah Harry. "Each member of the trio," asserted Alanna Nash of *Stereo Review,* "is a strong vocalist." But Exposé, despite their huge success with pop and dance music fans, are not entirely the darlings of music critics. Ralph Novak, reviewing *Exposure* in *People,* complained that some of the group's material was "undeniable disco fodder." He did, however, concede that Exposé's mixture of "Latin touches" with pop produced "often invigorating results," and concluded of the trio: "There is a lot of talent in evidence."

Exposé's second album, *What You Don't Know,* was delayed by legal battles, probably concerning the singers that Martinee had first hired to form the group. When it finally came out in 1989, Nash declared: "They'll love it in Europe, and probably on dance floors all across America." True, the title track—which made the Top 10—is an up-tempo dance number, but another hit from *What You Don't Know,* "When I Looked at Him," is a slow, romantic ballad. Again, though Exposé's 1989 effort has raced up the charts, it has not passed the reviewers unscathed. Even Nash's critique was mixed; she complained of repetitiveness in the material and felt the lyrics were immature. David Hiltbrand was even more harsh in *People,* calling the album "dizzyingly superficial dance music," and dismissing "When I Looked at Him" as sounding "like something the cat dragged in with some reluctance." Yet he recognized that Exposé was "giving the kids what they want to hear."

The trio, however, is undaunted by criticism, and takes pride in their work. Jurado announced to *People:* "We can work a crowd and get them going. We're the real stuff." Exposé also tries to do their part with public service messages; the album sleeve of *What You Don't Know* is printed with the slogan "Just say no to drugs."

Selected discography

Albums; on Arista Records

Exposure (includes "Come Go with Me," "Point of No Return," "Exposed to Love," and "Seasons Change"), 1986.
What You Don't Know (includes "What You Don't Know" and "When I Looked at Him"), 1989.

Sources

People, March 30, 1987; August 28, 1989; December 4, 1989.
Stereo Review, October 1989.

—Elizabeth Thomas

Dan Fogelberg

Singer, songwriter, guitarist

As one of countless singer/songwriter's to emerge from the conciousness-raising years of the early 1970s, Fogelberg became a success with his melodic, "light" rock songs that usually explored the bittersweet aspects of love and relationships. He was by no means a great critical success, but his sound was pleasing to a generation of rock fans whose musical tastes had tempered since the disonant, heavily electric, acid rock days of the late 1960s.

Fogelberg's smooth sound was the result of a tried-and-true approach that helped launch the careers of such similar artists as James Taylor, Paul Simon, Jackson Browne, Joni Mitchell, and Carole King. Though Fogelberg was not as commercially successful as those performers, his following has remained relatively strong to the present day, despite a growing impatience on the part of rock critics who have been waiting for some kind of evolution in Fogelberg's musical development. "Fogelberg is an incurable romantic, and after one or two songs you're ready for someone to find a cure," writes Mark Peel in a review of the 1987 album *Exiles* in *Stereo Review*. "It wouldn't be so bad if he had something new or interesting to say about love, but all he does is recycle the tired excuses and rationalizations couples use on one another when they're too lazy to *think*."

Growing up in Peoria, Illinois, in the 1950s, Fogelberg, the son of a band leader father and an opera student mother, was "constantly surrounded by good music, whether I liked it or not," he told *Rolling Stone*. He played the piano as a child and later began composing songs on the guitar. Fogelberg entered the University of Illinois as an art student, but after two years he became such a hit on the Midwest coffee-house circuit that he was compelled to head west in search of a recording contract. In Los Angeles Fogelberg tried to find work as a session musician and eventually caught the eye of singer Van Morrison, who made Fogelberg part of his touring band. Eventually he signed with Columbia and moved to Nashville to record his first album, *Home Free* (1972), a critically acclaimed effort that was nonetheless virtually ignored by the label, which eventually dropped Fogelberg from its roster.

But Fogelberg persevered in Nashville, working with such musicians as Roger McGuinn, Randy Newman, and Michael Stanley, and eventually things turned around for him. He was signed by the Epic label and came under the management of his old friend Irving Azoff (they had met when Azoff was scouting for talent in Champaign, Illinois), who had established his reputation as manager of Joe Walsh and the Eagles. The Fogelberg/Azoff relationship culminated in the 1974 LP *Souvenirs,* which featured backing by Don Henley,

For the Record. . .

Born August 13, 1951, in Peoria, Ill.; son of a band leader father and an opera singer mother. *Education:* Attended the University of Illinois.

Began performing original songs in coffee houses while student at University of Illinois, late 1960s; moved to Los Angeles and signed with Columbia Records, 1971; performed as back-up singer with Van Morrison's tour; released first LP, *Home Free,* 1972; signed with Epic Records and manager Irving Azoff after being dropped by Columbia; released first LP with Epic, *Souvenirs,* 1974; collaborated with jazz-pop flutist Tim Weisberg on 1978 LP *Twin Sons of Different Mothers,* which was double-platinum seller; appeared on soundtrack to 1980 film *Urban Cowboy;* has performed on LPs by, among others, Jackson Browne, Randy Newman, Roger McGuinn, and Michael Stanley.

Addresses: *Home—*Boulder, Colorado. *Record Company—*Epic Records/CBS Inc., 1801 Century Park West, Los Angeles, Calif.

Graham Nash, Glenn Frey, and Walsh (who also produced it). *Souvenirs,* helped along by the hit single "Part of the Plan," went gold and launched Fogelberg into stardom—a stardom that Fogelberg not only expected, but planned. "I planned every step of this," he told *Rolling Stone.* "I mean, this pop music isn't going to last forever. You gotta realize that there's a five-year period or so when your peak popularity is—you're lucky if it lasts that long."

Fogelberg certainly took advantage of his "peak popularity." He followed *Souvenirs* with the 1975 release *Captured Angel* and the 1976 album *Nether Lands,* both of which went gold. Then, in 1978, he collaborated with flutist Tim Weisberg on the platinum-selling LP *Twin Sons of Different Mothers.* This was followed by *Phoenix,* a 1980 release that sold more than two million copies, and *The Innocent Age,* another Top Ten-selling record. Despite his obvious appeal among record-buyers, Fogelberg, a recluse by nature, has never relished touring, preferring instead to remain secluded on the ranch he purchased near Boulder, Colorado, the moment he could afford to move away from the L.A. music scene. Nevertheless the singer

has established himself as a solid touring act with a top-notch road band, known as Fool's Gold, who have themselves cut a couple of relatively successful albums.

If Fogelberg does make a break in the future from the time-honored formula that has brought him success, it just might be in the unlikely area of classical composition. Fogelberg's music-loving parents exposed their son to a wide breadth of classical music when he was a child, and as he grew older he realized that those old records he was once forced to listen to actually contained some of the world's great music. He has dabbled in composing a concerto and even a ballet, though he admits that the stakes in that game are entirely different than those in popular music. "It's a little harder to compete against Tchaikovsky and Grieg," Fogelberg told *Rolling Stone.*

Selected discography

Solo albums

Home Free, Columbia, 1972.
Souvenirs, Epic, 1974.
Captured Angel, Epic, 1975.
Nether Lands, Epic, 1977.
Phoenix, Epic, 1980.
The Innocent Age, Epic, 1981.
Greatest Hits, Epic, 1981.
Windows and Walls, Epic, 1984.
High Country Snows, Epic, 1985.
Exiles, Epic, 1987.

With Tim Weisberg

Twin Sons of Different Mothers, Epic, 1978.

Sources

Books

Clifford, Mike, *The Harmony Illustrated Encyclopedia of Rock,* Harmony Books, 1986.
Pareles, Jon, and Patricia Romanowski, *The Rolling Stone Encyclopedia of Rock,* Rolling Stone Press, 1983.

Periodicals

Rolling Stone, August 25, 1977.
Stereo Review, October 1987.

—David Collins

Jerry Garcia

Singer, songwriter, guitarist

Something strange started to happen to rock and roll during the mid-1980s. Respected performers from the sixties, many of whom had become archival during the intervening years, began showing up on the charts again. Paul Simon won a Grammy Award for his *Graceland* LP, and Steve Winwood had a hit with "Higher Love." Yes scored its first Number 1 single—"Owner of a Lonely Heart"—and the rest of the comeback list included such venerable names as George Harrison, Deep Purple, and the Band's Robbie Robertson. The next thing you know, one pop music critic told some colleagues, the Grateful Dead will have a hit single. That brought a few chuckles.

But in 1987, the Grateful Dead—a 22-year-old group known for its fanatical devotees, despite a lack of commercial success since its West Coast origins in the psychedelic sixties—recorded its first hit ever with "Touch of Gray," a song about aging that the group had been performing for at least six years. The album it came from, *In the Dark*—the group's first studio recording in seven years—-became the Dead's biggest seller ever, raising the eyebrows of those who had written the band off long before. Only two years earlier, Jerry Garcia, the Dead's spiritual leader, admitted to the *Detroit Free Press* that the group's lack of commercial success was "of some concern to us. We make records at least partially with commercial intentions." But in that same interview, he expressed a certain amount of resignation towards the band's fate on the charts. "We're just different," he explained. "It's hard to describe how, but we are, and a lot of people don't understand that." In fact, when *In the Dark* was released, Garcia told United Press International that the album represented "us on a good night. Not necessarily on a great night, though."

So what happened? How did Garcia & Co. go from a formidable cult band to mainstream success? There's no single answer, but definitely a few factors—not the least of which is Garcia himself. In the early 1980s, in the wake of the film *The Big Chill,* radio programmers came up with a new format called Classic Rock. Playing music from the first generation of FM rock radio, it attracted legions of 25- to 54-year-old listeners who were turned off by the heavy metal direction album-rock stations had taken and by the slick, disco-oriented approach of Top 40. They wanted their Beatles and Stones and Led Zeppelin and Jefferson Airplane and Doors—and they also got the Grateful Dead, whose music was long gone from those other formats.

That little musical reminder made what happened next all the more important. In July of 1986, about 15 months after going through a drug treatment program, Garcia slipped into a diabetic coma brought on by his drug use. "I didn't feel any pain," he told *Rolling Stone.* "I just felt tired. . . . One day I couldn't move anymore, so I sat down. A week later, I woke up in the hospital, and I didn't know what had happened." The coma actually lasted five days, and it nearly claimed Garcia's life. And although he recovered, it also put his career in jeopardy; after being released from the hospital, he had to take lessons to get his guitar playing back in shape.

This event touched more than the group's most devout fans, a sizable group known as the Deadheads. Baby boom adults—coping with new roles as parents, partners, and providers—related to the tribulations of one of their generation's cultural leaders as further proof of their mortality. Reacquainted with the Dead through classic rock radio, they started to care about the band again, going back and embracing what rock critic Mikal Gilmore called the Dead's "ideals of humanity, benevolence, unity and even spirituality that most other Sixties-born bands long ago forgot and that most modern rock artists have forsworn in favor of more caustic values." Then came *In the Dark,* an album that hit the issues of aging right on the head; "Touch of Gray," with its chorus declaration that "We will survive!" became a veritable yuppie anthem and gave the Dead its place in the eighties rock pantheon. "We're ready for anything now," Garcia told *Rolling Stone* when "Touch of Gray" was well on its way up the charts. "It just took a while, that's all. I swear, it's like the Grateful Dead are the slowest-rising rock 'n' roll band in the world."

For Garcia, it was just another part of the "long, strange trip" he sang about in "Truckin'," the Dead's best-known song before "Touch of Gray." Born August 1, 1942, in San Francisco, Garcia was the product of music. His father, a Spanish immigrant named Jose, was a respected reeds player and swing bandleader in the Bay area, but he was blackballed by the local musicians union during the Depression because he was playing with two bands while other musicians had no jobs. He died in a fishing accident in 1952. Garcia's mother, Ruth, a nurse, moved the family around the Bay area after that and continued to foster her son's musical training. Garcia had started to play piano when his father was alive, but that was hampered by a lack of interest and a physical disfigurement—his older brother, Clifford, accidentally cut off half of the middle finger on Jerry's right hand when he was four. He had, however, developed an interest in the guitar and decided to move on it when, for his 15th birthday, his mother presented him with an accordion. "I said, 'God, I don't want this accordion. I want an electric guitar,'" he told *Rolling Stone.* "So we took it down to the pawn shop and I got this little Danelectro, an electric guitar with a tiny amplifier, and, man, I was just in heaven. I stopped everything I was doing at the time."

That included schoolwork, which had never been his forte during his years of moving around. "I was a f—k-up," Garcia—who began smoking marijuana when he was 15—told *Feature,* according to Blair Jackson's book *The Music Never Stopped.* "I was a juvenile delinquent. My mom even moved me out of the city to get me out of trouble. It didn't work. I was always getting caught for fighting and drinking. I failed school as a matter of defiance."

When he was 17, he finally dropped out of school, but he took a curious route from there—he joined the Army. After basic training, he was assigned to Fort Winfield Scott in San Francisco and began a tenure much like his time in school. "I treated the army like it was school or a bum job," he told *Feature.* "I was a nothing. I had been court-martialed twice and had tons of extra duty and was restricted to barracks. . . . I had seven or eight or nine AWOLS, which is a pretty damn serious offense in the Army." After nine months, he was discharged at the suggestion of the fort commander. There was an up side to Garcia's time in the service, however. He picked up an acoustic guitar and became enamored with traditional American folk and blues styles, using his ample barracks time to practice. "I was stuck because I didn't know anybody that played guitar," he told *Rolling Stone.* "I used to do things like look at pictures of guitar players and look at their hands and try to make the chords they were doing, anything, any little thing."

Upon his discharge, he traveled to Palo Alto to hook up

with some friends and there he found a burgeoning coffeehouse scene supported by the student body of Stanford University. It was there that he met Robert Hunter, another Army vet who would go on to become the Dead's chief lyricist. Also part of that scene were such future Bay-area rock stars as Janis Joplin, Jorma Kaukonen and Paul Kantner of the Jefferson Airplane, David Freiberg of Quicksilver Messenger Service, and future Dead bassist Phil Lesh, a trained jazz musician. There was also Ron "Pigpen" McKenna, a youth from San Francisco with a deep interest in the blues who would become the Dead's first frontman.

Together and separately, they played at clubs like the Chateau, the Tangent, and St. Michael's Alley in Palo Alto; the Boar's Head in San Carlos; the Off Stage in San Jose; the Jabberwock in Berkeley; and at several coffeehouses along San Francisco's North Beach area. Garcia—who was married briefly to a woman named Sarah—began playing banjo and indulged his interest in bluegrass with such ensembles as the Thunder Mountain Tub Thumpers, the Hart Valley Drifters, the Wildwood Boys and the Black Mountain Boys. When not playing music, Garcia worked at Dana Morgan's Music Shop in Palo Alto, where he sold equipment and gave lessons with future Dead drummer Bill Kreutzmann. And he hung out at the Palo Alto Peace Center, where he and other musicians, whom he dubbed "the opportunistic wolf pack," would talk with local teenagers, "preying on their young minds and their refrigerators," as he told Rolling Stone.

Like the rest of the world, the Beatles turned the Bay area upside down when they hit America in 1964. "All of a sudden there were the Beatles," Garcia remembered in Rolling Stone. "'Hard Day's Night,' the movie and everything. Hey, great, that really looks like fun." That coincided with the early consolidation of the Dead lineup. Joining Garcia, McKenna, Lesh, and Kreutzmann was Bob Weir, who came from an affluent family in nearby Atherton but who, like Garcia, didn't take to school. They started as a jug band, but the Beatles' influence shifted their interest to rock and roll and—as the Warlocks—they played their first show in a pizza parlor and honed their repertoire from British rock hits and standards from American blues performers like Jimmy Reed and Lightnin' Hopkins.

LSD also became an influence around this time. Robert Hunter, the lyricist, was part of a government drug testing program at Stanford, where he struck up a friendship with author Ken Kesey. By 1965, the drug—soon to be made illegal by the U.S. government—was on the streets and in the hands of area musicians. "The whole world just went kablooey," Garcia told Rolling Stone. "It freed me because I suddenly realized that my

attempt at having a straight life and doing that was really fiction and wasn't going to work out. . . . It was like a realization that just made me feel immensely relieved." It would take time before LSD would really influence the music, but its impact would be substantial. "Over the years, I've denied that it had any influence in that way," Hunter told Rolling Stone. "But as I get older, I begin to understand that I was reporting on what I saw and experienced. . . . Looking back and judging, those were pretty weird times. I was very, very far-out."

Things became exceptionally strange when Kesey formed his Merry Pranksters, an anarchistic, communal society based in nearby La Honda. The Warlocks began hanging out with Kesey and playing at his parties, and before long the two entities co-sponsored the famous Acid Test gatherings, which Dead biographer Blair Jackson described as "a night of having the senses assaulted in more ways than most people thought were imaginable." In Jackson's book, The Music Never Stopped, Garcia described the affairs as "open, a tapestry, a mandala. Anything was O.K. The Acid Tests were thousands of people, all hopelessly stoned, finding themselves in a roomful of other thousands of people, none of whom any of them were afraid of."

Because these gatherings attracted people from all over the Bay area, the Warlocks' audience began to spread and grow. Other bands were forming—including the Jefferson Airplane, the Great Society (with Grace Slick) and Big Brother & the Holding Company (with Janis Joplin)—and throughout 1966, San Francisco was awash with concerts that would make any music fan's mouth water, the biggest of which was probably the three-day Trips Festival in January of that year. Meanwhile, Kesey and the Warlocks took their Acid Tests on the road, rolling as far south as Los Angeles.

Somewhere along the line, the Warlocks, who had heard of another band by the same name, became the Grateful Dead. "We never decided to be the Grateful Dead," Garcia told Rolling Stone. "What happened was the Grateful Dead came up as a suggestion because we were at Phil's house one day; he had a big Oxford dictionary, I opened it up and the first thing I saw was The Grateful Dead. It said that on the page and it was so astonishing. It was truly weird, a truly weird moment."

The Dead was perfectly positioned for 1967, a watershed year that saw the Bay area become a center for the international youth culture with the Human Be-In in Golden Gate Park and the developing hippie populace of Haight and Ashbury streets. Record companies, looking for the next big thing to sell to teenagers, began signing local groups: RCA took the Airplane, while Columbia scooped up Joplin's Big Brother & the Holding Company. Because of its threatening name and skull-and-roses logo, there was some initial reticence to sign the Dead, but Warner Brothers finally offered a pact that was considered revolutionary at the time. "Basically, what we did was tear up the standard contract and write our own." Garcia told *Billboard,* according to Jackson. "We entered the business at a time when it was taking a 360-degree turn."

The Grateful Dead, released in 1967, got the band off to a slow start. Even Garcia told biographer Jackson that "it was mediocre performances of material we were able to do much better. It was uninspired, completely." The two following albums—*Anthem of the Sun* in 1968 and *Aoxomoxoa* in 1969—were more experimental (and more drug-influenced), complex, and inaccessible. The Dead simply weren't a hit singles band, and it had difficulty transferring the magnetic qualities of its live performances onto album. Appropriately, then, it was *Live Dead,* also released in 1969, that really showed what the Dead could do, with a 21-minute, improvisation-laden version of "Dark Star" and quintessential takes of several other tracks, including "St. Stephen" and "Turn on Your Love Light." It was a big seller; and, not surprisingly, the Dead's top selling releases in the future would also be live albums. "Our income doesn't come from records," Garcia told the *Detroit Free Press.* "It comes from [live] work. Making records is a different thing. It's not playing for warm human beings. It's a very artificial situation, with the overdubs and everything. In my mind, it's never really been making music."

But in 1970, the Dead turned out perhaps the best two studio albums of its career, *Workingman's Dead* and *American Beauty.* With acoustic instrumentation and country-oriented material, these records carried a relaxed, easygoing ambience that marked a pleasant departure from the comparatively labored late sixties albums. "We were into a much more relaxed thing about that time," Garcia told *Rolling Stone.* "We weren't feeling so much like an experimental music group but were feeling more like a good old band."

Hard times were ahead, however. McKenna died in 1973, the result of alcohol abuse. The Dead had a falling out with Warner Brothers in 1972 and started the misbegotten financial venture of its own record company. The group spent a considerable amount of money on a new sound system—comprised of 641 speakers and a deafening 26,400 watts—-that proved to be underwhelming. There were personnel changes, and the group even announced a "retirement" from performing in 1974. "Basically success sucks," Garcia told *Boston After Dark,* as reported by Jackson. "We've unconsciously come to the end of what you can do in America, how far you can succeed. And its's nothing.

It's nowhere. . . . It means high prices and hassling over extra-musical stuff. It's unnecessary, so we're busting it."

It turned out to be a short break, but it did give the group members time to work on projects away from the band. Garcia, who released his first solo album in 1971, came up with some of his best work during that period, captured on albums like *Old & In the Way* and *Reflections.* But it also ushered in what would be a long period of creative malaise that wouldn't be broken until 1987.

Those circumstances would have caused the end of lesser bands, but the Dead had a secret weapon: the Deadheads, unquestionably the largest, most devoted, best organized, and most varied group of fans ever assembled for one band. In his 1985 hit, "The Boys of Summer," ex-Eagle Don Henley sang of seeing "a Deadhead sticker on a Cadillac," an indication of just how broad the Dead's fan base really was. "My experience with the Deadheads is there's a tremendous width to them," Garcia told the *Detroit Free Press.* "There's all kinds, from three-PhD holders to bikers."

The group first began organizing its fans with the 1971 Grateful Dead album. Inside was a message from the band: "Dead Freaks Unite. Who are you? Where are you? How are you? Send us your name and address and we'll keep you informed." The reaction was overwhelming, and by 1972 there were newsletters that kept Deadheads in touch with the band and with each other, making it easy for fans to follow the Dead from city to city and to trade the bootleg tapes they made, with full cooperation from the band.

By the early eighties, the Deadhead network was considerably more sophisticated. The group started telephone hotlines that were kept busy day and night, and the advent of personal home computers spawned a batch of Deadhead electronic bulletin boards. The group's management also began offering ticket packages to guarantee Deadheads seats during the group's tours. "We're starting to pick up common and low-key ways to continue to do what the band wants to do, which is play and have a simple relationship to their audience," explained group publicist Dennis McNally to the *Detroit Free Press.*

It's hardly surprising, then, that the Deadheads were the first to sound the alarm about Garcia's deteriorating condition during the mid-1980s. Calls to the hotlines asked about his health, noting that he was putting on weight and that his playing was sluggish. The concern was well-placed. Garcia—the friendly, graying, Smurf-like father figure of the band—was indeed using cocaine and heroin, scaring those around him. "I was very afraid that Garcia was going to die," said Wyoming farmer John Barlow, the group's other lyricist, to *Rolling Stone*. "In fact, I'd reached a point where I'd just figured it was a matter of time before I'd turn on my radio and there, on the hour, I was going to hear, 'Jerry Garcia, famous during the sixties, has died.'" The scuttlebutt even prompted Garcia's bandmates, who Barlow said had drug problems of their own, to shift from the traditional laissez-faire attitude towards each other's habits and confront him. "Just before I got busted," Garcia told *Rolling Stone*, "everybody came over to my house and said 'Hey, Garcia, you got to cool it; you're starting to scare us.' There was something I needed or thought I needed from drugs. . . . I don't know what it was, exactly. Maybe it was the thing of being able to distance myself a little from the world. . . . But after awhile, it was just the drugs running me, and that's an intolerable situation."

Garcia never got a chance to act on his promise to the other Dead members to curb his drug habit. On January 18, 1985, he was arrested in Golden Gate Park and charged with possession of cocaine and heroin. A month later, a judge agreed to let him undergo treatment rather than serve time in jail. But after an early summer tour in 1986, his weakened system fell prey to his diabetes, resulting in the coma. Like the arrest, Garcia called the coma "another one of those things to grab my attention." But this was much more serious. "It was like my physical being saying, 'Hey, you're going to have to put in some time here if you want to keep on living.'" Garcia's new regimen included a set of guitar lessons from a Bay area friend, Merl Saunders, and by fall Garcia was back to playing and full of resolve to complete the *In the Dark* album.

Since it became a hit, Garcia—who continues to live in Marin County with his wife, Carolyn, and their daughters Annabelle and Teresa—has been enjoying his new health and new fame. In 1987 the Dead toured with Bob Dylan and on its own, and in the fall of that year, Garcia played a two-week stint on Broadway with his own bands. In the late 1980s and early 1990s, the Dead continued to tour, and Garcia took part in the Blues for Salvador benefit concert in San Francisco and worked with jazz artist Ornette Coleman.

But, he claimed in his infrequent interviews, the success of *In the Dark* had not modified his outlook on life or his musical ambitions. "No matter what happens," he told *Rolling Stone*, "if all these things fail, fall completely to the ground and shatter into a million pieces, it's not going to fundamentally affect us or what we do. We're going to keep on playing. It's just great to be involved in something that doesn't hurt anybody. If it provides some uplift and some comfort in people's lives, it's just that much nicer. So I'm ready for anything now."

Selected discography

With the Grateful Dead

The Grateful Dead, Warner Bros., 1967.
Anthem of the Sun, Warner Bros., 1968.
Aoxomoxoa, Warner Bros., 1969.
Live Dead, Warner Bros., 1969.
Workingman's Dead, Warner Bros., 1970.
American Beauty, Warner Bros., 1970.
Vintage Dead, Sunflower, 1970.
Historic Dead, Sunflower, 1970.
Grateful Dead, Warner Bros., 1971.
Europe '72, Warner Bros., 1972.
History of the Grateful Dead, Volume One: Bear's Choice, Warner Bros., 1973.
Wake of the Flood, Grateful Dead, 1973.
Skeletons from the Closet, Warner Bros., 1974.
From the Mars Hotel, Grateful Dead, 1974.
Blues for Allah, Grateful Dead, 1975.
Steal Your Face, Grateful Dead, 1976.
Terrapin Station, Arista, 1977.
What a Long, Strange Trip It's Been, Warner Bros., 1977.
Shakedown Street, Arista, 1978.
Go To Heaven, Arista, 1980.
Beckoning, Arista, 1981.
Dead Set, Arista, 1981.
In the Dark, Arista, 1987.

Solo LPs

Hooteroll, Douglas, 1971.
Garcia, Warner Bros., 1972.
Live at the Keystone, Fantasy, 1973.
Compliments of Garcia, Round, 1974.
Old & In the Way, Round, 1975.
Reflections, Round, 1976.
Cats Under the Stars, Arista, 1978.
Run for the Roses, Arista, 1982.

Sources

Books

Grushkin, Paul, Cynthia Barrett, and Jonas Grushkin, *The Official Book of the Deadheads,* Morrow, 1983.
Jackson, Blair, *Grateful Dead: The Music Never Stopped,* Delilah Books, 1983.
McDonough, Jack, *San Francisco Rock,* Chronicle Books, 1985.
The Rolling Stone Interviews, St. Martin's, 1982.
Santelli, Robert, *Sixes Rock: A Listener's Guide,* Contemporary Books, 1985.

Periodicals

Detroit Free Press, June 19, 1984.
Guitar Player, July 1988.
Musician, No. 36, 1981.
People, December 28, 1987.
Rolling Stone, July 16, 1987.
United Press International, August 31, 1987; March 24, 1988.

—Gary Graff

Art Garfunkel

Singer, songwriter

Whether performing folk-rock melodies with Paul Simon or delivering romantic ballads as a solo artist, Art Garfunkel has left a lasting impression with his finespun yet powerful voice. Described by Tony Schwartz in *Newsweek* as "an effortlessly lyrical voice that is as smooth and unfettered as any in pop music," Garfunkel's choirboy tenor lent a sparkling incandescence to the often dark and introspective compositions of partner Simon, when the duo recorded a string of hits as Simon & Garfunkel between 1964 and 1970.

Splitting to pursue separate interests in 1971, the two have forged successful solo careers, capitalizing on their individual strengths. Simon, the songwriter of the pair, has had continued success with his poetic, finely-crafted songs, experimenting with calypso, reggae, and gospel. Garfunkel has enjoyed success as a motion picture actor and as a singer of romantic standards. In an interview with Ron Givens for *Stereo Review* Garfunkel stated, "[I] attempt to do songs that have moved me as beautifully and interestingly as I can."

Growing up in the middle-class neighborhood of Forest Hills, New York, Garfunkel met classmate Simon in the sixth grade while preparing for their school's graduation play, "Alice in Wonderland." Garfunkel was the Cheshire Cat; Simon the White Rabbit. After rehearsals the two walked home together, discussing their mutual interests—sports and music. Fans of such fifties rock and roll performers as Elvis Presley, Bill Haley and the Comets, and Frankie Lymon and the Teenagers, the pair listened to the radio for hours, dabbled in composition, and practiced singing together, accompanied by Simon's acoustic guitar. Performing at school functions and parties, the pair cut a demonstration record that caught the attention of a Big Records executive, who offered them a contract and renamed them Tom & Jerry.

Singing simple teenage rock and roll tunes, the duo had their first hit single, "Hey! Schoolgirl," when they were just fifteen. Two years later, however, Big Records folded, and the duo went their respective ways, attending separate colleges after high school graduation. Garfunkel attended Columbia University, studying architecture and mathematics. There he crossed paths with Simon once more, who was studying at nearby Queens College. While neither seriously considered a professional musical career they began to perform together again, this time singing Simon's poetic folk pieces instead of their jointly-created rock and roll. The two attracted an enthusiastic local following and were offered a contract by Columbia Records.

Simon & Garfunkel's first album, *Wednesday Morning, 3 a.m.,* appeared in 1964. Released during the throes of Beatlemania, the album was largely ignored, although one of its songs, "The Sounds of Silence," was moderately popular. Late the following year, unbeknownst to the pair according to some accounts, Columbia overdubbed drums and bass guitar and re-released "The Sounds of Silence" as a single. This new version sold more than one million copies and became the title track for the pair's next LP, which went gold. Subsequent Simon & Garfunkel albums also proved top sellers, introducing such folk-rock classics as "I Am a Rock," "Homeward Bound," and "Scarborough Fair."

While Garfunkel arranged the occasional piece, Simon did the lion's share of the songwriting, and was paid commensurately from their recording and performing revenues; Garfunkel once explained that he didn't write songs "because Paul was so good . . . [and] it seemed foolish to go for equal time." Still, Garfunkel was often credited for much of the duo's success: it was his clear tenor voice that frequently soared above the pair's seamless harmonic blend; it was Garfunkel's easy manner and boyish looks (his bushy blond hair was described as "a huge dandelion gone to seed" by one

writer) that provided an appealing counterpoint to the dark, serious man that was Simon.

In 1968 Simon & Garfunkel provided original music for the hit motion picture *The Graduate;* "Mrs. Robinson," the film's theme song, earned a Grammy Award as record of the year. Nineteen seventy brought more Grammies for the duo, their album *Bridge Over Troubled Waters* becoming one of the top-selling LPs of all time, at nine million copies. The album's title song, featuring an inspirational Garfunkel solo, flooded the nation's airwaves. Yet ironically, while the two performers were at the height of their popularity—celebrating brotherhood in their hit song—their personal differences became so great that they abandoned their partnership.

Key to the split was Garfunkel's burgeoning acting career; the singer told Stephen Holden in a 1982 interview in *Rolling Stone* that "I think when I went off to make *Catch-22,* Paul was left feeling out of it and uncomfortably dependent. Looking back, I know, too, that I felt envious of Paul's writing and playing." While the pair did attempt to work together from time to time, it was not until 1982 that they laid old conflicts to rest, reuniting for an open-air concert in New York's Central Park, a television special, a double album, and an international tour—thrilling longtime fans.

Garfunkel made his acting debut as Captain Nately in Mike Nichols's 1970 film adaptation of the bestselling Joseph Heller novel *Catch 22.* The actor's efforts were well received by critics; Gary Arnold wrote in the *Washington Post,* for instance, "[Garfunkel] embodies a kind of youthful sweetness and idealism that the material desperately needs in the face of so many manic and inhuman characters." Garfunkel gave notable performances in Nichols's "Carnal Knowledge" and Nicholas Roeg's "Bad Timing" as well; nonetheless, in his interview with Holden, Garfunkel admitted that his acting career had fallen short of his expectations.

As a solo vocalist the performer has enjoyed greater success: his first album, *Angel Clare,* was a top seller and his second LP, *Breakaway,* went platinum. Reviewing the first release, Loraine Alterman wrote in the *New York Times,* "Not only does Garfunkel emerge as the excellent singer we all knew him to be but he also reveals himself as a romantic not afraid to luxuriate in lush sounds." Singing the soft-edged works of popular composers like Van Morrison, Randy Newman, and—especially—Jimmy Webb, Garfunkel has also recorded a number of ballad favorites: his rendition of "I Only Have Eyes for You" climbed the charts in 1975.

In his interview with Schwartz, Garfunkel revealed that his simple, sentimental stylings are far more thoughtful and complicated than they first appear: "I work a lot on the crafting . . . emptiness vs. busyness, peaks followed by valleys, tension and then resolve," he related. "I respond more to notes than to lyrics. . . . What I get caught up in is texture and sonority—the sound per se." Discussing his romantic inclinations, Garfunkel continued: "What that really means is that my leaning is more legato than percussive. I happen to like smooth, connected notes more than choppy, staccato ones. I find some songs too gritty, too sophisticated. My style is to sing bloody, from the heart."

Selected discography

Simon & Garfunkel LPs

Wednesday Morning, 3 a.m., Columbia, 1964.
The Sounds of Silence, Columbia, 1966.
Parsley, Sage, Rosemary & Thyme, Columbia, 1966.
Bookends, Columbia, 1968.
The Graduate (soundtrack), Columbia, 1968.
Bridge Over Troubled Waters, Columbia, 1970.
Simon and Garfunkel's Greatest Hits, Columbia, 1972.
Concert in Central Park, Warner Bros., 1981.

Solo LPs

Angel Clare, Columbia, 1973.
Breakaway, Columbia, 1975.
Watermark, Columbia, 1977.
Fate for Breakfast (Doubt for Dessert), Columbia, 1979.
Scissors Cut, Columbia, 1981.

Lefty, Columbia, 1988.
Garfunkel (greatest hits), Columbia, 1989.

Other

(With Amy Grant) *The Animals' Christmas*, Columbia, 1986.

Sources

Books

Simon, George T., and others, *The Best of the Music Makers*, Doubleday, 1979.
Stambler, Irwin, *Encyclopedia of Pop, Rock, and Soul*, revised edition, St. Martin's, 1989.

Periodicals

High Fidelity, May 1982.
Newsweek, October 8, 1973; April 3, 1978.
New York, June 29, 1970.
New York Post, May 26, 1973.
New York Sunday News, March 26, 1967.
New York Times, September 9, 1973.
New York Times Magazine, October 13, 1968.
Rolling Stone, August 3, 1972; October 30, 1980; March 18, 1982.
Seventeen, May 1968.
Stereo Review, April 1988.
Washington Post, June 25, 1970.

—Nancy Pear

Marvin Gaye

Singer, songwriter, guitarist, pianist

Marvin Gaye was one of the best-selling soul artists of his generation, a Motown prodigy whose work displayed everything from sexual passion to social consciousness. Gaye's murder at the hands of his own father in 1984 shocked all but his closest friends, who knew of his family quarrels, his cocaine dependency, and his despondency despite a brilliant 1983 comeback. *New York Times* contributor Robert Palmer called Gaye "one of the most gifted writer-arrangers, and one of the most musicianly singers, in pop music," adding that his songs "have enjoyed a life far longer than that of most pop and soul hits."

Gaye's tragic life was foreshadowed by his difficult childhood and rebellious teen years. He was born in 1939 in Washington, D.C., and was named after his father, Marvin Pentz Gay. The elder Gay was an evangelical minister who ruled his home with an iron fist, often beating his willful son. Although Marvin, Jr., first learned music in church, often performing after his father's sermons, he longed for a secular career. After serving briefly in the Air Force, he returned to Washington and joined a vocal group called the Marquees. He added the "e" to the end of his name because he thought it looked more professional.

The Marquees made several recordings and attracted a following among the rhythm and blues crowd. In 1958 singer Harvey Fuqua drafted them to replace his original backup group, renaming them the Moonglows. During a concert in Detroit in 1961 Gaye met fledgling music producer Berry Gordy, whose Motown Records business showed great promise. Gordy persuaded Gaye to sign with Motown as a solo artist, and shortly after joining the label Gaye married Gordy's sister, Anna. Gaye's first work for Motown was as a backup instrumentalist on disks by Smokey Robinson, among others. He was not long in proving himself as a vocalist, however. His fourth Motown single, "That Stubborn Kinda Fellow," was the first of a staggering number of pop-soul hits that he would accumulate through the 1960s.

As Motown Records flourished, so did Marvin Gaye. His solo recordings and duets with Mary Wells and Kim Weston quickly assured him superstar status. Gaye's best-known works from the 1960s—hits such as "Can I Get a Witness," "How Sweet It Is to Be Loved by You," and most importantly, "I Heard It Through the Grapevine"—are considered soul classics today. In the mid-1960s Gaye teamed with soprano Tammi Terrell for a series of romantic ballads, many of which also topped the charts. The Gaye-Terrell hit list included "You're All I Need to Get By," "Your Precious Love," "Ain't Nothin' Like the Real Thing," and "Ain't No Mountain High Enough."

For the Record. . .

Name originally Marvin Pentz Gay, Jr., changed name to Marvin Gaye for professional purposes; born April 2, 1939, in Washington, D.C.; died of gunshot wounds April 1, 1984; son of Marvin (a minister) and Alberta Gay; married Anna Gordy, c. 1964 (divorced, 1976); married Janis Hunter, 1976 (divorced, 1982); children: (first marriage) Marvin III, (second marriage) Nona, Frankie.

Singer, songwriter, guitar and piano player, 1956-84. Member of group the Marquees, 1957-58, and the Moonglows, 1958-61; solo or duet performer, 1961-84. Signed with Motown Records, c. 1961, had first hit record, "That Stubborn Kinda Fellow," 1962. Moved to Columbia Records, 1982. *Military service:* Served in United States Air Force.

Awards: Two Grammy Awards, 1983, for single "Sexual Healing." Numerous gold and platinum album citations.

Tragedy struck Gaye in 1967 when Terrell collapsed in his arms in the middle of a live concert. She died three years later after immense suffering caused by a brain tumor. Although Gaye claimed that he was not romantically involved with Terrell, her illness and death affected him profoundly. He took a hiatus from the business, and when he returned he insisted on retaining creative control of his work. At the time—1971—this demand was new to Motown; Gordy produced most of the albums and relied on a team of songwriters who churned out formula hits. Gaye was not the only artist who rebelled against the Motown system, but he was the first to do so. Late in 1971 he released *What's Going On,* an album of songs he wrote, sang, and played himself.

What's Going On was a milestone for Motown as well as for Gaye. The album addresses such timely issues as the Vietnam War, pollution, addiction, and the miseries of ghetto life—the first Motown work to deal with social ills. *down beat* contributor Steve Bloom describes the recording as "a blistering indictment of America's misguided priorities combined with God-is-the-answer proselytizing—clearly the work of a preacher's son." One single, "Mercy, Mercy Me," made the Top 10 on the pop charts, and Gaye was praised universally for his cogent musical statements.

Ironically, having established himself as more than a dance-stepping, crooning Motown star, Gaye returned to romantic music almost immediately. Here too he blazed a new trail, however, offering frankly sexual songs that heaped praises on unseen lovers. His last hit of the 1970s, "Let's Get It On," added volumes of suggestion to his reputation as a seductive ladies' man. Sadly, Gaye began a long downward spiral in the mid-1970s, largely because he became seriously involved with cocaine use. He divorced Anna Gordy in 1976 and immediately married Janis Hunter. That marriage too collapsed, with allegations of beating and mental harassment. At one point Gaye even arranged for his second son to be kidnapped and brought to him in Hawaii (Hunter endured a week of anguish before she discovered her son's whereabouts). During this period Gaye also attempted suicide by ingesting an ounce of cocaine in an hour.

By 1981 Gaye found himself deeply in debt to his ex-wives and the federal government. A tour of Europe, including a royal reception in England, revived his confidence somewhat, and he signed a new contract with Columbia Records. The executives at Columbia began to sort out his finances and brought him back to the studio to record. Gaye's 1982 release *Midnight Love* was hailed as a masterful comeback; the single "Sexual Healing" won him his first two Grammy awards.

Unfortunately, Gaye had been unable to kick his cocaine habit. A tour in the wake of the *Midnight Love* album was marred by fits of paranoia and stage fright, and after it ended Gaye retreated into the home he had bought for his parents and spent most of his time taking drugs. He was shot at point-blank range after a Sunday morning quarrel with his father, the last of many heated arguments between the two. He died one day short of his forty-fifth birthday.

Gaye died without a will, owing millions of dollars to the Internal Revenue Service. In the ensuing scramble to make money off his name, many of his family members revealed the details of his last months—he was portrayed as a distrustful, anxious, and desperately unhappy person who tried repeatedly to free himself from the use of cocaine. Some even suggested that he provoked his father into the shooting as a macabre form of suicide—he had been making suicide threats for some time.

In a *Rolling Stone* feature about Gaye's estate, Mary A. Fischer wrote: "The temptation is to think of Marvin Gaye as a reckless, selfish man who only took care of himself—and didn't even do a very good job of that. There was, of course, another side to him that was generous, charming and deep, and that produced so much memorable music. But he suffered from a lack of the thing he desperately longed for but never received—

his father's love. Finally, it did him in." Steve Bloom preferred to accent the positive contributions Gaye made to the world of pop and soul. Bloom called Gaye's legacy "a body of brilliant . . . music that will endure and continue to serve as inspiration to all," concluding: "Risk-taking, rule-breaking, and love-making were what Marvin Gaye was all about."

Selected discography

Soulful Mood, Motown, 1961.
That Stubborn Kinda Fellow, Motown, 1963, re-released, 1989.
Marvin Gaye Live on Stage, Motown, 1963.
When I'm Alone I Cry, Motown, 1964.
Marvin Gaye's Greatest Hits, Motown, 1964.
How Sweet It Is to Be Loved by You, Motown, 1964, re-released, 1989.
Hello Broadway, Motown, 1964.
(With Mary Wells) *Together*, Motown, 1964.
Tribute to Nat King Cole, Motown, 1965.
The Moods of Marvin Gaye, Motown, 1966, re-released, 1989.
Take Two, Motown, 1966.
(With Tammi Terrell) *United*, Motown, 1966.
(With Terrell) *You're All I Need to Get By*, Motown, 1968.
In the Groove, Motown, 1968.
MPG, Motown, 1969, re-released, 1989.
Marvin Gaye & His Girls, Motown, 1969.
Easy, Motown, 1969.
That's the Way Love Is, Motown, 1969, re-released, 1989.
Marvin Gaye's Greatest Hits, Motown, 1970.
What's Going On, Motown, 1971.
Troubled Man, Motown, 1972.
Let's Get It On, Motown, 1973.

(With Diana Ross) *Marvin & Diana*, Motown, 1974.
Marvin Gaye Live, Motown, 1974.
Marvin Gaye Anthology, Motown, 1974.
I Want You, Motown, 1976, re-released, 1989.
The Best of Marvin Gaye, Motown, 1976.
Marvin Gaye Live at the London Palladium, Motown, 1977.
Here My Dear, Motown, 1978.
In Our Lifetime, Motown, 1981.
Midnight Love, Columbia, 1982.
Dream of a Lifetime, Columbia, 1986.
Romantically Yours, Columbia, 1986.
Motown Remembers Marvin Gaye, Motown, 1986.
Compact Command Performance, Volumes 1 and 2, Motown, 1986.
I Heard It through the Grapevine, Motown, 1989.

Sources

Books

Ritz, David, *Divided Soul* (biography), 1986.

Periodicals

down beat, January 1986.
High Fidelity, April 1979.
New York Times, April 2, 1984.
People, January 24, 1983; April 16, 1984.
Rolling Stone, May 10, 1984; May 24, 1984; October 9, 1986.
Time, October 11, 1971.

—Anne Janette Johnson

Genesis

Rock band

Genesis is one of only a handful of rock music groups that has endured more than two decades in the ebb and flow of the show business spotlight, and this is more a tribute to the group's versatility and flexibility than any phenomenal and enduring popularity. Genesis has never been in the same league as such all-time great English supergroups as the Rolling Stones, the Beatles, or Led Zeppelin. They have never reached the absolute zenith of the pop world at any one moment, as each of the above groups have done—and yet they have been more consistent, quietly making music year in and year out without a lot of fanfare or dramatic personality clashes.

Which is not to say that Genesis has not undergone some major changes since its inception in the late 1960s. Indeed, the history of the band could be easily divided into two distinct phases. The first, stretching roughly from 1966 to 1975, could be called the "Art-Rock Years," or, more simply, the "Peter Gabriel Years" after the singer who was the group's driving creative force and chief vocalist before leaving for an outstand-

ing solo career. The second, current phase could well be called the "Phil Collins Years," for the man who stepped out from behind the drum-set in the mid-1970s to replace Gabriel on lead vocals. Collins's era saw the group move toward a simpler, more soulful sound that proved eminently more popular with record-buyers. Like Gabriel, Collins also decided to launch a career on his own, but he has since remained committed to keeping Genesis alive and has switched back and forth several times between his enormously successful solo projects and the less popular, though to him equally satisfying, Genesis collaborations. "Frankly, the term 'art-rock' has been a pain in the ass," Collins told *Rolling Stone* in 1982, as if to sound the territory the "Collins Era" would roam.

Though Collins is now the most famous member of Genesis, ironically he was not even an original member of the group, which came together as a "songwriters' collective" called Garden Wall in the exclusive London prep school Charterhouse in 1966. The group, consisting of Gabriel, bassist Mike Rutherford, keyboardist Tony Banks, and guitarist Tony Philips, came under the tutelage of producer Jonathan King, who suggested the new name Genesis. After their first LP, *From Gene-*

sis to Revelation, caused little fanfare, the members of the band retreated to an English country cottage to rehearse.

They emerged with the music for the *Trespass* album and a highly theatric road show which they immediately took to the far corners of Britain. During this time Philips and drummer John Mayhew quit the band and Collins and guitarist Steve Hackett joined to form the core of the first Genesis era. The band followed with the LPs *Nursery Cryme* and *Foxtrot,* which featured more of the layered, extended suites that were signature early-70s progressive rock. By this time, Gabriel's propensity for donning wild costumes and acting out the storylines of the music had begun to draw media attention and a growing cult following both in England and the United States. The crowning achievement of this period was 1974's double album *The Lamb Lies Down on Broadway,* which was accompanied by an elaborate world tour featuring Gabriel as Rael, a sojourner in a surreal Manhattan landscape.

Later that same year Gabriel inexplicably left Genesis, citing conflicts within the group over how much time he was expected to devote to the band, as opposed to how much time his wife and newborn child needed him at home. Gabriel recalled in *Rolling Stone* that before the birth of his daughter, "My wife remembers it that . . . I was away with the band all the time. The band remembers it that I was away with my wife all the time." Tony Banks added that "it was difficult for us to accommodate that, because at that stage in the group's career, we still wanted to do as much touring as we could."

After a long search to find a suitable replacement for Gabriel, Collins sort of took over the microphone by default, and the second Genesis era had begun. The musical output of Genesis in the following years stayed basically the same on such works as *Trick of the Tail* and *Wind and Wuthering.* Meanwhile, the group remained committed to the road, playing extended world tours that culminated in the double live LP *Seconds Out,* recorded in Paris. Though they had dropped the costumery and theatrics, Genesis in concert still relied on plenty of the long, complex tunes from their early years, but the departure of Hackett signalled a change in musical direction for the group. The aptly titled *. . .And Then There Were Three* was released in 1977 after Hackett left the band to pursue a solo career, and Genesis soon began producing shorter, more accessible rock songs that caught the attentions of radio programming, particularly in the United States. "Follow You, Follow Me" from *. . .And Then There Were Three* hit the top ten in Great Britain, and "Misunderstanding" from *Duke* and "Abacab" from *Abacab* both made the charts in the U.S.

It was 1981's *Abacab* that signalled the full arrival of the Collins era. The album featured extensive contributions from the horn section of the American group Earth, Wind & Fire, which had appeared on Collins's highly successful solo debut *Face Value* and lent the Genesis sound a fresher, more direct "pop" quality. Collins's second solo effort, *Hello, I Must Be Going* (1983), was a Top Twenty album that helped to bring even more attention to Genesis, which released *Three Sides Live* in 1982. Seemingly caught in the middle of his band loyalties and an expanding solo career, Collins simply capitalized on both. By 1987 Genesis had produced the Collins-esque *Invisible Touch* LP, which produced five top ten singles and was followed by a $60 million world tour.

In the meantime Collins released his third solo record, *No Jacket Required,* and Mike Rutherford had surprising success with the critically and financially successful album *Mike and the Mechanics* (1985). Almost out of nowhere, Genesis had become hot property—hot enough to become one of the first groups to fully capitalize on the lucrative, if not controversial, 1980s trend that saw several artists lend their names to ambitious product marketing campaigns. Suddenly Collins and Genesis were seen performing on television ads for Michelob beer, which had lent its name to the huge 1987 tour. Asked if he saw anything wrong with becoming a product spokesman, Collins told *Rolling Stone:* "Everyone has a beer—it's no big deal. We're not saying to go out and get legless every night. We're just saying a beer's a beer's a beer."

Despite the divergent solo interests of Collins, Rutherford, and even Tony Banks, who has developed a. career in film soundtrack composition, Genesis has repeatedly stated its intention to stay together, a fact that should come as good news to its longtime following. "Genesis is more than a rock institution," writes Mike Clifford in *The Harmony Illustrated Encyclopedia of Rock.* "Like an old family friend, they are always dependable, always faithful, and hopefully always there.

With room for solo projects, that should be the case for some time to come."

Selected discography

Trespass, ABC/Charisma, 1970; retitled *In the Beginning,* London/Decca, 1974.
Nursery Cryme, Charisma, 1971.
Foxtrot, Charisma, 1972.
Genesis Live, Charisma, 1973.
Selling England By the Pound, Charisma, 1973.
The Lamb Lies Down on Broadway, ATCO/Charisma, 1974.
A Trick of the Tail, ATCO/Charisma, 1976.
Wind and Wuthering, ATCO/Charisma, 1976.
Seconds Out, ATCO/Charisma, 1977.
. . .And Then There Were Three, ATCO/Charisma, 1978.
Duke, ATCO/Charisma, 1980.
Abacab, ATCO/Charisma, 1981.
Three Sides Live, ATCO/Charisma, 1982.
Invisible Touch, Atlantic, 1986.
And The Word Was. . ., London, 1987.

Sources

Books

Clifford, Mike, *The Harmony Illustrated Encyclopedia of Rock,* Harmony Books, 1986.
Hardy, Phil, and Dave Laing, *Encyclopedia of Rock,* Schirmer, 1988.
Pareles, Jon, and Patricia Romanowski, *The Rolling Stone Encyclopedia of Rock and Roll,* Rolling Stone Press, 1983.

Periodicals

Rolling Stone, March 18, 1982; February 3, 1983; April 9, 1987; July 16, 1987.

—*David Collins*

Benny Goodman

Clarinetist, bandleader

When clarinetist and bandleader Benny Goodman died in 1986, he was eulogized by Bill Barol in *Newsweek* magazine as "arguably the only white jazz player to be the best on his instrument." Known to critics and fans alike as "the King of Swing," Goodman—with the help of his arranger Fletcher Henderson—was largely responsible for the popularity of swing-style jazz during the late 1930s. As John McDonough writing in *down beat* put it, Goodman's "sharp, clean, legato clarinet solos performed against the smooth, unbroken, ensemble curves of his band were the perfect musical equivalent to an optimistic era marked by speed, sophistication, and streamlining." But though Goodman made famous such swing and jazz classics such as "Sing, Sing, Sing," "Let's Dance," and "The King Porter Stomp," he was also a brilliant classical musician and commissioned works for the clarinet from such composers as Bela Bartok and Aaron Copland.

Born May 30, 1909, in Chicago, Illinois, Benjamin David Goodman was the eighth child of eleven. His father was a tailor, and the family was poor, but the Goodmans believed in education of all kinds. When his father learned that the local synagogue gave music lessons and rented instruments at extremely low rates, he sent young Benny and two of his older brothers over. The biggest boy came home with a tuba, the middle with a trumpet, and Benny—as the youngest and smallest, came home with a clarinet. He took lessons first at the synagogue and later studied at philanthropist Jane Addams's Hull House, where he was taught by a member of the Chicago Symphony Orchestra. By the time Goodman was thirteen, he was playing professionally and had received his first union card. He performed on the excursion boats that skimmed Lake Michigan, and in 1923 was a steady player at a local dance hall called Guyon's Paradise.

When Goodman was sixteen years old, he traveled to Los Angeles, California, to play with the Ben Pollack Band. While he was with them he took part in the band's recording sessions; in addition to clarinet solos that showed the influence of players such as Jimmie Noone and Leo Rappolo, he also dabbled with the saxophone. After approximately four years, however, Goodman left Pollack and made his living as a freelance side man, working in recording and in radio. Though he was fairly successful, he was affected by the Great Depression, and did not turn down the opportunity to play college dances with bands that he had formed because, by this time, he was supporting his widowed mother.

The young clarinet player's fortune was forever altered in late 1933, when he made the acquaintance of jazz enthusiast John Henry Hammond. Hammond encouraged Goodman to form a jazz group, and though

Goodman's intent was to use the band in a recording session for English audiences, the resulting cuts were also released by Columbia in the United States, generating a cult following. By 1934 Goodman and his band had performed in famed promoter Billy Rose's Music Hall, and were featured on the National Broadcasting Corporation's radio program, "Let's Dance." Though a subsequent winter tour was discouraging to Goodman and his musicians, they were suddenly introduced to enormous popularity when they hit the Palomar Ballroom in Los Angeles. As Barol explained: "The kids went nuts, jitterbugging wildly. . . . The swing era was born."

From that point on, Goodman was a musical celebrity. He went on to play successful band concerts at places such as Carnegie Hall and, in one of his most memorable sessions, the Paramount Theatre in 1937. The strains of such swing songs as "One O'Clock Jump," "Stompin' at the Savoy," "Air Mail Special," and "Don't Be That Way," dominated the United States' radio waves. The clarinetist and his band also appeared in a few motion pictures. Along the way, however, Goodman made social history by becoming the first white bandleader to make a black musician part of his group when he hired pianist Teddy Wilson in 1936. With Wilson, Goodman's core bandmembers were Gene Krupa on drums and after 1937, Lionel Hampton, another black

jazz artist, on the vibraphones. According to *Maclean's* magazine, Goodman refused to play concert dates in the southern states, where audiences were segregated by race.

After World War II, the combination of a decline in the popularity of the big band sound and Goodman's health concerns prompted the clarinetist to break up his band. But as early as 1938 Goodman had begun to pursue his interest in classical clarinet; he performed works such as Wolfgang Amadeus Mozart's *Concerto in A Major for Clarinet,* and asked Bartok to compose an original work for the clarinet for him. After recording the result, *Contrasts,* on Columbia Records in 1940, he commissioned concertos from Copland and Paul Hindemith. Goodman, however, was dissatisfied with his own skills, and in 1949 began to study with famed classical clarinetist Reginald Kell. Kell taught him a completely new approach to the instrument, but critics concluded that Goodman's own unique style of playing had only been improved by these changes. As *Maclean's* put it: "For . . . classical music, Goodman used the pure, literate tone that Mozart required. But when digging into . . . pop hits . . . he produced a gritty and guttural sound that would earn an F from any conservatory professor." Actually, Goodman also spent some time as a conservatory professor himself, occasionally teaching at the Juilliard School of Music.

After 1955, the year when the story of Goodman's life was made into a feature film starring Steve Allen by Universal-International, renewed interest in his music stirred by the movie induced the clarinetist to form another jazz band. By 1956, he was performing again. In addition to prestigious dates in New York and other U.S. cities, Goodman took his music to the rest of the world. He toured the Far East from 1956 to 1957, and Europe in 1959. As part of a cultural exchange program, he became the first man to tour the Soviet Union with a jazz band—he was extremely well-received by Soviet audiences. Goodman continued to perform and record for the rest of his life and accumulated many honors, including recognition by the Kennedy Center, a Grammy award for life achievement, and—a month before his death from cardiac arrest on June 13, 1986—an honorary doctorate of music from Columbia University.

Selected discography

Singles

"Bugle Call Rag," Columbia, 1934.
"Let's Dance," 1935.
"Good-bye," MCA, Inc., 1935.
"King Porter Stomp," Victor, 1936.

"Stompin' at the Savoy," Victor, 1936.
"Down South Camp Meetin'," Victor, 1935.
"Moonglow," Victor, 1936.
"Sing, Sing, Sing," Victor, 1937.
"Avalon," Victor, 1937.
"Don't Be That Way," Victor, 1938.
"And the Angels Sing" Victor, 1939.
"Dizzy Fingers," Victor, 1947.
"Stealin' Apples," Victor, 1948.
"These Foolish Things Remind Me of You."
"One O'Clock Jump."

LPs

This Is Benny Goodman (two-album set; includes singles reissued from the 1930s and 1940s), RCA, 1971.
Benny Goodman: Trio and Quartet—Live, Columbia, 1976.
Benny Goodman Sextet, Columbia, 1986.
Benny Goodman: Clarinet a la King, Columbia, 1987.
Benny Goodman Sextet: Slipped Disc, 1945-46, Columbia, 1988.

Benny Goodman: Best of the Big Bands, Columbia, 1990.

Sources

Books

Goodman, Benny, and Irving Kolodin, *The Kingdom of Swing,* Stackpole Sons, 1939.

Periodicals

down beat, September, 1986.
Maclean's, June 23, 1986.
Newsweek, June 23, 1986.
New Yorker, December 1, 1986.
People, June 30, 1986.

—*Elizabeth Thomas*

Buddy Guy

Blues guitarist

"**B**uddy Guy," declared legendary British guitarist Eric Clapton in *Musician* magazine, "is by far and without a doubt the best guitar player alive . . . If you see him in person, the way he plays is beyond anyone. Total freedom of spirit." A musician bred in the purest traditions of American blues, Guy may be the best-kept secret in the music world. While a performer like Clapton could probably maintain a constant sold-out tour before huge arena crowds and has record companies beating down his door, Guy has not recorded a new album in more than twelve years and plays mostly in nightclubs before small crowds of intensely devoted fans.

Despite the respect he enjoys among his musical peers, Clapton being just one of his many notable devotees, Guy is not a household name, much less a wealthy, major recording star. He still struggles to make ends meet financially as well, but all of this is due in most part to the nature of Buddy Guy, to his own purist's devotion to the blues in general, and specifically to the blues as he wants to play it. He is true to himself first, and the result is a man completely focused on making music on his own terms. "I guess this is why I don't have a record company giving me a shot at it now," Guy told *Guitar Player* magazine, "because I really wants to be Buddy Guy. I wants to play the things that never came out of me that I know I have. And if I get that opportunity next time I go into the studio, I'm going to give it. If it sells, fine. If it don't, I will please myself inside because I know what I can do, and I'm not going to be shy about it anymore. I don't want anybody teaching me how to play when the tapes are rolling; I've had that happen to me a lot in the past. I've got to play what I already know."

Born in Lettsworth, Louisiana, in 1936 and raised in nearby Baton Rouge, Guy began picking on an acoustic guitar as a teenager, emulating such southern blues players as Lightnin' Slim and Guitar Slim, who have had a profound effect on Guy's stage act to this day. Of Guitar Slim, Guy told *Guitar Player*'s Dan Forte: "He wouldn't just stand there and play. He used to have a sort of heavy-set guy, and he'd play the guitar with this long 150-foot cord—which I have one now—and this guy would pick him up on his shoulders and walk him all through the crowd while he played. I was about 14 years old then—goosebumps just jumpin' all over me!" But times were tough in Louisiana in the 1950s, so Guy decided to take his best shot at Chicago, the home of the blues and at that time the stomping grounds of such greats as Muddy Waters, Howlin' Wolf, and Little Walter.

But Chicago, too, was hard on the broke, 21-year-old Guy—he was about to call his mother for the bus fare back home when he was rescued by none other than Muddy Waters himself. Shy and uncertain of his talent, Guy was offered an audition at the famous 708 Club, where he was spotted by Waters: "I was going on my third day without eating in Chicago, trying to borrow a dime to call my mom to get back to Louisiana," he told *Guitar Player.* "And Muddy Waters bought me a salami sandwich and put me in the back of his 1958 Chevy station wagon. He said, 'You're hungry, and I know it.' And talking to Muddy Waters, I wasn't hungry anymore; I was full just for him to say, 'Hey.' I was so overjoyed about it, my stomach wasn't cramping anymore. I told him that, and Muddy said, 'Get in the goddamn car.'"

Guy soon found out that this was the way of the Chicago blues fraternity—tough, but fair. Like a rookie ballplayer, Guy found himself having to prove what he could do in the very presence of his idols, even in competition against them in head-to-head "guitar battles," where he unleashed his trademark, hurricanelike Buddy Guy stage show. "So I just walked out there with this 150-foot cord," he told Forte in *Guitar Player,* "and it was snowing, and I just went straight on out the door. The next day the news media was there, wanting to know who I was. . . . When I came to Chicago, most guitar players in town did not stand up to play. . . . I stood up and played to make everybody know me. I started kicking chairs off the stage when I went up there at the battles of the guitars. They were sittin' there going, 'Who the hell is that?'"

By the early 1960s Guy's reputation in Chicago had become sufficient for him to find ample studio work. He recorded behind Muddy Waters, Howlin' Wolf, and Sonny Boy Williamson at the blues mecca Chess Records, and he also found time to record numerous singles of his own. His first album, however, did not appear until 1968's *A Man & the Blues,* and it became apparent at this stage that the true Buddy Guy sound was either impossible to capture on vinyl or was being confined by overzealous producers. Guy claims that the closest any recording has come to capturing his best can be heard on the live album *Stone Crazy,* recorded in 1978 in France.

The result, however frustrating for Guy, has been a blues purist's dream: Guy has remained almost exclusively a stage act. He has to be seen to be believed.In the 1970s Guy began a long association with the great harmonica player Junior Wells, who, before meeting Guy, was having a hard time finding a band that could adequately back him. In 1972 Guy opened the Checkerboard Lounge in the heart of Chicago's blues country, and his life then settled into something of a pattern. He is to this day a premier draw at top blues clubs and festivals, not only in the U.S. but around the world. He was a regular attraction at the Checkerboard Lounge until it closed in 1983, and in 1989 he opened a new club, Legends, on a street in Chicago that Guy was influential in having renamed "Muddy Waters Drive."

At Legends, Guy has tried to recreate the feel of the old blues bars where he started his career; playing before a constantly evolving band that never rehearses, Guy,

on any given night, will simply jump up on stage and take to heart the advice of his old mentors, who told him "Go get it, Buddy!" To some of his younger, more well-known peers, like Clapton, Bill Wyman, Ron Wood, Joe Walsh, and Jimmy Vaughan, Guy has become a kind of guitar guru, a wise old man on a mountaintop who has remained true to his own vision and never compromised it. Though he is often compared to Jimi Hendrix, Guy recalls that Hendrix once stopped by one of his shows and told him that he, Hendrix, had learned a great deal from Guy.

> "When I came to Chicago, most guitar players in town did not stand up to play. . . . I stood up and played to make everybody know me."

But if the essence of the blues is in the wanting of something you can't ever have, perhaps it is good that Guy has never had that big, popular crossover record he still dreams of. It is probable that many of the inimitable sounds that he creates can only be born of the feeling of hunger he had in his gut when Muddy Waters rescued him outside the 708 Club in Chicago that cold night in the 1950s. "A blues player like myself has so many ups and downs," Guy told Jas Obrecht in *Guitar Player,* "more downs than ups," but "I love it so much man, I even forgot what down is like. Even when I'm down, I think I'm up. If anybody in the business loves it better than me, they must eat it!"

Selected discography

Solo albums

A Man & The Blues, Vanguard.
Hold That Plane, Vanguard.
This Is Buddy Guy, Vanguard.
I Was Walking Through the Woods, Chess.
Left My Blues in San Francisco, Chess.
Buddy Guy, Chess.
First Time I Met The Blues, Chess Japan.
In the Beginning, Red Lightnin'.
The Dollar Done Fell, JSP.
D.J., Play My Blues, JSP.
Live at the Checkerboard Lounge, JSP.
Ten Blue Fingers, JSP.

Stone Crazy, Alligator.

Buddy Guy and Junior Wells

Buddy Guy and Junior Wells Play the Blues, Atco.
Drinkin' TNT, Smokin' Dynamite, Blind Pig.
The Original Blues Brothers, Intermedia.
Going Back, Isabel.
Live in Montreaux, Black & Blue.
Atlantic Blues: Chicago, Atlantic.

With Junior Wells

Hoodoo Man Blues, Delmark.
Southside Blues Jam, Delmark.
It's My Life, Baby, Vanguard.
Chicago/The Blues/Today, Vol. 1, Vanguard.
Coming At You, Vanguard.

With Muddy Waters

Folk Singer, Chess.
Baby Please Don't Go, Chess France.
The Super Duper Blues Band, Chess Japan.

Muddy Waters, Chess.

Also appears on numerous other recordings by Chess artists and on several Chess anthologies.

Sources

Books

Stambler, Irwin, *The Encyclopedia of Pop, Rock, & Soul*, St. Martin's, 1977.

Periodicals

Guitar Player, April, 1987; April, 1990.

—David Collins

Tom T. Hall

Singer, songwriter, guitarist

Nicknamed "The Storyteller" because of the narrative nature of most of his songs, country singer-songwriter Tom T. Hall "has broadened and deepened the country river significantly," according to Patrick Carr in *Country Music,* and "is one of the major architects of the music's modern form." Whether writing songs for other artists' interpretation, such as the famous "Harper Valley P.T.A.," or singing his own compositions, including the classics "The Year That Clayton Delaney Died" and "Old Dogs, Children, and Watermelon Wine," Hall has been a successful part of the country music genre since the 1960s. Yet he is not the "typical" country artist. Though some of his best-loved songs are simple, many others are sophisticated examinations of issues in story form, and Hall has attracted fans from the world of literature and politics, including author Kurt Vonnegut and former U.S. president Jimmy Carter.

Hall was born May 25, 1936, in Olive Hill, Kentucky, to a minister and his wife. Though he formed a musical group in his late teens that eventually performed on a local radio station, Hall did not initially consider music as a career. Rather, he wanted to become a writer or a journalist, but there were many obstacles in his way. When Hall was sixteen, his father was accidentally shot, and the young man had to quit school to help support his nine brothers and sisters by working in a factory. After an eight-year stint in the U.S. Army, where he picked up his high school diploma, he enrolled in Roanoke College in Virginia to pursue this goal. Though he admired authors such as Mark Twain and Ernest Hemingway, Hall soon came to believe that he was better at writing country songs than stories or articles. While working as a disc jockey in Roanoke, he sent some of his compositions to Nashville, Tennessee. Music publishers liked his work, and one company in particular, New Keys, urged Hall to relocate to Nashville. He did, and his first song recorded, "D.J. for a Day," was sung by Jimmy C. Newman.

"D.J. for a Day" did well for Newman, but Hall's most successful composition for another singer was 1968's "Harper Valley P.T.A.," recorded by Jeannie C. Riley. The song has sold over six million copies, and inspired a television movie and a series. Like many of Hall's musical narratives, "Harper Valley" is based on real incidents; apparently a woman in the songwriter's hometown threw wild parties, and the more upstanding citizens criticized her to such an extent that her child was singled out for extra discipline at school. The woman finally went to a P.T.A. meeting and publicly pointed out the hypocrisy of these so-called responsible people.

By the time "Harper Valley" was released, Hall had

For the Record. . .

B orn May 25, 1936, in Olive Hill, Kentucky; married, wife's name Dixie. *Education:* Attended Roanoke College.

Worked in a factory and as a disc jockey in Kentucky and Virginia; served eight years in the U.S. Army stationed in Germany; songwriter from the 1960s to present; recording artist and concert performer, 1967—. Has also written books, including *The Storyteller's Nashville* and the novel *The Laughing Man of Woodmont Cove.*

Awards: Inducted into the Nashville Songwriters' Hall of Fame.

Addresses: *Residence*—1512 Hawkins St., Nashville, TN 37203.

begun recording his own works on the Mercury label. He had resisted a recording contract for years, wishing first to gain a reputation in Nashville as a songwriter. But finally, during the late 1960s, Hall gave in—with astounding results. Through the next two decades his number of releases rivaled the most prolific country singers. His early hits include 1968's "The Ballad of Forty Dollars," depicting the memorial service of a man who died without paying back the money he owed the narrator, and 1969's "A Week in a Country Jail," describing the interesting conditions of the title locale. But perhaps Hall's most famous earlier release was the 1971 smash, "The Year That Clayton Delaney Died." Like "Harper Valley," it sprung from a true story, and the song is a tribute to a drunken guitar player fallen on hard times who taught Hall to play as a boy. As he confided to Carr, "It started out with just me sitting down with a guitar and thinking, 'Well, I want to thank Clayton.'" Another of Hall's songs, the philosophic "Old Dogs, Children, and Watermelon Wine," was taken from a conversation the songwriter had with an old black man in a bar in Miami, Florida. Reportedly Hall's own favorite from among his many hits is 1974's "I Love," in which he lists all the things most dear to him.

Some of Hall's hit songs, however, have strayed from the narrative mode to become singalong favorites. The gospel-flavored "Me and Jesus," while it advocates an individualistic approach to religion, is primarily a toe-tapping, feel-good song. So is the simplistic "I Like Beer," which has proved even more popular in Germany than in the United States. Carr reported that at least sixty different singers in Germany have recorded versions of the song. Hall's work has also earned him many fans in Poland; "people defy the authorities to buy his records on the black market and thank him for his music by sending him watercolor portraits of himself, [and] even Polish money," according to Carr.

During the 1980s, after Hall had switched from Mercury Records to RCA, his songwriting career fell somewhat into decline. "Now," he admitted to Carr, "there are so many writers and publishers; *everybody's* writing songs. Where there were maybe a dozen guys who were really putting the hot tunes together when I started in Nashville, now there must be hundreds." Hall also attributes his dry spell to a change in taste among country fans. Undaunted, he put more of his concentration into his prose, authoring the autobiographical history of country music *The Storyteller's Nashville,* and the novel *The Laughing Man of Woodmont Cove.* He also keeps active in charity work with his wife Dixie, but he continues to compose. "I've got the songs," Hall told Carr, "and one day next week someone will pick up that one tune that's just right for that one singer, and it'll be Number One."

Selected discography

Singles

"The Ballad of Forty Dollars," Mercury, 1968.
"A Week in a Country Jail," Mercury, 1969.
(With Dave Dudley) "Day Drinkin'," Mercury, 1970.
"The Year That Clayton Delaney Died," Mercury, 1971.
"Me and Jesus," Mercury, 1972.
"The Monkey That Became President," Mercury, 1972.
"Ravishing Ruby," Mercury, 1973.
"I Love," Mercury, 1974.
"This Song Is Driving Me Crazy," Mercury, 1974.
"Country Is," Mercury, 1974.
"I Care"/"Sneaky Snake," Mercury, 1975.
"Deal," Mercury, 1975.
"I Like Beer," Mercury, 1975.
"Faster Horses (the Cowboy and the Poet)," Mercury, 1976.
"Negatory Romance," Mercury, 1976.
"It's All in the Game," Mercury, 1977.
"What Have You Got to Lose," RCA, 1978.
"There Is a Miracle in You," RCA, 1979.
"You Show Me Your Heart (and I'll Show You Mine)," RCA, 1979.
"Son of Clayton Delaney," RCA, 1979.
"The Old Side of Town"/"Jesus on the Radio (Daddy on the Phone)," RCA, 1980.
"Soldier of Fortune," RCA, 1980.
"Back When Gas Was Thirty Cents a Gallon," RCA, 1980.
"I'm Not Ready Yet," RCA, 1980.

Also recorded singles "Margie's at the Lincoln Park Inn," "Salute to a Switchblade," "Turn It On," and "Shoeshine Man."

LPs

Has recorded many albums, including *Homecoming, Witness Life, One Hundred Children, In Search of a Song, We All Got Together, And. . ., The Storyteller, Tom T. Hall's Greatest Hits, Volume One, For the People in the Last Hard Town, Songs of Fox Hollow, Rhymer and Other Five and Dimers, Country Is, I Wrote a Song About It, Tom T. Hall's Greatest Hits, Volume Two, Faster Horses, Magnificent Music Machine, About Love, New Train . . . Same Rider, Places I've Done Time, Ol' T's in Town, Country Songs for Children,* and *The Essential Tom T. Hall.*

Sources

Country Music, March/April, 1987; January/February, 1989.

—*Elizabeth Thomas*

Emmylou Harris

Singer, songwriter, guitarist

Many country singers have achieved success by crossing over into the lucrative pop market. The dulcet-voiced Emmylou Harris has done just the opposite—she culls songs from pop and rock and transforms them into pure country fare. Harris, one of the most popular singers in Nashville, is praised on every side for the respect she holds for traditional country music. To quote Alanna Nash in *Esquire* magazine, the performer "has not only carried on the mission of taking pure, traditional country to a hip, pop audience, but through her own artistry and integrity has helped raise the music to a new position of respectability, carving an identity for herself unique in all of country music."

In *Country Music U.S.A.,* Bill C. Malone observes that Harris seems dedicated to the preservation of older country music, the sound of the Carter Family, Hank Williams, and George Jones. Still, Malone writes, "Harris is a true eclectic, borrowing from many styles. Her concerts and lps contain a mixture of contemporary and traditional material, rock-flavored songs and Appalachian-sounding ballads, and modern country-and-western numbers." It is Harris's vocal abilities that guarantee her an audience, no matter the style of her presentation. A *Time* magazine correspondent characterizes her singing as "more . . . melancholy Appalachian bluegrass than . . . western swing," adding: "Despite its range, her voice is most telling because of its feathery delicacy, an almost tentative dying fall capable of stirring deep emotions."

Harris was born in Alabama, but she grew up in the Maryland and Virginia suburbs of Washington, D.C. Her father was in the Marine Corps, and her family moved often, though never back to the Deep South. Harris has recollected that her older brother liked country music much more than she did; her own musical preferences included folk and pop/rock. As a teenager she was a cheerleader who played saxophone in her high school marching band. She told *Time:* "High schools are real hip now, but there was no counterculture in Woodbridge [Virginia]."

After a year of studies at the University of North Carolina, Harris took off for New York City in search of the counterculture. Like so many other young people, she drifted to Greenwich Village, where she sang country and folk music in coffeehouses and nightclubs, sometimes earning as little as ten dollars a night. In 1970 she and her first husband moved to Nashville to try their luck in the country format. She failed to hit there, and her marriage dissolved. With a newborn baby to care for, she returned to her parents' home in Maryland and began singing at clubs in Washington, D.C. Her performances at the Red Fox Inn and the Cellar Door were hailed by Washington audiences that were already

Could Only Win Your Love," A. P. Carter's "Hello, Stranger," and Buck Owens's "Together Again." Harris and Ahern were married in 1977.

Harris may have shown an unusual dedication to country music, but she also had an ear honed by folk and rock—she and Ahern recorded a trove of offbeat songs such as "Poncho and Lefty," by Townes Van Zandt, "The Boxer," by Paul Simon, and tunes by the Beatles and Bruce Springsteen. Her forte remained the ballad, however. Nash is one of many critics who suggest that Harris's best ballad work shows "a vulnerability rooted in the dark recesses of the soul."

Fueled by the "plaintive, piney-woods feeling evoked by her sweet, sinewy soprano," to quote *Newsweek,* Harris's albums went gold in America and Europe. Some of her best songs were written by members of her top-rate backup group, the Hot Band, whose membership included Ricky Scaggs and Rodney Crowell. From time to time she cut tracks with other country superstars, including Waylon Jennings, Dolly Parton, and

---

"Despite its range, her voice is most telling because of its feathery delicacy, an almost tentative dying fall capable of stirring deep emotions."

---

becoming known for a special receptivity to country-folk-bluegrass blends.

Harris met Gram Parsons in Washington in 1972. Parsons, formerly with the Byrds, was a primary force in the burgeoning country-rock movement. He was so impressed with Harris's voice and delivery that he invited her to join him in Los Angeles to sing backup on his first solo album. Harris was delighted by the offer, and over the ensuing two years she became Parson's protege, learning from him the special roots of country and honky-tonk music. "It was an ear-opening period for me," Harris told *Newsweek.* "I'd always liked Hank Williams and Buck Owens, but with Gram I discovered that country music was a natural form of singing for me."

In 1973 Parsons died of a heart attack, brought on by drug abuse. Left to her own resources, Harris formed a band and signed with Warner Bros. records. There she was paired with Brian Ahern, a gifted producer who gladly followed her natural tendencies *not* to strive for a pop sound. In short order Harris was climbing the country charts with hits like the Louvin Brothers' "If I

Linda Ronstadt. By 1980, when she was voted best female vocalist of the year by the Country Music Association, Harris was among the most successful pure-country performers in the nation. Unlike Parton and Ronstadt, she chose to adhere to the country format—and to singing in general.

Critics generally agree that Harris has recorded two "masterworks." The first is *Roses in the Snow,* a work from the early 1980s that is decidedly bluegrass in flavor. With its acoustic accompaniments and traditional songs, *Roses in the Snow* harks back to the work of the Carter Family, Ralph Stanley, and Flatt & Scruggs; it was a surprise commercial success for Harris. Her other outstanding accomplishment to date is the "country opera" album *The Ballad of Sally Rose,* a theme piece for which Harris wrote the lyrics herself. Based loosely on Harris's own life, *The Ballad of Sally Rose* follows a woman singer through the heights and depths of her career. In *Stereo Review,* Nash observes that the work "carries a desperation, a smoldering, aching passion to connect with the poignant realities that live in the heart and not just the head."

For many years Harris worked out of Los Angeles in studios she built with Ahern. When that marriage ended, she returned to Nashville and based herself there. Today she is married to Paul Kennerley, a Grammy Award-winning songwriter who helped her with *The Ballad of Sally Rose*. Harris has truly achieved success by following her own formula—by surrounding herself with a fine, distinctive backup band, by recording a quaint mixture of traditional, modern, and original tunes, and by presenting them all in a fine voice. "Even though my records don't go platinum," she said, "and I'm not a household word, I can do basically what I want, and get the same number of people to buy the records. That gives me a leverage to be able to experiment, and be able to do what I want. I'm very grateful for that. I really am aware of how important that is, to be able to enjoy what I do."

Selected discography

With Gram Parsons

GP, 1972.
Grievous Angels, 1973.

Solo Albums

Gliding Bird, 1969.
Pieces of the Sky, Reprise, 1975.
Elite Hotel, Reprise, 1976.
Luxury Liner, Warner Brothers, 1977.
Quarter Moon in a Ten-Cent Town, Warner Brothers, 1978.
Profile: The Best of Emmylou Harris, Warner Brothers, 1979.
Blue Kentucky Girl, Warner Brothers, 1980.
Roses in the Snow, Warner Brothers, 1980.
Light of the Stable, Warner Brothers, 1980.
Cimarron, Warner Brothers.

Last Date, Warner Brothers.
Evangeline, Warner Brothers, 1981.
White Shoes, Warner Brothers.
The Ballad of Sally Rose, Warner Brothers, 1985.
Thirteen, Warner Brothers, 1986.
Profile II: The Best of Emmylou Harris, Warner Brothers.
Angel Band, Warner Brothers, 1987.
Bluebird, Reprise, 1989.

Other

(With Dolly Parton and Linda Ronstadt) *Trio*, Warner Brothers, 1987.

Sources

Books

Malone, Bill C., *Country Music U.S.A.*, revised edition, University of Texas Press, 1985.
Nash, Alanna, *Behind Closed Doors: Talking with the Legends of Country Music*, Knopf, 1988.

Periodicals

Esquire, September, 1982.
High Fidelity, August, 1980.
Newsweek, April 17, 1978.
People, November 15, 1982.
Stereo Review, May, 1985.
Time, June 16, 1975.

—Anne Janette Johnson

Deborah Harry

Singer, songwriter

Referring to the brief fascination the public has with its celebrities before discarding them for a new set, Andy Warhol once said that everyone will have 15 minutes of fame before burning out. If that's true, Deborah Ann Harry has already had her shot. When she was lead singer for the New Wave group Blondie, which got its name from her distinctive peroxide-colored hair, Harry was the *femme fatale* of the rock crowd in the early 1980s. With her blonde bombshell good looks, pouty mouth, and come-hither-and-drop-dead expression, Harry was out-Madonnaing them while Madonna was still in pigtails.

But after three years of intense publicity and fame in the early 1980s, Blondie disbanded and Harry seemed to disappear. Her departure from the spotlight had to do with a number of things—fatigue, a life-threatening disease, soul searching—but after having been gone for close to 10 years Harry is undergoing one of those rarest of rock achievements: the comeback. And if the rave reviews of her latest solo album are any indication, Warhol may have been wrong. Perhaps some of us are allotted two 15-minute doses of fame.

Harry was born in Miami in 1945. At three months, she was adopted by Richard and Catherine Harry of Hawthorne, New Jersey. Although she has fantasized about being Marilyn Monroe's daughter ("A lot of pretty girls have the same fantasy," she told *People* magazine), Harry says she has no desire to track down her biological parents. ("I know who I am," she told *People,* "and it would be an insult to the Harrys.") Harry was a shy young girl. "People thought I had a speech impediment," she told *People.* "It turned out just to be globs of peanut butter stuck inside my mouth." A sweet child who sang in the church choir, she made her entertainment debut in a sixth-grade stage show. Yet even then, Harry was a bit of a fashion iconoclast. "I was never really satisfied with how I was supposed to look," she told *Vanity Fair* magazine. "My mother and I had huge battles. When we used to go shopping it was hell. She'd want me to wear little blouses with round collars and sweaters and I'd be looking at black turtlenecks. At that age—eight or nine—you can't be doing that. It was not the look in those days to be so, um, severe."

In 1963 Harry graduated from Hawthorne High, where she was voted Best Looking Senior. She spent two years at Centenary College, a junior college, but then dropped out, unsure of what she would do with her life. Eventually Harry drifted over to lower Manhattan, to an Italian/Ukrainian neighborhood on St. Marks Place, where she waited on tables at Max's Kansas City, a hangout for hippies, punk rockers, and Warholites like Nico, Ultra Violet, and the Velvet Underground. It was one of a series of jobs she held down—beautician, exercise instructor, Playboy bunny—and one she was not particularly good at. "I was just a hysterical waitress," she told *Vanity Fair.* "I was so timid in those days. They were just all so wild, they'd come in wrecked out of their brains, wanting a zillion things. I was extremely shy, and I was dealing with a lot of things I had to conquer within myself." One of those demons was a heroin addiction (although she says she never shot up) that she kicked while at an artists' colony in upstate New York.

When she returned to Manhattan she formed an all-female trio called the Stilettoes, came back to Max's sporting what she called "serious makeup," and began singing such original songs as "Dracula, What Did You Do to My Mother?" It was around this time that Harry met Chris Stein, a part-time band roadie from Brooklyn. Stein joined the Stilettoes. When the group broke up, he and Harry collaborated and formed Blondie (which at first was called Angel and the Snakes, then Blondie and the Banzai Babies). Harry and Stein acknowledged that their inspiration came from Buddy Holly, both in music and fashion.

"When we started Blondie in '73, our main goal was to be a dance band," Harry told *Vogue.* "The idea of performing rock and roll to a stand-up audience that danced was unheard of." But by 1979, Blondie had reached a level of preeminence in the rock world. Through her group, Harry had advanced the boundaries of the punk music scene. Within three years, Blondie had sold more than 11 million records with such hit songs as "The Tide is High," "Rapture," "Heart of Glass" and "Call Me," the theme from the film *American Gigolo.* She acted in two films—*Videodrome* and *Union City*—and although neither was a box office success, Harry received strong notices for both.

Then, in 1983, Harry dropped out of sight. Blondie disbanded. Harry had grown tired of the fast track and of the bottle-blonde, ditzy character she had created. "It was upsetting," Harry told *Savvy* magazine, "when businesspeople constantly condescended to me. Sometimes they went right to Chris (Stein) because they thought he was my Svengali. When they did talk to me, they did it as if I was a complete airhead created by some outside force." By dropping out, Harry was giving up a lot. But her plan wasn't to stay out of the limelight for long. Just to regroup and establish a more mature character. "I was looking for a short sabbatical," she told *Savvy,* "not a permanent retirement."

But soon months turned to years. Shortly after Blondie disbanded, Stein became gravely ill with pemphigus, a rare genetic disease. During his six-month stay in the hospital Harry would visit him by sneaking past papparazzi and sleeping on a cot in his room. After he was released from the hospital, Stein required years of personal care, and Harry soon found there were other things more important than rock music. "It wasn't a case of me being a martyr and throwing away my career for my man," she told *Savvy.* "I took it as a sign to stop, take a real rest, and see what we were doing. We hadn't taken a vacation since 1975, and Chris's illness was partly stress-related. It was a good lesson for both of us to learn."

While Harry tended to Stein, she watched as a host of other young women, principally Madonna, attempted to fill her pop-trash stiletto shoes. "I always knew that someone would come along, use similar things to what I had used and fit right in the pocket commercially," she told *Savvy.* "I always felt that if it wasn't me playing the blond, sexy nymphet, then it would be somebody else." Throughout this period Harry remained ephemerally on the consciousness of the Eighties. Through advertisements and small roles in films her distinctive face, with its high cheekbones and sultry mouth, never really vanished from the public eye.

Finally, in 1984, Harry prepared to reenter the pop market, only to face another setback. Legal entanglements with her record company forced her to postpone her comeback again. "It became obvious to me during this period how fast pop stars come and pop stars go," she told *Savvy*. "When you're hot like Blondie was hot, you've got so much momentum going for you that you don't realize how fragile it all is—even though the reality of what happens to fame is all around you, and you're so totally disposable, except to a small, devoted audience. It still sort of amazes me."

But by 1987, Harry's life was finally coming back together. First, Stein recovered. It would be nice—storybookish perhaps—if they were still together, but they are not. The two separated, but still collaborate on music projects. The legal problems were resolved, and in 1987 Harry released *Rockbird*, a comeback album that received rave music reviews. "When I first started the music business wasn't geared to marketing women," she told *Savvy*. "It wasn't the norm, and it was very difficult to get airplay. This has been the biggest change in the music industry—now, the marketing of women has gotten so sophisticated that practically anything can be sold. I wasn't alone in helping make that change. But I was one of the few involved in the transition."

By 1989, Harry was working on another album, *Def, Dumb & Blonde*. She had appeared to favorable reviews in the television series *Wiseguy*, playing a has-been rock star making a comeback. And she received positive notices for her work in the John Waters cult movie *Hairspray*. It is still a long way to the heights she once reached as Blondie, the ditzy yet seductive pop tart that ruled the charts, but Harry says she doesn't look back. Her return to the limelight is as a new person; more mature, with greater character. "Whatever scene people are involved in, it was always better six months ago," she told *Vanity Fair*. "Everybody's longing for some forgotten situation which was glorious just by the fact that it's fallen into memory. I'm not into nostalgia."

Selected discography

With Blondie

Blondie, Chrysalis, 1976.
Plastic Letters, Chrysalis, 1977.
Parallel Lines, Chrysalis, 1978.
Eat to the Beat, Chrysalis, 1979.
Autoamerican, Chrysalis, 1979.
The Best of Blondie, Chrysalis, 1981.
The Hunter, Chrysalis, 1982.

Solo LPs

Koo Koo, Chrysalis, 1981.
Rockbird, Geffen, 1987.
Def, Dumb & Blonde, Sire, 1990.

Sources

Harper's Bazaar, August 1981; July 1987.
Interview, October 1981; November 1981.
Penthouse, November 1981.
People, September 29, 1980; March 18, 1981; April 11, 1983.
Rolling Stone, December 25, 1980; October 29, 1981.
Savvy, May 1, 1987.
Vanity Fair, July 1989.
Variety, March 2, 1983.
Vogue, July 1980.

—*Stephen Advokat*

Jeff
Healey

Singer, songwriter, guitarist

Since the formation of his self-named band in late 1985, guitarist, singer, and songwriter Jeff Healey has attracted the attention of many with his searing guitar licks and imaginative blend of rock, jazz, and blues. Early in his career Healey was hailed as a blues guitar hero. According to Jas Obrecht of *Guitar Player,* B.B. King once told Healey "I've never seen anything like it. Your execution is the best I've ever seen. Stick with it, and you'll be bigger than Stevie Ray Vaughan, Stanley Jordan, and B.B. King."

Adopted into a middle-class Canadian family, Healey grew up in Natobico, an outlying suburb of Toronto. Healey lost his sight from eye cancer at age one. Two years later he received a small acoustic guitar, which he played flat on his lap, in open tuning with a slide until someone at the School for the Blind in Brantford showed him standard tuning. Healey attended the School for the Blind through the seventh grade and then the local high school.

When he first started playing the guitar, Healey often played country music in the style of Chet Atkins and Luther Perkins, but his musical experience was wide-ranging. He played guitar and trumpet in all the jazz and concert bands in his high school, and he and some other students organized a blues-based band—Blue Directions—that played in clubs. While in high school, Healey and his friends liked to listen to music by guitarists Eric Clapton, Jeff Beck, Jimi Hendrix, B.B. King, Albert Collins, and Buddy Guy. Although he did not graduate from high school, Healey privately studied music theory, earning a certificate in harmony and arranging. The young guitarist continued to perform on a free-lance basis, but at that time he did not become a permanent member of any band, Healey claims, because his unconventional style of holding the guitar made other band members uncomfortable.

Healey plays a black Fender Squire Strat, a white standard Strat, and a black Jackson six-and-twelve-string doubleneck on his lap. His right hand picks and strums, while his left runs wildly across the strings of the headboard. "I tried playing guitar the normal way, but I just wasn't very comfortable," declared Healey in an interview with the *Oregon Statesman-Journal* reporter Ron Cowan, "so I decided to hold it in my lap and work out all the chords that way."

One night in late 1985 Healey and a friend went to hear Texas bluesmaster Albert Collins at a club in Toronto. Healey's friend convinced Collins to let the then nine-teen-year-old Healey sit in for one song; Collins kept Healey on stage for an hour and invited him to come back a few nights later to play with Collins's friend, guitarist Stevie Ray Vaughan. After the later performance, Healey was flooded with calls for club dates. So he quickly put together a trio with drummer Tom Stephen, whom he knew from jam sessions, and studio bassist Joe Rockman, a friend of Stephen.

Stephen, who did not learn to play drums until he was twenty-eight, was happy to leave his job as an urban planner for the Ontario Land Corporation. After one rehearsal Rockman recognized the band's potential and cancelled other commitments. Shortly after its formation, the Jeff Healey Band toured extensively (200-300 concerts annually) in Canada for about two years. Not wanting to bore audiences visually, Healey adopted a more active concert style, roaming the stage, picking strings with his teeth, and playing with his guitar behind his head.

The self-managed band cut a single and made a video demonstration tape with the Toronto-based Forte Productions. Stephen presented the tape to New York City record producers but he returned, unable to spark any interest—or so he thought. Several weeks later the Jeff Healey Band was approached and signed by Arista Records.

For the Record. . .

Born c. 1966; adopted son of a Canadian family; raised in Natobico, Ontario, Canada.

Began playing guitar at age three; made performance debut at age six; played guitar and trumpet in school jazz and concert bands; formed blues band while in high school; formed the Jeff Healey Band with drummer **Tom Stephen** and bassist **Joe Rockman** in Toronto in 1985. Appeared in motion picture *Road House,* 1989.

Awards: Toronto Music Award for best new band and best new guitarist, 1987.

Addresses: *Record company*—Arista Records, 6 W. 57th St., New York, NY 10019.

When the band prepared to make its first recording, it needed a producer, and Jimmy Iovine was Arista's choice. Just as Iovine received the demonstration tape and video, he was asked to line up a band for a movie that needed a soundtrack. It called for a young, blind blues-rock guitarist who played with the guitar flat in his lap. The author of the script for the movie had seen the band in Toronto and been inspired by it. The Jeff Healey Band was asked to record the soundtrack and offered speaking parts in *Road House,* starring Patrick Swayze of *Dirty Dancing* fame.

While Iovine and the band started recording the twenty songs that make up the soundtrack in March and April of 1988, the movie itself was filmed in June and July. In the midst of the movie work, the Jeff Healey Band recorded its own album, *See the Light,* from which "Confidence Man" became a radio hit.

Five of the twelve songs on *See the Light* were composed by Healey, who wrote and taped hours of songs as a teenager. "I write about things that everyday people understand," Healey declared in an interview with *Musician*'s Ted Drozdowski. "I won't write about politics, which a lot of people can take or leave. But love between human beings is a natural thing, so we can all relate to it. And if I get to play some guitar in the bargain, then everybody's happy."

Healey is sometimes annoyed by the stereotypes that blindness engenders, but he does not view his lack of sight as a handicap. He has had few problems during performances with the band.

As a child, Healey began a record collection that now numbers over 10,000 early jazz, blues, and gospel 78s and reissued albums. His knowledge of diverse musicians is encyclopedic, but his all-time favorite is trumpeter Louis Armstrong. At one time Healey had considered a career in radio broadcasting. He worked for the Canadian Broadcasting Company for a while and has an hour-long radio show on CIUT, the University of Toronto FM station.

When asked about his plans, Healey told Obrecht, "I've really given up making plans because . . . you never know what's going to happen. When something comes along that I want to do, then I'll do it. The two main goals in life are to be happy and successful, and I would like to be both. That would satisfy me."

Selected discography

See the Light (includes "See the Light," "Confidence Man," "Hide-away," "Nice Problem to Have," "Blue Jean Blues," "My Little Girl"), Arista Records, 1989.
Hell to Pay, Arista, 1990.

Sources

(Baltimore, Maryland) *Sun,* April 7, 1989.
Guitar Player, August 1989.
Melody Maker, November 19, 1988.
Musician, March 1989.
The Oregonian (Portland), October 21, 1988.
(Salem) *Oregon Statesman-Journal,* October 24, 1988.

—David Collins

Highway 101

Country band

Country band Highway 101's songs "strike a nice balance between the stand-by-your-man country tradition and punch-your-man-in-the-nose modern feminism," according to Ralph Novak of *People.* Composed of vocalist Paulette Carlson, drummer Cactus Moser, bass player Curtis Stone, and guitarist Jack Daniels, Highway 101 made a stunning impact on the country charts in 1987 with their first album. Aptly titled *Highway 101,* the disc spawned three hit singles— "Whiskey, If You Were a Woman," "The Bed You Made for Me," and "Somewhere Tonight," and received rave reviews from critics, including Michael Bane in *Country Music,* who declared that "Carlson is the woman singer we've been waiting for, and she's backed by . . . one of the most versatile and off-beat bands in country music."

As Patrick Carr reported in *Country Music,* Highway 101 is "not a group of longtime friends who graduated to the recording studio and the concert circuit after years together in the honky tonks. It is in fact that supposedly most artificial and soulless of musical aggregates, a band which began as a businessman's

For the Record. . .

Formed in Nashville, TN, in 1986; group consists of **Paulette Carlson** (vocals); **Cactus Moser** (real name Scott Moser) on drums; **Curtis Stone** (bass); and **Jack Daniels** (guitar).

Signed recording contract with Warner Bros. in 1986. Recording artists and concert performers, 1987—.

Awards: Named vocal group of the year by the Country Music Association, 1987.

Addresses: *Record company*—Warner Bros. Records, Inc., 3300 Warner Blvd., Burbank, CA 91505.

bright idea." Carlson, however, was the core around which Highway 101 formed. She had been a songwriter in Nashville, Tennessee, and even had her own singing contract with RCA, but she didn't have a manager. When she found one—Chuck Morris, who also managed the Nitty Gritty Dirt Band and Lyle Lovett—he suggested that she try to make her mark as part of a group. Carlson had spent many years before coming to Nashville performing with various bands, and she was happily receptive to Morris's idea. Morris and Carlson rounded up a suitable drummer and bass player—Moser and Stone—and Stone contacted his friend Daniels. They got together to see how well they worked as a team, and everyone involved liked the results. The newly-formed band decided to take their name from a state highway that runs near Carlson's hometown, Winsted, Minnesota, and signed a recording contract with Warner Bros. in 1986.

The male members of Highway 101 had all come from a background of lots of studio work for other stars, and Stone confided to Carr about their initial recording sessions together: "It was an interesting thing when we first went into the studio. From all our session work we'd done . . . each of us had learned to go in and play what we thought the producer would want to hear, 'cause that's the way it is in this business." But Paul Worley, Highway 101's producer, felt that the band should come up with its own, original sound. Apparently, it was a struggle. Carlson told Carr that the first tracks they created "sounded sort of, well, country-pop." But when they went back to the studio, they decided to record one of Carlson's own compositions, "The Bed You Made For Me." As Carlson announced to Carr, "When we cut it, we knew we had the Highway 101 sound."

"The Bed You Made For Me" proved to be one of the debut album's hits. Reviewer Bane recalled: "The first time I heard [the song] on the radio, I stopped dead in my tracks . . . 'The Bed You Made For Me' is about hurt and strength, and I for one like to hear those kinds of sentiments." Another of *Highway 101*'s hits was "Whiskey, If You Were a Woman," which Bane praised as "the hands-down best drinking song . . . in years." He also "particularly liked" the album's third hit, "Somewhere Tonight," which laments a lost lover.

The band's second album, *101 Squared,* didn't fare as well with the critics, but did provide another big hit, "Just Say Yes." Novak hailed Highway 101's 1989 release *Paint the Town,* however, as being "full of lively, smart songs . . . with intensity . . . emotion . . . and . . . verve." Noteworthy cuts from *Paint the Town* include the hit "Walkin', Talkin', Cryin', Barely Beatin' Broken Heart," "I Can't Love You, Baby," and the title track. Carr summed up the band's feelings about the album as "accurately reflecting both the creative fire they had when they first found their sound and the creative growth since then."

Selected discography

LPs

Highway 101 (includes "The Bed You Made For Me," "Cry, Cry, Cry," "Whiskey, If You Were a Woman," and "Somewhere Tonight"), Warner Bros., 1987.
101 Squared (includes "Just Say Yes"), Warner Bros., 1988.
Paint the Town (includes "Paint the Town," "Walkin', Talkin', Cryin', Barely Beatin' Broken Heart," "I Can't Love You, Baby," and "Sweet Baby James"), Warner Bros., 1989.

Sources

Country Music, September/October, 1987; November/December, 1988; November/December, 1989.
People, August 31, 1987; October 9, 1989.

—Elizabeth Thomas

Joe Jackson

Singer, songwriter, pianist

In the modern music business, performers tend to hunt for a successful formula and then stick with it for as long as it continues to sell records. Joe Jackson has defied that convention, challenging himself and his listeners by making nearly every one of his albums in a different musical style. "There's this mentality in the music industry, 'Play it safe, stick to the format, give the people what they want,'" Jackson told David Wild in *Rolling Stone*. "I *hate* that expression, it makes me angry. The people don't know what they want—they just want something good." Jackson has proven his point by maintaining his popularity while experimenting with jazz idioms, pop conventions, Latin rhythms, Broadway-style tunes and even orchestral music.

At the age of twelve, Jackson was already writing instrumental music and developing his skills as a pianist. His great loves were Stravinsky and Beethoven, and he even attended the Royal College of Music in London for three years. Strangely enough, it was in this classical environment that he became convinced that the pop song was the most important musical form of his era. Accordingly, he tore up all his previous compositions, dropped out of the Academy, and began working on a repertoire of pop songs. He supported himself with various commercial gigs, including a stint as the house pianist at the Playboy Club in Portsmouth, England.

Eventually, he made his way to London, where he formed the Joe Jackson Band, featuring Graham Maby on bass, Gary Sanford on guitar, and Dave Houghton on drums. Before long the group had signed a contract with A&M Records and in 1979 they released their first album, *Look Sharp.* The album reflected Jackson's careful study of pop forms; despite a no-frills, stripped-down sound that led many to identify Jackson as a New Waver, it was full of catchy lyrics and irresistible hooks. Thanks to the single "Is She Really Going out with Him?," *Look Sharp* went gold in 1979, just before the release of the band's follow-up album, *I'm the Man;* it too went gold. Joe Jackson was on top of the pop music world.

He was growing restless, however. Having mastered one form, Jackson saw no sense in repeating it, no matter how lucrative such a move might have been. Accordingly, he began work on *Beat Crazy,* a collection of reggae-influenced songs. Released in November 1980, it was one of his only albums to draw both harsh reviews and sluggish sales. Two months later Jackson broke up his band. An extended illness followed. Jackson told *down beat* contributor Bill Milkowski that during his convalescence, he "was listening to [jazz great] Louis Jordan. I had split up my first band, I really didn't know what to do next. So I thought, 'What the hell, I don't

For the Record. . .

Born August 11, 1955, in Burton-on-Trent, Staffordshire, England; married wife, Ruth, in 1981. *Education:* Attended the Royal College of Music (London) for three years.

Began playing piano in childhood, was a composer of instrumental music by age 12; worked at various musical gigs after dropping out of college, including a stint as the house pianist at the Portsmouth, England, Playboy Club; leader of the Joe Jackson Band, 1977-80; released first album, 1979; solo artist, 1981—.

Addresses: *Record company*—A & M Records, 1416 N. LaBrea Ave., Hollywood, CA 90028.

have to do another album just yet. Why not do something just for the fun of it?'"

He proceeded to put together a swing group called Jumpin' Jive, and to write some songs in the style of Jordan. "I thought at first we'd just do a few gigs, maybe do an EP or something. And it just snowballed, until we did an album and A & M put it out. Next thing I knew we were doing a British tour and then an American tour. And that album seems to be pretty popular still. A lot of people come up to me and tell me they like it."

Following the *Jumpin' Jive* tour, Jackson rented an apartment in New York City's East Village. His intent was to absorb the city's unique atmosphere and then distill his impressions into his fifth album. That album, *Night and Day,* was a unique blend of jazz, salsa, and pop. "It's *not* nine songs about New York," Jackson explained to David Fricke in *People.* "It's nine very universal songs that are influenced by New York's rhythms and sounds." However it was categorized, the album quickly became Jackson's greatest success thus far. The single "Steppin' Out" became his first to reach the top ten, and it also won him Grammy nominations for record of the year and best pop male vocal performance. Even jazz critics, who had scorned *Jumpin' Jive,* responded enthusiastically to *Night and Day.* *down beat*'s Bill Milkowski admitted that Jackson deserved "newfound respect as a composer of alternately witty and sensitive songs, more sophisticated and worldly-wise than your average punk-rocker."

Experimentation with jazz and Latin idioms continued on *Body and Soul,* praised by Milkowski as Jackson's "most pure and personal statement to date. . . . This introspective album . . . [is] a direct expression of emotion rather than the detached, ironic observation that marked much of his earlier work." Mark Peel of

Stereo Review was also favorably impressed by the lush, emotional quality of *Body and Soul.* He commented: "Anyone without the kind of 'New Music' credentials Joe Jackson has would be hooted off to Las Vegas . . . for making music as unapologetically romantic as that on his new 'Body and Soul' album. But Jackson's honesty and intelligence let him get away with it."

Following the release of *Body and Soul,* Jackson took a two-year hiatus from recording. When he returned in 1986, it was with *Big World,* an album notable for both its eclectic collection of musical styles and for the unusual recording techniques used in making it. Reacting to the overproduced sound dominating pop music, Jackson had produced an entire album live, with no overdubs, retakes, or studio remixing. "I feel it's a very honest statement," the musician told Milkowski. "I want people to know, even if they don't like it, that it's a real performance and that no one's had his voice electronically altered to sound in tune. The drums haven't been triggered by drum machines but were actually played by a drummer, and that kind of thing. It's sort of like truth-in-advertising."

Big World included sounds ranging from folk, funk, and hard rock to waltzes, tangos, and honky-tonk soul. Concerning this wide variety, Rob Hoerburger wrote in *Rolling Stone* that "unfortunately, the big world proves just a little too big, even from someone as industrious as Jackson. In the past, his album concepts have been narrow enough for him to pay tribute, redefine, diverge and return. But there's no unity in *Big World.*" Milkowski did not concur, finding in the album a cohesive commentary "on how the very nature of travel allows one to step outside his or her own particular, nationalistic view of the world through an interaction with exotic cultures, customs, and musics."

Joe Jackson has given many reasons for his chameleon-like approach to music. He told Joe Contreras in *Newsweek,* "I don't think I'm original enough to have a definite style of my own that will stand up as a style. I use different musical styles in the same way I wear different clothes." On a more profound level, he told Milkowski, "I think my music is a mixture of a lot of different things because I am by nature, I think, a traveller and by nature pretty cosmopolitan." By working with various styles, he hopes to "promote openmindedness. . . . The world is getting pretty dangerous these days, and a lot of the problems are caused by the people in power being inflexible and not well-informed and not really understanding the other guy's point of view. So it's important to avoid being narrow-minded, and listening to the music of other cultures is not a bad start."

Selected discography

LPs; released by A & M

Look Sharp, 1979.
I'm the Man, 1979.
Beat Crazy, 1980.
Jumpin' Jive, 1981.
Night & Day, 1982.
Mike's Murder (soundtrack), 1983.
Body and Soul, 1984; reissued, 1986.
Big World, 1986.
Will Power, 1987.
Live:1980-1986, 1988.
Blaze of Glory, 1989.

Also wrote and recorded the film soundtrack *Tucker: The Man and his Dream.*

Sources

down beat, May 1986.
Newsweek, March 14, 1983.
People, February 14, 1983.
Rolling Stone, September 11, 1986; July 16, 1987; May 18, 1989.
Stereo Review, July 1984.

—Joan Goldsworthy

Waylon Jennings

Singer, songwriter, guitarist

Waylon Jennings, the quintessential Outlaw of country music, has successfully forged a distinctive sound best described as "redneck rock." For years Jennings chafed under the restraints imposed on his music by Nashville's tunnel vision, but when at last he was given creative control of his work his popularity soared. *Newsweek* contributor Maureen Orth credits Jennings with bringing "a new sophistication to country music and a welcome blast of country air to rock," noting that the singer "can make his music sound both pure country honest and stone-rock funky."

Jennings has managed simultaneously to return country to its roots and to revolutionize its beat and pitch. He has turned his back on the weepy strings and session orchestration most closely associated with modern country music, producing instead the exciting, gritty sound that has come to be the trademark of the Outlaw movement. "Maybe that's what has all these citified hippies so excited," writes Melvin Shestack in *The Country Music Encyclopedia,* "the fact that here's a big, mean-looking man with a band that could easily be a group of rock-and-rollers with their long hair and electric guitars, and they're playing music that has as much rhythmic guts as you could wish for, but still really isn't anything like what they get on the radio around here. It's country music, no mistake, and *do they ever love it to death.* It's genuine, no frills, no slickness, no pretensions. Just hard-hitting, hard-living country soul."

Jennings, who claims to have both Cherokee and Comanche ancestry, was born and raised in Littlefield, Texas. His father worked a succession of jobs from cotton farming to truck driving, and the Jennings family had little extra cash. Waylon himself began to pick cotton while still a youngster, but his heart was in music. As a child he immersed himself in the works of such country greats as Ernest Tubb and Hank Williams, then he discovered pop music and its nascent rock & roll beat. A performer from an early age, he saw singing as the only escape from a life of drudgery in the cotton fields.

By the time he turned fourteen, Jennings was a familiar sight in talent shows in his region, playing guitar and singing country or pop tunes. He dropped out of high school for a full-time job with the Littlefield radio station, where he spun discs and performed with his own band, the Texas Longhorns. In 1958 he took a job at a station in Lubbock, Texas, and there he met a young entertainer named Buddy Holly. Holly had already achieved national stardom with his country-rooted rock music, and before long Jennings was playing bass in Holly's band. Jennings toured with Buddy Holly and the Crickets for several months in late 1958 and early 1959, and

For the Record. . .

Full name Waylon Arnold Jennings; born June 15, 1937, in Littlefield, Tex.; son of a truck driver; married fourth wife, Jessi Colter (a singer), c. 1973; four children, including (fourth marriage) Waylon Albright. *Education:* Earned high school equivalency diploma, 1990.

Disc jockey in Littlefield, Tex. and Lubbock, Tex., c. 1950-58. Singer and guitar player, 1957—; played bass with Buddy Holly and the Crickets, 1958-59; formed own band, the Waylors, c. 1961, played in clubs in Phoenix, Ariz. Signed with RCA Records, 1965, moved to Nashville, had first number one single, "Only Daddy That'll Walk the Line," 1968. Became associated with the "Outlaw" movement in country music, 1972; had first platinum album (with Willie Nelson, Jessi Colter, and Tompall Glaser), *Wanted—The Outlaws,* 1976.

Has appeared in feature films and television dramas; has toured in the United States, Canada, and Mexico.

Awards: Numerous citations for country music performances, including male vocalist of the year from the Country Music Association, 1975; duo of the year (with Nelson) and single of the year from the Country Music Association, both 1976.

Addresses: *Office*—Utopia Productions, 1117 17th Ave. S., Nashville, Tenn. 37212.

with Johnny Cash. Shestack writes: "The following two years might well go down in history as the most spectacular era in the fine arts of door smashing, house wrecking, and general craziness." Jennings's career took off with albums such as *Love of the Common People* and *The One and Only Waylon Jennings,* and his reputation for hard-drinking rowdiness followed suit. He became a member of the Grand Ole Opry, appeared in the film *Nashville Rebel,* and generally began to cultivate a maverick personality.

According to Bill C. Malone in Country Music U.S.A., Jennings's artistic independence, lifestyle, and personality all contributed to the "Outlaw" label he attracted as the 1970s began. Still, Malone notes, "it is clear that the Outlaw phenomenon was largely a product of promotional hype, and most of it independent of Jennings himself." Whatever the case, Jennings embraced the Outlaw concept wholeheartedly—and proceeded to turn it to his use as an artist. In 1972 he hired Neil Reshen, a New York-based manager who helped his client win more control over the content of his albums.

> *Jennings's artisitic independence, lifestyle, and personality all contributed to the "Outlaw" label he attracted as the 1970s began.*

Almost overnight, the well-groomed and gaudily attired Jennings became the long-haired, leather-clad rebel rocker he is today. With the collaboration of friends such as Willie Nelson, Kris Kristofferson, Tompall Glaser, and Jack Clement, he "elevated country record production from cheap pap to soul art," to quote *New Times* contributor Patrick Carr.

Jennings had already seen the top of the country charts with songs like "Ruby, Don't Take Your Love to Town," but even he was amazed at the critical and commercial reception for his new work. His 1976 release *Wanted— The Outlaws,* an ensemble package with his wife, Jessi Colter, Nelson, and Glaser, was the first country album ever to go platinum in sales. He was showered with awards from the Country Music Association and was in demand as never before for live performances. Gradually, however, the down side of the Outlaw image began to take its toll. Jennings had long struggled with drug and alcohol abuse, but another drug—cocaine—almost claimed his life.

he would have died in the plane crash that claimed Holly's life if he had not offered his seat that night to J. P. Richardson (The Big Bopper).

Holly's untimely death was extremely traumatic for Jennings, who had established a genuine rapport with the star. For a time after the crash Jennings quit the music business and returned to radio announcing. Then, in the early 1960s, he moved to Phoenix, Arizona, and formed a new band. Waylon Jennings and the Waylors were soon regular performers at J.D.'s, a large club that drew an audience from every walk of life from cowboy to corporate attorney. Jennings met the challenge such an audience offered admirably, playing rock and pop with a country flavor as well as country in an up-tempo rock style. Before long his reputation transcended the bounds of Phoenix and drew talent scouts from Los Angeles and Nashville.

In 1965 Chet Atkins persuaded Jennings to sign a contract with the prestigious RCA label. Jennings then moved to Nashville, where he took bachelor quarters

Late in 1984 Jennings told *People* magazine that he was saved from cocaine addiction by his old friend Johnny Cash, himself a substance abuser. Jennings quit drugs cold turkey and cut down on the extensive touring that had contributed to his habit. He and Jessi Colter continue to provide vital material to the country music arena to this day, both as a duo and as solo artists. Malone writes: "Despite the hype surrounding the Outlaws, they did make a healthy challenge to Nashville's homogenization. And while they drew freely from other forms of music, such as rock, they also remained respectful of their own and country music's roots. In fact, if they used any term in private to describe themselves it was 'hillbilly' and not 'outlaw.' The ultimate irony for the Outlaws may be that, while drawing upon a diverse array of musical sources and reaching out to new audiences, they did more to preserve a distinct identity for country music than most of their contemporaries who wore the 'country' label."

Jennings put it another way in *The Country Music Encyclopedia*. "I couldn't go pop with a mouthful of firecrackers," he said. "I'm a country boy; I'm a hillbilly. . . . They talk about the Nashville Sound, y'know. My music ain't no Nashville Sound. It's my kind of country. It's not Western. It's Waylon."

Selected discography

Waylon Jennings at J.D.'s, Sound Limited, 1964.
Folk Country, RCA, 1965.
Leavin' Town, RCA, 1966.
Nashville Rebel, RCA, 1966.
Waylon Jennings Sings Ol' Harlan, RCA, 1966.
Love of the Common People, RCA, 1967.
The One and Only Waylon Jennings, RCA, 1967.
Hankin' On, RCA, 1968.
Only the Greatest, RCA, 1968.
Jewels, RCA, 1969.
Country Folk: Waylon and the Kimberleys, RCA, 1969.
Just To Satisfy You, RCA, 1969.
Waylon Jennings, Vocalion, 1969.
Don't Think Twice, A&M, 1969.
Best of Waylon Jennings, RCA, 1970.
Waylon, RCA, 1970.
Singer of Sad Songs, RCA, 1970.
The Country Style of Waylon Jennings, A&M, 1970.
The Taker, RCA, 1970.
Cedartown, Georgia, RCA, 1970.
Ladies Love Outlaws, RCA, 1971.
Good Hearted Woman, RCA, 1972.
Heartaches by the Number, RCA, 1972.
Lonesome, On'ry, and Mean, RCA, 1972.

The Taker/Tulsa, RCA, 1972.
Honky Tonk Heroes, RCA, 1973.
Ruby, Don't Take Your Love to Town, RCA, 1973.
This Time, RCA, 1974.
Ramblin' Man, RCA, 1974.
Ned Kelly, United Artists, 1975.
Dreaming My Dreams, RCA, 1975.
(With Jessi Colter, Willie Nelson, and Tompall Glaser) *Wanted— The Outlaws*, RCA, 1976.
Are You Ready for the Country? RCA, 1976.
Waylon Jennings Live, RCA, 1976.
Mackintosh & TJ, RCA, 1976.
Hits of Waylon Jennings, RCA, 1977.
Ol' Waylon, RCA, 1977.
(With Nelson) *Waylon & Willie*, RCA, 1978.
I've Always Been Crazy, RCA, 1978.
Music Man, RCA, 1980.
WWII, RCA, 1982.
It's Only Rock 'N' Roll, RCA, 1983.
Waylon and Company, RCA, 1983.
Never Could Toe the Mark, RCA, 1984.
Turn the Page, RCA, 1985.
Collector's Series, RCA, 1985.
Will the Wolf Survive, MCA, 1986.
A Couple More Years, RCA, 1986.
Sweet Mother Texas, RCA, 1986.
Waylon! RCA, 1986.
(With Johnny Cash) *Heroes*, Columbia, 1986.
Hangin' Tough, MCA, 1987.
The Best of Waylon, RCA, 1987.
(With Nelson) *Take It to the Limit*, CBS, 1987.
Full Circle, MCA, 1988.
A Man Called Hoss, MCA, 1988.
Waylon Jennings: The Early Years (1965-1968), RCA, 1989.
New Classic Waylon, MCA, 1989.
(With Nelson, Cash, and Kris Kristofferson) *Highwayman*, Columbia.
(With Nelson, Cash, and Kristofferson) *Highwayman II*, Columbia, 1990.

Sources

Books

The Illustrated Encyclopedia of Country Music, Harmony, 1977.
Malone, Bill C., *Country Music U.S.A.*, revised edition, University of Texas Press, 1985.
Shestack, Melvin, *The Country Music Encyclopedia*, Crowell, 1974.
Stambler, Irwin and Grelun Landon, *The Encyclopedia of Folk, Country, and Western Music*, St. Martin's, 1969.

Periodicals

After Dark, March 31, 1973.
Country Music, April, 1981.
Cue, February 24, 1975.
Newsday, January 22, 1978.
Newsweek, August 26, 1974.
New Times, February 20, 1978.
New York Daily News, May 31, 1981.
Penthouse, September, 1981.
People, October 22, 1984.
Stereo Review, August, 1983.

—Anne Janette Johnson

George Jones

Singer, songwriter

George Jones is often called the best honky-tonk performer of all time. An artist whose own life mirrors the defeat and despair of his song lyrics, Jones was one of the most popular male country singers of the 1960s. He has remained a Nashville favorite to this day despite numerous bouts of drug abuse, repeated legal entanglements, and even an arrest for assault. Jones has recorded so many albums and singles that even he has lost count, but since the 1980s began he has exerted more control over the direction of his music and the substance of his sound. This new control has meant that Jones's material has returned to the unembellished, hard-hitting honky-tonk style that brought him his first fame.

In her book *Behind Closed Doors: Talking with the Legends of Country Music,* Alanna Nash calls Jones "the greatest country singer of all time," a man "who understands, who can offer sympathy for the price of a quarter." Nash adds: "The quarter drops, and out comes the voice of Despair, anxious at first, then desperate, with Jones sliding up a wail meant to caress and exorcise his demons at the same time. He holds the cry as he might the last bottle on earth, and then plunges to the low notes in a moan that leaves no doubt—when you talk about pain and suffering, George Jones has *been* there."

Jones's miseries began literally at birth—the doctor who delivered him dropped him and broke his arm. Jones was raised in a succession of small Texas towns, his family finally settling in Beaumont, where his father took work in the shipyards. Life was hard for young George, who took what little consolation he could find from the guitar he learned to play at the age of nine. When his sister died of a fever, his grieving father turned to drink, often rousing George and the other children late at night to sing for him. George ran away from home at fourteen and began to support himself playing backup guitar for radio programs. By eighteen he had married—and deserted—the mother of his first child.

Jones spent three years in the Marine Corps and then returned to Texas to work as a house painter. Within months he was moonlighting as a radio performer, imitating his heroes Hank Williams, Roy Acuff, and Lefty Frizzell. Gradually his reputation spread, and he became acquainted with H. W. "Pappy" Daily, a producer for the Houston-based Starday label. Starday signed Jones and encouraged him to discover his own distinctive sound. In 1955 he had his first country hits, "Why Baby Why" and "You Gotta Be My Baby." The following year he realized a dream that he had held since childhood—he was invited to join the Grand Ole Opry. He switched to the more prestigious Mercury label in 1958, where according to Nash he recorded his first "honky-tonk classics"—"White Lightning" and "The Race Is On"—and developed "the emotional wail-and-moan delivery that would become his trademark."

Between 1958 and 1971 Jones placed at least one song in the country top ten each year. Only Merle Haggard rivals Jones for the most number-one country hits in the history of the business. Jones's number-one singles include "Window Up Above," which he wrote himself, "She Thinks I Still Care," "We Must Have Been out of Our Minds," "Take Me," "Things Have Gone to Pieces," "Love Bug," "I'm a People," and "You Can't Get There from Here." Record companies bid for Jones's services, and he switched several times, working at United Artists, Musicor, and finally Epic. For more than a decade he turned out albums at a staggering rate and toured almost without a break.

The relentless pace Jones set inevitably began to take its toll. By the mid-1960s the singer began to drink heavily and behave erratically, missing concert dates entirely or playing only abbreviated programs. His reputation received a reprieve in 1967, when he began to tour with Tammy Wynette. Both Jones and Wynette were at the peak of their careers at the time, and they proved a winning duo. They were married in 1968. For a time the marriage seemed to steady Jones—he and Wynette even ended their concerts with a song version of their wedding vows—but turbulence developed and Jones began drinking heavily again. Jones and Wynette divorced in 1975 and quarreled openly for some years thereafter.

The late 1970s proved a nadir for Jones. He had to declare bankruptcy after a number of show promoters sued him for missed dates. Alcohol abuse led to automobile accidents, fights with lovers, and one instance where he fired a gun at a male friend. By 1983 he had been hospitalized and arrested repeatedly for alcohol and cocaine use and sued by a legion of creditors and ex-wives. Nash notes, however, that his problems "only made him more irresistible to his fans." Even as he wrestled with the shambles of his personal life, Jones made a momentous professional decision: he vowed to return to the traditional country sound that he had always loved, a sound that had too long been submerged in over-produced tracks.

Jones told *High Fidelity* that he allowed his producers—among them the celebrated Billy Sherrill—to orchestrate his material in such a way that it might appeal to the "crossover" audience. "I went along with the record company against my better judgment," he said. "I didn't wanna do it, but I let them put strings on my sessions just out of curiosity, more or less, just to see what they might do. . . . When you use strings and

> *Jones's miseries began literally at birth—the doctor who delivered him dropped him and broke his arm.*

horns and all these things, you just don't have country music anymore . . . you abuse it. To try to sell two or three hundred thousand more records . . . hell, a man could always use the money, but I wouldn't go out of my way to have that big a production on my records, because I'm never gonna sell pop."

Jones's return to his roots salvaged his career. Works such as *He Stopped Loving Her Today, My Very Special Guests,* and *Shine On* assured Jones a front-runner position in the resurgent honky-tonk format. *High Fidelity* contributor Nick Tosches concludes that Jones has remained so popular over the years because of his singular voice. "Unlike most country singers," the critic writes, "there is no cheap melodrama in his singing. He works his rough Texas voice with a noble gravity, wringing from every work its full color and power. He has a poet's sense of rhythm: the most pedestrian lyrics emerge from his mouth with teutonic dignity." In *Stereo Review,* Nash likewise suggests that Jones might prove to be "the last poor boy to give traditional country music everything he has in him."

Many times Jones has said that he plays, sings, and writes country music out of a deep love for the genre. He told Nash: "I wouldn't care if I even got paid for the dates, because how can you put a price on it?. . . It's really not that important to me, as far as glory, popularity, and those things. I just feel like I'm makin' people happy, that they're likin' what I'm doin'. And they durn sure make me happy when I walk out on that stage. That's all that's really important to me."

Selected discography

George Jones Sings, Mercury, 1960.
Country Church Time, Mercury, 1960.
Country and Western Hits, Mercury, 1961.
Greatest Hits of George Jones, Mercury, 1961.
Crown Prince of Country, Starday, 1961.
The Fabulous Country Music Sound of George Jones, Starday, 1962.
George Jones' Greatest Hits, Starday, 1962.
George Jones Sings from the Heart, Mercury, 1962.
Ballad Side, Mercury, 1963.
Duets Country Style, Mercury, 1963.
Novelty Styles, Mercury, 1963.
Homecoming in Heaven, United Artists, 1963.
Blue and Lonesome, Mercury, 1964.
The Great George Jones, Mercury, 1964.
George Jones Salutes Hank Williams, Mercury, 1964.
Number One Male Singer, Mercury, 1964.
Bluegrass Hootenanny, United Artists, 1964.
Grand Ole Opry, United Artists, 1964.
I Get Lonely, United Artists, 1964.
More Favorites by George Jones, United Artists, 1964.
George Jones Sings Like the Dickens, United Artists, 1964.
What's in Our Hearts, United Artists, 1964.
Heartaches and Tears, Mercury, 1965.
My Very Special Guests, Epic, 1980.
Shine On, Epic, 1983.
Jones Country, Epic, 1985.
Best of George Jones, Epic, 1986.
Country, By George! Epic, 1986.
Honky Tonks and Heartaches, Mercury, 1987.
One Woman Man, Epic, 1989.
(With Melba Montgomery) *Close Together*, Musicor.
If My Heart Had Windows, Musicor.
I'll Share My World with You, Musicor.
I'm a People, Musicor.
In a Gospel Way, Epic.
Love Bug, Musicor.
Mr. Music, Musicor.
My Boys, Musicor.
My Country, Musicor.
New Hits with the Jones Boys, Musicor.
Nothing Ever Hurt Me, Epic.

Oh Lonesome Me, Epic.
Old Bush Arbors, Musicraft.
(With Montgomery) *Party Pickin'*, Musicor.
The Race Is On, RCA.
Songs of Dallas Frazier, Musicor.
Songs of Leon Payne, Musicor.
The George Jones Story, Musicor.
Walk through this World, Musicor.
We Found Heaven Here, Musicor.
Where Grass Won't Grow, Musicor.
Will You Visit Me on Sunday? Musicor.
With Love, Musicor.
You Gotta Be My Baby, RCA.
Famous Country Music Makers, RCA.
The Best of the Best, RCA.
George Jones Sings His Songs, RCA.
We Must Have Been Out of Our Minds, RCA.
Alone Again, Epic.
The Battle, Epic.
A Picture of Me, Epic.
Memories of Us, Epic.
The Best of Times, Epic.
Anniversary: Ten Years of Hits, Columbia.
Bartender's Blues, Epic.
Burn the Honky Tonk Down, Rounder.
By Request, Epic.
Encore, Epic.
First Time Live! Epic.
Heartaches & Hangovers, Rounder.
I Am What I Am, Epic.
Ladies' Choice, Epic.
Live at Dancetown U.S.A., Ace.
The Lone Star Legend, Ace.

With Tammy Wynette

George and Tammy and Tina, Epic.
Greatest Hits, Epic.
Let's Build a World Together, Epic.
Me and the First Lady, Epic.
Together Again, Epic.
We Go Together, Epic.
We Love To Sing about Jesus, Epic.
We're Gonna Hold On, Epic.

Sources

Books

The Illustrated Encyclopedia of Country Music, Harmony, 1977.
Malone, Bill C., *Country Music U.S.A.*, revised edition, University of Texas Press, 1985.
Malone, Bill C. and Judith McCulloh, *Stars of Country Music*, University of Illinois Press, 1975.

Nash, Alanna, *Behind Closed Doors: Talking with the Legends of Country Music,* Knopf, 1988.

Shestack, Melvin, *The Country Music Encyclopedia,* Crowell, 1974.

Stambler, Irwin and Grelun Landon, *The Encyclopedia of Folk, Country, and Western Music,* St. Martin's, 1969.

Periodicals

High Fidelity, May, 1977.
People, January 15, 1979.
Stereo Review, September, 1983.

—*Anne Janette Johnson*

Rickie Lee Jones

Singer, songwriter

The story of Rickie Lee Jones is a classic rock 'n' roll fable, a story with a moral of its own that shows, in all of its extremes, the ups and downs of the rock life and the way that rock 'n' roll contains within itself the seeds of destruction and regeneration. In the years since her smash debut album, *Rickie Lee Jones,* which contained her trademark hit single "Chuck E.'s In Love," Jones has endured the downside of success, the kick in the head fame saves for you after its first magical kiss, and arrived at the second, more lasting and valuable stage of rock stardom—that of the survivor. "Same old story," writes Jay Cocks in *Time.* "A unique gift, a fresh voice, a knack for psychic immolation. When Rickie Lee Jones broke onto the scene with her surprising and successful 1979 debut album, she seemed to signal a fresh trail for rock. But uncertainty and self-destruction crowded close. An equivocal second album was followed by an enterprising third and diminishing commercial returns. Confusion enveloped, and Jones seemed to lunge toward the flash point. Then she pulled back, in a two-step away from the brink, consolidating and reconsidering her work. With personal turmoil put in perspective, Jones produced a new life and a new record.

That new record was 1989's *Flying Cowboys,* a work that signalled the return of Rickie Lee Jones to fame, but also, more importantly, to a more mature, even plateau from which she can commit to a long-term artistic stance. Cocks continues: "Even the casual listener who knows Jones mostly from her 1979 hit single, 'Chuck E.'s in Love,' will recognize the smoky snap of her voice in the opening moments of the fine first track, "The Horses." But just as quickly, the changes will be obvious. The jazz inflections and beat intonations are still intact, but all the mannerisms have been pared away. Jones isn't hiding behind artifice anymore. Her lyrics may be enigmatic, her music an eccentric mixture of rock, electrified hipster jazz and reggae, but she makes it all flow by the sheer force of her feeling."

The saga of Jones's early childhood would sound strangely familiar to many artists. Born in Chicago, Jones was uprooted and dragged to a new home as soon as she had gotten settled down in the last one. Her father was primarily a waiter, but, coming from a family of vaudevillians himself, the elder Jones was also an amateur musician who wrote and sang songs for his children. Jones's mother was a waitress. The couple had a stormy relationship and once broke up, only to reunite again. The family moved almost every year, Jones told *Rolling Stone,* mostly back and forth from Chicago to Phoenix. "All of us were so much trouble that my parents would say 'Well, let's try it someplace else.'"

For the Record. . .

Born November 8, 1954, in Chicago, Ill.; married Pascal Nabet-Meyer (a musician); children: Charlotte Rose.

Began working as a waitress and club singer in Los Angeles, where she met musician Tom Waits, 1977; signed recording contract with Warner Bros., 1978; released debut album, *Rickie Lee Jones*, 1979 (hit single "Chuck E.'s in Love" went to number four on charts); recorded three additional albums in early 1980s; took five-year hiatus from recording industry, 1984-88; recorded critically acclaimed comeback LP *Flying Cowboys*, 1989.

Addresses: *Residence*—Ojai, Calif. *Record company*—Geffen Records, 9130 Sunset Blvd., Los Angeles, Calif. 90069-6197.

In 1969, while living with her father, Jones went off with some friends to a rock concert in California. She never came back, instead living a hippie road life and finally settling down, sort of, in Los Angeles, where she fell in with friends Tom Waits and Chuck E. Weiss, a local musician who became the inspiration for Jones's first hit single. What happened next, according to *Interview*'s Dewey Nicks, was "Rickie Lee Jones made her public debut as a model. She was the silent after-hours siren slouched seductively on a chrome-laden auto on the dust jacket of Tom Waits's *Blue Valentine*. A few months later she stepped out of the shadows and up to the mike for her own vinyl solo, and she carved out a niche in Coolsville with her hit single, 'Chuck E.'s in Love.'"

It wasn't quite that easy, however. Jones struggled for a few years, singing in L.A. bars, living in a dilapidated section of town which was peopled with many of the characters she later incorporated into her songs. At the insistence of her manager, Nick Mathe, Jones cut a demo tape that soon attracted the attention of several record companies, including Warner Bros. Warners' executive Lenny Waronker, producer of Randy Newman, among others, had heard Jones performing at L.A.'s Troubador and signed Jones with the stipulation that he was to produce her first record. The result was an album, perplexing at first, which slowly grew upon the public. Jazzy, hip, decidedly uncontrived, the first LP was a fresh breath of air in the disco-saturated atmosphere of the late 1970s. "Jones's sound, gracefully old-time, never turns antique," wrote *Time*'s Jay Cocks in 1979. "She likes Van Morrison, Marvin Gaye and Laura Nyro, but she also talks of Peggy Lee and Sarah Vaughan with respect, performs a stops-out version of an old Louis Prima tune to close out her concerts. Her

songs have their origins in, and owe a friendly debt to, the work of such all-night-joint bards as Tom Waits."

After a successful first LP honeymoon, which included a spot on television's *Saturday Night Live,* Jones continued to produce (three albums over the next five years), but with diminishing success. Part of the problem was Jones's sudden slide back down the spiral of success. "Her sudden success could have made her a kept songbird in a gilded sound booth, but royalties slipped through her fingers like quicksilver, and platinum success fueled her desire for the forbidden fruit of the Golden Triangle," wrote Dewey Nicks in *Interview*. "She became a regular at the Physician's Desk Reference Cafe. Excess took a toll, turning her chimerical songs into bulletins from the abyss."

Jones's salvation finally came with a long turn inward. She dropped out of the music scene for nearly five years in the mid-1980s. While traveling in Tahiti, she met French musician Pascal Nabet-Meyer. The two never parted, and in 1988 Jones had her first child, daughter Charlotte Rose. Having regained control of her personal life, Jones was ready to regain control of her musical life as well. The result was *Flying Cowboys,* produced by Walter Becker (formerly of Steely Dan) and Jones's most critically acclaimed LP since her debut. "The music on *Flying Cowboys* is spare but not starved," writes David Gates in Newsweek. "Guitars, tastefully deployed synthesizers (I don't like them either) for supplementary texture and color. Muscular, rocking rhythms. Jones's singing is as wild and free as ever—from childlike piping to sluttish slurring, sometimes in overdubbed girl-group harmonies. And her unscrutinized metaphors tell all we need to know." Writes *Time*'s Jay Cocks of Jones's return to the work she was born to do: "Now she's back, looking like her old self: the most gifted woman on the scene."

Selected discography

Rickie Lee Jones, Warner Bros., 1979.
Pirates, Warner Bros., 1981.
Girl at Her Volcano, Warner Bros., 1983.
The Magazine, Warner Bros., 1984.
Flying Cowboys, Geffen, 1989.

Sources

Interview, November, 1989.
Newsweek, October 16, 1989.
Rolling Stone, May 31, 1979.
Time, May 21, 1979; October 23, 1989.

—David Collins

Kris Kristofferson

Singer, songwriter, guitarist, actor

Kris Kristofferson's success in movies and on television tends to obscure his considerable accomplishments as a songwriter and vocal performer. In fact, the lanky Texas native established his career by writing and singing country music; his mournful lyrics and deceptively simple melodies helped to define the "progressive" Nashville sound in the late 1960s. *Esquire* contributor Tom Burke notes that Kristofferson is "one of the most respected, and his work among the most often performed, of contemporary songwriters. He is highly paid not only for the writing of songs but for the singing of them." In *Best of the Music Makers,* George T. Simon calls Kristofferson "a balladeer of the dispossessed, the troubadour of losing and losers," who has brought "a gentle intensity to his portraits of frustration, defeat, and lost romance."

Kristofferson emerged in Nashville at the time when performers such as Johnny Cash, Waylon Jennings, and Willie Nelson were beginning to challenge the clean-cut, all-American image expected of country performers. It is no surprise that the scruffy, hard-living Kristofferson forged close friendships with these stars and has since performed with them on stage and on television. Indeed, Kristofferson's songs—many of them celebrations of drifting in the wrong direction—have established him as one of country music's "outlaws." *TV Guide* correspondent Neil Hickey finds the artist a leading member of "a new breed of Nashville songwriters who [are] more literary, more poetic, less insular in their approaches."

Kristofferson's "outlaw" image is a product of his adult years. As a young man he was every American family's model son: a Golden Gloves boxer who earned Phi Beta Kappa grades in college, winner of a prestigious *Atlantic Monthly* collegiate short-story contest, and recipient of the coveted Rhodes Scholarship to Oxford University. The son of a career major general in the U.S. Air Force, Kristofferson seemed to be destined for the same sort of conservative success. The golden youth had one Achilles heel, however. He was passionately fond of country music, especially Hank Williams, and he liked to sing folk songs and accompany himself on guitar. While studying literature at Oxford he managed to sing and tour as Kris Carson, even appearing on British television.

Never particularly fond of academic life, Kristofferson eventually became disillusioned with Oxford. In 1960 he returned to the United States and joined the army. For a time it appeared that he might follow in his father's footsteps, as he moved through ranger school, parachute-jump school, and pilot training, eventually becoming an able helicopter pilot. When his first tour of duty ended he reenlisted for another three years and

For the Record. . .

Full name Kristoffer Kristofferson; born June 22, 1936, in Brownsville, Tex.; son of U.S. Air Force major general; married Fran Beir, 1960 (divorced); married Rita Coolidge (a singer), August 19, 1973 (divorced, 1979); married Lisa Meyers (an attorney), February 18, 1983; children: (first marriage) Tracy, Kris; (second marriage) Casey; (third marriage) two. *Education:* Pomona College, B.A., 1958; attended Oxford University as a Rhodes Scholar, 1959.

Helicopter pilot for United States Army, 1960-65. Songwriter, singer, and composer, 1965—; actor, 1970—. Signed with Monument Records, 1969. Author of numerous songs, including "Me and Bobby McGee," "Sunday Mornin' Comin' Down," "Help Me Make It Through the Night," "Loving Her Was Easier (Than Anything I'll Ever Do Again)," "For the Good Times," and "Why Me, Lord?" Has worked as a solo performer, a duet performer with former wife, Rita Coolidge, and part of an ensemble with Johnny Cash, Waylon Jennings, and Willie Nelson.

Actor in feature films, including *Cisco Pike*, 1971, *Alice Doesn't Live Here Anymore*, 1975, *A Star Is Born*, 1976, *The Sailor Who Fell from Grace with the Sea*, 1976, *Semi-Tough*, 1977, *Heaven's Gate*, 1980, *Trouble in Mind*, 1986, and *Amerika*, 1987.

Awards: Song of the year citation from Country Music Association, 1970, for "Sunday Mornin' Comin' Down"; Grammy Award nominations for best song, both 1971, for "Help Me Make It through the Night" and "Me and Bobby McGee"; Grammy Award nominations for best country song, 1971, for "For the Good Times," and 1973, for "Why Me, Lord?"; Grammy Award for best vocal performance by a duo (with Rita Coolidge), 1973; Grammy Awards for songwriting, 1973, for "From the Bottle to the Bottom," and 1975, for "Lover Please." Honorary doctorate awarded by Pomona College, 1974.

Addresses: *Other*—3179 Sumacridge Dr., Malibu, Calif. 90265.

was sent to Germany. There a friend persuaded him to send a few songs to a Nashville agent. In 1965 Kristofferson was on the verge of accepting a teaching position at West Point when he decided to move to Nashville instead. Against the wishes of his parents and his wife, he embarked for the South with little to sustain him but a handful of songs he had written.

The following four years became "a struggle just to stay alive and write," according to Paul Hemphill in a *New York Times Magazine* feature. Kristofferson's struggle was the classic sort—he tended bar and even worked as the night janitor at a Columbia Records studio in order to make ends meet while he peddled his songs to the reigning country stars. Eventually two performers responded to Kristofferson's talent and persistence— Johnny Cash and Roger Miller. Miller was the first to record a Kristofferson song, the winsome "Me and Bobby McGee." Cash accepted Kristofferson's "Sunday Mornin' Comin' Down" and turned it into a Number 1 hit. No one was more surprised than Kristofferson when the Country Music Association named "Sunday Mornin' Comin' Down" the 1970 song of the year. In a vision of country music's future, the long-haired Kristofferson ambled to the stage and shyly accepted his prize.

By that time Cash and Kristofferson had become fast friends. Cash persuaded Kristofferson to perform his own music, and the artist signed with Monument Rec-

> *Kristofferson's songs—many of them celebrations of drifting in the wrong direction—have established him as one of country music's "outlaws."*

ords. From the outset Kristofferson's music had its roots squarely in folk and country, but he found fans in the pop-rock arena as well. Even though every live concert became a battle with stage fright, Kristofferson achieved great popularity. He earned two gold singles on his own for "Silver Tongued Devil and I" and "Why Me, Lord?," and he watched with satisfaction as Janis Joplin made "Me and Bobby McGee" into a major rock classic.

Hollywood discovered Kristofferson in the early 1970s, and he added film appearances to his already-busy schedule of touring and recording. In 1973 he married singer Rita Coolidge, and they performed as a country-pop duo, earning a number of Grammy nominations and awards together. Nevertheless, as Cheryl McCall notes in a *People* magazine article, Kristofferson's "peculiar insecurity led to near panic in the face of adulation and stardom." Between 1973 and 1977 Kristofferson took roles in more than a half-dozen feature films, some of which—particularly *A Star Is Born*—became major embarrassments for him. Plagued with drug and alcohol abuse, he divorced Coolidge and tried to set his life straight. The process took almost five years.

Kristofferson told Roger Ebert: "Getting high was supposed to be a method of opening the doors of perception for me, and what it was doing was shutting them. . . . It took me thirty years to admit I had a problem." With his newfound sobriety, Kristofferson remarried and gravitated back to country music, where he found his friends Cash, Nelson, and Jennings undergoing similar dryouts. In 1987 Kristofferson released a new album, *Repossessed,* that earned widespread praise. Once again he found himself in demand for live performances, and he also made several well-received films, including *Amerika* and *Trouble In Mind.* Hickey described the resurgent Kristofferson as "a middle-aged gent who's dead serious about his fathering, husbanding, songwriting, acting, record-making, and concert-giving."

In 1990 Kristofferson teamed with Cash, Nelson, and Jennings for a tour to promote the *Highwayman II* album. Kristofferson is indeed in his element as a member of that foursome of road-weary troubadours. His songs address familiar themes in country music— lost love, loneliness, aimless wandering, and maverick lawlessness—but they do so with a degree of sensitivity and sophistication one might expect from a Rhodes Scholar who wanted to be a novelist. Like his fellow "outlaws," Kristofferson has gained a measure of respect from his well-publicized struggle for sobriety as well as for his artistic integrity. The bashful singer told *TV Guide* that he now looks at life "like an old alcoholic" who "is trying to take it one day at a time."

Selected discography

Singles

"Loving Her Was Easier (Than Anything I'll Ever Do Again)," Monument, 1971.
"Why Me, Lord?," Monument, 1973.
(With Rita Coolidge) "From the Bottle to the Bottom," Monument, 1973.
(With Coolidge) "Lover Please," Monument, 1975.

Albums

Kristofferson, Monument, 1970, rereleased as *Me and Bobby McGee,* 1988.

The Silver Tongued Devil and I, Monument, 1971, rereleased, 1988.
Border Lord, Monument, 1974.
Jesus Was a Capricorn, Monument, 1974.
Spooky Lady's Sideshow, Monument, 1974.
(With Rita Coolidge) *Full Moon,* A & M, 1975.
(With Barbra Streisand) *A Star Is Born,* Columbia, 1977.
Surreal Thing, Monument, 1978.
Big Sur Festival, Monument, 1978.
Songs of Kristofferson, Monument, 1978, rereleased, 1988.
Easter Island, Monument, 1978.
Who's To Bless and Who's To Blame, Monument, 1978.
Shake Hands with the Devil, Monument, 1979.
(With Coolidge) *Breakaway,* Monument.
To The Bone, Monument, 1981.
My Songs, Monument, 1986.
Repossessed, Mercury, 1987.
(With Waylon Jennings, Johnny Cash, and Willie Nelson) *Highwayman,* Columbia.
(With Jennings, Cash, and Nelson) *Highwayman II,* Columbia, 1990.

Sources

Books

Contemporary Theatre, Film, and Television, Volume 5, Gale, 1989.
Ebert, Roger, *A Kiss Is Still a Kiss,* Andrews & McMeel, 1984.
The Illustrated Encyclopedia of Country Music, Harmony, 1977.
Shestack, Melvin, *The Country Music Encyclopedia,* Crowell, 1974.
Simon, George T., *Best of the Music Makers,* Doubleday, 1979.

Periodicals

Esquire, December 1976; November 1981.
Globe & Mail (Toronto), January 31, 1972.
Newsday, September 11, 1971.
New York Times, July 26, 1970; June 3, 1973.
New York Times Magazine, December 6, 1970.
Saturday Review, February 3, 1973.
TV Guide, October 12, 1985.

—Anne Janette Johnson

K.D. Lang

Singer, songwriter

Her music has been called cow-punk or new wave country. With her spiked short hair and cut-off cowboy boots, she looks like a cross between Dale Evans and Johnny Rotten. Canadian singer K.D. Lang transcends easy labelling but one thing is certain—her expressive voice and wild stage shows are bringing a whole new generation of listeners back to country music. With the release of her third album, *Shadowland,* Lang joined young singers like Dwight Yoakam and Randy Travis as new stars in the country music firmament. But unlike Yoakam, a country purist who rejects Nashville "schmaltz," Lang embraces both the old and the new. While some have called her unusual renderings of classic tunes campy or even sarcastic, Lang insists her music is sincere.

Kathy Dawn Lang, who likes to go by K.D., seems to have a broad appeal. She has garnered standing ovations everywhere from Vancouver punk clubs to the Grand Ole Opry. The *Nashville Banner* called her "one of the most exciting new artists to come around in a while." At the same time, *Rolling Stone* applauded her already "legendary" live performances. Among her many influences, Lang lists Patsy Cline and Boy George. This eclecticism has its drawbacks. She has yet to have a major hit record because radio programmers have a difficult time slotting her in their playlists. Edmonton, Alberta, music director Larry Donohue summed up the problem in *Western Report,* "A lot of her stuff isn't country enough to go country, and it isn't pop enough to go pop." And Robert K. Oermann, music critic for the *Tennessean,* explained, "She is in some kind of weird place between artsy new wave and country."

Lang's focus, however, seems to be narrowing as her music matures. She has discarded some of her props, like the Elvis Costello horn-rimmed glasses and the rhinestone-studded cowboy skirts. She says she doesn't want to become known simply as an "act" like Bette Midler's Divine Miss M. Her concern may be warranted. The *Nashville Banner* once referred to her as a singer with "Patsy Cline's sublime power . . . inside Pee Wee Herman's mind."

K.D. Lang has country roots. She was born Katherine Dawn Lang in 1961 in the tiny town of Consort (pop. 672), Alberta, Canada. Her father ran the local drugstore and her mother was the second grade schoolteacher. As a teenager, K.D. earned summer money driving a three-ton grain truck for local farmers. But despite her rural surroundings, Lang's early musical influences were not country. She trained on classical piano and listened to her older sister's rock music collection. "I grew up not liking country music," she told Jay Scott in *Chatelaine.* "I was brought up in a family that studied classical music, at the piano. We also listened to Broadway shows. And I listened to Janis Joplin and the Allman Brothers." Besides music, young Kathy Dawn was interested in athletics. She was able on the volleyball court, and she claims her first professional ambition was to be a roller derby queen. Later, in college, she dabbled in performance art. She played in productions that ranged from a seven hour re-enactment of Barney Clark's plastic heart transplant to filling up an art gallery with garbage.

But music remained her first love. As a teenager, she was a would-be professional, doing numbers like "Midnight Blue" and the "Circle Game" on her acoustic guitar at weddings and other functions. At college, she discovered the music of Patsy Cline, whose emotional approach drew Lang back to the golden age of country, when singers like Johnny Horton and Hank Williams sang simple tributes to the everyday life of ordinary people.

In 1982 she answered an ad in an Edmonton newspaper for a singer for a Texas swing fiddle band. Her future manager, Larry Wanagas, was at the audition. He knew immediately that a unique talent was ready to be developed. "The first show she did," he told Perry Stem in *Canadian Musician* magazine, "surprised her-self as well as me. I knew she could sing, but what she brought to the stage was this undeniable presence."

For the next two years, Lang and her band, the Reclines, toured throughout Canada. They played country, college, and rock bars. K.D. would stomp out wearing ugly, rhinestone-studded glasses (without lenses) and cowboy boots with the tops sawn off. She would fling herself to the stage in the middle of her version of the 1960s girl-pop classic "Johnny Get Angry." But no matter how contorted her hijinks, her voice rang deep and melodious. She was clearly capable of vocal gymnastics, tumbling from a full-throated alto line one moment to a yelping yodel the next. It didn't take long for the word to spread—this weird-looking woman from the plains of Alberta was singing country tunes like they had never been sung before.

Her first album, *A Truly Western Experience,* was recorded during this period on an independent Edmonton label. It showed that her voice could be transposed successfully to vinyl, but it didn't sell well. Then, in the spring of 1985, after playing a gig at New York's Bottom Line club, the head of Sire Records signed her to his label. Seymour Stein was already recording the Talking Heads, Madonna, the Pretenders, and the Ramones. After witnessing her Bottom Line show, he decided she was ready for big-time exposure. "You are what should have happened to country music 30 years ago," he told her at the time.

Her star was on the rise. In November, she was named Canada's "most promising female vocalist." But in 1986, Lang disappeared from the concert circuit. When she reappeared, she had abandoned the persona that had won her headlines. A restrained, new Kathy Dawn Lang emerged, without the cat glasses and the studied attempts to make herself ugly. "The reason I've tempered my style is because I'm taking my music more seriously," Lang told *Western Report.* "I'm tired of being written about as some zany, crazy kid. I think the gap between K.D. and Kathy has lessened to the point where I'm almost completely Kathy on stage now." Lang clearly sought to defy the critics who doubted her artistic commitment.

Lang's second album, but first major release, *Angel With a Lariat,* was the product of K.D.'s new devotion to her music. It was a complex collection of Lang's own pieces and country classics, like Patsy Cline's heartbreaker "Three Cigarettes in an Ashtray." Produced in England by rocker Dave Edmunds, it featured the spontaneity of a live performance. And at the same time, it strove to recapture the honesty and purity that Lang found lacking in contemporary country music. The reviews were generous. The *Toronto Globe and Mail,* for example, called the production "a breathlessly paced, musically adventurous album that's unlike anything in contemporary or rock music."

With the release of her first major commercial effort, K.D. began to look south of the Canadian border. In May, 1987, she made her television debut on "The Tonight Show." Johnny Carson was so impressed that he invited her back three times. She quickly became a television regular, appearing on the Smothers Brothers' program, "Late Night with David Letterman," "Hee Haw," and on pay-TV alongside Bruce Springsteen and Elvis Costello. She also teamed up with music legend Roy Orbison to record a stirring version of the rock veteran's classic ballad "Crying." Their co-production sold more than 50,000 copies in the United States. Nonetheless, major radio airplay still seemed to elude Lang.

In the summer of 1988, Lang released the album that was to feature her vocal talents in a way that *Angel With a Lariat* never did. *Shadowland* was produced by country legend Owen Bradley, the man who developed Patsy Cline's talent. Indeed, *Shadowland* seemed to be a coming-to-terms of Lang's long-time obsession with her mentor and role model. None of the songs on the album are her own. Instead, they are nostalgic, sincere interpretations of emotional ballads known in the country music business as "weepers." There is no wacky sarcasm in these songs; one track, "Honky Tonk Angels' Medley," features country stars who are former Bradley protegees and contemporaries of Cline.

The album has done well, garnering respectable sales and laudatory reviews. *Rolling Stone* called it a celebration of country music, and *Maclean's* suggested the collection of Nashville classics was "richly nostalgic" and "a major turning point." A single from the album, Patsy Cline's "I'm Down to My Last Cigarette," climbed both the country and pop charts. And it has been credited with sparking a revival of interest in Cline's work. Her label, MCA Records, has re-released Cline's greatest-hits collection and has issued two previously unreleased recordings.

Her 1989 release, *Absolute Torch and Twang*, "splits the difference between the unbridled high spirits . . . of *Angel With a Lariat* and the more studied, Patsy Cline-influenced studioscapes crafted by legendary country producer Owen Bradley on *Shadowland*," noted Holly Gleason in a *Rolling Stone* review. "There are more

obvious records Lang could have made," Gleason continued, "ones designed to make her a country queen. Instead, she opted for songs that challenge her abilities and make a case for artistic vision. . . . This album isn't gonna win her any points with the Nashville Network or country-radio programmers, but it shows what country music, when intelligently done, can be."

Lang continues to defy the easy labels. Even without her spiked hair, K.D. Lang stands in stark contrast to the pronounced femininity of Nashville's female country artists. She may mimic country music's golden years, but her mannish looks do not fit in with the bouffant hairstyles of earlier times. When *Chatelaine* magazine chose Lang as it's 1988 Woman of the Year, she defiantly posed for the magazine cover without makeup. "I am a woman of the 1980s and have been influenced by punk and Boy George," she explained to *Maclean's* magazine.

Selected discography

A Truly Western Experience, independently produced in Edmonton, Alberta, Canada, c.1984.

Angel With a Lariat, Sire, 1987.

Shadowland (includes "I'm Down to My Last Cigarette," "Honky Tonk Angels' Medley," and "Busy Being Blue"), Sire Records, 1988.

Absolute Torch and Twang (includes "Full Moon Full of Love," "Three Days," "Trail of Broken Hearts," "Big Boned Gal," "Luck in My Eyes," "Nowhere to Stand," "Didn't I," and "Big Love"), Sire, 1989.

Sources

Calgary Herald, February 14, 1987.
Canadian Composer, December 1985; November 1987.
Canadian Musician, April 1987.
Chatelaine, January 1988.
Maclean's, July 6, 1987; August 3, 1987; May 30, 1988.
People, July 4, 1988.
Rolling Stone, June 16, 1988; July 13, 1989.
Vancouver Sun, March 15, 1986.
Western Report, March 2, 1987; September 28, 1987.
Winnipeg Free Press, April 12, 1986.

—*Ingeborg Boyens*

Little Feat

Blues-rock band

Little Feat is an enormously versatile rock band with an ever-growing cult following in the United States and Europe. *Detroit Free Press* contributor Gary Graff describes Little Feat as "one of those groups that baffled record company executives and radio station program directors [with] a Cuisinart blend of rock, country, jazz, soul, blues and gospel, chopped and mixed into a dish that defied categorization." In fact, the band probably owes its current existence to the popularity of album-rock and classic-rock radio stations. Many Little Feat albums from the 1970s are still selling today thanks to the enduring allure of Feat hits such as "Dixie Chicken" and "Oh Atlanta," and the group's new work is finding enthusiasts as well.

Little Feat's down-and-dirty blues-rock was primarily the invention of Feat founder Lowell George. George and bass guitarist Roy Estrada were veterans of the Frank Zappa band Mothers of Invention before they formed their own group in 1970. The original incarnation of Little Feat also included keyboardist Bill Payne and drummer Richard Hayward, both of whom had

spent years establishing themselves in the California rock scene. Much of the early Little Feat material was composed and sung by George, a talented songwriter and producer. The group's first live gigs were performed under the dubious name Country Zeke and the Freaks, but George eventually hit upon the name Little Feat when he recalled how former band companions had teased him about his feet.

George was so well-connected in the music business that he had little trouble persuading Warner Brothers to sign his new band. Their debut album, *Little Feat,* was released in 1970. A "fine set of post-psychedelic country-influenced rock," to quote the *Rolling Stone Record Guide, Little Feat* sold steadily behind the group's spirited concert performances. A second album, *Sailin' Shoes* (1972), was hailed by critics for its ground-breaking fusion of widely varied musical elements and for its catchy lyrics, most of them provided by Lowell George. Unfortunately, the band's eclectic sound defied easy categorization, so pop stations were not quick to play Little Feat cuts. As a result the band sold more albums in Europe than it did in America, although concert attendance was hefty on both sides of the Atlantic.

Roy Estrada left Little Feat in 1972, and George recruited several new members to fill the gap. That year bass guitarist Ken Gradney, guitarist-vocalist Paul Barrere, and conga player Sam Clayton joined the group. These performers form the nucleus of the current version of Little Feat, and in the early 1970s they proved to be valuable members of a promising band. The first album produced by the expanded Little Feat band was *Dixie Chicken,* released in 1973. The title song from this

release is probably the best-known Little Feat number, a swinging, good-natured rocker with elements of gospel in its sound. A 1974 album, *Feats Don't Fail Me Now,* also sold well and produced another popular single, "Oh Atlanta."

A rock band's success is measured in increments of one million, and under those criteria Little Feat did not seem so successful. Album sales in the United States averaged a half-million per title or less, despite critical acclaim. Still, the band was prosperous enough to continue recording and performing, with Payne and Barrere contributing more and more material to the albums as the decade wore on. George gradually diminished his role in the group as he sought a solo career, but he was still a member of Little Feat and can be heard singing on the 1979 album *Down on the Farm,* which was released after his death from a heart attack.

George's untimely death proved to be the undoing of Little Feat. For several years the band suffered caustic reviews that suggested its reputation rested solely on George's talent. Rather than put that hypothesis to the test, the group disbanded in 1979. Then a curious thing happened. Little Feat actually *gained* popularity. Copies of the classic Little Feat albums continued to sell, much to the delight of Warner Brothers executives. The group's best numbers began to be featured on classic-rock radio stations. Like other hard-rocking bands of the early 1970s, Little Feat got a second wind from the music public's taste for vintage recordings.

Little Feat re-formed in 1988 with a fine representation of original members—Payne, Hayward, Gradney, Barrere, and Clayton—and with new associates Fred Tackett and Craig Fuller. In little more than two years the group released two albums of new material, *Let It Roll* and *Representing the Mambo,* which both sold more initial copies than any of the classic Little Feat works. The group's music was also used in the soundtracks of two feature films, *Pink Cadillac* and *Twins.* On tour once again, Little Feat played to appreciative audiences in smaller arenas, drawing the kind of devoted followers usually associated with cult bands like the Grateful Dead.

The comparison between Little Feat and the Grateful Dead is not an idle one. Both groups are at their most brilliant in live settings—a fact not lost on Little Feat's critics over the years. Little Feat's virtuoso instrumentation plays extremely well in mid-size theatres. The band's current audiences are as eclectic in make-up as is the music itself—young rockers who list the group as an influence on their work, middle-aged business people with a fondness for real rock, and vintage hippies rejoicing over the rediscovery of an old friend. In the *Encyclopedia of Pop, Rock & Soul,* Irwin Stambler describes Little Feat as "a premier concert band, one able to involve the crowd passionately in its constantly changing mixture of vocal and instrumental sounds."

Needless to say, Little Feat's original aim was to ascend to the highest pinnacles of rock music fame. That ambition has been denied the group, but more satisfying accomplishments have come in droves—praise from critics, influence, and most importantly, lasting music. "What we do is rather special," Bill Payne told the *Detroit Free Press*. "Basically, what we're trying to do is develop this thing into a nice, long run. It takes work to bring that growth, and we're willing to do it."

Selected discography

Little Feat, Warner Brothers, 1970.
Sailin' Shoes, Warner Brothers, 1972.
Dixie Chicken, Warner Brothers, 1973.
Feats Don't Fail Me Now, Warner Brothers, 1974.
The Last Record Album, Warner Brothers, 1975.
Time Loves a Hero, Warner Brothers, 1977.
Down on the Farm, Warner Brothers, 1979.
Let It Roll, Warner Brothers, 1988.
Representing the Mambo, Warner Brothers, 1990.

Sources

Books

Lillian Roxon's Rock Encyclopedia, Grosset, 1978.
The Rolling Stone Record Guide, Rolling Stone Press, 1979.
Stambler, Irwin, *The Encyclopedia of Pop, Rock & Soul,* revised edition, St. Martin's, 1989.

Periodicals

Detroit Free Press, May 11, 1990.
High Fidelity, December 1988.

—Anne Janette Johnson

Madonna

Pop singer, songwriter; actress

The reigning queen of pop music is Madonna Louise Veronica Ciccone, a sultry singer-dancer born in Bay City, Michigan. Madonna has dominated the concert scene, the pop charts, and the music-video airwaves since 1985, with nary a rival able to nip at her heels. Her engaging blends of hip dance music and suggestive, campy lyrics have found audiences on every continent and have made her one of the wealthiest active performers in the world. *Vanity Fair* correspondent James Wolcott writes that Madonna "could be the American star who fulfills the [ultimate] erotic promise. . . . Madonna clearly has the nerve to confront a sexual equal on his own turf, redefine the boundaries of desire, then walk away from the bed unscathed."

Madonna's music videos and live concert performances have indeed featured some of the most erotic dancing and posing ever seen in the music industry. Feminists have been quick to complain that the singer perpetuates the "woman as sexual plaything" stereotype, with her lingerie costumes and "boy toy" belt buckles. Madonna herself couldn't disagree more. She told *Rolling Stone:* "People have this idea that if you're sexual and beautiful and provocative, then there's nothing else you could possibly offer. People have *always* had that image about women. And while it might have seemed like I was behaving in a stereotypical way, at the same time, I was also masterminding it. I was in control of everything I was doing, and I think that when people realized that, it confused them. . . . You *can* be sexy and strong at the same time."

Madonna was born August 16, 1958, and was named after her mother, who was also Madonna Ciccone. The singer had a very abbreviated childhood—when she was five, her mother died of cancer after a long and painful illness. At first Madonna and her five siblings were shuttled among relatives, then they were placed under the care of a housekeeper who eventually married their father. Remembering her days at home with a new parent, Madonna told *People:* "I felt like Cinderella with a wicked stepmother. I couldn't wait to escape." Madonna was tapped for child care and babysitting chores to such an extent that she had little time to be a child herself. She also attended Catholic school, where she earned top grades despite a tendency to decorate her dull uniforms and cavort in class.

In junior high Madonna discovered the world of drama and dance. She began taking private ballet lessons with Christopher Flynn, a teacher who encouraged her to dream of fame. During her high-school years at Rochester Adams High in suburban Detroit, Madonna was able to make the honor roll and be a cheerleader while still pursuing dance with great seriousness. Even then she had the determination to succeed, an attitude in the lead. This group, simply called Madonna, caught the eye of Camille Barbone, who became Madonna's manager in 1981.

From new wave Madonna moved to funky, rap-influenced dance music, which she performed in New York's thriving dance clubs with great success. This shift from rock to funk alienated her first manager, but it won her the attention of Mark Kamins, a deejay with wide contacts in the industry. Through Kamins, Madonna signed with Sire Records, a division of Warner Brothers. She cut her first album, *Madonna,* early in 1983 and engaged the services of Freddie DeMann, Michael Jackson's manager.

Sales of Madonna's debut album were hardly brisk at first, but she found powerful allies in the dance clubs. Eventually the exposure led to more radio coverage of her first singles, "Holiday," "Lucky Star," and "Borderline." The latter two songs finally began to inch up the pop charts until both made it into the top twenty in 1984. While stuffy critics predicted that she would be just

> *"Madonna will still have her detractors, but somehow little girls across the world seem to recognize a genuine hero when they see one."*

another flash-in-the-pan, the energetic performer set out to win the world—and she did just that in 1985.

Like a Virgin, Madonna's second album, was released early in 1985 and quickly went platinum in sales. Madonna had the rare treat of seeing two of her singles, "Material Girl" and "Crazy for You," in the top five simultaneously, while her funky tune "Into the Groove" became the rage in the dance clubs. Her fame was sealed, however, by the music videos she released with *Like a Virgin*—and with the white-hot performance she delivered in the film *Desperately Seeking Susan.* The "Like a Virgin" video featured the singer flirting from beneath a lace wedding gown, and the even campier "Material Girl" offered a tongue-in-cheek imitation of a famous Marilyn Monroe dance number. The "Like a Virgin" tour began in three thousand-seat halls, but quickly moved to the largest arenas as shows sold out in a matter of hours.

International fame brought with it the usual troubles. Critics accused Madonna of releasing only the simplest

that she took no pains to hide. She graduated early and won a full scholarship to the University of Michigan.

After only two years at Michigan, Madonna left for New York City with the clothes on her back and less than one hundred dollars in pocket money. She worked for some months as an artist's model and even posed for some nude pictures while waiting for a break into the entertainment business. Her first professional work came with the Alvin Ailey Dance Theater, where she earned a spot in the third company. She left that troupe and studied briefly with Pearl Lang, but she soon became convinced that dancing alone would not provide her an avenue to fame.

Madonna gravitated to music, especially the new wave sounds of the Pretenders and the Police. Between 1979 and 1982—with a brief hiatus in Paris as a backup singer to disco star Patrick Hernandez—she performed with a number of post-punk groups, including the Breakfast Club, Emmy, and the Millionaires. She soon tired of a backup role, and with a former Michigan boyfriend, Steve Bray, she formed a band with herself of pop schlock. The news media hounded the star, making a mockery of her short marriage to actor Sean Penn. Still, Madonna conducted herself with dignity, eventually winning over some of the hardest-to-please rock writers. Her album *True Blue* was the first to earn critical acclaim for its message song "Papa Don't Preach," about unwanted pregnancy, and its lovely ballad "Live To Tell." As she confronted her own marital difficulties and disappointments, the so-called "Material Girl" began to write and sing about deeper subjects—much to the dismay of those who accused her of pandering to mediocrity.

In 1989 Madonna released *Like a Prayer,* an album containing brutally frank music about her childhood, her marriage, and her Catholic upbringing. As usual, the music video of the title track caused the biggest sensation, with its sly mixture of religious and sexual symbolism. Behind the sensationalism, though, was some serious music, as J. D. Considine notes in his *Rolling Stone* review. The songs on *Like a Prayer,* Considine writes, are "stunning in their breadth and achievement. . . . as close to art as pop music gets." The critic adds: "*Like a Prayer* is proof not only that Madonna should be taken seriously as an artist but that hers is one of the most compelling voices of [the times.]"

Madonna's 1990 album, *I'm Breathless,* marks a return to the funky dance-and-flirt style that made the performer famous. Having put her marriage behind her without answering the sensational press reports, the singer seems ready to have fun again. Still in her early thirties, Madonna is head of a multimillion-dollar corporation—Madonna, Inc.—that employs hundreds of people. The beautiful star shows little sign of flagging in either her ambition or her vitality; in fact, her 1990 tour was tagged the "Blond Ambition" tour.

All the hype surrounding her career notwithstanding, Madonna does have enormous talents upon which to draw. She is an able songwriter who has contributed original material to every album she has released, she is a fine dancer who can set trends, and she covers a somewhat thin voice with sophisticated but never dominating instrumentation. It is not surprising, then, that she complained to *Rolling Stone:* "There are still those people who, no matter what I do, will always think of me as a little disco tart." The singer is not about to tamper with her image, however—she is content to fulfill audiences' need for a sultry, campy vamp, at least until she ages some more and moves permanently into film work. *Rolling Stone* contributor Mikal Gilmore concludes that Madonna need offer no apologies for her hard-won fame. "Madonna will still have her detractors," the critic writes, "but somehow little girls across the world seem to recognize a genuine hero when they see one."

Selected discography

Madonna, Sire, 1983.
Like a Virgin, Sire, 1985.
True Blue, Warner Brothers, 1986.
You Can Dance, Sire, 1988.
Like a Prayer, Sire, 1989.
I'm Breathless, Sire, 1990.

Also contributed cuts to the film soundtracks of *VisionQuest,* 1985, and *Desperately Seeking Susan,* 1985.

Sources

Mademoiselle, December 1983.
New Republic, August 26, 1985.
Newsweek, March 4, 1985.
New Yorker, April 22, 1985.
New York Times, April 14, 1985.
People, March 11, 1985; September 2, 1985; December 23, 1985; December 14, 1987.
Playboy, September 1985.
Record, March 1985.
Rolling Stone, November 22, 1984; May 9, 1985; May 23, 1985; December 19, 1985; June 5, 1986; September 10, 1987.
Spin, May 1985.
Time, March 4, 1985; May 27, 1985; April 6, 1989.
Vanity Fair, August 1985.
Village Voice, June 18, 1985.
Vogue, May 1989.
Washington Post, May 26, 1985; November 25, 1985.

—*Anne Janette Johnson*

Barbara Mandrell

Country singer; instrumentalist

Barbara Mandrell is one of the brightest stars of contemporary country music. She has scored hits with songs such as "Sleeping Single in a Double Bed," "I Don't Want to Be Right," and "Fooled by a Feeling," and has garnered numerous awards, including the Country Music Association's Entertainer of the Year in 1980 and the People's Choice Award for Favorite All-Around Female Entertainer for six consecutive years beginning in 1982. Mandrell also hosted her own variety show with her sisters, Louise and Irlene, "Barbara Mandrell and the Mandrell Sisters," from 1980 to 1982.

Mandrell was born on Christmas Day, 1948, in Houston, Texas. Her father, Irby Mandrell, owned a music shop, and her mother, the former Mary McGill, was a music teacher, so it was natural that Barbara was interested in music from her early childhood. The first instrument she learned to play was the accordion, and she performed a solo at the family's church when she was only five. When she was a little older she took pedal steel guitar lessons from family friend Norman Hamlet—famed in country circles for his ability with the instrument. By the time Mandrell was eleven years old, she was paid to demonstrate steel guitars at a music trade show in Chicago that she attended with her father. When they returned to Oceanside, California, where they had moved from Houston, country performer Joe Maphis—who had heard Mandrell's work in Chicago—got her a job as a regular on a local country variety show, "Town Hall Party." The following year, she performed on the nationwide ABC television show "Five Star Jubilee." And the year after that, Mandrell took part in a three-week tour of the Southwest with country greats such as Patsy Cline, Johnny Cash, and George Jones. Meanwhile, she was adding to her repertoire of instruments—they now include saxophone, banjo, guitar, dobro, mandolin, and bass in addition to the accordion and the pedal steel guitar.

But country music was not as popular around the year 1960 as it was to become in later decades, and Mandrell suffered socially for her childhood stardom in the field. She told *Country Music* reporter Michael Bane that after "doing a four-hour live television show. . .I would go back to school on Monday and the kids would yell 'Yee-haw!' or 'Hillbilly!'—poking fun at me. It continued through high school." During some of these high-school years she managed to find the time to travel with her father's band, entertaining U.S. servicemen stationed in the Pacific and the Far East.

Mandrell intended to curtail her performing when she married Ken Dudney in 1967, but this was not to be. Fearing loneliness when Dudney was shipped overseas for Air Force duty, she decided to live with her parents for the duration of his assignment—and her

Born December 25, 1948, in Houston, Texas; daughter of Irby (a music shop owner, entertainer, and talent manager) and Mary (a music teacher; maiden name, McGill) Mandrell; married, husband's name Ken Dudney; children: Matthew, Jaime (daughter), Nathaniel. *Religion:* Christian.

Demonstrated steel guitar at music trade shows at age eleven; performed on country variety shows "Town Hall Party" and "Five Star Jubilee," c. 1960; toured with country stars Patsy Cline, Johnny Cash, and George Jones, c. 1962; entertained U.S. Armed Forces with father's band in the Pacific and Far East, c. 1965; played and sang with the Curly Chalker Trio, c. 1969; recording artist and concert performer, 1969—. Had television variety show with sisters, Louise and Irlene, "Barbara Mandrell and the Mandrell Sisters," on NBC, 1980-82.

Awards: Numerous awards, including six consecutive People's Choice Awards for Favorite All-Around Female Entertainer, 1982-87; Academy of Country Music's Entertainer of the Year, 1981; Country Music Association's Entertainer of the Year, 1980; Country Music Association's Female Vocalist of the Year and Academy of Country Music's Female Vocalist of the Year, 1979; and "Sleeping Single in a Double Bed" named Single of the Year by the American Music Awards, 1979.

Addresses: *Home*—Whites Creek, Tenn. *Other*—P.O. Box 332, Hendersonville, Tenn. 37075.

father had taken a job in Nashville. When she accompanied him to a Grand Ole Opry show, Mandrell was filled with determination to become a major country star. She landed a spot with a Nashville band called the Curly Chalker Trio; she of course played steel guitar, but she also sang, and when producer Billy Sherril of Columbia Records sat in on their show, he signed Mandrell to a recording contract in 1969.

Mandrell's first releases earned respect from her country peers, but her first big breakthrough with the fans came in 1973 with the single "Midnight Angel." As she recalled for Bane, the cheating song struck a chord with her female audiences: "To my knowledge, that was the first time a girl had said, 'Say, I'll cheat.' It had always been him who was slipping around. . . . The timing was right on." Mandrell followed with other hits throughout the 1970s, including "Standing Room Only," "That's What Friends Are For," and "Love Is Thin Ice." She had big smashes with "Married, But Not to Each Other" in 1977 and "Sleeping Single in a Double

Bed" in 1979. The latter was voted single of the year by the American Music Awards, but that wasn't enough for Mandrell; she quickly scored two more hits with "I Don't Want to Be Right" and "Fooled by a Feeling."

During the 1980s Mandrell had more hits, including "Crackers" and "Wish You Were Here," but perhaps more importantly, in terms of gaining exposure, she started off the decade by starring in her own television variety show, supported on screen by her two sisters, Louise and Irlene, who were also talented on a wide variety of instruments. The show, "Barbara Mandrell and the Mandrell Sisters," fared extremely well for a variety program, and lasted two seasons. Possibly the increased recognition Mandrell received from being seen by millions of television viewers helped her garner six consecutive People's Choice Awards for Favorite All-Around Female Entertainer during the span from 1982 to 1987.

While Mandrell was at the peak of her popularity, she had a major setback when she was involved in a serious automobile accident in 1984. According to Toni Reinhold in *Redbook* magazine, the singer "sustained multiple fractures in her right leg, including a broken thigh bone, knee and ankle. She also suffered lacerations and abrasions and a severe concussion that caused temporary memory loss, confusion and speech difficulties." Though after a year and a half of rehabilitation she recovered and returned to recording and performing, Mandrell has told interviewers that the accident made her reassess her priorities; thus she spends more time with her family and limits the number of concerts and recording dates. She continues to be active, however, and has been at work on an autobiography. In 1990, she released the album *Morning Sun*, which features a duet performance of "Crazy Arms" with Ray Price and a remake of that singer's "You Wouldn't Know Love if It Looked You in the Eye."

Selected discography

Singles

(With David Houston) "After Closing Time," Epic, 1970.
"Show Me," Columbia, 1972.
"Give a Little, Take a Little," Columbia, 1973.
"Midnight Oil," Columbia, 1973.
(With Houston) "I Love You, I Love You," Epic, 1974.
(With Houston) "Ten Commandments of Love," Epic, 1974.
"This Time I Almost Made It," Columbia, 1974.
"Standing Room Only," MCA, 1975.
"That's What Friends Are For," MCA, c. 1976.
"Love Is Thin Ice," MCA, c. 1976.
"Woman to Woman," MCA, c. 1977.

"Married, But Not to Each Other," MCA, c. 1977.
"Hold Me," MCA, 1977.
"Tonight," MCA, 1978.
"Sleeping Single in a Double Bed," MCA, 1979.
"I Don't Want to Be Right," MCA, 1979.
"Fooled by a Feeling," MCA, 1979.
"Years," MCA, 1980.
"Crackers," MCA, 1980.
"The Best of Strangers," MCA, 1980.
"Love Is Fair"/"Sometimes, Somewhere, Somehow," MCA, 1981.
"Wish You Were Here," MCA, 1981.
(With Ray Price) "Crazy Arms," Capitol, 1990.
"You Wouldn't Know Love if It Looked You in the Eye," Capitol, 1990.

LPs

Treat Him Right, Columbia, c. 1973.
(With Houston) *Perfect Match,* Epic, c. 1974.
This Is Barbara Mandrell, MCA, 1975.

Midnight Angel, MCA, c. 1976.
Lovers, Friends, and Strangers, MCA, c. 1976.
Ups and Downs of Love, MCA, c. 1977.
Love Is Fair, MCA, c. 1978.
Moods, MCA, c. 1979.
Best of Barbara Mandrell, MCA, 1979.
Just for the Record, MCA, 1980.
Greatest Hits, MCA, 1985.
Morning Sun, Capitol, 1990.

Sources

Country Music, January/February 1990.
McCall's, May 1988.
Redbook, April 1988.

—Elizabeth Thomas

Paul McCartney

Singer, songwriter, guitarist

No one could have predicted that an English youth raised in poverty-stricken Liverpool would become the world's wealthiest musician. Paul McCartney has done just that, principally by virtue of his memorable songs for the Beatles and his subsequent group Wings. McCartney's wholesome good looks and affable manner helped to attract fans to the Beatles, but it was his songwriting abilities that kept those fans enthralled year after year. He is the only former Beatle whose solo career has matched, dollar for dollar, the success of the legendary Fab Four.

The *Guinness Book of World Records* lists McCartney as history's most commercially successful musician, with more than 100 million albums and 100 million singles sold since 1961. Estimates of the singer's wealth vary greatly, but most sources place it in the $500 million range, with annual revenues of $48 to $60 million. Such a fantastic fortune could hardly be achieved without talent, and over the years McCartney has proven his—both with and without the other Beatles. As a *Time* magazine contributor puts it, McCartney's "bounteous melodic gifts [seem] to be reflected in the brightness of his step, the openness of his smile. His impishness, and his considerable charm, always had an ironic undercurrent of worldliness and assurance. Even now,. . . he has the surprised sophistication of a gremlin who has just been caught under the drawbridge compromising the fairy princess."

McCartney was born June 18, 1942 in Liverpool, England. He grew up in public housing projects, the son of a school nurse and a cotton salesman. From his father he learned to play the piano by ear, but as a teenager he gravitated to the guitar, influenced by the American music of Elvis Presley, Little Richard, and Jerry Lee Lewis. Although McCartney is righthanded, he restrung his guitar and played it lefthanded, a quirk that has lasted throughout his career. By 1956 he was sufficiently versed in guitar and vocals to seek work with a local band.

McCartney joined the Quarrymen, a "skiffle" (jug) band founded by John Lennon. Before long Lennon and McCartney were bosom buddies who spent long hours in McCartney's home writing songs and improvising on their guitars. McCartney made his debut with the Quarrymen in 1957 at the Broadway Conservative Club in Liverpool. Under the name Johnny and the Moondogs the group toured Scotland and the smaller working-class towns outside of London, then signed for several lengthy engagements in Hamburg, Germany. The Hamburg audiences were notoriously demanding, and it was there that the group—renamed the Beatles—developed a confident stage presence and a generally outrageous act. Upon their return to Liverpool, the Beatles attracted a gifted manager, Brian Epstein.

For the Record. . .

Full name James Paul McCartney; born June 18, 1942, in Liverpool, England; son of James (a cotton salesman) and Mary (a nurse) McCartney; married Linda Eastman (a photographer), March 12, 1969; children: James, Mary, Stella.

Joined group the Quarrymen, founded by John Lennon, in June, 1956; group included George Harrison (guitar) and Pete Best (drums) and performed under names Johnny and the Moondogs, the Moonshiners, and Long John and the Silver Beatles. Name changed to the Beatles in 1962; Ringo Starr replaced Best on drums.

Group performed in Liverpool area and in Hamburg, Germany, 1960-62; signed with Capitol/EMI Records, 1962; released first single, "Love Me Do," 1962; had first Number 1 hit, "Please Please Me," 1963. Group subsequently sold more than 100 million singles and 100 million albums and toured in the United States, Europe, and the Far East. Appeared in motion pictures, including *A Hard Day's Night,* 1964, *Help,* 1965, *Yellow Submarine,* 1969, and *Let It Be,* 1970. Group disbanded, 1970, and legally dissolved, December 30, 1974.

Released first solo album, *McCartney,* 1970. With wife Linda and others (principally studio musicians), formed group Wings, 1971; had first Number 1 hit with group, "Band on the Run," 1973; subsequently produced numerous platinum singles and albums, including *Band on the Run, Live and Let Die, Wings at the Speed of Sound,* and *Pipes of Peace.* Has made live concert appearances in United States, Europe, and the Far East. Owner of MPL Communications, Ltd., a music publishing firm.

Awards: Numerous Grammy Awards for albums and singles both as a member of the Beatles and as a solo performer. Named Member of the Order of the British Empire, 1965.

Addresses: *Office*—MPL Communications, Ltd., 1 Soho Sq., London W1V 6BQ, England.

The Beatles phenomenon has never been equalled in the history of popular music. In one year—1964—the group had five hits in the Top 10 simultaneously, another seven in the Top 100, and four albums in the Top 10 as well. Most of these songs were McCartney-Lennon collaborations. The pair had decided early on to attach both names even to songs that just one of them had written, so it is difficult to sort out exactly who wrote what. "John and Paul went together like peanut butter and jelly," writes John Milward in the *Philadelphia Inquirer.* "They brought out the best in each other. Even in the later years of the Beatles, when the majority of Lennon-McCartney songs were written solely by one or the other, each man acted as the other's most trenchant critic."

Certainly Lennon and McCartney were pop music's most successful songwriters as a team, but McCartney also authored timeless songs of his own, including the engaging ballads "Yesterday," "Eleanor Rigby," and "Hey, Jude." As the Beatles matured—discover-

McCartney's fans of the 1990s include those of his own generation as well as youngsters who were not even born when the Beatles disbanded.

ing social consciousness, hallucinogenic drugs, and Eastern religion—McCartney managed to maintain a comic perspective with songs such as "When I'm Sixty-Four." This tongue-in-cheek wit, in sharp contrast to Lennon's pessimism, would follow McCartney into his solo career.

The Beatles disbanded in 1970 and for some years thereafter quarrelled bitterly in legal and personal disputes. The period was traumatic for McCartney, especially since the critics panned his first solo efforts, *McCartney* and *Ram.* Lennon also stung his former partner with a song "How Do You Sleep," that spoke of McCartney's "pretty face" and his "Muzak" in pejorative terms. Undaunted, McCartney formed a group called Wings and continued to record, using his wife Linda as a backup singer and keyboardist. Within three years of the Beatles' demise he was back on the charts with a platinum album, *Band on the Run,* and two hit singles, "My Love" and "Band on the Run." The theme song he wrote for the motion picture *Live and Let Die* was nominated for an Academy Award.

Epstein "cleaned up" the Beatles somewhat, dressing them in matching suits and suggesting new hairstyles. Within a year the group had a recording contract with EMI Records and its American counterpart, Capitol. By January of 1963 two Beatles songs, "Love Me Do" and "Please Please Me," had made the British Top 20; both were written by Lennon and McCartney. The group—which had added Ringo Starr on drums and George Harrison on guitar—made its triumphant debut in America in the early months of 1964.

With Wings or on his own, McCartney has achieved a success that rivals his Beatles days. For one thing, he owns the royalty rights to the Wings songs (Michael Jackson owns the entire Beatles library, to McCartney's chagrin). His business concerns are managed by personnel he considers trustworthy. Most important, however, is the fact that Linda McCartney accompanies him in the studio and on tour—the two have been inseparable since they married in 1969. A *Time* reporter writes: "Smarmy as all this may sound to any fan used to high-voltage tales about the profligate life of rock stars, McCartney draws . . . sustenance from his rigorously imposed family structure. . . . Unlike most rock superstars, the McCartneys try to stay in touch with reality."

McCartney's solo work has been described as "middle of the road" pop, a somewhat disparaging classification for his catchy tunes and singable lyrics. It *is* fair to say that McCartney's music fits in the pop format, but it falls into the same "pop as art" category as do the works of Phil Collins, Elton John, and Billy Joel. "As a Beatle, McCartney ebulliently proved that he could mix with the best of them," writes the *Time* critic, "but at the moment he is having fun being flippant about rock's old insistence on relevance. His tunes are elaborately homespun, lined with shifting, driving rhythms and coy harmonics, their lyrics full of flights of gentle, sometimes treacly fantasy. . . . Even during his Beatle days, McCartney was something of a sentimentalist, and not embarrassed about it. At this point in his development, he seems pleased to be a first-rate performer and a composer of clever songs."

McCartney's fans of the 1990s include those of his own generation as well as youngsters who were not even born when the Beatles disbanded. "McCartney still draws many of the Beatles faithful, to be sure," writes the *Time* critic. "He has also found a whole new audience, his audience. They have come to hear him, not history." In a candid interview for the CBS-Television series "48 Hours," McCartney said that he has no intentions of retiring from songwriting or performing. "I'm just in the middle of my career," he said. "I'm only 47, I don't feel like I'm finished." He concluded: "I'm still planning to write better songs."

Selected discography

With the Beatles

Introducing the Beatles, Vee Jay, 1963.
Meet the Beatles, Capitol, 1964.
The Beatles Second Album, Capitol, 1964.

A Hard Day's Night, United Artists, 1964.
Something New, Capitol, 1964.
The Beatles Story, Capitol, 1964.
Beatles '65, Capitol, 1964.
The Early Beatles, Capitol, 1965.
Beatles VI, Capitol, 1965.
Help, Capitol, 1965.
Rubber Soul, Capitol, 1965.
Yesterday . . . and Today, Capitol, 1966.
Revolver, Capitol, 1966.
This Is Where It Started, Metro, 1966.
Amazing Beatles and Other Great English Group Sounds, Clarion, 1966.
Sgt. Pepper's Lonely Hearts Club Band, Capitol, 1967.
Magical Mystery Tour, Capitol, 1967.
The Beatles (White Album), Apple, 1968.
Yellow Submarine, Apple, 1969.
Abbey Road, Apple, 1969.
Hey Jude, Apple, 1970.
Tony Sheridan and the Beatles, Polydor, 1970.
Let It Be, Apple, 1970.
In the Beginning (Circa 1960), Polydor, 1970.
The Beatles 1962-1966, Apple, 1973.
The Beatles 1967-1970, Apple, 1973.
Rock 'N' Roll Music, Capitol, 1976.
The Beatles at the Hollywood Bowl, Capitol, 1976.
The Beatles Live! At the Star Club in Hamburg, Germany: 1962, Lingasong, 1977.
Love Songs, Capitol, 1977.
Rarities, Capitol, 1979.
The Decca Tapes, Circuit, 1979.
Rock 'N' Roll Music, Volume II, Capitol, 1980.
Reel Music, Capitol, 1982.
Twenty Greatest Hits, Capitol, 1982.

With Wings

McCartney, Capitol, 1970.
Ram, Capitol, 1971.
Wild Life, Capitol, 1973.
Red Rose Speedway, Apple, 1973.
Band on the Run, Apple, 1973.
Venus and Mars, Capitol, 1973.
Wings at the Speed of Sound, Capitol, 1976.
Wings over America, Capitol, 1977.
London Town, Capitol, 1978.
Wings Greatest Hits, Capitol, 1978.
Back to the Egg, Columbia, 1979.
McCartney II, Columbia, 1980.
Tug of War, Columbia, 1982.
Pipes of Peace, Columbia, 1983.
Give My Regards to Broad Street, Columbia, 1984.
Press To Play, Capitol, 1986.
All the Best, Capitol, 1987.
Flowers in the Dirt, Capitol, 1989.

On Video

The Beatles: Alone and Together, Fox Hills.
The Beatles Live: Ready, Steady, Go, SVS.
Beatles Scrapbook, Discvid.
Fun with the Fab Four, Goodtimes.
A Hard Day's Night, MPI.
Help! MPI.
Magical Mystery Tour, MPI.
Yellow Submarine, MGM/UA.
I Wanna Hold Your Hand, Warner.
The Compleat Beatles, MGM/UA.
Give My Regards to Broad Street, CBS/Fox.
The Paul McCartney Special, SVS.

Sources

Books

Carr, Roy and Tony Tyler, *The Beatles: An Illustrated Record,*
Harmony Books, 1978.

Flippo, Chet, *Yesterday: The Unauthorized Biography of Paul McCartney,* Doubleday, 1988.
Norman, Philip, *Shout! The Beatles in Their Generation,* Simon & Schuster, 1981.
Schaffner, Nicholas, *The Beatles Forever,* McGraw, 1978.
Schaumburg, Ron, *Growing Up with the Beatles,* Harcourt, 1976.

Periodicals

New Republic, December 2, 1981; October 31, 1988.
Newsweek, February 24, 1964; October 29, 1973; May 17, 1976; May 3, 1982.
New York Times Magazine, February 16, 1975.
Oakland Press Sunday Magazine, February 4, 1979.
People, November 14, 1983.
Philadelphia Inquirer, December 28, 1989.
Playboy, December, 1984.
Rolling Stone, June 17, 1976; July 12, 1979; June 26, 1980.
Time, May 31, 1976; December 22, 1980.
Washington Post, October 29, 1984.

—Anne Janette Johnson

Roger Miller

Singer, songwriter

Country singer-songwriter Roger Miller is perhaps best known for his 1965 smash, "King of the Road," which has sold over two and one-half million copies, been recorded over three hundred times by other artists, and been translated into approximately thirty different languages. He is responsible for other classics in the genre as well, including "Chug-a-lug" and "Dang Me," but gained critical acclaim later for his work on the 1985 Broadway musical *Big River: The Adventures of Huckleberry Finn.*

Miller, born January 2, 1936, in Fort Worth, Texas, had a severely disadvantaged childhood. His father died less than a year after he was born, and his mother was unable to support her three sons. Thus each was given to one of their uncles to raise, and Roger found himself with his Uncle E.D. and his Aunt Armella Miller on a cotton farm near Erick, Oklahoma, with no electricity. The boy hated farm work, and from early childhood developed the ambition of becoming a singer in order to escape the farm; as Miller told Alan Wallach in *Newsday:* "I hated it all. . . . A lot of people who grew up on a farm will know why I said, 'Lord, give me a guitar and let me get out of here and make something of the world.'" He was also influenced by the fact that one of his cousins was married to Sheb Wooley, a country and novelty song performer. When Miller was twelve, he took the earnings from picking four hundred pounds of cotton and bought a secondhand guitar; he had also learned to play the fiddle and the drums. Not able to wait until someone discovered his musical talent and made him a star, Miller quit school a short time afterwards and began to wander through both Oklahoma and Texas, working odd jobs that included cattle herding and driving tractors. He also tried his hand at riding in rodeos.

Throughout this period of his life, however, Miller continued to pursue his interest in music. He sang and played for any audience he could scrape up, and was occasionally invited to sit in with local bands. Eventually when he was seventeen, he joined the U.S. Army and was sent to Korea during the latter part of the Korean War. Though Miller saw some active duty, his talent was quickly recognized and he was transferred to Special Forces as an entertainer. He became part of a group that performed country music for the troops, and his efforts—often his own compositions—were well received by his fellow servicemen. Also, one of Miller's sergeants was the brother of Jethro, of the country duo Homer and Jethro; this acquaintance helped persuade him to try his luck in Nashville, Tennessee after his release from the army.

The first time Miller did so, he received an audition with RCA Records before famed country guitarist Chet Atkins.

Apparently the young performer was so nervous that he sang in one key and played in another; Atkins was not impressed. So Miller went back to odd jobs, including a short stint as a firefighter in Amarillo, Texas. He was fired because he slept through the alarm for the second fire that took place after he was hired. Eventually he decided to try his luck in Nashville again. He made a slow start, having to work as a bellhop in one of the city's luxury hotels. But Miller also began to find work as a musician for other country artists; during the late 1950s he served as a fiddler for Minnie Pearl, a bandleader for Ray Price, a drummer for Faron Young, and a guitarist for George Jones. He managed to sell some of his songs, too; Price recorded his "Invitation to the Blues," Ernest Tubb his "Half a Mind," Jim Reeves did "Billy Bayou," and Jones did "Tall, Tall Trees."

By the early 1960s, Miller was recording for RCA. He was only moderately successful; one of his bigger hits was a song he wrote with country singer Bill Anderson, "When Two Worlds Collide." But in 1964 Miller was no longer with RCA and was so frustrated with his singing career that he decided to go to Los Angeles, California, and take acting classes. To earn extra money for this project, he first did a recording session for Smash Records because they were willing to give him an advance of nearly two thousand dollars. While he was in California, the songs he had recorded for Smash started attracting attention. Disc jockeys liked the tracks,

and gave them lots of airplay. "Dang Me" and "Chug-a-lug" became quick hits, and much bigger ones than any of his previous recordings for RCA. The tunes also won praise from the musical establishment; 1964 saw Miller garner five Grammy Awards, including the writer's award for best country and western song for "Dang Me," and Best New Country and Western Artist.

The following year was an even better one for Miller. He released four huge hits: "Engine, Engine Number Nine," "Kansas City Star," "One Dyin' and a-Buryin'," and the classic "King of the Road." And he scored six Grammy Awards in 1965; because of the broad appeal of "King," these included both Best Contemporary Male Vocal Performance and Best Country and Western Male Vocal Performance. Such phenomenal success led the National Broadcasting Corporation to offer Miller his own television variety program. The result, "The Roger Miller Show," ran during the fall of 1966.

Despite Miller's fame, the show failed. In addition to being aired against the extremely popular "I Love Lucy," it apparently didn't take Miller's style into consideration. He told William Whitworth in the *New Yorker* that "they were trying to make a country Andy Williams out of me. Writing things for me, putting things in my mouth that didn't fit. . ." Unfortunately, the cancellation of "The Roger Miller Show" marked the beginning of a downturn in the singer's career. This was further complicated by Miller's problem with amphetamine addiction, which he conquered in 1969.

Though Miller scored minor hits throughout the 1970s and early 1980s, such as "I Believe in Sunshine" and "Everyone Gets Crazy Now and Then," he didn't grab the spotlight again until his involvement with the Broadway show *Big River*. He was approached by the show's producer, Rocco Landesman, in 1982; Landesman asked Miller to write lyrics and music for the project. He worked on the show for the next three years, but the results were apparently worth it. Mel Gussow in the *New York Times* affirmed that "the songs are tuneful," and Clive Barnes concluded in the *New York Post* that "the defiantly countrified Roger Miller score . . . comes up as fresh and original." Not only did Miller receive an Antoinette Perry Award for his work on the score, but in 1986 *Big River* provided the venue for his acting debut when he played the drunken father of Huckleberry Finn. Miller also continued writing songs for other country artists during the late 1980s; one of his later successes was composing "Walkin', Talkin', Cryin', Barely Beatin' Broken Heart," a 1990 hit for the group Highway 101.

Selected discography

Singles

"When Two Worlds Collide," RCA, 1961.
"Chug-a-Lug," Smash, 1964.
"Dang Me," Smash, 1964.
"King of the Road," Smash, 1965.
"Engine, Engine Number Nine," Smash, 1965.
"Kansas City Star," Smash, 1965.
"One Dyin' and a-Buryin'," Smash, 1965.
"Rings for Sale," Mercury, 1972.
"I Believe in Sunshine," Columbia, 1973.
"Our Love," Columbia, 1975.
"Everyone Gets Crazy Now and Then," Elektra, 1981.

Albums

Roger Miller, RCA, 1964.
The Return of Roger Miller, Smash, 1965.
Words and Music, Smash, 1967.

Walkin' in the Sunshine, Smash, 1967.
Waterhole Number Three, Smash, 1967.
Roger Miller 1970, Smash, 1970.

Also released albums *Roger Miller Supersongs,* Columbia; *Country Side,* Starday; *Best of Roger Miller,* Mercury; and *Trip in the Country,* Mercury.

Sources

Chicago Tribune, March 2, 1986.
Christian Science Monitor, April 26, 1985.
Newsday, June 9, 1965; November 2, 1970.
New Yorker, March 1, 1969.
New York Post, April 26, 1985.
New York Times, May 5, 1985.

—*Elizabeth Thomas*

Milli Vanilli

Pop/rap duo

European pop and rap duo Milli Vanilli began their recording career on a West German label in 1987, and met with such success that their music was introduced to the United States in 1989. Their U.S. debut album, *Girl, You Know It's True,* has sold over three million copies and spawned four hit singles: the title track, "Baby, Don't Forget My Number," "Girl, I'm Gonna Miss You," and the smash ballad, "Blame It on the Rain." Rob Pilatus and Fab Morvan, who make up Milli Vanilli, have become international stars and are so popular that, according to Jeff Giles in *Rolling Stone,* they "have been making *Hard Day's Night*-style escapes from fans all over Europe."

The two members of Milli Vanilli each have interesting histories. Pilatus was born in New York, New York during the mid-1960s, the biological son of a black U.S. serviceman and a German striptease dancer. Soon after birth he was adopted by a German couple and raised in Munich. Morvan was born at about the same time on the island of Guadeloupe, but moved to Paris, France with his parents at an early age. Pilatus got

For the Record. . .

D uo is comprised of **Rob Pilatus**, born c. 1966 in New York City, and **Fab Morvan**, born c. 1966 in Guadeloupe.

Recording artists and concert performers in Germany, beginning 1987; in United States and internationally, 1989—.

Addresses: *Residence*—Both reside in London, England. *Record company*—Arista Records, Inc., 6 W. 57th St., New York, NY 10019.

interested in music through the break-dancing craze that swept Europe and the United States during the early 1980s; he performed in a group of dancers who competed in international competitions. He also worked as a model and as a disc jockey in dance clubs. But break dancing went the way of many fads, and Pilatus told Giles that he tried to convince the members of his group to adapt to the situation: "Break dancing went down and down and down. I said, 'Hey, listen, guys, why don't we try to sing and make music?'" They were not receptive to his idea, so he struck out on his own.

Morvan was not originally interested in a career in music. During his youth he trained as a gymnast, seeking to compete in the European championships, but this ambition ended when a trampoline accident left him paralyzed for a time. Though he regained the use of his limbs, he was not able to continue the strenuous activity of gymnastics, and began to explore the possibilities of dance. As Giles reported, Morvan was attending a dance seminar in Los Angeles, California, when he met Pilatus. Pilatus saw Morvan, he explained to Giles, and noticed his extravagantly long hair: "I said, 'I have to hook up with this guy, he's dangerous for me.'"

The duo decided to settle in Munich to work on their careers. Meanwhile, Pilatus set about finding a gimmick for Milli Vanilli, a name reportedly chosen because both men liked the music of pop group Scritti Politti. "I looked at all the superstars," he confessed to Giles. "What is their different thing? Their *hair*. Beatles, Elvis, James Dean, James Brown, Marilyn Monroe. I wanted to be a star. I said, 'I have to fix my hair.'" So the two men adapted a style of several long, thin braids. This coif-

fure has gotten attention, but a gimmick without talent underneath does not create the level of success that Milli Vanilli has achieved.

Though they received their first contract from a German company, they went to London, England, to make the actual recording. There, Milli Vanilli tried to tell the English that they were an American group, feeling that German musical groups did not have a very exciting reputation, but their English was not good enough to pull off the ruse. Indeed, in order to sing English lyrics on their album, they had to be taught the songs syllable by syllable by an American accent coach. The effort was worthwhile. "Girl, You Know It's True" hit number one on the German charts, and attracted the notice of Arista Records, who decided to export Milli Vanilli's music to the United States. Arista changed the German album somewhat for American consumption, replacing four songs with four others, including a remake of the Isley Brothers' hit "It's Your Thing" and "Blame It on the Rain."

Released in the United States in 1989, *Girl, You Know It's True* was very well-received by music fans. It also received some praise from the critics; a *People* reviewer lauded the title track for its "catchy, limber little groove." He did not care for some of the cuts, particularly what he termed the "rap ballads," but concluded that Milli Vanilli was "most listenable" on "It's Your Thing." Milli Vanilli's plans include another album, and Pilatus and Morvan are considering roles in a film about the life of black performer Josephine Baker.

Selected discography

Girl, You Know It's True (includes "Girl, You Know It's True," "Baby, Don't Forget My Number," "Girl, I'm Gonna Miss You," "Blame It on the Rain," and "It's Your Thing"), Arista, 1989.
Quick Moves: The Remix Album, Arista, 1990.

Sources

People, May 8, 1989.
Rolling Stone, November 30, 1989.

—Elizabeth Thomas

Anne Murray

Pop/country singer

Anne Murray is one of Canada's most successful vocalists. She scored her first hit in 1970 with "Snowbird," which made her the first Canadian woman ever to sell one million copies of a song. Murray has since had many other smashes on both the country and pop charts, including "Danny's Song" and "You Needed Me," and her long and fruitful career has also yielded her twenty-two Juno Awards, four Grammy Awards, and three awards from the Country Music Association.

Murray was born Morna Anne Murray on June 20, 1945, in Springhill, Nova Scotia, Canada. The daughter of a doctor and a nurse, and the only girl in a family of six, she had a happy childhood except for the trauma of mining disasters which occasionally devastated Springhill. "It was horrifying," Murray recalled for Edwin Miller of *Seventeen*. "Many of my girlfriends had their fathers killed. Just standing at the pit head, waiting for days on end for them to find people. You're not aware of it at the time, but it has a profound effect on you. Growing up in that environment made me fairly strong."

Murray's smalltown Canadian environment also drove her to entertain herself with music. "After a long winter," she confided to Miller, "people are ready to slash their wrists waiting for spring. . . . The people along the entire coast amuse themselves singing." Her parents recognized her talent during family sing-alongs, and paid for approximately eight years of piano lessons and three years of voice training. Murray had to travel one hundred miles every Saturday to get to her singing teacher. Of course, like most young people of her generation, she also listened to the radio. Her influences ranged from Rosemary Clooney to Odetta, from Dusty Springfield and Peter, Paul and Mary to Buddy Holly and the Beatles.

But as a teenager Murray did not have enough faith in her vocal abilities to depend upon them for her livelihood, and after graduating from high school she decided to enter college to become a physical education teacher. While earning her bachelor's degree from the University of New Brunswick, however, she auditioned for a Canadian summer replacement television program called "Sing-Along Jamboree." She came close to winning a spot in the show's chorus, but the producers decided they already had enough altos. Two years later, though, when Murray had already taken a job as a high-school gym teacher on Prince Edward Island, Bill Langstroth, the host of "Sing-Along," urged her to try out again. By 1967 she was a regular soloist on the show, and quickly "became Canada's country music sweetheart," in the words of Bob Levin of *Maclean's*.

Murray appeared barefoot and sang country and folk-flavored tunes, and Canadian fans warmed to her strong voice and wholesome image. In 1968 she recorded an album on the Canadian label Arc.

Brian Ahern, one of the producers of "Sing-Along," believed Murray could be successful on an international level as well, and he encouraged her to seek a recording contract with a label that had a U.S. affiliate. Capitol of Canada met those requirements and was eager to sign the young singer. Her first two albums for them were sufficiently well-received in Canada, but did not get much attention in the United States. But "Snowbird," a song written by another "Sing-Along" regular and recorded as the B-side of what they thought would provide a hit for Murray, brought her to the notice of U.S. audiences. It raced up both the pop and country charts in 1970, and Murray was an international star. Ironically, "Snowbird" brought Murray controversy as well. "Some people called it a drug song!" she exclaimed to Miller. "I couldn't believe it. I didn't even know what cocaine was! A guy wrote it because he was walking alone on a beach in the spring and there was snow around and birds."

Though Murray continued her efforts after "Snowbird," she went for three years without another major hit. Her

fears of being a "one-hit wonder" were greatly alleviated when "Danny's Song," written by the songwriting team of Kenny Loggins and Jim Messina —also veterans of "Sing-Along"—proved successful with both pop and country audiences in 1973. The following year, she scored with another Loggins and Messina tune, "Love Song." Even with these triumphs, however, Murray was becoming frustrated with her career. Attempts to spice up her image and give her a more sophisticated appeal went nowhere, and in 1975 she went into semi-retirement after marrying former "Sing-Along" host Bill Langstroth. In 1976, Murray gave birth to her first child, William; a daughter, Dawn, followed three years later.

But while she concentrated on starting a family, Murray also did some studio work, and recorded what is perhaps her biggest hit, "You Needed Me." The song's phenomenal success encouraged Murray to return to the limelight after its 1978 release—it netted her both a Juno and a Grammy for best female pop vocalist. With the awards came a new self-confidence. Murray admitted to Christopher Petkanas in *High Fidelity* that at first she was daunted by her fellow 1978 Grammy nominees—stars such as Donna Summer, Olivia Newton-John, Carly Simon, and Barbra Streisand—and asked herself "What the hell am I doing in this category? Those singers are in show business." But the Canadian songstress finally came to terms with her own abilities. "I listened to my performance [on 'You Needed Me']," she told Petkanas, "and realized that I can sing as well as the next girl."

Since the breakthrough of "You Needed Me," Murray has produced a flurry of pop and country smashes, including 1979's "Shadows in the Moonlight," "I Just Fall in Love Again," and "Broken-Hearted Me" and 1980's remake of the Monkees' "Daydream Believer," and "Could I Have This Dance," a single from the film *Urban Cowboy.* Her concerts continue to attract large crowds in both Canada and the United States, even though she tries to schedule her appearances and recording sessions to allow her at least four days a week with her husband and children. In 1986, Murray again went for a more sophisticated pop sound with the album *Something to Talk About*—as she concluded for Levin, "I'm doing what I think is right. . . . I want to reach as many people as I can."

Selected discography

Singles; on Capitol Records

"Snowbird," 1970.
"Cotton Jenny," 1972.

"What About Me?" 1973.
"Send a Little Love My Way," 1973.
"Danny's Song," 1973.
"You Won't See Me," 1974.
"Love Song," 1974.
"Just One Look," 1974.
"He Thinks I Don't Care," 1974.
"Son of a Rotten Gambler," 1974.
"Things," 1976.
"Walk Right Back," 1978.
"You Needed Me," 1978.
"I Just Fall in Love Again," 1979.
"Shadows in the Moonlight," 1979.
"Broken-Hearted Me," 1979.
"Could I Have This Dance?" 1980.
"Daydream Believer," 1980.
"I'm Happy Just to Dance With You," 1980.
"It's All I Can Do," 1981.
"Now and Forever (You and Me)," 1986.

Also recorded singles "Another Sleepless Night," "Just Another Woman in Love," and "A Little Good News."

Albums; on Capitol Records

Snowbird, 1970.
Anne Murray, 1971.
Talk It Over in the Morning, 1971.

Annie, 1972.
Love Song, 1974.
Country, 1974.
Highly Prized Possession, 1974.
Together, 1975.
Keeping in Touch, 1976.
Let's Keep It That Way, 1978.
New Kind of Feeling, 1979.
I'll Always Love You, 1980.
A Country Collection, 1980.
Anne Murray's Greatest Hits, 1980.
Where Do You Go When You Dream, 1981.
Something to Talk About, 1986.
Anne Murray's Greatest Hits, Vol. 2, 1989.

Sources

Maclean's, October 20, 1980, April 7, 1986.
People, December 17, 1979.
Seventeen, April 1980.

—Elizabeth Thomas

Alannah Myles

Singer, songwriter

Shortly after the 1989 release of Alannah Myles's solo hit "Black Velvet," the song hit the Number 1 spot on *Billboard* magazine's Top 100, and the name and face of this remarkable singer, previously unknown, shot into the limelight. This raven-haired, green-eyed beauty has an amazing self-confidence, described by some as arrogance. She possesses a strong sense of bravado, and a joy derived from the rewards that have come to her after years of relentless pursuit of a precise musical identity. Few performers, especially those as new to the scene as Myles, have her strong sense of direction and drive. Her voice has a wide dynamic and expressive range; she can belt out a raunchy, Madonna-like rock sound, or slip into a smokey torrid blues voice. There is a strong country flavor to her sound that shows the influence of singers like Mavis Staples and the Judds.

Myles has a no-nonsense, aggressive approach to her music. Her self-titled debut album was released in 1989, and was an immediate success. An eclectic mixed bag, it seems to have come out of nowhere, but, in actuality, five years of preparatory work went into its making. Much of her success comes from the combined teamwork of Myles, producer/songwriter David Tyson, and manager/songwriter (and former boyfriend) Christopher Ward. The team did not come about by accident. As Myles told *Music Express:* "I made the choice of working with David Tyson because I thought he was a really good producer. I made the choice of Christopher Ward because he writes songs that no one else in the world writes. I knew if I had challenging songs, I could meet the demands of pushing myself."

Myles was born on Christmas day (she refuses to give her age but is reported by *Maclean's* to be in her 30s) and spent her childhood alternately living in Toronto and on the family ranch in a little northern Ontario town, Buckhorn. By the age of five she knew that she would be a singer and began playing guitar, an old Spanish classical guitar that belonged to her mother, at age eleven. At that stage Alannah was a fan of such singers as Leonard Cohen and Joni Mitchell. By fifteen she was writing her own songs. At nineteen, Myles got herself an agent and began performing solo in and around Toronto, singing mostly original compositions. A couple of years later she put together her own rock and roll band, which has been called the Alannah Myles Band ever since.

Everything about Myles is fiery and intense. Her speech, her singing and her devotion to music. After ten years of being rejected by Canadian record companies, Myles shifted her sights to landing a deal with a U.S. record company. She picked the three songs that were to appear on the demo tape and recorded them her way. This resulted in a contract with Atlantic Records in the U.S., an unusual move for a Canadian artist—particularly one with no proven track record. The people at Atlantic were so impressed that they gave her free rein to make the entire album as she wanted it. Their faith was rewarded with a quadruple platinum record in Canada. Four of her singles hit the Top 5 in Canada, with "Love Is" and "Black Velvet" hitting the Number 1 spot. "Love Is," re-released in the U.S. after it became a winner in Canada, fared much better there than after its original release.

Myles loves to do live shows. Following the release of her first album, she toured Europe and the U.S. as the opening act for Robert Plant. Myles, a musician who marches to the beat of her own drummer, feels that she has learned to hone her skills sharply enough to give her audience exactly what they want. Her act has definite sexual overtones, but as she told *Music Express:* "I'm not ashamed of that. . . . Perhaps I can bring a 1990's contemporariness to that image that doesn't have to be submissive." Myles feels she can take her place in the rock scene without sacrificing her femininity. With that conviction and her intense drive, she cannot fail to create waves on the music scene in the years ahead.

Selected discography

Alannah Myles (includes "Black Velvet," "Still Got This Thing," "Love Is," "Lover of Mine," and "Just One Kiss"), Atlantic, 1989.

Sources

Canadian Musician, June 1990.
Maclean's, April 2, 1990.
Music Express, February 1990.

—*Heather Rhodes*

The Neville Brothers

Rhythm and blues, soul group

"I had one guy tell me it was great music, but it wasn't black enough," Art Neville told *down beat* in the mid-1980s. "I don't know what it is. It's good. And I figure that we're getting through that barrier now." Although generally ignored by radio programmers and probably unheard of by the majority of today's contemporary music audience, the Neville Brothers, collectively and separately, have been a mainstay of rhythm and blues and soul since the 1950s.

While still regarded in many circles as one of the greatest unknown bands in the world, they have come to epitomize the sound and party atmosphere of their home state, Louisiana. "New Orleans's first family of soul . . . is as much a part of that melting pot's culture as blackened redfish, as pervasive an ingredient to the town's atmosphere as humidity," wrote Dan Forte in *Guitar Player*.

Their legacy stretches all the way back to 1954, when the eldest brother, Art, scored a hit with "Mardi Gras Mambo" with his high school band, the Hawkettes (over the years "Mambo" has become a million-seller

For the Record. . .

Following individual solo careers, the Neville Brothers (originally from New Orleans) formed in 1977 with **Aaron Neville** (vocals), **Art Neville** (keyboards), **Charles Neville** (saxophone), and **Cyril Neville** (percussion); band also features **Brian Stoltz** (guitar), **Willie Green** (drums), and **Tony Hall** (bass; replaced **Daryl Johnson**).

Addresses: *Record company*—A & M Records, 1416 N. La Brea Ave., Los Angeles, CA 90028.

and is now recognized as the Crescent City's theme song). Aaron Neville performed with the Avalons during this time and fronted the Hawkettes in 1958 when Art joined the Navy.

Along with brothers Charles and Cyril, the Nevilles paired up in different groups like the Nevilles Sounds and Soul Machine until the 1960s, when Art formed the Meters. For nearly ten years the Meters worked as producer Allan Toussaint's studio band while churning out albums loaded with funky instrumentals: "Cissy Strut," "Ease Back," "Ney Pocky-yay," "Look-ka Py Py," "Meter Man," and many more. Along with Joseph "Zigaboo" Modeliste on drums, Leo Nocentelli on guitar, and George Porter on bass, the Meters were the premiere groove band. Cyril joined Art's unit in 1975 as a percussionist during their *Fire on the Bayou* LP.

While those two brothers were burning it up with the Meters, Charles was playing jazz licks on his sax in New York clubs. Vocalist Aaron Neville was working on a solo singing career and scored a Number 1 hit in 1966 with "Tell It Like It Is," an all-time classic featuring one of the finest falsetto voices ever to be recorded.

The four brothers did not appear as a whole until recording an album with their uncle, Big Chief Jolly (George Landry), titled *Wild Tchoupitoulas*. With the Meters as backup, the Nevilles helped capture the rhythms and chants associated with their Indian heritage and the city of New Orleans, of which Art told *down beat,* "reminds me of the closeness of the family scene and how this stuff is being passed on. It's like a tribal situation, that's the only way I can think to describe it." Pleased with the results of *Wild Tchoupitoulas,* the four brothers decided to finally form a band in 1977. "My Uncle Jolly suggested, 'You cats should all get together a family band. Your parents would like to see you all working together,'" Charles said to Josef Woodard in *down beat.* "So we talked about it and said, 'That's a good idea. That's worth moving back to New Orleans for.'"

While the Meters were mainly recording instrumentals, the Neville Brothers, produced by Allen Toussaint for the Capitol label, was more vocal oriented, with Aaron's sweet voice as the focal point. With their funk, jazz, and soul backgrounds, the brothers were able to shift effortlessly between different musical idioms. "The things about playing with the Nevilles is that it's so limitless," guitarist Brian Stoltz said in *Guitar Player.* "I mean, there's no telling which direction they're going to go in."

Unfortunately Capitol wasn't very enthusiastic about a band that was too hard to categorize and the brothers found themselves playing in clubs without a label to back them up. That's when producer Joel Dorn heard them in New York and, along with Bette Midler, convinced A & M to sign the Nevilles in 1981.

The resulting *Fiyo on the Bayou* was voted one of the top LPs of the 1980s by *Rolling Stone* but the band was still ignored by the public. The fact that the album was similarly titled to an earlier Meter's LP and contained a version of that band's "Hey Pocky Way" confused matters more. "I knew it wasn't going to get played on the radio. So I didn't build up any false hopes," Cyril said in *Rolling Stone.* "We just made the best record we could." Aaron's rendition of Nat King Cole's "Mona Lisa" with the New York Philharmonic was a sure-fire hit that somehow missed.

The band then decided to record in their prime element with the live *Neville-ization,* on Black Top's label, from one night at New Orleans's famous Tipitina's nightclub. One listen to Aaron's stirring "Tell It Like It Is" redo made one wonder how much longer this band could remain the Big Easy's best-kept secret, but the album still did not give the Neville Brothers the recognition they deserved. As Jim Roberts wrote in his *down beat* review, "I get the feeling that the Nevilles have still not delivered the album they are capable of, but this is a promising step in the right direction."

Nineteen eighty-seven's *Uptown,* on EMI, was definitely a step in the wrong direction. The brothers abandoned their New Orleans sound in an effort to broaden their appeal but the results were less than pleasing. John Sinclair, writing in Detroit's *Metro Times,* called the album "an unlistenable mishmash of commercially oriented pop pap which succeeded only in reducing their idiosyncratic attack to an exercise in faceless blandness."

Finally, in 1989, after four albums and four different labels, the band seemed to make some headway with *Yellow Moon,* recorded with their first record company, A & M. The Nevilles recruited ace producer Daniel

Lanois (whose track record included Peter Gabriel and U2 hits) to help bring the band into mainstream recognition. Movie director Jonathan Demme filmed their video for "Sister Rosa" (telling the story of Rosa Park's role in the birth of the modern Civil Rights Movement during the 1950s) and the Neville Brothers were soon appearing on MTV with a message. "As sensuous and as stylistically inclusive as their work is, the Nevilles don't view their music as strictly a call-to-party," wrote Josef Woodard in *down beat*, "but also as a source of social enlightenment and as a warning signal."

After receiving the type of promotion needed to break through, the Neville Brothers began opening for major artists by the decade's close and were gathering a broader audience for their unique sound. And if they somehow still don't get the recognition they deserve, second-generation Nevilles like Ivan, Charmaine, and Jason are right behind them ready to continue the tradition until it happens.

Selected discography

(With Big Chief Jolly [George Landry]) *Wild Tchoupitoulas* , Antilles.
The Neville Brothers, Capitol, 1979.
Fiyo on the Bayou, A & M, 1980.
Neville-ization, Black Top, 1984.
Uptown, EMI, 1987.
Treacherous: A History of the Neville Brothers (1955-1985), (compilation of individual and collective recordings), Rhino, 1987.
Yellow Moon, A & M, 1989.
Brother's Keeper, A & M, 1990.

Solo LPs; Aaron Neville

Orchid In The Storm, Passport.
Tell It Like It Is, Minit.
Greatest Hits, Curb/CEMA, 1990.

Solo LPs; Art Neville

Mardi Gras Rock 'N' Roll, Ace, 1987.

Solo LPs; Ivan Neville

If My Ancestors Could See Me Now, Polydor, 1988.

Sources

Books

Christgau, Robert, *Christgau's Record Guide*, Ticknor & Fields, 1981.
The Illustrated Encyclopedia of Rock, compiled by Nick Logan and Bob Woffinden, Salamander, 1977.
The Rolling Stone Record Guide, edited by Dave Marsh with John Swenson, Random House/Rolling Stone Press, 1979.

Periodicals

down beat, September 1984; December 1984; March 1985; June 1989.
Guitar Player, September 1987.
Metro Times (Detroit), June 28, 1989.
Rolling Stone, November 16, 1989.

—*Calen D. Stone*

The New Grass Revival

Bluegrass band

The New Grass Revival has been called "the premier progressive-bluegrass band." The group's members play traditional bluegrass instruments—guitar, fiddle, mandolin, banjo, and bass—and their vocal harmonies reflect a bluegrass pattern. What distinguishes this band, however, is its incorporation of rock, jazz, reggae, and even rhythm & blues influences for a strikingly modern sound. Some listeners even hesitate to call this work "bluegrass," so far does it depart from the classic bluegrass approach.

Bluegrass Unlimited contributor Ronni Lundy notes that the New Grass Revival's songs bear no resemblance to the "pop-rock influenced pap . . . being touted as 'newgrass.'" The critic adds: "Yes, this music [borrows] heavily from the realms of rock, jazz and blues, but it [has] lost none of the drive and melancholy that characterizes bluegrass music. It [is] as old and poignant as sepia photographs . . . and, at the same time, full of the powerful pace of modern life, rushing by like the city traffic." Needless to say, this innovative fusion of old and new has found enthusiastic followers among younger listeners. *Stereo Review* correspondent Alanna Nash claims that the New Grass Revival is talked about in bluegrass circles as "the ultimate progressive supergroup."

The band formed in 1971, essentially by splitting *en masse* from a group called the Bluegrass Alliance. Original members of the New Grass Revival included fiddle and mandolin player Sam Bush, banjo picker Courtney Johnson, and guitar and dobro player Curtis Burch. All three musicians grew up in bluegrass country—Bush and Johnson in Kentucky and Burch in Georgia—and they all gravitated to bluegrass out of their love for such classic groups as Flatt & Scruggs, the Stanley Brothers, and Jim & Jesse McReynolds. Bush, Johnson, and Burch all cut their professional teeth with the Bluegrass Alliance, joining within several years of one another. When they formed their own band they added Ebo Walker on upright bass.

The earliest New Grass Revival work reflects the influence of bluegrass pioneers such as Flatt & Scruggs and Jim & Jesse. The band departed from that path in 1973 when Walker was replaced by electric bass player John Cowan. Cowan's was *not* a bluegrass background. He had begun playing bass as a young teen because he loved Elvis Presley and the Beatles, and he had matured with an interest in soul, acid rock, and country rock. Cowan brought these interests—and a strident tenor voice—to the New Grass Revival. He had never played bluegrass before. Bush told *Bluegrass Unlimited:* "When John came into the band, he had to change more for us than we did for him. . . . He had to learn how to play without a drummer, how to approach bluegrass music."

In fact, Cowan's country-rock experience started the band in the direction it has taken to this day. The evolution continued in 1982 when Johnson and Burch left and were replaced by banjo virtuoso Bela Fleck and singer-songwriter Pat Flynn. Flynn's own songs have a rock feel to them, and the band has also recorded work by the Beatles and rocker Marshall Crenshaw, among others. Many New Grass Revival tunes—especially the instrumental ones—owe a debt to jazz, with improvisational solos and coordinated breaks. Lundy describes the New Grass Revival's material as "fusion music, not just a technical fusion of style, but the fusion of a rich and complex past with a powerful, fast paced present. It is . . . the poignant country man taken one generation further into the world of cities, factories and alienation, but never losing contact with the heritage that is his strength and joy."

Nearing its twentieth anniversary as a group, the New Grass Revival is on tour some forty-two weeks per year. The band's move to Capitol Records in 1989 reflects its growing prestige both within and outside the bluegrass community. Lundy concludes: "The road has often been rough and rocky, but the incredible talent and solid professionalism of the band members are winning

For the Record. . .

Band formed in 1971 with **Sam Bush** (vocals, mandolin, fiddle, guitar), **Courtney Johnson** (banjo), **Curtis Burch** (vocals, guitar, dobro), and **Ebo Walker** (upright bass). **John Cowan** (vocals, electric bass) replaced Walker, 1973. **Bela Fleck** (vocals, banjo) and **Pat Flynn** (vocals, guitar) replaced Johnson and Burch, 1982.

Signed with Flying Fish Records, 1972; have also recorded with EMI America and Capitol Records. Group has made numerous live appearances in the United States and Canada; television appearances include "Hee Haw" and "Nashville Now."

Addresses: c/o Vector Management, P.O. Box 128037, Nashville, Tenn. 37212.

them great respect from their contemporaries. . . . For those of us who consider ourselves living offspring of [the bluegrass] culture, New Grass provides not only an echo of our past but a meaningful musical expression of our present and future."

Selected discography

Fly through the Country, Flying Fish, c. 1973.
The New Grass Revival, Starday, c. 1974.
To Late To Turn Back, Flying Fish, 1977.
When the Storm Is Over, Flying Fish, 1979.
Barren Country, Flying Fish, 1979.
On the Boulevard, Sugar Hill, 1985.
New Grass Revival, EMI America, 1986.
(With Leon Russell) *Commonwealth,* Flying Fish.
The New Grass Revival Live, Sugar Hill, 1989.
Friday Night in America, Capitol, 1989.

Sources

Bluegrass Unlimited, November 1978.
Stereo Review, May 1985.

—Anne Janette Johnson

Randy Newman

Singer, songwriter, composer.

Randy Newman was born November 28, 1943, a Jewish boy growing up in the south, with a poet's sensitivity and a severe disfigurement that left him badly cross-eyed. He soon moved with his family to Los Angeles, where he was surrounded by the glitz, glamour, and fast-talking pulse of the American recording industry, and as he grew up he became almost the antithesis of everything he saw around him. Short and chubby with wildly disheveled hair, his face enveloped by an enormous pair of his trademark tortoise-shell glasses, which slump characteristically down on his stubby nose, Newman openly admits that he's a lousy singer, and the thin smile that only occasionally crosses his face is more likely to be a sarcastic sneer.

But Newman has found his niche, both among his small, cult-like following of devoted fans, as well as with the mainstream of the L.A. recording industry. Long before he had ever experienced the urge to perform his music before an audience, Newman was well-known in industry circles as a successful arranger and composer, and his songwriting abilities were apparent by the time Newman was a teenager. "Los Angeles mainstay Randy Newman will probably never top the charts," wrote Lilian Roxon in her *Rock Encyclopedia*. "But it is doubtful that he'll ever need to during the course of his career. Newman is one of the world's foremost songwriters (and alleged singers) and, although his albums sell moderately well, his songs have been heard more often than not being performed by other singers."

Indeed, long before music lovers had ever heard of Newman, Judy Collins scored a hit with Newman's song "I Think It's Going To Rain Today" in 1966; the composition has been so successful that such artists as Joe Cocker, Dave Van Ronk, and Joni Mitchell have also made minor-hit recordings of the same song. In 1970 Newman started receiving greater notoriety when he had two songs, both performed by other artists, in the national Top 10. Peggy Lee had a hit with Newman's "Love Story," a song which Newman would later sing before a national television audience on a Liza Minelli variety special, and Newman's song "Mama Told Me Not To Come" became a Number 1 hit for the rock group Three Dog Night in July of that year. In the early 1970s Newman's close friend, the charismatic singer Harry Nilsson, performed an entire album of Newman compositions on the record *Nilsson Sings Newman*.

If Newman's lyrics reflect a characteristic bitterness, cynicism, and sarcasm, the motivation may have come from the experiences of Newman's childhood. Though he was born in Los Angeles, Newman lived his first years in such places as New Orleans, Louisiana; Jackson, Mississippi; and Mobile, Alabama, while his father, Irving, an internist, spent several years serving in World

For the Record. . .

Born November 28, 1943, in Los Angeles, CA; married Roswitha (a boutique owner) 1967, separated; children: Amos, Eric, John. *Education:* UCLA, B.A. in music composition.

Began writing songs for Metric Music Co. as a teenager; began collaborating with singer Harry Nilsson and performers Glen Campbell, Leon Russell, late 1960s; hit single "I Think It's Going to Rain Today," performed by Judy Collins, 1966; signed recording contract with Warner Bros., 1967. Released first LP, *Randy Newman*, 1968; hit single "Mama Told Me Not to Come," performed by Three Dog Night, hits number one 1970; hit single, "Short People," number two, 1977; diagnosed with Epstein-Barr virus, 1986; comeback LP, *Land of Dreams*, released 1988.

Addresses: *Residence*—Los Angeles, Calif. *Record company*—Reprise Records, 3300 Warner Blvd., Burbank, CA 91510.

War II. Newman had a rough time growing up as a Jewish boy in the south, and the situation was made worse by the relentless teasing due to his eye disfigurement, a problem which required four operations to correct. "School was painful," Newman told *People* magazine. "It was not the best time of my life, like they said it was going to be. Life got harder later, but it got more interesting too . . . I've had a low opinion of myself since childhood." But Newman was fortunate to have a fine musical tradition to fall back on—his uncles, Alfred and Lionel Newman, were successful conductors and film score composers—and by age eleven he was playing the piano and writing songs. "I think he would have flipped his cork if he didn't have his own words to sing back," his father told *People*. By age fifteen Newman was selling some of his work to the Metric Music Company, but, encouraged by his family to get a solid music education, he enrolled in a music composition program at UCLA.

After graduating in the mid-1960s, the admittedly lazy Newman spent several years bumming around Los Angeles, writing songs only sporadically and doing some arranging for record companies. But by 1968 Newman was married, a father, and his songs were increasingly in demand by performers. Convinced by friends that he should be performing his own songs, Newman released his first album, *Randy Newman*, on the Warner Bros. Reprise label, and he began accepting invitations to appear at a small number of concert venues, mostly on college campuses. With his discor-

dant, off-color voice and frumpy appearance, Newman is definitely an acquired taste, but his undeniable talent lay in his songwriting ability. "Newman is one writer whose style is not strictly personal," wrote Phil Hardy and Dave Laing in their *Encyclopedia of Rock*. "He rarely writes about his own situation and prefers to create songs from inside the characters of others . . . he helped immeasurably to broaden the scope of the pop song in terms of subject-matter by exploring the other side of sex in his songs—inadequacy, impotence, even perversion."

Through the next two decades Newman continued to work sporadically, and with varying degress of success. His 1972 release, *Sail Away*, was a definite high-water mark, and in 1977 Newman became something of a national phenomenenon when his sarcastic song "Short People," off the *Little Criminals* LP, reached number two on the U.S. charts and evoked the kind of outrage that Newman probably craves for each of his compositions. But by the mid-1980s Newman's life and career became turbulent. He was separated in 1985 from his wife of eighteen years, Roswitha. And in 1986, Newman was diagnosed with the Epstein-Barr virus, a debilitating condition (some physicians maintain that it is a mental condition) that leaves a person in a long, entrenched state of depression and fatigue. "I'd get so tired," Newman told *Rolling Stone*. "It was hard. There's nothing to look forward to. I couldn't think of anything to do that I liked . . . Probably a philosophy I was looking for. 'Lie down and do nothing for three years.'"

But Newman bounced back strong from these setbacks. He even tried holistic medicine and acupressure to help him snap him out of his doldrums, and in 1988 he released the widely acclaimed LP *Land of Dreams*, a probing, sometimes painful journey into parts of himself and his past that Newman has always kept under guard. It was the first album Newman ever recorded without the help of longtime friend and producer Lenny Waronker, who became too busy when he took over as president of Warner Bros. Records. Much of the album was instead produced by another friend of Newman's, Dire Straits guitarist Mark Knopfler. Though Newman had high hopes for the album, after two decades in the business he has pretty much come to realize that his success will always be limited when it comes to record sales, a fact that of course makes him grouchy. "What do you think people would think if Dylan made this record?" Newman asked *Rolling Stone*. "They'd think it was the greatest thing since Beethoven, that's my opinion. My last record too. I just wonder. I read a review of [Brian] Wilson or a review of Dylan, and I'll think, 'I'd like a break like this. I'd like them to look at me someday with these rose-colored glasses.'"

Selected discography

Albums

Randy Newman, Reprise, 1968.
Twelve Songs, Reprise, 1970.
Randy Newman Live, Reprise, 1972.
Sail Away, Reprise, 1972.
Good Old Boys, Reprise, 1974.
Little Criminals, Reprise, 1977.
Born Again, Reprise, 1979.
Trouble in Paradise, Reprise, 1983.
Land of Dreams, Reprise, 1988.

Film Soundtracks

Ragtime.
Performance, 1970.
Cold Turkey, 1971.
The Natural, 1984.

Sources

Books

Hardy, Phil, and Dave Laing, *Encyclopedia of Rock,* Macdonald, 1982.
Lilian Roxon's Rock Encyclopedia, compiled by Ed Naha, Grosset & Dunlap, 1978.
Stambler, Irwin, *Encyclopedia of Pop, Rock, and Soul,* St. Martin's, 1977.

Periodicals

People, December 5, 1988.
Rolling Stone, August 27, 1987; September 22, 1988; October 20, 1988; May 18, 1989.

—*David Collins*

Oak Ridge Boys

Country group

For more than a decade the Oak Ridge Boys were among the top gospel quartets in the nation. Then, at the height of their success in the mid-1970s, the group decided to go secular and record pure country music. The move was risky—Christian crowds loved the spirited Oaks and bought their records by the fistful—but country audiences too embraced the group's energy, sure singing, and rowdy stage shows. Named Vocal Group of the Year in 1978 by the Country Music Association, the Oak Ridge Boys managed to find a new audience in Nashville without alienating their gospel fans.

The history of the Oak Ridge Boys is a case study in the evolution of a vocal group. An ancestral ensemble called the Country Cut-Ups was formed during the years of World War Two in Oak Ridge, Tennessee. The group disbanded after the war and did not form again for ten years. Then it was merely a pick-up band that served as weekend entertainment for the workers at the nuclear energy research station in Oak Ridge. Originally a gospel group called the Oak Ridge Quartet (after the atomic-energy plant that has become nation-

ally famous), the members began to travel and record as professionals in the 1960s. The name was changed to the Oak Ridge Boys as the group branched into up-tempo, rollicking gospel work.

More than twenty-nine singers have come and gone through the ranks of the Oak Ridge Boys. The current group consists of Bill Golden, Duane Allen, Richard Sterban, and Joe Bonsall. Golden is the dean of the group, having been an Oak Ridge Boy for twenty-five years. Golden was a member when the band hit the top ranks in the gospel market—he has estimated that he earned a phenomenal $250,000 per year for personal appearances and religious record sales. Still, he and other members faced a creativity crisis in 1975. The gospel industry began to frown on the Oak Ridge Boys' long haircuts and beards as well as on their rock-flavored sound. Finally the current members agreed to move into the country market.

Bonsall remembered the gospel years in a *People* magazine profile. "We were always the subject of gossip," he said. "When we added a rock drummer we were talked about for months. At one time our only goal was to make gospel as prestigious as any other kind of music. The gospel establishment wouldn't let us do it, so we took our business elsewhere." Golden told *High Fidelity* that gospel music actually had an adverse effect on the group's style. "In gospel music, you're usually working with very little background instrumentation," he said. "The singers compensate for the rela-

tively thin sound by holding out phrases longer, and they tend to get over-dramatic."

Making up for lost time, the Oak Ridge Boys incorporated a large country-rock backup band, complete with drums and electric guitars. Soon they were vying for top country honors with the ever-popular Statler Brothers. By mid-1979 they had earned five Number 1 country hits, including "Y'all Come Back Saloon" and "You're the One," and they sang backup vocals on the immensely popular Paul Simon hit "Slip Slidin' Away." The group dominated the country charts for the rest of the 1970s and had a major crossover pop hit with "Elvira," a swinging, bass-dominated comic song.

Most critics note that the Oak Ridge Boys are best appreciated in live concert settings—they have even been called the "Beach Boys of country music." Member Richard Sterban attributes this stage presence to the group's long tenure in the gospel ranks. "The gospel industry is such a competitive one, we learned how not to be denied onstage," he said. "In a gospel sing everybody is there to outdo you. I think we still carry that. We're going to get to a crowd regardless of what it takes." This attitude has made the Oaks perennial favorites in Nashville, where they give numerous live concerts at the Opryland Theatre.

Fortunately for the Oak Ridge Boys, their defection from gospel did not alienate them from their former fans—or from their religious roots. They still perform gospel numbers, even in such unlikely environments as Las Vegas showrooms. "A change of style doesn't cancel off fans," Golden told *People*. "They stay with you and new fans pile up. Inevitably our music will cross all borders and all labels. Some day we're going to run across something that everybody will like at the same time." That is a tall prediction, but one that *High Fidelity* contributor Todd Everett feels the group may just fulfill. Everett praises the Oak Ridge Boys for their subtle harmonies and their "shouts of melodic joy," adding: "In all, the exultation and constantly changing textures are pretty damned irresistible."

Selected discography

Sky High, Columbia.
Oak Ridge Boys, Columbia.
Old Fashioned Music, Columbia.
Super Gospel Hits, two volumes, Columbia.
The Sensational Oak Ridge Boys, Starday.
The Oak Ridge Boys, Power Pak.
Old Fashioned, Down Home, Hand Clappin', Foot Stompin', Southern Style, Gospel Quartet Music, Columbia.
American Made, MCA.

Deliver, MCA.
Best of the Oak Ridge Boys, MCA.
Bobbie Sue, MCA.
Christmas, MCA.
Christmas Again, MCA.
Fancy Free, MCA.
The Oak Ridge Boys' Greatest Hits, MCA.
The Oak Ridge Boys' Greatest Hits, Volume 2, MCA.
The Oak Ridge Boys' Greatest Hits, Volume 3, MCA.
Heartbeat, MCA.
Monongahela, MCA.
The Oak Ridge Boys Have Arrived, MCA.
Our Favorite Songs, Columbia.
Room Service, MCA.
Seasons, MCA.
Smokey Mountain Gospel, Columbia.
Step On Out, MCA.
Together, MCA.

Where the Fast Lane Ends, MCA.
Y'All Come Back Saloon, MCA.

Sources

Books

The Illustrated Encyclopedia of Country Music, Harmony, 1977.

Periodicals

High Fidelity, April 1979.
People, May 28, 1979,
Stereo Review, September 1979.

—*Anne Janette Johnson*

Billy Ocean

Pop/rhythm and blues singer

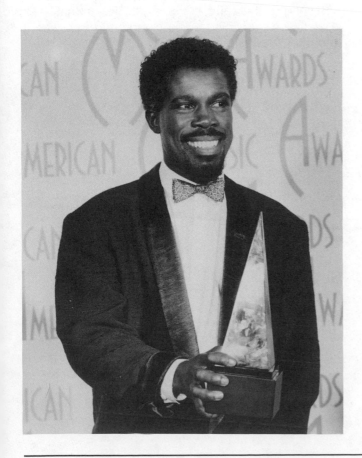

Smooth and glamorous, with a soothing voice and a charisma that makes him appear larger than life, Billy Ocean falls easily into the category of rhythm and blues/pop superstars that includes Lionel Richie, Luther Vandross, and Jefferey Osborne. Even his stage name evokes images of a suave, glittering persona. His songs, such unmistakable hits as "Caribbean Queen," "Love Zone," and "Suddenly," are filled with sexy, romantic lyricism and danceable rhythms that speak to a crowd that wants to feel good.

But a closer look reveals a man in contradiction with his public image. Most music fans probably assumed, on first hearing Ocean's voice over the radio, that he was American. In fact, Ocean was born in Trinidad and grew up in London. Though being black may have been an advantage to the American r & b stars Ocean idolized as a young man, Ocean explains that he had trouble gaining notoriety as a black singer in London. "It's very difficult for black artists to get their records played on the radio [in London]," he told *Rolling Stone*. "When something comes from America, it's ten times more successful than something that comes from here."

Even more contrary to his bona fide superstar status, Ocean seems, even on the heels of three immensely successful LPs in the 1980s, remarkably unaffected by his financial success. "He doesn't have a mansion," writes *Rolling Stone*'s Michael Azerrad. "He drives a Volkswagen Golf. 'Material things are too much for the mind,' Ocean says dismissively. He is vaguely spiritual, but he doesn't go to church. He has been married for ten years, has three kids and helps support his mother and three sisters. Ocean doesn't touch cigarettes or alcohol and stays out of the whirl of publicity and parties that he calls 'the socializing thing.' In his leisure time he likes to do a bit of gardening."

To better understand the humility that lies behind the glittering character dancing and singing on television videos, it is best to retreat to Ocean's childhood in Trinidad, where he was born Leslie Sebastian Charles in 1950. Music was a big part of young Charles's life; his father, an amateur calypso musician, used to push his son toward center stage to sing at parties. The boy was even forced to sing in an all-girls choir when his sister/babysitter dragged him to her choir practices rather than leave him home alone. He received his first musical instrument, a ukulele, from a friend of the family when he was three. "The other kids in the village all had guns to play war," Ocean told *People*. "I got a guitar and played calypso."

Ocean was eight when his family moved to London's East End in search of better opportunity. But as his interest in music grew, his grades in school deteriorated badly, so, to satisfy his parents wishes, Ocean became a tailor's apprentice. At night, however, he began singing with local bands. He was working successfully on London's Savile Row as a tailor when, one day on the job, he heard one of his singles on the radio. Ocean was promptly fired from that job because he "wasn't one hundred percent with the firm," but he continued recording under such stage names as Piggy Bank and Sam Spade. At age twenty-five he was working in a Ford auto assembly plant when his single "Love Really Hurts" hit number two on the U.K. charts. He quit the job and never went back.

It was around this time that the "man with a hundred names" finally decided to call himself Billy Ocean for the rest of his career. He took the name from a football team he had followed in Trinidad called Oceans Eleven, then added Billy. Billy Ocean continued to have minor successes with a number of singles in late 1970s Great Britain. His 1982 hit single "Nights (Feel Like Gettin' Down)" became popular in America when it was chosen to play on a popular Jane Fonda aerobics video. But when GTO, the label Ocean recorded for, was bought out by CBS Records, Ocean's career stalled. The new label's plans for Ocean were sketchy, at best, and contract squabbles kept the singer out of the recording studio for a couple of years. To make matters worse, Ocean's depression was compounded by the tragic death of his infant son.

But the singer's career received a huge boost in 1984 when he was signed by the Jive label. That year he released the LP *Suddenly,* which took the world by storm with several hit singles, including "Caribbean

Queen," Ocean's biggest hit ever. *Suddenly* has sold more than two million copies to date, and "Caribbean Queen" won Ocean a Grammy award. Ocean followed this success with two more platinum albums, *Love Zone* (1986) and *Tear Down These Walls* (1988). He also had a runaway hit with "When the Going Gets Tough, the Tough Get Going," which appeared on the soundtrack to the film *Jewel of the Nile.*

Though his popularity has been proven with consistently strong record sales, Ocean is not without his critics, some of whom take issue with Ocean's tendency to write his songs according to a pop formula. "Billy Ocean's voice is no more innocuous, and no more distinctive, for that matter, than that of Freddie Jackson, James Ingram or Jeffrey Osborne," writes *Rolling Stone*'s Rob Hoerburger. "The reason Ocean's had more pop success than the others seems to have been his uncanny ability to recycle past hits. 'Caribbean Queen' was merely a dressed-down 'Billie Jean'; 'Loverboy' just a bit less than 'Urgent'; and 'Suddenly' an echo of 'Hello.' Familiarity, it seems, breeds the Top Ten."

But Ocean acknowledges these shortcomings readily, without bitterness. He knows what he is trying to accomplish with his music, and he knows his own limitations. He's only giving his fans more of what they want. "I just try to instill happiness in my music," he told *Rolling Stone.* "You know, my songs may not be the best songs in the world, but I really think that what I lack in talent and everything, I gain in approach. I just want it to be fun. I just want it to be loose."

Selected discography

Suddenly, Jive, 1984.
Love Zone, Jive, 1986.
Tear Down These Walls, Jive, 1988.

Also recorded several singles, including "Love Really Hurts," and "Nights (Feel Like Gettin' Down)."

Sources

Ebony, January 1987.
People, September 15, 1986; April 11, 1988.
Rolling Stone, February 28, 1985; July 17, 1986; July 14, 1988.

—David Collins

Jimmy Page

Guitarist, songwriter

Though the argument over who is the greatest rock guitarist of all time will probably rage on forever, one name that seems to appear on everyone's list is that of Jimmy Page, the heavy-metal guitarist who most prominently wielded his chain-saw-like guitar for the legendary British rock group Led Zeppelin, a band that dominated the rock world with an imperial arrogance throughout the 1970s. Coming of age along with an impressive generation of British musicians, among them such other legendary guitarists as Eric Clapton and Jeff Beck, Page was able to take advantage of both a recurrence of interest in traditional American blues and a period of quantum breakthroughs in music technology to forge a distinctive guitar style. The resulting sound blossomed to full flower in the Led Zeppelin years, when Page realized his dream of creating a music that held a balanced combination of bluesy emotional content and modern, earth-shattering rock and roll power. "The rock guitarists of his generation are probably the greatest in rock history," said Atlantic Records chairman Ahmet Ertegun in *People*. "But Jimmy Page is the least conventional, the most personal. He developed a magical, distinctive style."

A self-described "introspective loner" as a child, Page, who was born January 9, 1944, grew up the son of a corporate personnel officer in the town of Surrey, outside London. As a young art student, Page, like nearly all of England, had become swept away with the rock and roll craze that reached Europe in the form of Elvis Presley in the 1950s. Deciding to take up guitar, Page started out in a band called Neil Christian and the Crusaders, where he learned to imitate such star guitarists of the day as Scotty Moore, James Burton, and Hank B. Marvin. But due to physical problems involving a glandular disorder that induced travel sickness, Page was unable to perform live, so he began to make his mark in London as a guitarist in recording sessions, some that were credited to him and some that were not, for various groups. Much controversy has swirled around Page's work during this period, such as the claim by some that Page contributed greatly to such hits by the Kinks as "You Really Got Me" and "All Day and All of the Night." Nevertheless, it is certain that during this time Page performed on recordings by such a diverse array of artists as the Rolling Stones, the Who, Joe Cocker, Donovan, Petula Clark, and Tom Jones.

But the session work began to drag on Page, particularly the work on easy-listening and Top 40 records that reined in his budding talent (though the control Page learned in these years would later add significantly to his trademark style). One of the path-burning groups in London in the mid-1960s was the Yardbirds, and when Eric Clapton, another up-and-coming guitarist with whom Page had played and recorded, left the group,

For the Record. . .

Full name, Jimmy Page; born January 9, 1944, in Middlesex, England; son of a corporate personnel officer.

Rock guitarist, began playing in first band, Neil Christian and the Crusaders, early 1960s; unable to perform live due to illness, he began to work as a session musician for various groups recording in London; joined rock group The Yardbirds, 1966-68; formed own band The New Yardbirds (later to become Led Zeppelin), 1968; first tour of America with Led Zeppelin, 1969; started own recording label with Led Zeppelin, Swan Song Records, 1975; appeared in Led Zeppelin concert film *The Song Remains the Same*, 1976; Led Zeppelin breaks up, 1980, following death of drummer John Bonham; appears occasionally on solo records or collaborations with, most notably, Robert Plant and rock group the Firm; composer of soundtrack for film *Deathwish II*; appeared at A.R.M.S. and Live Aid benefit concerts.

Addresses: c/o Phil Carson, Atlantic Records, 75 Rockefeller Plaza, New York, NY 10019.

his vacated position was offered to Page, who turned it down because of concerns over his illness and then because he was earning a good living in session work. The position was filled by Jeff Beck. But when Yardbirds' bassist Paul Samwell-Smith left the group a year later, Page again was offered a spot in the band and this time he accepted, starting out initially on bass and then moving to guitar to form a twin-lead. This Beck-Page guitar duo not only recharged the group at the time, but has piqued the imaginations of rock lovers since as a dream pairing.

The situation was short-lived, however. Beck left the group a short time later, leaving Page as the sole lead guitarist until the Yardbirds folded for good in 1968. Firmly established in the business as a solid name with a formidable reputation, Page then set about forming his own group, which he initially intended to call the New Yardbirds. Page knew bassist John Paul Jones from session work, and a friend recommended vocalist Robert Plant, who, in turn, recommended the drummer John Bonham. After a brief Scandinavian tour to fulfill previous Yardbirds obligations, and after deciding, with manager Peter Grant's help, to rename the group Led Zeppelin, the foursome went into the studio. The group grooved so instantly that, two weeks later, after just thirty hours of recording time, they had completed their first album, which featured such rock classics as "Dazed and Confused" and "Communication Break-

down." After negotiating a worldwide contract with Atlantic Records, Page and Grant, deciding that their "heavy-metal" sound would do best in America, took the group on its first tour of the U.S. in 1969.

Led Zeppelin soon took America by storm. By May of 1969, *Led Zeppelin* was a Top Ten album, and the group's intense, three-hour concerts were fast becoming the hottest talk on the music scene. In the next two years, the band recorded two more albums (*Led Zeppelin II* and *Led Zeppelin III*) and followed each with another American tour. By this time the group had become almost as famous for its road-life carousing as for their music. Everywhere they went, Led Zeppelin were besieged by throngs of girls that they were all too happy to oblige, and the bouts of drinking and violent hotel room smashing, particularly by Bonham, have become legend. Once Bonham was said to have taken exception to a pool table in his suite and smashed the entire thing to pieces.

But throughout the entire joyride Page and Plant were particularly prolific musically. The 1972 release *Led Zeppelin IV* contained such songs as "The Battle of Evermore," "Black Dog," "Misty Mountain Hop," and the band's trademark work "Stairway to Heaven," all of which became fixtures on FM album-rock stations for more than a decade. By the mid-1970s Led Zeppelin had become the largest-drawing touring band in the world, amassing huge gate draws at stadiums around the world. They had an enormous entourage and flew to each city in their own private jet. In 1975 they released their first LP on their own record label, Swan Song Records, and 1976 saw the release of their follow-up album soundtrack to their concert film *The Song Remains the Same*. By the late 1970s Led Zeppelin had become a bit outdated musically, and the symbolic end to the band came with the death of Bonham, who died drowning in his own vomit at Page's home outside London in 1980.

While Plant and Jones moved on to other projects, Page was so distraught over Bonham's death that he could not pick up his guitar for nearly a year. "I couldn't even look at it because it was part and parcel of the band," Page told *People*. "I had made such a major statement being in a group like Zeppelin. It's the best of my playing, and one could never eclipse that." Indeed, one could say that Led Zeppelin dominated the music of the 1970s the way the Beatles dominated the '60s, and entire books have been written about the group, most notably Stephen Davis's *Hammer of the Gods: The Led Zeppelin Saga,* which traces the group's swift ascension to superstardom along with its notable Bacchanalian excesses.

But life had to go on for Page, and in the 1980s he

slowly began putting his career back on the right track. Picking his spots carefully, Page in the 1980s appeared on a wide variety of projects, including two LPs by former Zeppelin mate Plant, a touring group he helped form called The Firm, the A.R.M.S. tour to fight multiple sclerosis, and Live Aid. "Page's future projects, given his consummate skills onstage and in the studio, might take him anywhere," writes Rich Kienzle in his book *Great Guitarists.* "So far, he has created some outstanding, much imitated music. He has managed to create guitar music of high artistic value that works on a commercial level as well—no small achievement. Jimmy Page's musical spark and durability will create much of interest, though he could easily rest on his Yardbirds/Zeppelin laurels forever. We have not heard the last from him."

Selected discography

With Led Zeppelin

Led Zeppelin, Atlantic, 1969.
Led Zeppelin II, Atlantic, 1969.
Led Zeppelin III, Atlantic, 1970.
Led Zeppelin IV, Atlantic 1972.
Houses of the Holy, Atlantic, 1973.
Physical Graffiti, Swan Song, 1975.
Presence, Swan Song, 1976.
The Song Remains the Same, Swan Song, 1976.
In Through the Out Door, Swan Song, 1979.
Coda, Swan Song, 1982.

With Albert Lee and John Paul Jones

No Introduction Necessary, Thunderbolt, 1984.

Solo LPs

Don't Send Me No Flowers, Marmalade, 1969.
Sonny Boy Williamson, Springboard, 1975.
Jam Session, Charly, 1975.
Outrider, Geffen, 1988.

Sources

Periodicals

Creem, October 1988.
Newsweek, June 20, 1977.
People, April 8, 1985.
Rolling Stone, January 31, 1985; July 4, 1985; July 14, 1988; December 15, 1988.
Stereo Review, July 1988.

Books

Kienzle, Rich, *Great Guitarists: The Most Influential Players in Blues,*
Country Music, Jazz and Rock, Facts on File, 1985.

—*David Collins*

Michael Penn

Singer, songwriter, guitarist

Singer-songwriter Michael Penn "is a thinking person's pop musician," according to critic Parke Puterbaugh in *Stereo Review*. Though Penn is the older brother of actor Sean Penn, the critical consensus is that his talent is more than strong enough to stand on its own merits. As reviewer Jeffrey Ressner put it in *Rolling Stone:* "Yeah, Penn is the brother of you know who, but who cares? It's a moot point." David Wild, writing in the same publication, echoed that just "one listen" to the singer's debut album, *March,* "is sufficient evidence that Penn's music warrants attention in its own right." *March* has spawned the hit single "No Myth," and launched critical comparisons of Penn to such musical legends as the Beatles and Bob Dylan.

Penn was born into a show-business family; aside from the fact that his brothers Sean and Christopher would eventually become actors, his father is actor-director Leo Penn and his mother is actress Eileen Ryan. But Michael Penn was interested in music rather than acting from an early age. As Wild reported, one of his best early memories was of receiving the Beatles' album *Something New* from a family friend when he was five years old. Penn learned to play the guitar by the time he was in junior high, and even belonged to a band that played songs made famous by the likes of David Bowie, Cream, and the Rolling Stones in school talent shows.

By the time he attended high school in Santa Monica, California, Penn's musical tastes had become more eclectic, and he had begun to write what Wild described as "earnest, downbeat songs." Penn himself recalled for Wild that he "leaned towards the gloomy and pretentious back then. . . . Everyone told me I should see [the black comedy film] *Harold and Maude,* because I *was* Harold." During the early 1980s, Penn became involved with a band called Doll Congress. Though the recording they made was unsuccessful, they established something of a local cult following in the Los Angeles, California, clubs; once Doll Congress even served as the opening act for rock group R.E.M. But the band's work did not provide Penn with enough to live on, and he did other jobs to support himself, such as working as a customer services representative for a photography firm. He also appeared as an extra on the television show "St. Elsewhere."

Eventually Penn realized that Doll Congress, as Wild put it, "wasn't going anywhere," and left the group in 1986. Some time afterward, he was invited to perform a musical number on the television comedy/variety program "Saturday Night Live" when his brother Sean was serving as guest host. But Michael found the experience uncomfortable. He told Wild: "I was scared. . . . I have no idea how I came off, and I certainly haven't

For the Record. . .

Full name Michael Penn; son of Leo Penn (an actor and director) and Eileen Ryan (an actress).

Rock/vocals, guitar, bass, drum machines, songwriter; member of rock band Doll Congress beginning in the early 1980s until 1987; solo recording artist and concert performer, c. 1989—. Appeared on television shows "St. Elsewhere" and "Saturday Night Live."

Addresses: c/o Nick Wechsler, RCA Records, 6363 Sunset Boulevard, Los Angeles, CA 90028.

As many have since, the people at RCA immediately liked Penn's music. They signed him to a contract, and *March* was recorded. The video for the single "No Myth" received lots of airplay on the video channels MTV and VH-1, and helped Penn's album up the charts, making it successful enough to merit a 1990 concert tour. *March* also received much praise from the critics; on it, Ressner claimed, "Penn maintains a delicate balance between rhythmic pop and sensitive folk music, pulling off the perilous feat with surprising clarity." Puterbaugh liked *March* also, citing the tracks "Brave New World," "Half Harvest," "Bedlam Boys," and "Evenfall" as particularly noteworthy. He concluded that Penn had "real soul" and "real daring."

gone back to find out." Following this, he and former Doll Congress keyboardist Patrick Warren began working on some of the material that would become part of the album *March*. Penn said of the recording in an RCA publicity release: "I really wanted to make a record that utilized the benefits of technology, but still retain a real warmth and earthiness. We spent a long time trying to find a way to make the drum machine feel and sound good . . . and trying to find ways to integrate it with the sound of acoustic guitars. Most of the sounds on the record are acoustic sounds, even if they're sampled; everything has its footing in real life." Former entertainment lawyer Nick Wechsler, who had been a fan of Doll Congress, offered Penn his services as a manager, and showed Penn's demo tape to executives at RCA Records.

Selected discography

March (includes "No Myth," "Brave New World," "Half Harvest," "Bedlam Boys," "This and That," "Innocent One," "Disney's a Snow Cone," "Cupid's Got a Brand New Gun," "Big House," and "Battle Room"), RCA, 1989.

Sources

Rolling Stone, November 30, 1989; February 22, 1990.
Stereo Review, February 1990.
RCA publicity packet (available from address above).

—*Elizabeth Thomas*

Peter, Paul & Mary

Folk group

One of the few folk groups to survive the shift in the music industry from folk to rock in the late 1960s, Peter, Paul & Mary are considered by many to be the quintessential folk act. They came together in Greenwich Village early in the 1960s, clearly a product of the day. The music they delivered was deeply rooted in folk tradition, incorporating the sound of another age with the moral and political issues of a turbulent decade.

Born November 30, 1937, in Baltimore, Maryland (Birmingham, Mich., according to one source), Noel Paul Stookey's early musical interests were rooted not in folk music but in 1950s rock and roll. He learned to play electric guitar while in high school, a handy skill which helped him work his way through college at Michigan State University. After graduation, he moved to Pennsylvania with his family, working odd jobs until the lure of music became too strong. In New York he sought work as a musician, battling starvation until finally accepting a job in a chemical company. While still hoping to be involved with the music scene, by the end of 1960 Stookey was better known as a stand-up comic in

192

For the Record. . .

Group formed in New York City by Milt Okun, 1961, made debut in New York, 1962; disbanded, 1970; reunited, 1978; original members include:

Peter Yarrow—Guitars, vocals. Born May 31, 1938, in New York City; B.A. in psychology from Cornell University; learned to play guitar and violin during youth; performed in various folk groups after graduating from Cornell; discovered on CBS-TV special, "Folk Sound, U.S.A."; performed at 1960 Newport Folk Festival.

Paul Stookey—Guitar, vocals. Full name, Noel Paul Stookey; born November 30, 1937, in Baltimore, Md. (some sources say Birmingham, Mich.); son of George William and Dorothea (St. Aubrey) Stookey; married Mary Elizabeth Bannard, September 4, 1963; children: Elizabeth Drake, Katherine Darby, Anna St. Aubrey. *Education:* Attended Michigan State University, 1955-58. Played guitar in rock and roll bands while in school; released first album, *Birds of Paradise*, 1954; worked at odd jobs, including one with a chemical company; worked as a stand-up comic in Greenwich Village, N.Y. clubs prior to joining group.

Mary Travers—Vocals. Full name, Mary Ellin Travers; born November 7, 1937, in Louisville, Ky.; moved to New York City during childhood; sang in folk groups while a teenager; appeared at Carnegie Hall with folk group the Songswappers; appeared briefly on the musical stage; worked in advertising prior to joining group.

Awards: Recipients of numerous awards, including five Grammy Awards.

Addresses: *Record company*—Gold Castle Records, 3575 Cahuenga Blvd. West, Suite 470, Los Angeles, CA 90068.

Greenwich Village clubs. It was there he would meet Mary Travers and folksinger Milt Okun.

Mary Ellin Travers was born November 7, 1937, in Louisville, Kentucky. Her family moved to New York when she was still very young and she took an early interest in folk music, later singing in teenage folk groups. With a group called the Songswappers she actually made two appearances at Carnegie Hall. Following school Travers landed a chorus part in "The Next President." When the show flopped, she turned her attention to various advertising day jobs, leaving her weekends and evenings free to explore the local music scene. It was there she met Stookey and folksinger

Milt Okun. As Okun was currently focusing on managing young talent, he took an interest in promoting Stookey and Travers. It was he who felt the duo would do better as a trio.

Peter Yarrow proved an able musician from a young age. Born May 31, 1938, in New York City, Yarrow was adept at both guitar and violin by the time he enrolled at Cornell University to major in psychology. Though he played in school functions and at local clubs, his intention upon graduation was to work in the field of psychology. Like Stookey, though, he found the lure of music strong and soon he was working with various folk groups. Yarrow gained exposure through a CBS television special "Folk Sound, U.S.A." and went on to play in the 1960 Newport Folk Festival. His decision to remain in music could only have been strengthened by Milt Okun's proposal that he become the third party in a promising new trio: Peter, Paul & Mary.

After seven months of intensive rehearsing and making their debut in New York in 1962, the group signed with Warner Bros. Records. Already they were considered one of the major up-and-coming new acts on the Manhattan folk scene. Their 1962 self-titled debut album of standard and original folk-style material won them great recognition and two hit singles, "Lemon Tree" and "If I Had a Hammer." The latter provided the group with their first Grammys for best performance by a vocal group and best folk recording. For three years *Peter, Paul & Mary* remained on the charts, its namesakes becoming one of the most popular bands on the college circuit, not to mention their involvement in protest marches and various political rallies. Two albums followed in 1963, each doing better than the last. *Peter, Paul & Mary—Moving* included the smash hit "Puff (the Magic Dragon)," "Stew Ball," and Woody Guthrie's folk-anthem "This Land Is Your Land." With *Peter, Paul & Mary—In the Wind,* the group featured music of the then-unknown Bob Dylan ("Blowin' in The Wind" and "Don't Think Twice It's All Right"), giving a great boost to the growing "folk-protest" movement. Their rendition of "Blowin' in The Wind" earned them two more Grammys—again for best performance by a vocal group and for best folk recording. Throughout the 1960s the group was greatly in demand for TV and live performances, appearing at a number of folk and rock music festivals.

In 1965 the group brought Canadian songwriter Gordon Lightfoot, whose "Early Morning Rain" they recorded on the album *See What Tomorrow Brings* to the attention of the United States. In the latter part of the decade they introduced the music world to yet another talented unknown—John Denver—when they recorded his touching "Leavin' On a Jet Plane" in 1967. A succession of hit singles and best-selling albums continued until 1970 when the group disbanded to follow individual pursuits. Their final album of the decade, *Peter Paul & Mommy* was a delightful collection of children's music including traditional and original works as well as songs by Tom Paxton ("The Marvelous Toy," "Going to the Zoo"), Shel Silverstein ("Boa Constrictor"), and others. A Grammy winner for best recording for children, the album was largely recorded live, featuring the singing and spontaneous reactions of the children involved.

For Stookey, the group's disbanding meant spending more time with his wife and daughters and seriously pursuing a commitment to the Christian faith. "After the discovery that I needed God in my life, it became obvious that I had allowed a great distance to develop between me and my family," he said. "But since my body moves about two years after my mind, it wasn't until 1970 that I spoke about retiring." Among his projects were three albums on biblical parables and the solo album *Paul And,* which contained a major hit with the classic-sounding ballad "Wedding Song (There Is Love)" written in celebration of Peter Yarrow's marriage.

Other solo albums, by all three members, were to fare poorly. Though Yarrow continued in folk music, taking part in concerts, festivals, and appearing on folk radio shows early on, he later became involved in political activism as well as record and television production. His co-produced animated special "Puff, the Magic Dragon" aired on CBS in 1978 and was an Emmy nominee. Mary Travers remained the most consistent performer after the trio's breakup, appearing at nightclubs and on college campuses. She even lectured on "Society and Its Effect on Music," something the group she had been a part of knew and demonstrated well.

Peter, Paul & Mary joined together again in 1978, and the resulting album, *Reunion,* included such classics as Bob Dylan's "Forever Young," Shel Silverstein's "Unicorn Song" (made popular by the Irish Rovers), and new material co-authored by Yarrow with Barry Mann. They toured early in 1980, then again for their 25th anniversary concert. Said one reviewer, "Their jokes and sweet-'60's observations of life may date Peter, Paul & Mary now. But their songs don't get old."

From other directions, however, the trio was met with sizzling contempt for their supposedly misinformed political involvement with everyone from the Democratic party to dissidents on several continents. Said one especially irate critic in *New Republic,* "They have for months been humming and strumming a remarkably cacophonous hymn, lazily called 'Nicaragua.' Its aggressively credulous message about the revolution probably would not have passed the lips of even so

genial a comrade as Pete Seeger, banjo Bolshevik extraordinaire. . . . The freedom cause in South Africa deserves more discerning friends than those dewy-eyed apologists for dictatorship."

Their 1987 album, *No Easy Walk to Freedom,* their first in six years, met with similar mixed reviews. While they earned compliments for the harmonies they are so well known for, "it's a little puzzling," said one critic, "why so many of the tracks are done as solos . . . and there is so little of the harmonizing that was always one of PPM's most charming qualities." The album's content was heavily influenced by the call for a 1980s brand of social justice. The trio are featured on the album cover being arrested for protesting apartheid. The songs run the gamut from U.S. military intervention in El Salvador to saving whales to racism in South Africa. According to one critic, all of these are worthy subjects, but "to cram them all into one album is reminiscent of bad political speech making, in which issues are tossed out wholesale in the hope that there's something there for every-

---

> *To ask "where have all the flowers gone" is to return to a decade of fading innocence, and Vietnam, and a thousand questions whose answers never seemed sufficient.*

---

body." He favored the "less pretentious" love songs. The title track, an anti-apartheid tune, and "Light One Candle," a song for Jewish dissidents in Russia, were nevertheless singled out by another critic who maintained that they "rank with their best protest material."

Throughout a turbulent decade Peter, Paul and Mary sang protest songs, calling for social justice. They sang timeless love songs, children's songs, and classic folktunes, blending their voices in unsurpassed harmony. Their impact on culture and on the developing concept of the sixties generation was far-reaching. To ask "where have all the flowers gone" is to return to a decade of fading innocence, and Vietnam, and a thousand questions whose answers never seemed sufficient. Of their development, Travers commented that "we came from the folk tradition in a contemporary form where there was a concern that idealism be a part of your music and the music a part of your life . . . the music becomes an extension of your caring and your soul—there's no schism between what you can do on stage and who you are. What we're trying for is a kind of health—and that's what we were always trying for."

Selected discography

Peter, Paul & Mary, Warner Bros., 1962.
Peter, Paul & Mary—Moving, Warner Bros., 1963.
Peter, Paul & Mary—In the Wind, Warner Bros., 1963.
Peter, Paul & Mary in Concert, Warner Bros., 1965.
A Song Will Rise, Warner Bros., 1965.
See What Tomorrow Brings, Warner Bros., 1965.
Peter, Paul & Mary Album, Warner Bros., 1966.
Album 1700, Warner Bros., 1967.
Late Again, Warner Bros., 1968.
Peter, Paul & Mommy, Warner Bros., 1969.
The Best of Peter, Paul & Mary: Ten Years Together, Warner Bros., 1970.
Reunion, Warner Bros., 1978.
No Easy Walk to Freedom, Gold Castle, 1987.

Solo LPs; Paul Stookey

Paul And, Warner Bros., 1971.
Noel—One Night Stand, Warner Bros., 1973.

Solo LPs; Mary Travers

Mary, Warner Bros., 1971.

Morning Glory, Warner Bros., 1972.
All My Choices, Warner Bros., 1973.
Circles, Warner Bros., 1974.
It's in Every One of Us, Chrysalis, 1978.

Solo LPs; Peter Yarrow

Peter, Warner Bros., 1972.
That's Enough for Me, Warner Bros., 1973.
Hard Times, Warner Bros., 1975.
Love Songs, Warner Bros., 1975.

Sources

Books

Encyclopedia of Folk, Country and Western Music, St. Martin's, 1983.

Periodicals

High Fidelity, May 1987.
New Republic, August 25, 1986.
People, February 23, 1987.

—Meg Mac Donald

Charley Pride

Singer

Charley Pride, hailed as "the Jackie Robinson of the Rhinestone Cowboys" by Dolly Carlisle in *People* because blacks are rare in the field of country music, has gone way beyond being a novelty to rank as one of the genre's greatest superstars. Famed for hits like "Is Anybody Goin' to San Antone," "Kiss an Angel Good Morning," and "I Don't Think She's in Love Anymore," he became the first black to perform onstage at country music's most famous showcase, the Grand Ole Opry in Nashville, Tennessee. In his long and prolific career, Pride has garnered many of his industry's major awards, including being named top male country artist of the 1970s by *Cash Box* magazine in 1980.

In Sledge, Mississippi, where Pride was born in 1938, whites listened to country music and blacks listened to the blues. But from his early childhood, Pride escaped the drudgery of the sharecropper's life he was born to by listening to radio broadcasts of the Grand Ole Opry. Despite chiding from his ten brothers and sisters, he walked around singing the songs he loved—the songs of country greats such as Hank Williams (by whom he was deeply influenced) and Roy Acuff. When Pride was fourteen years old, he bought his first guitar from Sears and Roebuck, and taught himself to play it by trying to imitate the various picking styles he heard on the radio.

Around the same time, young Pride began to formulate a plan so that he would not have to follow in his father's footsteps and pick cotton all of his life. Oddly enough the plan did not involve music, but rather baseball. Encouraged by the growing acceptance of blacks in the major leagues, Pride aimed for a career as a professional ballplayer; he figured he might become a country singer after he broke all the important records and retired from sports. When he turned seventeen, he left home to seek his fortune; by 1955 he had won a spot in the Negro American Leagues. Pride played for teams in Detroit, Michigan; Memphis, Tennessee; and Birmingham, Alabama; taking time out for two years of service in the U.S. Army. In or around 1960 he left the Negro league for a class C team in Great Falls, Montana, and even won a brief trial with the major league Los Angeles Angels (now the California Angels) in 1961. The latter stint did not work out, and Pride returned to Great Falls, where he supplemented his income working as a tin smelter. He also occasionally sang between innings during the games he played in, and was well-received by the crowds. At some point during this stage of his life, Pride also noticed the country band practicing in the apartment next to his. He went over and introduced himself, and the band occasionally invited him to play and sing with them at local nightclubs.

Soon Pride was getting club engagements on his own,

"Snakes Crawl at Night," and Pride's succeeding song, "Just Between You and Me," did well on the country charts. At his first large concert, however, before ten thousand fans in Detroit, the preliminary applause faded to shocked silence when the black man walked onstage. Fortunately, he was more than able to get the crowd cheering again when he began to sing. As *Ebony* put it: "It is the concerts, more than the recordings, that reveal Charley Pride the man, the entertainer." By 1967, he was so popular that he was invited to perform at the Grand Ole Opry.

Throughout the 1970s, Pride continued to rack up hits and honors at a phenomenal rate. His singles from that decade include perhaps his biggest smash, "Kiss an Angel Good Morning" from 1970, "Amazing Love" from 1973, "We Could" from 1974, "Hope You're Feelin' Me (Like I'm Feelin' You)" from 1975, "My Eyes Can Only See as Far as You" from 1976, and "You're My Jamaica" from 1979. In 1971 he was voted Entertainer of the

> "I'm not a black man singing white man's music. I'm an American singing American music. I worked out those problems years ago—and everybody else will have to work their way out of it too."

Year by the Country Music Association; in that year Pride also won his first two Grammys. Oddly enough they were for gospel rather than country and western—his album *Did You Think to Pray?* won the award for best sacred performance, and its single, "Let Me Live," garnered him best gospel performance.

While it is Pride's success in the field of country music that has brought him the most fame, it has also brought him controversy. When his race first became widely known, some country disc jockeys boycotted his records. And as he became a star, many blacks looked down on him for promoting what they felt was an essentially white genre. Pride responded to his critics for Carlisle: "I'm not a black man singing white man's music. I'm an American singing American music. I worked out those problems years ago—and everybody else will have to work their way out of it too." He also predicted in *Ebony* that "sooner or later Black people are going to start coming out of the closet and

and in 1963, country star Red Sovine saw him perform at one of these establishments. Sovine liked what he heard, and urged Pride to go to Nashville, telling him who to audition for. But Pride still held on to his dream of becoming a major league ballplayer, and did not heed Sovine until a 1964 tryout with the New York Mets convinced him that he did not have what it took to make it in professional baseball. On the way back to Great Falls after his rejection by the Mets, Pride decided to stop in Nashville. He sang for manager Jack D. Johnson, and, in the words of *Ebony* magazine: "Impressed that a Black man could sing country music, Johnson asked Pride to sing in his natural voice. Pride told him he was." Johnson took some of his new discovery's demo tapes to famed country guitarist Chet Atkins, who was also head of RCA Victor Records. Atkins decided to sign Pride, but, unsure that the then predominantly white, Southern audiences that enjoyed country music were ready to welcome a black performer, released the singer's first single, "Snakes Crawl at Night," in 1966 without the usual publicity photographs.

admitting they like country music. And I think it's about time."

Pride has continued to score hits in the 1980s, cutting an album in tribute to Williams entitled *There's a Little Bit of Hank in Me* that yielded the Number 1 country single "Honky Tonk Blues." He's also had hits like "I Don't Think She's in Love Anymore," "Mountain of Love," and "Roll on Mississippi"; his later chart-climbers include 1988's "Shouldn't It Be Easier Than This" and 1989's "Amy's Eyes."

Selected discography

Major single releases; on RCA, except as noted

"Snakes Crawl at Night," 1966.
"Just Between You and Me," 1966.
"Does My Ring Hurt Your Finger," 1967.
"I Know One," 1967.
"The Day the World Stood Still," 1968.
"The Best Part's Over," 1968.
"Kiss an Angel Good Morning," 1970.
"Let Me Live," 1971.
"Amazing Love," 1973.
"We Could," 1974.
"Then Who Am I?" 1975.
"I Ain't All Sad," 1975.
"Hope You're Feelin' Me (Like I'm Feelin' You)," 1975.
"The Happiness of Having You," 1976.
"My Eyes Can Only See as Far as You," 1976.
"A Whole Lotta Things to Sing About," 1976.
"I'll Be Leavin' Alone," 1977.
"More to Me," 1977.
"When I Stop Leavin' I'll Be Gone," 1978.
"Burgers and Fries," 1978.
"You're My Jamaica," 1979.
"Where Do I Put Her Memory?" 1979.
"Missin' You," 1979.
"Honky Tonk Blues," 1980.
"You Win Again," 1980.
"Roll on Mississippi," 1981.
"Never Been So Loved," 1981.
"I'm Missin' Mississippi," 1984.
"I'm Gonna Love Her on the Radio," Capitol, 1988.
"Shouldn't It Be Easier Than This," Capitol, 1988.
"Amy's Eyes," Capitol, 1989.

Also recorded the singles "Is Anybody Goin' to San Antone" and "Mountain of Love."

LPs; on RCA Records, except as noted

Country Charley Pride, 1966.
Pride of Country Music, 1967.
Make Mine Country, 1968.
Songs of Pride . . . Charley, That Is, 1968.
Charley Pride in Person at Panther Hall, 1968.
The Sensational Charley Pride, 1969.
The Best of Charley Pride, 1969.
Just Plain Charley, 1970.
Christmas in My Home Town, 1970.
From Me to You, 1971.
Did You Think to Pray? 1971.
I'm Just Me, 1971.
Charley Pride Sings Heart Songs, 1971.
The Best of Charley Pride, Vol. 2, 1972.
A Sunshiny Day With Charley Pride, 1972.
Songs of Love by Charley Pride, 1973.
Sweet Country, 1973.
Amazing Love, 1973.
Country Feelin', 1974.
Pride of America, 1974.
Charley, 1975.
The Happiness of Having You, 1975.
Sunday Morning With Charley Pride, 1976.
She's Just an Old Love Turned Memory, 1977.
Someone Loves You, Honey, 1978.
When I Stop Leavin' I'll Be Gone, 1979.
You're My Jamaica, 1979.
There's a Little Bit of Hank in Me, 1980.
The Power of Love, 1984.
I'm Gonna Love Her on the Radio, Capitol, 1988.
Moody Woman, Capitol, 1989.

Sources

Ebony, September 1984.
Newsday, November 15, 1971.
People, June 9, 1980.
Time, May 6, 1974.

—Elizabeth Thomas

Public Enemy

Rap group

Public Enemy is widely acknowledged to be the most important group to emerge in the rap medium since the mid-1980s. Self-proclaimed "prophets of rage," the three main members of Public Enemy have sought to become a major force of social change, disturbing white America's complacency with highly-charged political statements reminiscent of the 1960s Black Power movement. In the *Chicago Tribune*, Greg Kot notes that PE "is not just a great rap group, but one of the best rock bands on the planet—black or otherwise." The critic adds that the group courageously "challenges listeners to step into their world."

The world Public Enemy describes is not a pretty one. It is, quite simply, the United States as seen by young black men—a land of limited opportunities, drug deaths, and active oppression by a fearful white majority. Until recently, few rappers chose to address these issues as part of their work, but PE does so as its highest priority. As Richard Harrington puts it in the *Washington Post*, the PE message is "a rap-opera reflecting America's social malaise and Public Enemy's ongoing challenge to political and economic systems that have dehumanized and exploited minorities for centuries." *New York Times* contributor Peter Watrous observes that, almost singlehandedly, "the band has jerked rap music into an active political sphere. The music outdistances other

political pop with both its urgency and its visionary approach to the dance floor. And the group has made pop music that is vital in the contemporary debate about race in American culture for the first time since the 1960s."

The principal members of Public Enemy are all from Long Island, New York. The group is headed by rapper Chuck D and his partner Flavor Flav. Much of the pulsing background accompaniment is provided by DJ Terminator X and a production team that includes Hank Shocklee, Carl Ryder, Eric Sadler, and Keith Shocklee. The group cut its first album in 1987 and released it through Def Jam, a division of Columbia devoted specifically to rap music.

Public Enemy burst on the scene at a time when rap was moving into the mainstream as entertainment for blacks and whites. What Public Enemy has brought to the medium since 1987 is a sense of higher purpose—the hardly novel notion that music should have a message for its listeners. Group members have been influenced by many of black America's most controversial spokesmen, including Malcolm X and the leader of the Nation of Islam, Louis Farrakhan. Needless to say, this has meant rough riding for the young rappers as their public utterances and album lyrics have been combed for anti-Semitic and other racist remarks.

In May of 1989, a satellite member of Public Enemy, Richard "Professor Griff" Griffin, gave an interview to the *Washington Times* in which he made several disparaging remarks about Jews. The fallout from that interview stunned the other band members, who clearly stated that they held no malice for any racial or religious group. Professor Griff was asked to leave the band (he had been a backup performer at concerts), but then was reinstated when the members decided not to cave in to social pressure. Public Enemy subsequently released a single, "Welcome to the Terrordome," that chronicled their frustrating battle with the media. Some of the lyrics in that work were attacked too for anti-Semitism, especially the lines "Crucifixion ain't no fiction; so-called chosen, frozen."

Chuck D answered the charges against his band in a profile for the *Los Angeles Times*. "I'm not anti-Semitic," he said. "I think it is a waste of time being anti-anything. But I also won't let this [controversy] keep me, as a black nationalist, from talking about problems of the black people and asking questions about how these problems came about. What is happening now is that people are . . . reading racism or anti-Semitic thoughts in everything we do. . . . I'm not a racist, but I am inquisitive and I hope that when I keep asking questions, people don't respond to them by saying it's

For the Record. . .

Membership includes **Chuck D** (Charles Ridenhour), **Flavor Flav** (William Drayton), and **DJ Terminator X** (Norman Rogers); group formed on Long Island, N.Y., in mid-1980s, signed with Def Jam Records (a division of Columbia), 1986, released first album, *Yo! Bum Rush the Show,* 1987. Group's song "Fight the Power" was featured in the film *Do the Right Thing,* 1989.

Awards: Best album award from *Village Voice* national critics poll, 1988, for *It Takes a Nation of Millions To Hold Us Back.*

Addresses: *Record company*—Def Jam, CBS Records, 51 West 52d St., New York, NY 10019.

a racist question because there is no such thing as a racist question. There are only racist answers."

The Public Enemy platform asserts that, genetically speaking, all people are descended from black ancestors (a theory long accepted by human evolutionists) and that whites oppress blacks out of a suppressed fear of this fact. In its music Public Enemy attacks the sources of that fear and the machinery used to keep blacks at bay. *Commentary* correspondent Terry Teachout writes that in the group's songs, "policemen kill blacks casually and deliberately, and the federal government, usually personified by Ronald Reagan or, more recently, George Bush, is the mortal enemy of all blacks. White racism, one and indivisible, is the principle of American social organization, all blacks are its perpetual objects; white and black America are in a state of de-facto war."

It comes as no surprise that three black men under thirty might feel this way about America. It is also not surprising that Public Enemy concerts—in which the band is surrounded by plastic Uzi-toting uniform-clad dancers—are received enthusiastically by young blacks. The message is not merely one of rage, however. Public Enemy exhorts its listeners to learn something about their culture and to disdain the tools of enslavement such as gold jewelry, drugs, and designer clothing. Chuck D told the *Los Angeles Times:* "Rappers can do a lot of good because we have control of the media and that's why we're not liked because never before has the black man or so many black males spoken their opinion on so many things."

In a review of the PE album *Fear of a Black Planet,* *Rolling Stone* correspondent Alan Light writes: "Public

Enemy has never aimed for anything less than a comprehensive view of contemporary black America. . . . Chuck D and Flavor Flav and DJ Terminator X complement this ambition with stunning maturity and sophistication." Most critics agree that Chuck D commands one of rap's most compelling voices, with his harsh and resonating sermons on rage and pride. The group's multi-layered accompanying sounds—the work of Terminator X and his crew—are dense and insistent, occasionally showing a moment of humor. Watrous describes the PE sound as "an unattended machine gone berserk. It's the sound of urban alienation, where silence doesn't exist and sensory stimulation is oppressive and predatory. But Public Enemy has conquered it. Through the mess comes the redemptive beat; the group makes some of the best dance records around."

The Public Enemy song "Fight the Power" was featured in the 1989 Spike Lee film *Do the Right Thing,* principally because Lee finds Public Enemy's work an accurate reflection/reaction to America in the 1990s. Critics see a new level of understanding in recent Public Enemy raps, a more pragmatic worldview born of their conflicts with the media. "Public Enemy is looking to the future," writes Light, "not with apocalyptic despair but with fiery eyes firmly fixed on the prize. The group's determination and realism, its devotion to activism and booty shaking, make [its work] a welcome, bracing triumph."

Selected discography

Yo! Bum Rush the Show, Def Jam, 1987.
It Takes a Nation of Millions To Hold Us Back, Def Jam, 1988.
Fear of a Black Planet, Def Jam, 1990.

Sources

Chicago Tribune, April 15, 1990.
Commentary, March 1990.
Detroit News, May 14, 1990.
Ebony, January 1989; June 1990.
Los Angeles Times, February 4, 1990.
Mother Jones, February/March 1990.
Newsweek, March 19, 1990.
New York Times, April 22, 1990.
People, March 5, 1990
Rolling Stone, October 19, 1989; November 16, 1989; May 17, 1990.
Time, February 5, 1990.
Washington Post, April 15, 1990.

—Anne Janette Johnson

Martha Reeves

Singer

As a member of the Motown label's Martha and the Vandellas, Martha Reeves was a large part of what *Ebony* magazine described as "the rousing pop sound that rocked Detroit and shook the world." Her lead vocals enriched a string of hits during the 1960s, including "Dancing in the Streets," "Heatwave," and "Jimmy Mack." After the final break-up of the Vandellas in the 1970s, Reeves became a solo artist; though she never achieved the same success as she had with the group, nostalgia for the pop music of the 1960s helped her regain her status as a popular concert attraction during the 1980s.

Reeves went to work at Motown Records in Detroit, Michigan, without much thought of becoming a singer. Rather, she served as a secretary for the company shortly after she left high school. She occasionally sang lyrics onto demonstration tapes to enable Motown's artists to learn new songs, and when one of the company's regular studio back-up singers was too ill to participate in a recording session, Reeves was allowed to take her place. From there it was only a short step to becoming a regular Motown background vocalist; with Rosalind Ashford and Annette Sterling, who had at-

tended high school with her, Reeves contributed her talents to the records of Marvin Gaye and other Motown proteges.

By 1963, the Motown executives felt that Reeves, Ashford, and Sterling had enough talent to form their own group, particularly with Reeves's strong voice on lead vocals. The women were signed to the Gordy label, a Motown subsidiary, and quickly released the hit single "Come and Get These Memories," which was soon followed by an even bigger smash, "Heat Wave." Though she hadn't aimed for that kind of success, Reeves told *Ebony:* "I sang because it made me happy *and* helped me to help my family. It allowed me to develop from a little girl in the ghetto to someone who could pay my bills."

After "Heat Wave," Sterling quit the Vandellas and was replaced by Betty Kelly. This personnel change failed to have much impact on the trio's hitmaking ability; with 1964's "Dancing in the Street," Martha and the Vandellas continued to trademark the rougher, more raucous rhythm and blues sound that distinguished them from the Supremes and other Motown female groups. According to Geoffrey Stokes in *Rock of Ages: The Rolling Stone History of Rock and Roll,* "Dancing in the Street"'s catchy beat was produced, in part at least, by one of the producers banging on the floor with some snow chains from an automobile.

Hits like "Nowhere to Run," "I'm Ready for Love," and "Honey Chile" took Reeves and the Vandellas through to the late 1960s. Kelly was replaced by Reeves's sister Lois in 1968, but the following year saw Reeves sidelined by illness. When the group reformed in 1970, it was composed of Martha and Lois Reeves and another woman named Sandra Tilley. Though this set of Vandellas scored some minor hits on the rhythm and blues charts, including "Bless You," "I Gotta Let You Go," and "Tear It on Down" during the early 1970s, they could not match the success of Reeves's earlier years. She obtained her release from Motown, and broke up the Vandellas in 1972.

The success of Reeves's early solo career was no match for that of her heyday with the Vandellas, either. She bounced from record company to record company—MCA, Arista, and Fantasy all held her contract at one time or another—and only scored a minor hit in 1974 with "Power of Love." According to *Ebony,* Reeves experienced problems with depression and drug abuse during this period, but was healed by what that magazine termed a "religious rebirth" in 1977. Not long afterward, in the 1980s, nostalgia for her music brought her better luck with her career. She was also helped by

For the Record. . .

B orn July 18, 1941, in Detroit, Michigan; children: Eric. Pop vocalist; worked as a secretary for Motown Records in Detroit, Michigan, during the early 1960s; studio backup singer for Motown, 1962-63; lead singer for Martha and the Vandellas, 1963-69, 1970-72; solo recording artist, 1974-80, and concert performer, 1974—. Featured in the cable television special "Legendary Ladies of Rock 'n' Roll," about 1987.

Addresses: *Residence*—Detroit, Michigan; *Record company*—Fantasy Records, 1775 Broadway, Suite 617, New York, NY 10019.

other artists doing remakes of her Motown hits, such as Linda Ronstadt's cutting a version of "Heat Wave." Reeves told *Ebony:* "I really appreciate them and love them for doing it."

Reeves continues to tour England and tours the United States with other former Motown stars, including Eddie Kendricks and Mary Wells. Commenting on one such excursion in July, 1987, she announced to *Ebony:* "It was fantastic. I am very proud that after all these years, we could still produce the quality of sound and remember all the things we were taught—the things that still make us happen." And, apparently, she no longer needs back-up singers. "Now that everybody knows the music, the people in the audience are the Vandellas," she explained in *Ebony.*

Selected discography

Singles; with the Vandellas; on the Gordy label

"Come and Get These Memories," 1963.
"Heat Wave," 1963.
"Quicksand," 1963.
"Dancing in the Street," 1964.
"Nowhere to Run," 1965.
"My Baby Loves Me," c. 1966.
"I'm Ready for Love," 1966.
"Jimmy Mack," c. 1968.
"Honey Chile," c. 1968.
"Bless You," 1971.
"I Gotta Let You Go," 1971.
"In and Out of My Life," 1972.
"Tear It on Down," 1972.

Solo albums

Martha Reeves (includes "Power of Love"), MCA, 1974.
The Rest of My Life, Arista, 1976.
We Meet Again, Fantasy, 1978.
Gotta Keep Moving, Fantasy, 1980.

Sources

Books

Ward, Ed, Geoffrey Stokes, and Ken Tucker, *Rock of Ages: The Rolling Stone History of Rock and Roll,* Summit Books, 1986.

Periodicals

Ebony, February 1988.
Jet, July 17, 1989.

—*Elizabeth Thomas*

Jean
Ritchie

Folk singer/songwriter, guitarist, dulcimer player; folk scholar

When Jean Ritchie moved from eastern Kentucky to New York City forty-odd years ago, she brought along 300 folk songs. Singing them in her pretty, untrained voice while accompanying herself on mountain dulcimer, she sparked a nationwide love for traditional music. Today she's revered as a folk-music matriarch throughout the English-speaking world. As the *New York Times* observed, "Miss Ritchie Is something of a national treasure whose clear soprano ballads have [long] thrilled 'folkies.'"

Focusing on music from England, Ireland, Scotland, and the United States, Ritchie has discovered countless traditional songs that might otherwise have been forgotten, traced their origins, and preserved them in her many books and recordings. She's equally renowned for her own songs, several of which—"Blue Diamond Mine," "Black Waters," and "The L&N Don't Stop Here Anymore"—have become classics. Crucial to her sound is the simple, sweet drone of the dulcimer, a stretched-out fiddle that originated in the Appalachian Mountains. She's widely credited with popularizing the instrument: because of her concerts, recordings books and workshops, there are now dulcimer players

and festivals as far afield as Germany, Japan, and Jerusalem. "I used to tell people how easy it is to play, and they wouldn't believe me, she told the *Boston Globe* in her soft southern voice. "I couldn't understand why people just didn't pick it up and play it. I learned it from my dad, just from listening." Joseph Hickerson, head of the Archive of Folk Culture in Washington, D.C., told the *Courier-Journal* that Jean is "probably the single most important factor in the revival of the Appalachian dulcimer as a popular instrument."

Jean Ritchie was born in 1922 in Viper, Kentucky, which is the heart of Southern Appalachia. According to local history, the first Ritchies came from Scotland in 1768 to settle the area. "They continued to farm the rugged hillsides," Ritchie wrote in a press biography referring to her family, "and to entertain themselves with the old ballads, love plaints and play-parties handed down from their Scottish, Irish and English ancestors." Jean was born the youngest of 14 children. As a child, she watched her father, Balis, plow his fields and plant his crops with handmade tools and her mother, Abigail, make butter with a wooden churn. Though her childhood coincided with the advent of commercial country music, the Cumberland Mountains surrounding her home remained as isolated culturally from the rest of the country as it was geographically. "When Jean was growing up," she wrote in her press bio, "the favorites were not the new 'hillbilly' tunes . . . but 'Barbry Ellen,' 'Over the River, Charlie,' 'Sourwood Mountain,' 'Lord Randal' . . . People made up songs, too—news accounts of hangings, elections, groundhog hunts, elopements, feuds—all meaningful, each a living part of the growth of a people."

Ritchie's childhood is beautifully recounted in her autobiographical first book, *The Singing Family of the Cumberlands*. Writing in the dialect of her Kentucky brethren, she described how music was a vital accompaniment to work, family gatherings, bedtime, socializing, and virtually every other part of their lives. One of Jean's favorite music-making rituals, as she recounted in *Singing Family* was "singing the moon up." It took place summer evenings after dinner, when the whole family would gather on the L-shaped porch of their four-room house.

As she grew up, Jean pursued the two interests that would later merge in her career—Anglo-American folk music and its history. She was also fascinated by the sociological background of the music. "It was always a wonder to me how families living close to one another could sing the same song and sing it so different," she wrote in *Singing Family of the Cumberlands*. "Or how one family would sing a song among themselves for years, and their neighbor family never knew that song

For the Record...

Born December 8, 1922, in Viper, Kentucky; daughter of Balis (a farmer) and Abigail Ritchie; youngest of 14 children; married George Pickow (a photographer), 1950; children: Peter (born 1954), Jon (born 1958). *Education:* Attended Cumberland Junior College; University of Kentucky, B.A. in social work.

Worked at the Henry Street Settlement (an inner-city school for children), 1947; began to perform locally, singing, playing dulcimer and guitar; discovered by folklorist Alan Lomax, who recorded her songs for the Archive of the American Folksong at the Library of Congress; performed in the first Newport Folk Festival, 1959 (one of seven original directors); numerous international concerts and festival appearances, recordings, books, TV and radio shows, and dulcimer workshops; has represented U.S. folk-music history at international folk conferences, and served a three-year term on the folklore panel of the National Endowment for the Arts; president of Geordie Music Publishing Company, vice-president of Greenhays Recordings, partner in Folklife Productions, all New York-based companies created by her and her family. Appeared in a 1989 PBS documentary (with Bill Moyers) on the song "Amazing Grace," and in a cameo role in the 1989 film, *Next of Kin*.

Awards: Recipient of numerous awards, including University of Kentucky founders Day Award; Phi Beta Kappa Certificate of Honor; Fulbright Scholarship, 1952; *Rolling Stone* Critic's Award and *Melody Maker* Award, both for best folk album, 1977, for *None But One*; proclamations from the City of Lexington, Kentucky, the State of Kentucky, and the U.S. Congress, along with a Capitol flag and letter from President Reagan honoring her and her family's contribution to music, 1986.

Addresses: *Office*—Folklife Productions, 7A Locust Ave., Port Washington, NY 11050.

at all. Most curious of all was how one member of a family living in a certain community could have almost a completely different set of songs than his cousins living a few miles away."

Commenting on her family's music-making, she illustrated the haphazard way in which folk music tends to spread: "Because we Ritchies loved to sing so well, we always listened to people singing songs we didn't know, and we caught many good ones that way. Soon we learned from many different folks and without trying

to, so when someone asks us, 'Where'd you learn that one?' we just can't say for sure. But with others we can name the very person that sang them to us."

At Cumberland Junior College, Ritchie studied teaching, the profession chosen by most of her sisters. After a brief teaching stint during her freshman year at a one-room school, however, she decided it wasn't for her. She enrolled at the University of Kentucky to study social work. Graduating with highest honors and a Phi Beta Kappa key, she moved to New York in 1947 to take a job at Henry Street Settlement, an inner-city school on Manhattan's Lower East Side. As part of her teaching, she would play party songs for the children, accompanying herself on guitar and dulcimer.

Both students and co-workers became intrigued by her clear, ringing voice, the strange, sweet dulcimer, and the enchanting Anglo-American songs. Without meaning to, Ritchie was building a following. She began giving small concerts at the school and playing at parties in the city. At one of her performances, she met her future husband, photographer George Pickow. At first, she told the *Courier-Review,* Pickow "thought I was an act, that I was putting on my accent and I wasn't for real." Soon he realized otherwise, and became— and remains—one of her most ardent fans. They married in 1950, and a few years later moved to the suburbs of Long Island.

Around this time Ritchie met Alan Lomax, the preeminent folklorist who had fostered the careers of Woody Guthrie, Leadbelly, and other noted contributors to America's music. In the *Courier-Journal* Lomax recounted that meeting: "I was in an office about 14 floors up on 57th Street working on a folk music project for Decca Records when this young lady came in—this beautiful, golden-haired woman from the mountains with a gorgeous voice. She said her friends had told her she should sing for me and she wondered If she could, so I said, 'Yes, sing.' She hadn't gone very far when suddenly the tears came to my eyes and I was crying at the beauty. In my mind she's one of the finest pure mountain singers ever discovered."

In 1948 Lomax arranged for Ritchie to give her first formal concert, which was held at Columbia University. He also recognized the importance of documenting her work, and arranged for her to record some of her songs for the Archive of the American Folk Song at the Library of Congress. "It's the rare person who know's how the flow of the poem enhances the melody of the song," he told the *Courier-Journal*. "Jean has a pure, instinctive knowledge for that. The true folk singer sings a new tune for every verse. All folk singers, if they're good, do this, but Jean handles it with extraordinary grace. . . . There is no one else in her category. She has devoted herself to her heritage and the struggle to convey it in all its majesty and beauty."

The 1950s were a time of rich artistic and scholarly growth for Ritchie. In 1952, on a Fulbright Scholarship, she traveled through England, Ireland, and Scotland to trace the roots of certain folk songs. Pickow accompanied her, and together they made several documentary films on the subject. Meanwhile, she decided to document her childhood, as those years are part and parcel of her music. The result was the aforementioned *Singing Family of the Cumberlands*, now considered an American classic. Skillfully written, the book offers not only a charming story but valuable information for folk scholars and performers—the music and lyrics of 42 songs, as well as comments on interpretation and how a particular song was learned and preserved through the generations. In 1959 she was chosen to help direct the first Newport Folk Festival. She also performed, sharing the stage with Pete Seeger, Odetta, Flatt and Scruggs, John Jacob Niles, Sonny Terry, and Brownie McGhee.

The 1960s saw a great commercial folk revival, and Ritchie was among its leaders. As she continued to record and publish books on folk music, she grew even stronger as a performer. In an interview with the *Courier-Journal* she recalled a telling moment during the 1969 Newport Folk Festival. Arlo Guthrie was onstage, and the audience was yelling for him to sing his hit song, "Alice's Restaurant Massacree." Guthrie, who was tired of the song, refused, but the audience wouldn't relent. "Everybody was stamping and yelling for 'Alice,'" Jean recounted. "It was getting ugly, and that's when Pete [Seeger] pushed me out on the stage and said, 'Close the festival, Jean. Sing something gentle.' I was scared to death. So I started singing 'Amazing Grace' the old way. I lined it out and everything. And you know, it calmed them right down. It's a truly powerful song."

Though the folk scene had already peaked by the 1970s, Ritchie continued to build her career. She began to prove herself as a songwriter, with tunes so true to the music's history that they were often mistaken as traditional. With her 1977 album *None But One,* she strayed a bit from the purist path, using electric guitar and drums alongside authentic instrumentation, as well as highly polished production. Her departure, however, was to good effect. Featuring sons Peter and Jon Ritchie on vocals, as well as several noted folk musicians, the LP won her a well-deserved *Rolling Stone* Critics' Award.

Ritchie often performs side-by-side with Pickow. While she sings and tells stories, he shows photo essays and slide shows that he has created of her family and hometown. Pickow has not missed a single concert of his wife's. From their home in Port Washington, New York, Ritchie and Pickow run Greenhays, their own record label, as well as Geordie Music, which publishes her songs, and Folklife Productions, which markets her books and videos on folk culture. During the warm months, they spend time in Viper, Kentucky. "We built a house back in the hills out of some old relatives' cabins," she told *Long Island Monthly*. "Virgin timber, old hand-hewn logs. It's good to go back and get into the swing of talking Kentucky—be a hillbilly, a mountaineer." That part of Ritchie's life can be seen in *Next of Kin,* the 1989 film that's set not far from her birthplace. Ritchie appears in her debut role as Patrick Swayze's on-screen aunt. "I got to sing one of Mama's old hymns, 'Leaning On Everlasting Arms,'" she told *Long Island Monthly.*

In an interview with *New York Newsday,* Ritchie spoke of a woman who was singing songs by Joan Baez and other folk musicians until Ritchie encouraged her to research her own family's folk heritage. To the woman's

> *"The tears came to my eyes and I was crying at the beauty. In my mind she's one of the finest pure mountain singers ever discovered."*

amazement, she discovered that her grandfather and his brother played fiddles for dances near their home. "She started collecting folk songs and now has hundreds of them," Jean reported. "Like others, she thought she had to import folk music from people like me. She never thought it was right there in her own background. That's one of my missions . . . to get people to sing their own music . . . to take an interest in their local backgrounds and heritage. It really is something that grows and grows once you get started." Ritchie added that she becomes distressed when people tell her they don't sing because their voices are untrained. "I want to take them by the shoulders and shake them. I never would have had any lullabies sung to me if my mother had to study first."

Selected discography

Jean Ritchie at Home, Pacific Cascade, 1971.
None But One, Greenhays, 1977.

High Hills and Mountains, Greenhays, 1979.
The Most Dulcimer, Greenhays, 1984.
O Love is Teasin', (reissue), Elektra/Asylum, 1985.
Kentucky Christmas, Old and New, 1988.

Writings

Singing Family of the Cumberlands (illustrated by Maurice Sendak), 1955; University Press of Kentucky, 1988.
The Swapping Song Book, Henry Walck, Inc., 1952; revised, 1964 (available from Folklife Productions, 7A Locust Ave., Port Washington, NY 11050).
The Dulcimer Book, 0ak Publications, 1963.
Folk Songs of the Southern Appalachians, Oak Publications, 1965.
The Dulcimer People, Oak Publications, 1974.
Celebration of Life, Geordie Music, 1971.

Other Projects

Wrote and performed theme song for *Caring and Sharing,* a documentary (made by husband George Pickow and son Jon Pickow) about underprivileged children in Long Island.

Sources

Boston Globe, November 12, 1987.
Courier-Journal Magazine (Louisville, Kentucky), July 23, 1989.
Frets, April 1980; August 1989.
Long Island Monthly, January 1990.
New York Newsday, February 13, 1980.
New York Times, January 11,1980.
Rolling Stone, December 29, 1977.
Press biography (available from Folklife Productions).

—Kyle Kevorkian

Run-D.M.C.

Rap group

Run-D.M.C.'s musical identity is easy to pinpoint— pure, city-bred rap. But the group's message is a little harder to figure. The first group to come to genuine superstardom under the banner of rap music, a sparse, tough-talking street sound that features staccato rhymes and a heavy beat, Run-D.M.C. uses a violent, gangster image to get across its mostly peaceful, anti-drug, anti-gang message. When the band's 1986 LP *Raising Hell* rose to Number 3 on the pop charts and sold more than three million copies, the contradictions between the group's oft-stated good intentions and its often violent repercussions came to a head when violence erupted at several of Run-D.M.C.'s sold-out tour dates. The backlash and controversy that followed, including several condemnations of both Run-D.M.C. and rap music itself, prompted an exhaustive discussion of both the causes of street violence and the proper channels of communication that are needed to condemn it.

But Joe "Run" Simmons, chief lyricist and spokesman for Run-D.M.C., sees no contradiction in his group's appeal. He says that what young, disadvantaged kids

need is precisely the kind of message he can give them. "A lot of kids who like us are impressionable," Simmons told *New York* magazine's Peter Blauner. "But they listen to me *because* I act tough and cool. I got a lot of juice with them. It's like I'm cooler than their teacher, I'm cooler than their mother, I'm cooler than their father. So when we say don't take drugs and stay in school, they listen." Adds Johnny Johnson, a Run-D.M.C. fan, in the same article: "They got the power . . . they're like homeboys. If they came on stage in suits and ties, it wouldn't have the same impact."

Still, despite Simmons's insistence, on stage, in interviews, and in his song lyrics, for kids to stay in school, keep away from drugs, and avoid the trappings of gangs, the tone Run-D.M.C. sets has an undeniably violent quality about it. Whether or not that tone is needed to reach the group's audience is a question for sociologists, but from their all-black outfits, gangster-style hats and swinging, gold-rope chains, to the way Simmons characteristically hurls his microphone stand around stage, the group comes across very aggressively. They even made a film called *Tougher Than Leather,* which, during the planning stages, the group described as a "cross between *48 Hrs* and *Rambo*" and which involved a plot of violent revenge. "In our new movie," said the group's on-stage DJ Jason "Jam

Master Jay" Mizell in *New York,* "people are gonna get shot in the face."

Despite Run-D.M.C.'s hardened street image and strong appeal among ghetto youth, all three members of the band grew up quite comfortably in a middle-class section of Queens, New York. Simmons actually was led into the recording business by his older brother, Russell, who had helped establish such pioneer rap acts as Kurtis Blow and Grandmaster Flash and the Furious Five by booking them in Harlem clubs through his company, Rush Productions. Blow and Russell Simmons were close friends, and young Joe Simmons would tag along with the two of them, particularly fascinated with Blow's distinctive rap style and record-scratching technique. Soon, Joe was being called the "Son of Kurtis Blow," and was even allowed to perform a few of his own raps during Blow's concerts. "He was a slick kid," Blow recalled in *New York* of those days in the late 1970s. "Always running his mouth. A nice kid,

> *"It's like I'm cooler than their teacher, I'm cooler than their mother, I'm cooler than their father. So when we say don't take drugs and stay in school, they listen," said Simmons in* New York *magazine.*

though. I taught him a lot, but he was good, really good."

Only fifteen years old at the time of this first exposure to the glamorous music business, Simmons could have easily been tempted to drop out of school. But his father, Daniel, a New York Board of Education employee, was adamant that all his sons finish high school and find something useful to do. Joe enrolled at LaGuardia Communiity College to study, of all things, mortuary science, and it was while studying a cadaver in one class that he came up with a new rap: "One thing I know is that life is short/ so listen up home boy, give this a thought/ The next time someone's teaching why don't you get taught?/ It's like that/ and that's the way it is."

Simmons then showed the rap to his best friend since childhood, Darryl "D.M.C." McDaniels, who was then studying at St. John's University. The two friends extended the rhyme into a full-scale rap and, together, recorded "It's Like That" as a single on the small, independent Profile label. The single sold more than 250,000 copies in 1983, and the group followed it up with the equally successful single "Hard Times." It was at this time, under the eye of Russell Simmons, that the band adopted its now customary gangster style of dress, and it was not entirely without reason. "That's a lot of the appeal," Russell told *New York*. "It's not for the Bill Cosbys. People talk about how there aren't black role models around, but what they mean is there aren't enough white black people on television. Rap groups like Run-D.M.C. aren't like that. They talk directly to the kids. It's more authentic."

Ironically, it was in the wake of Run-D.M.C.'s greatest success that the group began coming under increasing fire from the media. Their third LP, *Raising Hell*, skyrocketed up the charts on the strength of the immensely successful single "Walk This Way," which was originally recorded in 1977 by the heavy-metal group Aerosmith. But rap purists immediately cried foul, claiming that the group had gone "soft" by recording a song popular with white rock audiences. Simmons was outraged with this claim, telling *Rolling Stone* that "I made that record because I used to rap over it when I was twelve. There were lots of hip-hoppers rapping over rock when I was a kid. . .As for my trying to get more radio play, I'll never. . . I always say what I feel."

But the real trouble started when Run-D.M.C. embarked on a fifteen-week, sixty-two-city tour to promote the album. Although most of the concerts were peaceful, positive events, violence erupted at several locations, such as Pittsburgh, New York, and especially Long Beach, California, where more than forty people were injured when rioting broke out before Run-D.M.C. reached the stage. The violence turned out to be a turf war between L.A.'s two notorious gangs, the Bloods and the Crips—which is exactly the kind of thing that Run-D.M.C. claims to be against. "We like their rhymin'," a gang member told *Rolling Stone*. "It's hip, it says something to me, and I like their clothes—it's B-boy [gang] style to the highest degree. So gangs want to see them, and when you put all these groups together, you're lookin' for trouble."

Which only leaves Simmons all the more exasperated. Clearly worn out by all the negative publicity he's received, and with the way Run-D.M.C.'s message has been misconstrued, Simmons tried to sum up the precise reason why violence has been so close on the heels of rap music. "The broke crackheads can make money if they come out and beat up on my little fan who's got $30 in his pocket because he wants a Run-D.M.C. T-shirt or a booklet," he told *Newsweek*. "Which leaves me hurt. They come to make money. They come to fight. They're scum." A family man with a wife and a daughter, Simmons, like the other Run-D.M.C. members, remains as committed to rap as he is to his family and his community. The band members still live in their old Queens neighborhood, and are trying to make a stand there. "I don't want money," Simmons told *Rolling Stone*. "I've made money. Right now I don't need ten cars, but I have enough money for fifty cars. I don't want anything. I'm so happy. I look at my daughter sleeping. I kiss her while she's asleep. I sit with a pen and see if I can write something. If not, I go shine up my '66 Oldsmobile, gas it up, and drive my wife to work."

Selected discography

Run-D.M.C., Profile.
King of Rock, Profile.
Raising Hell, Profile, 1986.
Tougher Than Leather, Profile, 1988.

Sources

New York, November 17, 1986.
Newsweek, September 1, 1986.
People, December 22, 1986; June 22, 1987.
Rolling Stone, December 4, 1986.

—David Collins

Joe Satriani

Guitarist, songwriter, singer

In 1988, Joe Satriani blasted into public consciousness with an entrance that was as unexpected as it was grand. For the past fifteen years he inhabited the crowded world of lesser-known rock guitarists, honing his virtuosity away from the celebrity limelight. But with his second album, *Surfing with the Alien,* he rose from the multitudes to a place where Jimi Hendrix, Eric Clapton, Eddie Van Halen, and other guitar greats once stood. In fact, by the end of the year Satriani had already cut some deep marks into the history of rock guitar.

Surfing shot to Number 29 on the charts, becoming the first rock guitar instrumental LP to enter the Top 40 since Jeff Beck's 1980 *There and Back.* (Remarkably, it remained at that spot for seventy-seven weeks.) In the nineteenth annual readers poll of *Guitar Player Magazine,* he won the categories of best overall guitarist, best new talent, and best guitar album—the only guitarist other than Beck (in 1976) and the late Stevie Ray Vaughan (1983) to score a triple victory in the poll's history. To the critics, the meaning of all of this was clear: The rock guitar messiah of the '90s had arrived.

Satriani is indeed a guitar hero. "He has amazing chops," declared Jas Obrecht in *Guitar Player,* "unorthodox approaches to whammy and one- and two-handed techniques, and a talent for melodies that venture beyond the common." What gives wings to his music is a desire to transcend everyday life. His mission, as he told *Guitar Player* in a tongue-in-cheek nod to the TV series "Star Trek," is "to boldly go where no man has gone before. To seek peace and harmony." His songs on *Surfing,* though wordless, explore the realms of science fiction—one of his favorite authors is Kurt Vonnegut, Jr.—and the supernatural. "Echo," for instance, "deals with the reincarnation of lost loved ones," as he explains in the liner notes; in other songs on the album, he seeks to evoke dreams, "the journey of our spirits through time," and the site of Jesus's execution. On the whole, his songs are aptly described by both the title of his previous album—*Not of This Earth*—and the name of his music publishing company, Strange, Beautiful Music.

As a child Satriani grew up in a musical environment. Each of his four older siblings played instruments; he himself took up piano and then drums. It was a Hendrix solo, though, that ignited his passion for guitar. He was eleven at the time, he told the *Los Angeles Times,* and "Purple Haze" came on the radio. "It's still vivid when I think about it sometimes," he recalled, referring to the guitar solo, "like it happened this morning or something. His music was overwhelming. I felt it deep inside. He was talking to me. It opened up a new world for me. I had tunnel vision all of a sudden. I could only focus on

For the Record. . .

Born c. 1957 in Carle Place, New York; married; wife's name, Rubina. *Education:* Attended Five Towns College.

Guitarist and songwriter; began teaching himself guitar and playing local clubs on Long Island, N.Y., at the age of 14; at age 17 began teaching guitar; played with pop-rock trio the Squares in Berkeley, Calif., 1979-84; recorded and toured with Mick Jagger's world tour, 1988; solo performer. Studio work includes collaborating with drummers Tony Williams and Danny Gottlieb, writing commissioned pieces for PBS, Dole Pineapple, and Otari, singing back-up vocals for Crowded House, co-producing Possessed's EP *Eyes of Horror,* and contributing to the soundtrack for the 1989 film *Say Anything.*

Awards: Named best overall guitarist and best new talent, and cited for best guitar album in *Guitar Player Magazine* reader's poll, 1988.

Addresses: *Home*—Berkeley, Calif. *Office*—c/o Relativity Records, 187-07 Henderson Ave., Hollis, N.Y. 11423.

the radio. It was like there was this tuning fork in my body waiting for someone to come along and play the right note and make me vibrate." The full impact of that experience hit him about three years later, on the day that Hendrix died. "My life, my purpose was different," he told the *Los Angeles Times.* "After I heard about his death, I went home and played my Hendrix records. Then I *had* to play." Abandoning his drums and quitting the school football team, he turned instead to a Hagstrom III solid-body guitar. His parents, recognizing the seriousness of his new interest, supported and encouraged him. "My father taught me discipline," he told *Pulse!* "If he knew I didn't practice one day, he'd wake me up in the middle of the night and march me downstairs in my pajamas to sit there and practice."

It wasn't long before Satriani was playing local gigs on Long Island. At home, during marathon practice sessions, he would play along with records, absorbing styles and techniques from Hendrix, Beck, Led Zeppelin, the Beatles, the Who, the Stones, and Johnny Winter. Though he never took guitar lessons, high school studies in music theory enabled him, at the age of seventeen, to take on a few students—one of whom was his classmate and future guitar great Steve Vai. His background in music theory carried a second bonus: "When I got to Five Towns College to study music," he told *Guitar Player,* "there was absolutely no point in my being there." Dropping out and confused about what musical direction to take, he tried a variety of things:

lessons with jazz pianist Lennie Tristano for a couple of months; a cross-country tour with a several-piece dance band called Justice; a brief stay, mostly spent practicing, in Los Angeles; and then, desiring a complete change of pace, six months in Japan. His time in Japan, he told *Rolling Stone,* refreshed his attitude and boosted his playing: "I lived in a tiny little house way up in the mountains in Kyoto. It was great for my playing because I only played by myself and it was just Japanese nature all around me. It was starting all over, and there were no distractions, no one telling me that what I was playing wasn't relevant."

Returning to the States in 1977, Satriani settled in Berkeley and set up shop teaching guitar—a part-time job that helped pay the bills and soon established him as the whiz who had coached Vai and Metallica's Kirk Hammett. Beginning in 1979, he put in five years with the Squares, a pop-rock group whose style—an unlikely cross between the Everly Brothers and Van Halen—impressed critics but failed to win them a record contract. In 1984 he struck out on his own, recording and producing a self-titled EP that showcased his experimental side. "For the few people who heard the EP," wrote *Guitar Player,* "the much-needed clarification 'every sound on this record was made on an electric guitar' was hard to believe, especially after hearing the sound effects of 'Talk To Me' and the popping bass in 'Dreaming Number Eleven.' "

Not of This Earth was born of the same adventuresome spirit. Satriani financed the project with a credit card—"I couldn't get anyone to lend me a *dime,"* he told *BAM Magazine*—and, in his strong, melody-based style, unleashed more of his unique guitarisms. "His writing, arranging, and production kept the guitar center stage," *Guitar Player* noted, "with tones ranging from dentist drills and record-scratch rubs to crunch metal and the squeaky clean." He also outdid himself in the recording process. "The guitars were recorded in a different way, just to be different," he told the *Los Angeles Times.* "Why compromise and go for something commercial? I figured people would hate it and no one would buy it, so why not make the kind of record I wanted?" At the urging of Vai, who is still close with his former teacher, Relativity Records gave the record a listen. An independent label that had Metallica and Megadeth as young bands, Relativity has had experience in selling new artists; in Satriani they saw both artistry and accessibility. Their vision proved correct: *Not of This Earth,* which they released in 1986, sold 30,000 copies—no small feat for an all-instrumental LP. While most mainstream listeners unknowingly passed the album by, musicians were flipping over it, hailing its maker, according to the *Los Angeles Times,* as "the new king of the two-handed tap technique." But as Joe wrote in the album's liner notes, the best was yet to come: His next effort would "turn heads" and "drop jaws."

He was right, of course. With over 360,000 copies sold, his 1987 *Surfing with the Alien* represented a quantum leap over his previous work. Initial momentum for the album sprang from a few radio stations that were adventurous enough to feature a little-known instrumentalist. Then came the big break. Mick Jagger had scheduled a tour of Japan for the spring of 1988, and he needed a lead guitarist. Again through Vai's recommendation, Satriani got an audition. "Mick wanted someone fresh and new," Satriani told the *Los Angeles Times*. On the other hand, he added, "A lot of the younger guitarists don't know [the] music—but I did. I grew up playing the Stones and Hendrix and old blues." Needless to say, he got the gig—a role that cast him alongside Beck, who had played lead on Jagger's solo LP *Primitive Cool.* In Japan Satriani was mobbed for autographs; upon returning to the States three weeks later, the media were upon him. *Surfing* began a swift ascent up the charts, eventually surpassing Jagger's *Primitive Cool.* Meanwhile, he toured almost constantly throughout the year, alternating between Jagger's band and his own.

Having recorded his third LP in the spring of 1989, Satriani plans to hit the road. For him, the rigors of touring actually help to improve his playing. "Having a constant outlet for your ideas just increases your ability to play better," he told *Guitar Player,* "and finding acceptance in the musical community gives you more confidence. . . . I remember when there was so much music I wanted people to hear, and they didn't hear it. They only heard me at my musical job, doing these other things, and this had a negative effect on my playing. That's why I dropped out of playing in traditional-type bands and decided to go into doing instrumentals." Yet at that time, going solo brought its own share of disappointment: The world simply was not ready for what Joe Satriani had to offer. "People would tell me, 'You gotta use a vocalist or nobody will want to listen to it,'" he told *Pulse!* "Or they would say, 'It's not fusion, it's not metal—what is it?' But I never got so frustrated that I put it on the shelf. I just kept working on it. And I thought, 'One of these days people will like it, they'll be ready for it.' I just really believed all along that it would eventually happen."

Yet while Satriani hoped for public acceptance of his music, he never set out to achieve fame. "I've never been a career-minded, guitar-solo kind of guy," he told *Rolling Stone.* Ironically, he is now a premier "guitar-solo kind of guy"—and remarkably, his outlook as a musician has not much changed. Unlike the many rock guitarists who are motivated by stardom, his concern is still simply to grow as an artist. And as he told *Guitar Player,* that means forging ahead on his own path: "I try to do what people say they won't do. Whatever is considered standard operating procedure, I generally try to go the other way, just to see what happens— usually with good results. I take chances a lot. A year or two goes by, and I look back at what we've worked on, and I like it because it's so outrageous and strange."

Selected discography

Solo LPs

Joe Satriani (EP), Rubina Records, 1984.
Not of This World, Relativity, 1986.
Surfing with the Alien, Relativity, 1987.
Dreaming #11 (EP), Relativity, 1988.
Flying in a Blue Dream, Relativity, 1989.

Other

(With the Greg Kihn Band) *Rock & Roll & Love,* EMI.
(With Danny Gottlieb) *Aquamarine,* Atlantic Jazz.
Say Anything (soundtrack), 1989.

Sources

Cash Box, May 7, 1988.
Guitar Player, February 1988; January 1989; November 1989.
Guitar World, December 1987.
Los Angeles Times, April 24, 1988.
Pulse!, March 1988.
Rolling Stone, April 21, 1988.
USA Today, May 6-8, 1988.

—*Kyle Kevorkian*

Neil Sedaka

Singer, songwriter, pianist

Singer-songwriter Neil Sedaka has enjoyed two different periods of success during his career. He first caught the music industry's attention when one of his compositions, "Stupid Cupid," provided a smash for singer Connie Francis in 1958. Sedaka went on to record his own hits, including "Oh, Carol," "Stairway to Heaven," and "Breaking Up Is Hard to Do," but the British invasion of the 1960s forced him to concentrate solely on his writing. He made an amazing comeback during the 1970s, however, with songs like "Laughter in the Rain" and "Bad Blood."

Sedaka was born March 13, 1939, in Brooklyn, New York, to a musical family. Both parents played the piano, though his father drove a taxi for a living, and Sedaka's grandmother was a concert pianist who had studied with the founder of the Juilliard School. One of Sedaka's elementary school teachers noticed his own potential with the instrument, and urged his parents to get him private lessons. Soon afterwards he was given a scholarship to Juilliard's preparatory school division, where he studied for eight years.

But while Sedaka earnestly tried to develop his skills as a classical pianist, he also became interested in popular music, and listened to it on the radio. He was encouraged in his interest by one of the other teenage boys in his family's apartment building; one day, neighbor Howard Greenfield asked him to write some music to go with one of his poems. Thus, when they were thirteen and sixteen respectively, the songwriting team of Sedaka and Greenfield was born. Meanwhile, Sedaka's interest in popular music was helping him adjust in other areas of his life. Something of a social outcast in his adolescence, Sedaka saw his social status improve as a result of performing pop songs. "It worked in my favor," he told Norma McLain Stoop in *After Dark*. "Not only was I invited to parties, but I was suddenly the life of every party I attended."

Even while they were teenagers, however, Sedaka and Greenfield tried to put their talents on display for a wider audience than just their immediate friends. Especially after 1954, when Sedaka was captivated by the Penguins' rendition of "Earth Angel" and convinced Greenfield to turn their efforts towards rock and roll and rhythm and blues, they attempted to market their compositions to record companies and music publishers. They managed to sell a few songs to Atlantic Records; some of them were recorded by artists such as LaVern Baker and Clyde McPhatter. As for Sedaka's progress towards a classical career, he was chosen to play on the radio for the *New York Times*'s Musical Talent in Our Schools competition in 1956; shortly afterwards he graduated from high school and matriculated at Juilliard at the college level.

While Sedaka was still at Juilliard, he and Greenfield found work as songwriters with Aldon Publishing Company, owned by Don Kirshner and Al Nevins. Kirshner and Nevins also employed other talented composers: Carole King, Gerry Goffin, Barry Mann, and Cynthia Weil. One of the Sedaka-Greenfield efforts, "Stupid Cupid," was forwarded to singer Connie Francis. It climbed the Top Forty charts, and its success gave Sedaka the incentive to leave Juilliard and concentrate more fully on his pop career. "Stupid Cupid" helped Sedaka gain more attention from the music industry as well. At the urging of his Aldon employers, he cut a demonstration tape singing his own songs. When Steven Sholes of RCA Records heard it, he signed Sedaka to a recording contract.

Sedaka's first hit single for RCA was "The Diary," which did fairly well in 1958, rising to number fourteen on the charts. "Oh! Carol," which he and Greenfield wrote for colleague King, fared even better, hitting the Top 10. Amazed at his success, Sedaka confided to Tom Nolan in *Rolling Stone:* "I had to keep pinching myself to believe it. . . . I can't describe to you the feeling of pushing the buttons in the car and . . . there were my songs blaring on the radio." He also did well with concert performances, and appeared on the television shows "American Bandstand" and "The Ed Sullivan Show." Sedaka continued to ride the charts through the early 1960s, scoring hits with "Little Devil," "Calendar Girl," "Sweet Sixteen," and "Next Door to an Angel." In 1962, he surpassed his previous popular height with the chart-topping "Breaking Up Is Hard to Do."

But like many other pop and rock-and-roll acts that bloomed during the same period, Sedaka's appeal as a performer was severely reduced by the onslaught of new musical groups from Great Britain, including the Beatles. He also held RCA responsible, however, for not giving him enough creative freedom to vary his style: "The most I could do was change the tempo a bit," he complained to Nolan. "'Little Devil' sounded like 'Stairway to Heaven,' 'Next Door to an Angel' was very similar to 'Breaking Up Is Hard to Do.' So . . . I blew a good thing." Undaunted by this turn in his fortunes as a recording artist, Sedaka concentrated on his songwriting, and continued to compose hits for acts like the Fifth Dimension and Tom Jones.

He also continued to perform abroad, and, ironically, the stage for his later comeback was set in England—whose artists helped cause him to lose his first popularity. In 1970 Sedaka moved to England for a while, and though he played medleys of his old hits during concerts, he put most of his efforts into new songs. He released a few albums in England, and made the charts there with singles like "That's Where the Music Takes Me" and the smash ballad, "Laughter in the Rain." While in England, Sedaka also became acquainted with British pop superstar Elton John, who had formed his own record label, Rocket Records. By 1974, John had agreed to help him with his U.S. comeback, re-recording some of Sedaka's British hits on Rocket for American release.

The result was the aptly titled album *Sedaka's Back.* In addition to "Laughter in the Rain," which succeeded in bringing Sedaka back to the attention of U.S. fans as a performer, the disc also included a song he had written with Greenfield called "Love Will Keep Us Together." The pop duo the Captain and Tennille also recorded this number, making it a smash hit and scoring a Grammy for Best Record of the Year. But Sedaka had a smash of his own waiting in the wings. In 1975 he released *The Hungry Years,* and along with it, the hard-driving single "Bad Blood." It raced up the charts rapidly. Somewhat controversial, it was labeled misogynistic because it included the word "bitch" in the lyrics. Sedaka, however, was pleased with the change it made in his image, feeling that the public had previously perceived him as too wholesome. *The Hungry Years* also included a remake of his previous hit, "Breaking Up Is Hard to Do"—this time sung as a mellow, torchy ballad. This version proved successful enough to make the Top 10, just as the original had years before.

Shortly afterwards, Sedaka switched from Rocket to Elektra Records. He has not fared as well as he did with John's company, but he did garner a hit in 1980 from a duet single he recorded with his daughter Dara, "Should've Never Let You Go." Later he changed to MCA/Curb Records. Sedaka also published his autobiography in 1982, *Laughter in the Rain: My Own Story*.

Selected discography

Singles

"The Diary"/"No Vacancy," RCA, 1958.
"I Go Ape," RCA, c. 1959.
"Oh! Carol," RCA, 1959.
"Stairway to Heaven," RCA, 1960.
"Calendar Girl," RCA, 1961.
"Little Devil," RCA, 1961.
"Happy Birthday, Sweet Sixteen," RCA, 1961.
"Breaking Up Is Hard to Do," RCA, 1962.
"Alice in Wonderland," RCA, 1963.
"Let's Go Steady Again," RCA, 1963.
"Bad Girl," RCA, 1963.
"Laughter in the Rain," Rocket, 1974.
"That's Where the Music Takes Me," Rocket, 1974.
"The Immigrant," Rocket, 1974.
"Bad Blood," Rocket, 1975.
(slow version) "Breaking Up Is Hard to Do," Rocket, 1975.
"Love in the Shadows," Rocket, 1976.
(With daughter, Dara) "Should've Never Let You Go," Elektra, 1980.
(With Dara) "Your Precious Love," MCA/Curb, 1983.

LPs

Neil Sedaka, RCA, 1959.
Circulate, RCA, 1961.
Little Devil and Other Hits, RCA, 1961.
Italiano, RCA, 1964.
Sedaka's Back, Rocket, 1974.
The Hungry Years, Rocket, 1975.
Steppin' Out, Rocket, 1976.
A Song, Elektra, 1977.
All You Need Is the Music, Elektra, 1978.
In the Pocket, Elektra, 1980.
Now, Elektra, 1981.

Writings

Laughter in the Rain: My Own Story, Putnam, 1982.

Sources

After Dark, September 1976.
Rolling Stone, December 4, 1975.
Seventeen, September 1976.

—Elizabeth Thomas

Pete Seeger

Singer, songwriter, banjo player

T he indomitable Pete Seeger has weathered a number of storms to become, at age seventy, the most influential folk artist in America. Seeger was instrumental in popularizing both the five-string banjo and the songs of populist America that could be played on it; his own works such as "If I Had a Hammer," "We Shall Overcome," and "Where Have All the Flowers Gone?" served as anthems in the anti-establishment protests of the late 1960s. In *Best of the Music Makers,* George T. Simon calls Seeger "an uncanny mixture of saint, propagandist, cornball, and hero" whose "emotional generosity and companionship with his audiences around the world has invariably been returned affectionately by the . . . people he has entertained and inspired."

Peter R. Seeger was born into a family "whose chromosomes fairly burst with music," to quote *Philadelphia Inquirer* contributor Amy Linn. His father was an ethnomusicologist and composer, his mother a classical violinist who taught at Juilliard. While Seeger was young his parents moved from university to university across the country. He grew up longing for roots but accustomed to travel, a boarding school student who dabbled in Marx, sang in choirs, and played the ukelele.

In 1936 Seeger accompanied his father on a trip to a North Carolina music festival. As Linn puts it, during the festival "young Seeger took one look at a five-string banjo and fell in love." Although he enrolled in Harvard University that fall, Seeger found college much less fascinating than the banjo. He practiced relentlessly until he had taught himself to play in the various Appalachian picking styles. Seeger—along with bluegrass musician Earl Scruggs—is credited with saving the five-string banjo from extinction. A line of banjos made by Vega Instrument Company bears his name.

Through his father's friends Seeger met the finest folk singers of the Depression era, Huddie "Leadbelly" Ledbetter and Woody Guthrie. Guthrie became Seeger's mentor, and the youth quit college to travel with him. Together Guthrie and Seeger sang for the striking workers and displaced farmers of the nation; they proudly associated themselves with the Communist Party and other left-wing groups. "I knew it wasn't a quick way to get jobs—to sing for the Communist Party," Seeger told the *Philadelphia Inquirer.* "It was something that you do, because you think it's the right thing at the time. And in the long run, you realize the value in doing what you think is right."

After wartime service as an entertainer for enlisted men, Seeger formed a quartet, the Weavers, in 1948. A full decade before the so-called "folk revival," the Weavers placed several songs on the pop charts, including the winsome "On Top of Old Smokey" and a

For the Record. . .

Full name Peter R. Seeger; born May 3, 1919, in New York, N.Y.; son of Charles (a conductor, musicologist, and educator) and Constance de Clyver (a concert violinist and teacher; maiden name Edson) Seeger; married Toshi Aline Ohta, July 20, 1943; children: Daniel Adams, Mike Salter, Virginia. *Education:* Attended Harvard University, 1936-38.

Folksinger, banjo and guitar player, and songwriter, 1939—. Assistant at the Archive of American Folk Song, Washington, D.C., 1939-40; founding member of the Almanac Singers, 1940-41; toured the Southern and Southwestern states and Mexico with Woody Guthrie, 1941-42. Co-founder and national director of People's Songs, Inc., 1945.

Founding member of the Weavers (folk quartet), 1948-52, other members were Lee Hays, Fred Hellerman, and Ronnie Gilbert. Cut Top 40 singles, "On Top of Old Smokey" and "Goodnight, Irene," both 1950. Group disbanded, 1952, and re-formed, 1955. Solo performer, 1957—, appearing in concert in United States, the Soviet Union, and Europe. Appeared in movies *To Hear My Banjo Play*, 1946, and *Tell Me That You Love Me, Junie Moon*, 1970. Organizer of Newport (R.I.) Folk Festivals, and co-founder of Hudson River Sloop Restoration, Inc. *Military service:* U.S. Army Special Services, entertained troops in the United States and the South Pacific, 1942-45.

Address: *Home*—Duchess Junction, Beacon, N.Y. 12508.

gress and sentenced to ten years in prison. The sentence was overturned on appeal, but the blacklisting endured. Undaunted, Seeger continued to perform wherever he was welcome, and he wrote numerous songs and books about music.

A changing political and musical climate brought Seeger back into prominence in the mid-1960s. The younger generation—many of them rootless as Seeger had been—embraced the simplicity and passion of folk music. Seeger was one of the organizers of the prestigious Newport Folk Festival, and one of its most popular performers. Having stood his ground in the McCarthy era, he finally achieved respect for his strength—and his music.

With civil rights activists singing "We Shall Overcome" and anti-war demonstrators singing "Where Have All the Flowers Gone?" Seeger found himself compared to his former teacher, Woody Guthrie, in terms of influence. Although he did not appear on television again

> *The motto etched on his banjo—"This machine surrounds hate and forces it to surrender"—perhaps best sums up the essence of his musical message.*

country favorite, "Goodnight, Irene." The Weavers were also the first to perform "If I Had a Hammer," and as the Cold War era dawned, the group—and Seeger in particular—faced a hostile government. Linn writes that as anti-communist sentiment rose, "simple concerts turned into melees between a rising tide of 'patriots' and the people who were branded as commies. Hundreds of concertgoers and singers . . . were caught in the violence, including Pete Seeger and his family. Cars were overturned, crosses burned, a man was stabbed. It was an omen."

One year after compiling four million record sales, the Weavers found themselves blacklisted as communist sympathizers. Seeger was called before the dreaded House Un-American Activities Committee in 1955 and questioned about his communist activities. When he evoked his First Amendment rights of free speech, rather than the Fifth Amendment rights against self-incrimination, he was charged with contempt of Con-

until 1967—some twelve years after his appearance before the House Un-American Activities Committee—he was a favorite at outdoor festivals and on college campuses. Beginning in 1965 he launched a campaign to save the environment, especially the filthy Hudson River. With a cadre of friends Seeger organized a series of "sloop concerts," the proceeds from which he donated to a foundation. In 1968 the sloop *Clearwater* was built to carry the environmental message along the Hudson, and the river's conditions began to improve significantly.

Today Seeger still makes at least one hundred personal appearances per year, most of them at intimate concerts in small theatres. Linn writes that the artist "is as capable as ever of getting a crowd to sing along." Seeger has said that the term "folk music" has lost its meaning through misuse—he prefers to think of his work as aurally-transmitted music, the kind learned "by ear." Seeger told the *Philadelphia Inquirer* that he relishes the *participation* possibilities that folk music offers the audience. "The modern world has a tendency to say, 'Just pay your money and let the experts do it for you.' Or, let the machines do it for you," he said. "My father used to tell me that one must not judge the musicality of a nation by the number of its virtuosos, but by the number of people in the general population who are playing for themselves."

Called "America's tuning fork" and "the living embodiment of native folk tradition," Seeger has certainly left a mark on music in the twentieth century. The motto etched on his banjo—"This machine surrounds hate and forces it to surrender"—perhaps best sums up the essence of his musical message. Linn concludes: "For fifty of his years Pete Seeger [has] been wedding his songs to history, and making history with his songs."

Selected discography

Singles; with the Weavers

"Kisses Sweeter than Wine," Decca, 1950.
"Tzena, Tzena, Tzena," Decca, 1950.
"On Top of Old Smokey," Decca, 1950.
"Goodnight, Irene," Decca, 1950.

LPs

Champlain Valley Songs, Folkways.
American Industrial Ballads, Folkways.
The World of Pete Seeger, Columbia.
Pete Seeger Sampler, Folkways.
Pete Seeger with Brownie McGhee and Sonny Terry: Washboard Band Country Dance Music, Folkways.
American Favorite Ballads, five volumes, Folkways.
Pete Seeger Sings Woody Guthrie, Folkways.
Pete Seeger Sings Leadbelly, Folkways.
Little Boxes, Folkways.
Pete Seeger Sings American Ballads, Folkways.
Darling Corey, Folkways.
The Rainbow Quest, Folkways.
Goofing Off Suite, Folkways.
Pete Seeger and the Almanac Singers: Talking Union and Other Union Songs, Folkways.
Pete Seeger and Frank Hamilton: Nonesuch, Folkways.
Pete Seeger and Mike Seeger: Indian Summer, Folkways.
Banks of Marble, Folkways.
Clearwater Classics, Folkways.
The Essential Pete Seeger, 2 volumes, Vanguard.
Gazette, Folkways.
Pete Seeger's Greatest Hits, Columbia.
With Voices Together We Sing, Folkways.
(With Arlo Guthrie) *Precious Friend*, Warner Brothers.
Pete Seeger and Arlo Guthrie Together in Concert, Reprise.
(With Jeanne Humphries) *Ballads of Black America*, Folkways.

(With Ed Renehan) *Fifty Sail on Newburgh Bay*, Folkways.
(With others) *Carry It On!*, Flying Fish.

With Woody Guthrie

American Folksay, 3 volumes, Stinson.
Chain Gang, Stinson.
Southern Mountain Hoedowns, Stinson.

Newport Folk Festival recordings

Volume 1, Vanguard, 1959.
Volume 1, Folkways, 1960.
Volume 1, Vanguard, 1960.
The Evening Concerts II, Vanguard, 1963.
Evening Concerts I, Vanguard, 1964.

Recordings for children

Song and Play Time, Folkways.
Folk Songs for Young People, Folkways.
American Folk Songs for Children, Folkways.
American Playparties, Folkways.
Games and Activity Songs for Children, Folkways.
Abiyoyo and Other Songs for Children, Folkways.
Birds, Beasts, Bugs and Little Fishes, Folkways.
Children's Concert at Town Hall, Columbia.
Birds, Beasts, Bigger Fishes and Fookish Frog, Folkways.
Song and Play Time with Pete Seeger, Folkways.
Stories and Songs for Little Children, High Windy.

Writings

American Favorite Ballads, Oak, 1961.
(With Jerry Silverman) *The Folksinger's Guitar Guide*, Oak, 1962.
(With Julius Lester) *The Twelve-String Guitar as Played by Leadbelly*, Oak, 1965.
How To Play the Five String Banjo, Oak, ca. 1965.
The Incomplete Folksinger, Simon & Schuster, 1972.
Henscratches and Flyspecks: Or, How to Read Melodies from Songbooks in Twelve Confusing Lessons, Berkeley Press, 1973.
Carry It On!, Simon & Schuster, 1985.
Abiyoyo, Macmillan, 1986.

Sources

Books

Lawless, Ray, *Folksingers and Folk Songs in America*, Longmans, 1960.
Simon, George T., *Best of the Music Makers*, Doubleday, 1979.

Periodicals

Audubon, March 1971.
Conservationist, June 1969.

High Fidelity, January 1963.
Look, August 1969.
National Wildlife, February 1970.
Philadelphia Inquirer, May 12, 1989.
Popular Science, August 1970.
Ramparts, November 30, 1968.
Rolling Stone, March 10, 1977; October 18, 1979.
Saturday Review, May 13, 1973.
Sing Out!, May 1954.

—*Anne Janette Johnson*

The Seldom Scene

Bluegrass band

A group that formed to play "just for the fun of it," the Seldom Scene has become one of the most popular bluegrass bands in America. Members of the Seldom Scene never intended to make a living together as musicians—some of them were retired from other bluegrass bands, and all of them had white-collar jobs in the Washington, D.C., area. Even the group's name implies a resistance to the limelight, but as Robert Kyle notes in *Pickin'* magazine, "from the very start they possessed all of the necessary elements to become a bluegrass supergroup."

Bluegrass Unlimited magazine reviewer George B. McCeney once observed that the Seldom Scene has been unique virtually since it formed in 1971. "Rarely has a bluegrass band been blessed with such talent from the start," wrote McCeney, "and perhaps even less often has a band been able to stabilize that talent over an extended period." The critic is right on both counts. The Seldom Scene formed around a nucleus of seasoned musicians, including the top-ranked John Duffey (mandolin and tenor vocals) and Mike Auldridge

For the Record...

Group formed in 1971 with **John Duffey** (mandolin and vocals), **Tom Gray** (upright bass), **Mike Auldridge** (dobro), **Ben Eldridge** (banjo and vocals), and **John Starling** (guitar and vocals); Starling quit in 1977 and was replaced by **Phil Rosenthal**. Gray has been replaced by **T. Michael Coleman** (electric bass) and Rosenthal has been replaced by **Lou Reid** (guitar and lead vocal). Signed with Rebel Records, 1972, and cut first album, *Act One*, the same year. Moved to the Sugar Hill label, 1979. Performed for President Carter at the White House, June, 1978.

Addresses: *Record company*—Sugar Hill Records, Box 4040, Duke Station, Durham, NC 27706.

(dobro); amazing though it may seem, the band has had only one major personnel change in twenty years. At the same time the Seldom Scene has attracted a host of well-known "guest" performers, including Linda Ronstadt, Ricky Skaggs, Emmylou Harris, and Jonathan Edwards. *Bluegrass Unlimited* contributor Don Rhodes concludes that the members of the ensemble "have shown that they can stay at home during the week and still be one of the top groups in America today."

The initial roots for the Seldom Scene took hold on the University of Virginia campus in the early 1960s. There, two college students—John Starling, a pre-med major, and Ben Eldridge, a math major—spent their few spare moments playing bluegrass music. Graduation separated the two friends, but they were reunited in Washington, D.C., in 1967. By that time Starling was serving an internship in preparation for becoming an army surgeon, and Eldridge was working as a mathematician for a Virginia firm. They formed a basement band with a few other pickers. One of these pickers, Mike Auldridge, played dobro, an instrument so rare in the 1960s that he had to build one himself.

When Starling was sent to Vietnam, the band broke up. Auldridge and Eldridge joined Cliff Waldron and the New Shades of Grass, one of the first "progressive" bluegrass bands. In that environment they were encouraged to experiment with bluegrass versions of rock, jazz, and pop music—quite a challenge for a dobro player used to providing the sliding wail to country songs. Starling returned from his tour of duty in 1971, and by that time Auldridge and Eldridge had had enough of professional musicianship. All of them set-

tled down to full-time jobs—Starling in medicine, Eldridge in mathematics, and Auldridge in commercial art for the *Washington Star*.

The informal picking parties continued, however, and they attracted a seasoned veteran in John Duffey. Duffey had been a founding member of the Country Gentlemen, an immensely popular band. He had retired from that group to run an instrument repair business near Washington, D.C. The last member to join was bass player Tom Gray, a cartographer with *National Geographic*. Starling was actually the only member who had no professional musical experience, and he encouraged the group to find small gigs—"fun" outings that would not interfere with the members' regular jobs.

In January of 1972 the Seldom Scene had its debut at the Red Fox Inn just outside Washington. Kyle writes: "Assembled in the small club for their 'weekly card

---

"Scattered throughout their musical selections are instrumental breaks that put chill bumps on your skin and vocal harmonies so sweet you need a fly swatter handy to ward off bugs after the nectar."

---

game,' the Seldom Scene unknowingly began a career with the deck stacked in their favor with wild cards galore." Word of the band soon spread—the Washington area is a bluegrass "hot spot"—and within months the group was playing to standing-room-only crowds. Duffey arranged a recording session with Rebel Records, and a debut album, *Act One*, appeared that summer.

Virtually since that day, the Seldom Scene has been playing selected tours and recording albums at the rate of one almost every year. In 1977 Starling left the group and was replaced by singer-songwriter Phil Rosenthal, also a veteran performer. Oddly enough, some members of the Seldom Scene have held onto their day jobs even in the wake of the band's success. They continue to perform live at the Birchmere, a club in Alexandria, Virginia, every Thursday night, and they also continue to restrict their concert appearances to the bluegrass festivals held May through October in the Eastern states.

Its "basement band" mystique notwithstanding, the Seldom Scene has risen to the forefront principally through first-class musicianship. Duffey, Gray, and Auldridge have all won awards for their instrumental prowess—Auldridge in particular is a sought-after session player with a score of solo albums to his credit. The group appeals to all age groups, offering bluegrass versions of songs by Eric Clapton, Bob Dylan, and other rock artists for younger listeners and classic gospel works and traditional tunes for older fans. Rhodes writes: "Scattered throughout their musical selections are instrumental breaks that put chill bumps on your skin and vocal harmonies so sweet you need a fly swatter handy to ward off bugs after the nectar."

The Seldom Scene enters its third decade as a major force on the bluegrass scene. Kyle calls the band's evolution "a Cinderella story whose creation has been a significant catalyst in the coming-of-age of bluegrass. . . . By updating the music while still retaining its traditional roots, the band has achieved and preserved the proper proportions of both old and new." The critic concludes: "In giving bluegrass music a more contemporary representation and wider audience appeal, the Seldom Scene has successfully extended a new awareness of the acoustic music native to America's heritage."

Selected discography

Act One, Rebel, 1972.

Act Two, Rebel, 1973.
Act Three, Rebel, 1973.
(With Linda Ronstadt) *Old Train*, Rebel, 1974.
The Seldom Scene Recorded Live at the Cellar Door in Washington, D.C., Rebel, 1975.
The New Seldom Scene Album, Rebel, 1976.
Baptizing, Rebel, 1978.
Act Four, Sugar Hill, 1979.
After Midnight, Sugar Hill, 1981.
. . . At the Scene, Sugar Hill, 1983.
(With Jonathan Edwards) *Blue Ridge*, Sugar Hill, 1985.
(With Ronstadt, Edwards, Emmylou Harris, Ricky Skaggs, and others) *15th Anniversary Celebration*, Sugar Hill, 1987.
(With Lou Reid and T. Michael Coleman) *A Change of Scenery*, Sugar Hill, 1988.
Best of the Seldom Scene, Rebel, 1989.
Scenic Roots, Sugar Hill, 1990.

Sources

Books

The Illustrated Encyclopedia of Country Music, Harmony, 1977.
Malone, Bill C., *Country Music U.S.A.*, revised edition, University of Texas Press, 1985.

Periodicals

Bluegrass Unlimited, July 1980.
Pickin', April 1978; November, 1978.

—Anne Janette Johnson

Michelle Shocked

Singer, songwriter, guitarist

One of the new breed of angry young women to burst onto the music scene is Michelle Shocked (nee Johnston). She chose her stagy surname to reflect outrage over a troubled past and uses her music to deliver stinging social commentary and recount dreamy Texas memories. Her songs seem headed for the top of the charts, but Shocked isn't sure she wants to follow suit.

Thin and pale with close-cropped hair often hidden under a British sailor's cap, Shocked is defiantly reluctant to answer personal questions. A sassy Texan who's achieved more professional success in Europe than her homeland, she's a difficult talent to categorize. Her music has been described as country, punk, protest, folk, blues, rock and pop.

She's the daughter of Bill Johnston, who has been described as a former teacher, part-time carnival ride operator, and sixties-style hippie, and a mother whose name Shocked won't reveal but cynically describes as a "Tammy Bakker-type." When her parents divorced in 1963, Michelle lived with her converted-Mormon mother and career-Army stepfather, who moved them from Maryland to Massachusetts, to West Germany, and then Texas. In 1979, at age 16, she quit school and left home to live with her father in Dallas. Johnston encouraged her musical talent, convinced her to buy a second-hand guitar, and took her to local blues and country music festivals.

Shocked enrolled at the University of Texas but didn't stick with classes for long. She began a period of restless wanderings, which took her from the homes of relatives and friends to student housing co-ops, then on to San Francisco and involvement with local hardcore bands and a squatters' movement. Shocked calls this her period of homelessness, when she aligned herself with a number of causes, from save-the-whales to anti-nuclear activities. Evictions drove her back to Texas where her mother, alarmed over Michelle's wild lifestyle, had Shocked hospitalized in mental institutions. "They kept me till the insurance ran out," Shocked told *People* magazine. "I guess you can't be crazy without insurance."

In 1984 she continued her political involvement and was arrested twice during public protests—once at the Republican Convention, then again in a protest against a defense contractor. For the next two years, she bounced from California to New York to Europe. "I was never gonna come back. If I could actually survive in a foreign country with no money, taking care of myself, I couldn't be crazy," she explained to *Musician*. Things didn't work out as she planned. She was raped while wandering through Italy and retreated back to Texas.

For the Record. . .

Surname originally Johnston; name changed, 1984; born c. 1963; raised in Maryland, Massachusetts, West Germany, and Texas; daughter of Bill Johnston (described variously as an English teacher and/or part-time carnival ride operator) and a mother Shocked refuses to identify; stepfather was in the military. *Education:* Attended University of Texas, briefly.

Became interested in music at age 16 when she went to live with her father in Texas, and he introduced her to blues and country music; after periods of being committed to two mental institutions by her mother, went on the road in the United States and Europe, singing and participating in peace protests; signed a recording contract, 1986; has toured throughout the United States.

Addresses: Home—London, England. *Record company*—c/o Mercury/Polygram Records, Worldwide Plaza, 825 Eighth Ave., New York, NY 10019.

It was there, while performing at the Kerrville Folk Festival in 1986 that Shocked was accidentally discovered by English producer Pete Lawrence. He taped her performance on his Sony Walkman, complete with background crickets chirping, then released the crude recording as *The Texas Campfire Tapes* and watched it soar to the top of British independent charts. A surprised Shocked moved to London and was received with open arms.

Polygram offered her a $130,000 advance on a second album, but Shocked would only accept $50,000. "When it comes to it," she explained to *Musician,* "I have to confess I'm not that committed to the medium of making albums. It's a nice means, but it's not the end as far as I'm concerned. If it gets people to the live shows where I can spit my two cents worth of politics, it's done the job. . . . I knew if I was going to keep the album as simple as I wanted, it was never gonna take that much money."

A dramatic photo of a raging Shocked being restrained and arrested by riot police that appeared in the *San Francisco Examiner* serves as the cover of her second album, *Short Sharp Shocked.* Her third release, *Captain Swing,* appeared in November 1989. Some record industry observers believe Shocked is on the verge of becoming as big a star in the United States as she is in Europe. Meanwhile, Shocked is content to return to the houseboat on the Thames she now calls home.

Selected discography

The Texas Campfire Tapes, Cooking Vinyl, 1987.
Short Sharp Shocked, Polygram, 1988.
Captain Swing, Mercury, 1989.

Sources

Musician, June 1988.
Newsweek, October 3, 1988.
New York Times, September 4, 1988.
People, November 7, 1988.
Rolling Stone, November 3, 1988; October 6, 1988.
Stereo Review, March 1989.

—*Sharon Rose*

Carly Simon

Singer, songwriter

Pop singer-songwriter Carly Simon first gained attention in the music world in 1971 with her first hit single, "That's the Way I've Always Heard It Should Be." Though perhaps most famous for her 1972 smash "You're So Vain," she has had many other hits, including "Anticipation," "The Right Thing to Do," and "Coming Around Again." After a career slump in the mid-1980s, Simon returned with the latter song, and also won a 1989 Academy Award for best film theme for her hit "Let the Rivers Run."

Simon was born into a famous family; her father, Richard Simon, was a co-founder of the Simon & Schuster publishing company. Yet both her parents were musically inclined, and introduced her to the music of composers Richard Wagner and George and Ira Gershwin. Simon continued expanding her musical horizons, being exposed to the folk genre as a schoolgirl. One of her teachers at her private school was folk great Pete Seeger, and one of her first boyfriends took her to many of Odetta's concerts. She attended Sarah Lawrence College for a few years, but dropped out to form a folk duo with her sister Lucy. Meanwhile, her eldest sister, Joanna, was pursuing a career as a professional opera singer.

Carly and Lucy billed themselves as the Simon Sisters, and managed to obtain gigs in small clubs on the east coast. Eventually they won an opportunity to perform on the television variety program "Hootenanny," and recorded an album on Kapp Records. This was not an overwhelming success—the most popular single, "Winkin', Blinkin', and Nod," reached the dizzying height of seventy-eighth on the charts. The sisters stopped working together after Lucy's marriage in 1965.

After going solo, Simon encountered rock manager Albert Grossman, who wanted to bill her as the female Bob Dylan, but she was uncomfortable with that style. For a brief period in 1969, she served as one of the lead singers for a rock band called Elephant's Memory. She had also formed a songwriting partnership with one of her childhood friends, Jacob Brackman. In 1970, Simon sang a demonstration tape of some of their songs; it circulated among some record companies, was rejected by Columbia, but provoked great interest at Elektra. Simon's solo debut was a self-titled 1971 album that received almost immediate critical acclaim. Timothy Crouse in *Rolling Stone* claimed that "some of the songs on [*Carly Simon*] sound like [John] Updike or [J.D.] Salinger short stories set to music." He was also impressed by Simon's "superbly controlled voice." The disc featured a hit single, "That's the Way I've Always Heard It Should Be." That year, Simon garnered a Grammy Award as best new artist.

Simon followed her debut with *Anticipation,* which fea-

For the Record. . .

Born June 25, 1945, in New York, N.Y.; daughter of Richard Simon (a publisher); married James Taylor (a singer-songwriter) in November, 1972 (divorced 1981); children: Sarah, Ben; married Jim Hart (a writer), December 23, 1987. *Education:* Attended Sarah Lawrence College.

Pop, rock, ballads singer and songwriter; member of folk duo the "Simon Sisters" with sister Lucy during the early 1960s; lead singer for rock group Elephant's Memory, 1969; solo recording artist and occasional concert performer, 1971—. Wrote film score for *Heartburn,* c. 1987.

Awards: Grammy Award, 1971, for best new artist. Academy Award, 1989, for best motion picture theme, "Let the Rivers Run," from *Working Girl.*

Addresses: *Residence*—Martha's Vineyard, Mass. *Record company*—Arista Records, 75 Rockefeller Plaza, New York, N.Y. 10019.

tured the hit title track, and another minor hit, "Legend in Your Own Time." "Anticipation" supposedly took its inspiration from Simon's brief relationship with fellow singer-songwriter Kris Kristofferson, but by November, 1972, she had married another singer-songwriter, James Taylor. At roughly the same time, Simon launched what was to become her trademark smash, "You're So Vain," from the album *No Secrets.* The latter became her first gold album, and also included the hit, "The Right Thing to Do." She followed this triumph with 1974's *Hotcakes,* which was cited by *Cue* magazine as the year's top album in the pop category, and featured the hit singles "Haven't Got Time for the Pain" and a duet remake with Taylor of the old rhythm and blues song, "Mockingbird."

But with success came problems. It is a good idea to tour in order to promote a recording career, but Simon suffered from severe stage fright. She managed to get through her earlier concerts without audiences sensing her fear, but temporarily abandoned public performances in 1974 after the birth of her first child. When she was persuaded by Elektra executives to do a tour in 1981, she collapsed from fright in the middle of a concert. She also had many personal stresses at the time—she was divorcing Taylor and her young son had just undergone kidney surgery. Simon finally managed to give another concert in 1987 near her home in Martha's Vineyard, Massachusetts.

Meanwhile, Simon's popularity continued. She had a hit

in 1977 with "Nobody Does It Better," the theme from the James Bond film "The Spy Who Loved Me," and another in 1978 with "You Belong to Me." The latter came from the album *Boys in the Trees,* which went platinum. But from this peak, Simon's career began to descend. She scored in 1980 with "Jesse," but the rest of the early 1980s were bleak, and her 1985 album *Spoiled Girl* "just bombed," she admitted to Jane Hall in *People.*

Simon started a comeback in 1987 when she was asked to score the film *Heartburn.* The theme she wrote for it, "Coming Around Again," became her biggest hit in years. She included the song on an album of the same title; she switched to Arista Records to release it. *Coming Around Again* also featured the hits "Give Me All Night" and "The Stuff That Dreams Are Made Of," in addition to an interesting remake of "As Time Goes By." Simon followed this up with yet another triumph, writing and performing the theme for the film *Working Girl.* The inspiring "Let the Rivers Run" garnered its composer an Academy Award for best motion picture theme.

Selected discography

(With sister, Lucy) *The Simon Sisters* (includes "Winkin', Blinkin', and Nod"), Kapp, 1964.
Carly Simon (includes "That's the Way I've Always Heard It Should Be"), Elektra, 1971.
Anticipation (includes "Anticipation" and "Legend in Your Own Time"), Elektra, 1971.
No Secrets (includes "You're So Vain," "The Right Thing to Do," and "We Have No Secrets"), Elektra, 1972.
Hotcakes (includes "Haven't Got Time for the Pain" and "Mockingbird"), Elektra, 1974.
Playing Possum (includes "Attitude Dancing," "Slave," "Waterfall," and "More and More"), Elektra, 1975.
Another Passenger (includes "It Keeps You Runnin'"), Elektra, 1976.
Boys in the Trees (includes "You Belong to Me"), Elektra, 1978.
Spy, Elektra, 1979.
Come Upstairs (includes "Jesse"), Warner Bros., 1980.
Torch, Warner Bros., 1981.
Spoiled Girl, Warner Bros., 1985.
Coming Around Again (includes "Coming Around Again," "Give Me All Night," "The Stuff That Dreams Are Made Of," and "As Time Goes By"), Arista, 1987.
My Romance, Arista, 1990.
Have You Seen Me Lately?, Arista, 1990.

Also recorded the singles "Nobody Does It Better" and "Let the Rivers Run."

Sources

Cue, December 9, 1974.

McCall's, May 1987.

People, April 27, 1987; August 17, 1987; January 11, 1988.

Rolling Stone, April 29, 1971; June 18, 1987.

—Elizabeth Thomas

Phoebe Snow

Singer, songwriter

Singer-songwriter Phoebe Snow, proficient in many musical genres—including pop, folk, blues, and rock—first came to fans' attention in 1974 when her self-titled debut album was released. *Phoebe Snow* launched her first hit, "Poetry Man"; since then the recording artist has also scored critical acclaim with songs like "Cash In," "No Regrets," "Every Night," and her 1989 comeback "Something Real," from the album of the same name. *People* reviewer David Hiltbrand has lauded her "mercurial, often thrilling vocal style," and Holly Gleason cited her "shimmering alto" and "impeccable phrasing" in *Rolling Stone*.

Snow was born Phoebe Laub in New York City, New York, on July 17, 1952. From a musical standpoint she had an interesting childhood and adolescence; her mother was a friend of many of the folk artists who were prominent during the 1950s and 1960s. One of them was famed musician Pete Seeger, who taught young Phoebe her first blues song, and introduced her to the standards of folk and blues singers of even earlier eras. Thus Snow's early artistic influences included the likes of Seeger, Woody Gutherie, and Leadbelly. Yet she also enjoyed the pop and rock she was exposed to by watching television programs such as "American Bandstand." In her teens, she took guitar lessons; later she tried out for a jug band that had been formed by one of her friends, and was rejected because the other band members felt she was too good to squander her talent upon them.

By the time Snow became a young woman, she was interested in becoming a performer, but frightened of trying to entertain people by herself. She began to study singers whom she felt had extraordinary stage presence, especially Judy Garland. Snow finally found the courage to begin singing and playing in clubs in and around New York City, and though later commentators have speculated that the reason that she is more of a critical success than a popular one is that her talent does not come across as well in live performance as it does in the recording studio. She put on a brave show during one of her early gigs at a club called the Bitter End. One of her guitar strings broke in the middle of a song, but she coolly borrowed one from another musician, restrung her instrument, and continued to sing. Both her presence of mind and her vocal talent impressed an executive of Shelter Records who sat in the audience, and he signed her to a recording contract.

Shelter was responsible for the change of her last name from Laub to Snow, which they apparently thought would make her more attractive to record buyers. They released her first album, *Phoebe Snow,* in 1974, and the single "Poetry Man" set the critics gushing with praise and became one of her biggest hits. But despite her newfound success, Snow was dissatisfied with Shelter and tried to get out of her contract. The legal wrangling had some ugly moments; Shelter claimed that they—and not the singer herself—had the exclusive rights to the stage name Phoebe Snow. Eventually, however, the young woman emerged triumphant, signed with Columbia Records, and released her second album in 1976, *Second Childhood.* This disc, like her debut, earned her a gold record and critical acclaim, and included trademark cuts such as "Inspired Insanity" and "All Over."

But while Snow was expanding as a recording artist, she was suffering personal setbacks. Just before the release of *Second Childhood,* she gave birth to a daughter, Valerie, who proved to be handicapped. As might be imagined, Snow had a great deal of difficulty adjusting to the child's problems. She managed, however, and her music actually provided her with a means of temporary escape from her woes—she continued to release albums on Columbia throughout the late 1970s.

Columbia dropped Snow at the beginning of the following decade, however, because her record sales did not keep pace with her critical acclaim; she bounced back by signing with Atlantic Records' Mirage label, and releasing a more hard-driving sound on the 1981 album *Rock Away.* But her professional relationship with Mirage was not to last long. After *Rock Away,* Snow sent them a demo tape for her next album; when they asked her to recut it, she "got very defensive," as she explained to Sheila Rogers in *Rolling Stone.* "I said, 'No, I like it the way it is.'" Snow promptly left Mirage and tried to find another company to release it, but none of them were interested.

Meanwhile, Snow had developed a love relationship with guitarist Gary Roda, who encouraged her to tour

with him. So she spent almost eight years performing on the road, which she "considered to be a lot of touring for someone who's not signed [to a recording contract]," she told Rogers. But while Snow toured, she began to put new material on demo tapes, and she also earned money by singing commercial jingles. When the relationship with Roda ended in 1987, she began to think about recording again, and she won a contract with Elektra. Some of the material she had recorded on demos over the past several years eventually became part of her successful 1989 comeback album, *Something Real.* The title cut, a tribute to her mother who died in 1986, has brought Snow back to the attention of music fans. The album, which has also been praised for tracks like "Touch Your Soul" and "If I Can Just Get Through the Night," prompted Hiltbrand to declare: "she's still got it." Gleason went even further, concluding that "Phoebe Snow has never sounded better."

Selected discography

Phoebe Snow (includes "Poetry Man"), Shelter, 1974.
Second Childhood (includes "Two Fisted Love," "Cash In," "Goin' Down for the Third Time," "No Regrets," "Sweet Disposition," "All Over," "Isn't It a Shame?" "Inspired Insanity," "Pre-Dawn Imagination," and "There's a Boat That's Leavin' Soon for New York"), Columbia, 1976.
It Looks Like Snow (includes "Autobiography," "My Faith Is Blind," "Teach Me Tonight," and "Shaky Ground"), Columbia, 1976.
Never Letting Go (includes "Love Makes a Woman," "Elektra," "Something So Right," and "Garden of Joy Blues"), Columbia, 1977.
Against the Grain (includes "Every Night"), Columbia, 1978.
Best of Phoebe Snow, Columbia, 1981.
Rock Away, Mirage, 1981.
Something Real (includes "Something Real," "Best of My Love," "Touch Your Soul," "I'm Your Girl," and "If I Can Just Get Through the Night"), Elektra, 1989.

Also released a duet single with Paul Simon in 1975, "Gone at Last."

Sources

Audio, April 1988.
People, May 1, 1989.
Rolling Stone, May 18, 1989; June 15, 1989.
Time, May 1, 1989.

—*Elizabeth Thomas*

Martial Solal

Pianist

Considered one of Europe's best jazz musicians, pianist Martial Solal is relatively unknown in the United States. Solal was born in Algiers, Algeria, North Africa, where he grew up listening to jazz pianists Fats Waller and Art Tatum and was exposed to bebop. In the forties Solal worked in Algiers as a pianist before settling in Paris in 1950. During the fifties he performed in Parisian clubs, often as backup, with many American expatriate jazz musicians.

The early 1960s were productive years for Solal. He performed for several months at the Hickory House, a club in New York City, and appeared at jazz festivals in Newport, Rhode Island; Montreal, Canada; and Berlin, West Germany. When asked in the sixties what he thought the future of jazz and his place in it would be, Solal recalled to Jerome Reese of *Musician,* "I said that in order for jazz to survive it had to have a repertoire, jazz musicians had to write important works. Just after that stupid declaration everyone did exactly the opposite, playing totally improvised music. Presently there is a return to traditionalism, and I persist in believing that the future of jazz lies in written music, in longer and longer written sequences, which does not exclude improvisation, of course. I also believe that once one

has a very definite style, the only way to evolve is through composing."

While most jazzmen went the alternate route, emphasizing improvisation, Solal has scored pieces for big band and various trios with which he has performed since the sixties. "Freedom, for me, means being able to go as far as possible in a certain direction, established and prepared in advance," he told Reese. "But I don't like the idea of 'anything goes.' That's why I play jazz standards, which give the audience something they can follow more easily and which will perhaps entertain them while having to put up with my, shall we say, busy style. Even when playing my own pieces, a major part of my performance consists of humourous musical citations I'll throw in as they pop into my head. But this humorous aspect can only be appreciated if the audience knows the standards I'm quoting. I like music that can surprise you at any given moment, not to show off, but in order to produce something different each time."

At one point in his career, Solal seriously studied classical music to help perfect his technique. Regular daily practice, often consisting of scales, maintains the virtuoso technique that has given him the ability to express whatever he has to say musically. When improvising he explores a melody in a seemingly endless stream of variations, which has given rise to his reputation as a highly technical musician. When the French government commissioned a work from Solal in the early eighties, Solal composed a concerto for piano and orchestra that was played by the big band that eventually involved into the government-supported Orchestre National de Jazz.

While Solal is best known in France for his duo albums with saxophonists Sidney Bechet and Lee Konitz and violinist Stephane Grappelli, he has also composed more than thirty movie scores, including the original French version of *Breathless,* conducted by Jean-Luc Goddard and starring Jean Paul Belmondo. With the advent of pop music and highly improvisatory jazz in the late sixties, the opportunites for film-score composing vanished.

Through his composing, arranging, and performing, Solal seems to want to legitimize jazz in Europe in general and his distinct style of jazz in particular. "Even if it doesn't sound modest, I think that one must listen to my music several times because of its density," Solal declared to Reese. "If you are surprised by the technical aspect, then the musical content may escape you on the first listening. I have always had very high hopes for jazz. I want people who love classical music to find that same perfection in jazz, and 90 percent of jazz doesn't satisfy that demand."

For the Record. . .

Born August 23, 1927, in Algiers, North Africa.

Jazz pianist, composer, arranger; played in Paris during 1950s; formed trio with Humair on drums and Guy Pedersen on bass; performed at Hickory House in New York City, 1963; played at jazz festivals in Newport, R.I., Montreal, Canada, and Berlin, West Germany; formed new trio with Gilbert Rovere (bass) and Charles Bellonzi (drums) 1965; began composing music for films in early 1960s, with more than 30 to his credit including three for Jean Paul Belmondo *(Breathless)*; best known in France for recordings with saxophonists Bechet and Konitz, and violinist Grappelli, 1974-80s.

Address: *Home*—Suburb of Paris, France.

Selected discography

Bluesine, Soul Note, 1983.
Duplicity (Martial Solal/Lee Konitz), Horo, 1977.
Four Keys (Martial Solal/Lee Konitz), MPS.
Happy Reunion (Stephane Grapelli/Martial Solal), Owl Records.
Impromptu (solo piano), 1985.
Jazz Gaveau, Columbia, 1960.
Key For Two (Martial Solal/Hampton Hawes), Affinity.
Martial Solal Big Band, Gaumont Musique, 1981.
Martial Solal Life 1962/85, (four-album set).
Mystere Solal (big band), 1962.
Suite for Trio (Solal/Pedersen/Humair), MPS, 1978.
Solal 56, Vogue Jazz Legacy.

Sources

Jazz Magazine (in French), December 1981; July/August 1983; January 1986.
Musician, March 1989.

—*Jeanne M. Lesinski*

Phil Spector

Producer, songwriter

C onsidered a rock-and-roll legend, Phil Spector is credited with revolutionizing the recording industry. From 1962 to 1965 he produced a number of rock classics and made stars of such groups as the Crystals, the Ronnettes, and the Righteous Brothers. His influence declined, however, with the "British invasion" of the mid-1960s. Ironically, the vanguard of that invasion—the Beatles—later helped to revive his career. Today, the reclusive and somewhat volatile Spector serves as president of his own record label.

Born in the Bronx, Spector moved to Los Angeles with his family when he was 12. He became interested in music (particularly rhythm and blues) while in high school and was influenced by the work of Jerry Leiber and Mike Stoller, who had produced a number of hits for Elvis Presley, the Coasters, and other performers. Spector eventually met the producers and became something of a regular at their studio. Spector wrote his first song, "To Know Him is to Love Him," in 1958. He recruited a local high school student to sing the female lead, sang the background harmonies himself, and named the duet the Teddy Bears. "To Know Him," which sold over one million records, was the Teddy Bears' only hit. In 1959 Spector recorded two singles under the name Spectors Three. Both records, however, failed to make the charts.

Three years later Spector founded Philles Records and began producing what *Time*'s Jay Cocks called "some of rock's greatest records." Spector-produced hits include "He's a Rebel," "Da Doo Ron Ron," "Then He Kissed Me," "Be My Baby," "You've Lost That Loving Feeling," and "River Deep-Mountain High." During this time he perfected his trademark "wall of sound," which was dubbed by Cocks as "vaulting arrangements and majestic delirium." In *Out of His Head: The Sound of Phil Spector,* Richard Williams noted that the producer used his singers "as tools, manipulating their every musical move with infinite care." It was, Williams continued, "'spontaneous' excitement through precise preplanning."

As British rock came into prominence in the mid-1960s, the Spector era drew to a close. Though semiretired, in 1970 he produced several tracks on the Beatles' *Let It Be* album; he worked with John Lennon on *Imagine* and with George Harrison on *All Things Must Pass.* He also produced *A Concert for Bangladesh,* as well as records by Cher, Dion, Leonard Cohen, Nilsson, and the Ramones.

Spector has been variously described as a mad genius, an eccentric, and a recluse. "In a recording studio, he throws tantrums as easily as other producers turn dials," wrote Cocks. "His excesses of style and manner

Born December 25, 1940, in Bronx, N.Y.; mother's name, Bertha; married Veronica Bennett (a singer), 1968 (divorced, 1974); children: Gary and Louis (twins), Donte, Nicole and Phillip (twins). *Education:* Attended University of California at Los Angeles.

Member of musical groups the Teddy Bears, 1958-59, and Spectors Three; producer with Atlantic Records, 1960-61; founder, Philles Records, 1962; currently president of Phil Spector Records International. Has produced records and albums for numerous artists, including Gene Pitney, Connie Francis, the Crystals, the Ronnettes, the Righteous Brothers, the Beatles, Ike and Tina Turner, John Lennon, George Harrison, Yoko Ono, Cher, and the Ramones. Composer of songs, including "To Know Him Is to Love Him," "Oh Why," and "I Really Do"; also composed, with others, "Spanish Harlem," "Da Doo Ron Ron," "Then He Kissed Me," "Be My Baby," "Chapel of Love," "You've Lost That Loving Feeling," "River Deep—Mountain High," and numerous other songs. Producer of television documentary "A Giant Stands 5 Ft. 7 In." and of movie *The Big T.N.T. Show.* Appeared in films *The T.A.M.I. Show* and *Easy Rider.*

Addresses: *Office*—Phil Spector Records International, P.O. Box 69529, Los Angeles, CA 90069.

are legend, and some call him mad." In a review of a documentary on Spector, the *New Statesman's* Mary Harron commented: "He had one perfect moment in the early 60s, and never recovered. And maybe that was all he could have because, as Sonny Bono said, 'everything he did was perfect, but it was always that one wall of sound.' But what a sound."

Selected discography

"To Know Him Is to Love Him" (single), Dore, 1958.
The Teddy Bears Sing!, Imperial, c. 1958.
"I Really Do" (single), Trey, c. 1959.
"My Heart Stood Still" (single), Trey, c. 1959.

Sources

Books

Williams, Richard, *Out of His Head: The Sound of Phil Spector,* Outerbridge & Lazard, Inc., 1972.

Periodicals

High Fidelity, June 1977.
Interview, March 1980.
Los Angeles Times, April 1, 1983; November 4, 1983.
New Statesman, August 19, 1983.
Newsweek, April 22, 1985.
New York, July 18, 1977.
New York Times, March 15, 1984.
Time, March 10, 1980.

—Denise Wiloch

Tiffany

Singer

I don't want anyone to think I'm controlled," Tiffany Darwish declared. "I'm not. I'm the only one who can tell you when I can and can't work, what I will and will not do. There's not some drill sergeant ordering me around." Speaking to the *Detroit Free Press* via a cellular phone in a limousine that was taking her to the Los Angeles International Airport, the 17-year-old pop singer sighed. She was once again on The Topic, the dreaded line of questioning that dogged her throughout 1988. The question—Who's in charge of Tiffany?

It was a valid question. In 1987, seemingly out of nowhere, the young singer had popped into shopping malls, singing to the accompaniment of backing tapes to shoppers clutching bags from the Gap and Sibley's Shoes. The stench of prefab contrivance was heavy in the air. This'll never work, said the critics. But because of that mall tour, Tiffany's debut album sold more than five million copies and became the first No. 1 record by a teenager since Stevie Wonder did the same at age 13 in 1963. She also had three Top 10 singles, including remakes of Tommy James's "I Think We're Alone Now" and the Beatles' "I Saw Her Standing There"—songs Tiffany claims she wasn't familiar with until she recorded them.

The media world, however, doesn't give teen stars a whole lot of respect. Visions of David Cassidy, Donny Osmond, Leif Garrett, Shaun Cassidy, and all those Phil Spector-produced singers come to mind. They were young, modestly talented performers who were jerked, pulled, and hyped towards success by calculating businessmen. Tiffany certainly has the svengali quotient in manager George Tobin. A onetime Motown Records staffer, Tobin found Tiffany, at age 12, singing with a country band in Southern California. He once told *Rolling Stone* that "Tiffany is signed to me, 100 percent to me." And he told *Life* magazine that "She *is* the girl next door. I've done nothing to change her. My role is to make sure nothing does."

That sounded like a frightening amount of control. And things got scarier in early 1988, when Tiffany filed for emancipation from her mother's custody. "My mother was not making smart career moves," Tiffany told *Rolling Stone.* But there were many who felt this move was engineered by Tobin. A compromise was reached by the California courts: Tiffany controlled the finances, and her mom was still her legal guardian, though the star—who would get lump-sum payments of her previous earnings at 18, 21, and 25—continued to live with her paternal grandmother in Norwalk, Calif. "I like the way it's done," she told the *Orange County Register,* "because it keeps me working now." In acknowledgment of the concerns and criticism raised by the public regarding Tobin's role, she told the *Free Press,*

For the Record. . .

Full name, Tiffany Renee Darwish; born October 2, 1972, in Norwalk, Calif.; daughter of Jim Darwish (a pilot) and Janie Christine Williams. *Education:* Attended high school in Norwalk, Calif.

Began singing publicly at age nine with country-western bands in Norwalk, Calif.; signed a contract with MCA Records, 1987, and recorded her first album; has performed in concert throughout North America, Europe, and Japan; has appeared on television programs, including "The Tonight Show" and "Entertainment Tonight."

Addresses: *Home*-La Mirada, Calif. *Record company*-c/o MCA Records, 70 Universal City Plaza, Third Floor, Universal City, Calif. 91607. *Other*—c/o Winterland Fan Asylum, 13659 Victory Blvd., Van Nuys, Calif. 91401.

"I'm fine. I'm not working too hard. I work at my own pace. George says to me, 'This is what we can do. Do you want to do this?' No one can force me to do anything."

Tiffany's career began singing before audiences at age nine, and within three years, she was appearing with country bands around the Los Angeles area. Things got rolling for her in 1981, when Tiffany agreed to sing on a demo tape by a local songwriter. The session took place in Tobin's North Hollywood studio, where he was producing a Smokey Robinson album. One of his assistants suggested that Tobin give a listen to the girl singing in the next room, and he was hooked. "I was enthralled by her voice," Tobin told *Rolling Stone*. "It was like taffy—you could pull it anywhere. In under 10 minutes, I decided to sign her."

Tobin kept in close contact, helping Tiffany and her mother look for a manager so that he could begin producing records for her. In 1986 Tobin got tired of searching and decided to manage Tiffany himself. He signed a seven-album exclusive production and management contract that gave him complete control of any records, videos, and performances by Tiffany during that period. "I learned a lot working at Motown," Tobin explained to *Rolling Stone* when asked about the possibility of excessive control.

The quarrels between Tobin and Tiffany's mother started early, according to the *Rolling Stone* feature. Mom wanted Tiffany to be a straight country singer; Tobin had his eye on the more lucrative pop market. "Her mother did think covering a Beatles song was sacrilegious, so we just never sent those tapes home," Tobin

said. "But her mother doesn't get involved. The family has decided that I manage the act." The Tobin-Tiffany deal also meant that record companies would sign a contract with George Tobin Productions, which would, in effect, lease them the Tiffany material. The only problem was that, early on, no one was biting. "Teen acts had burned so many record companies in the past that they were afraid," Brad Schmidt, Tobin's partner, told the *Free Press*. "They were all saying that they didn't know how to promote her."

So Tobin played hardball. He took Tiffany to the hotel room of Arista Records chief Clive Davis so that she could perform live for him. He barged in on countless executives and badgered others with phone calls. The persistence paid off; MCA signed a $150,000 deal for Tiffany's first album in early 1987. "The main reason I went with MCA is because their offices are one mile from my office," Tobin told *Rolling Stone*. "If I want to get something done, I can drive down there and block their cars on their driveway with my car, which I have done, and not let them out until it's settled."

It took a while to settle Tiffany into a niche into the marketplace, however. While she went about the business of being a teenager—going to malls, talking on the phone, and watching TV, according to a *Life* magazine profile—Tobin and MCA mulled over marketing plans while her album sat in record stores, unable to interest buyers or radio programmers. MCA's own promotion department, in fact, told Tobin that Tiffany's record didn't have the hit song necessary to garner attention. "To market a 14 or 15-year-old to the record industry was a tough sell," Larry Solters, MCA's vice-president of artist development told *Advertising Age*. The "Beautiful You" shopping mall tour idea was a bolt from the blue for Solters and Tobin. It came from simple deduction. Who's likely to buy an album by a teenager? they asked. Other teenagers. Where do you find teenagers? At shopping malls! It was a novel idea for the music industry, but not for the marketing world. Manufacturers like the Campbell Soup Co., Clairol, and General Foods had staged successful promotions in which they gave away free samples. So MCA was going to give away a free sample of Tiffany. "It was the first time a record company tried it," Phil Rosenthal of the Miami-based Shopping Center Network, which set up the tour, told *Advertising Age*.

Tiffany wasn't an immediate smash in the malls, however. The tour, which started in July 1987, drew tiny crowds at first, and, as Tiffany told *Rolling Stone,* "people were laughing and giving me weird reactions." That was OK, because it was odd for her, too. "I was singing to backing tracks," she told the *Detroit Free Press,* "and when the guitar solo came on, I was left filling in that time. When you have a live band, people can look at the guitar player, but in that situation, all people had to look at was me." But as the tour went on, the crowds got bigger, and scores of teenagers began calling their favorite radio stations and requesting Tiffany music. By the time the tour hit Salt Lake City in September 1987, an overflow crowd of more than 4,000 packed the stagefront.

Tiffany's album soared up the charts after that, as did her single. "I Think We're Alone Now" knocked Michael Jackson out of the No. 1 spot. Tours of Europe and Japan boosted album sales there; in Japan, she even starred in a TV commercial for an M&Ms-like candy. In America her story was splashed across the pages of everything from *People* to *Sixteen*.

Her success also opened the doors of record companies to other teen artists. Following in her wake were: Debbie Gibson, an accomplished 17-year-old from Long Island who composed most of her own material; Glenn Medeiros, a 17-year-old from Hawaii who had a Top 20 hit with "Never Gonna Change My Love for You"; 14-year-old Shanice Wilson; and Tracie Spencer, the 12-year-old winner of the TV talent contest *Star Search*. "Kids buy kids," co-manager Schmidt told the *Free Press*. "The record companies are starting to be open to the possibility of there being a youth market out there. They're trying to find the best of the talent out there that will accommodate that." Added Tom Arndt, associate editor of *Tiger Beat*, a teen-oriented magazine, "A lot of kids are surprised to hear that Tiffany and Debbie Gibson are as young as they are."

Tiffany, meanwhile, tried to keep the perils of success at bay. She toured with a tutor—27-year-old Craig Yamek, who doubled as the drummer in her band—to keep up with her studies. She told *Life* that her friends still "don't care if they come over and I'm lying in bed." And, she contended, she was still able to "hang out," just like in the pre-star days. "I went to Knot's Berry Farm the other day," she told the *Free Press*. "Not a lot of people recognized me. Most seemed to be thinking, 'That looks like Tiffany, but why would she be here by herself, with just friends, no bodyguards or anything?' Even if they do ask for autographs, they've always been nice people."

Approaching the end of 1988, Tiffany and Tobin were already mulling over her next album. Tobin had recorded 48 songs for the first record, but they kept working up new music, including a remake of the Young Rascals' "I Ain't Gonna Eat Out My Heart Anymore," another of those oldies that was new to Tiffany. The new record, *Hold An Old Friend's Hand*, was released in December 1988 to unenthusiastic critical response. Reviews in both *Rolling Stone* and *People*, for instance, both referred to Tobin's overbearing influence over the album's material (he wrote two of the songs) and the young singer herself. But, as Tiffany told *Advertising Age* earlier, "this is my dream," adding that "I've never thought of anything else, and now that it's happening, it's almost too overwhelming, but it's great."

Selected discography

Tiffany (includes "I Think We're Alone Now," "Could've Been," and "I Saw Him Standing There"), MCA, 1987.
Hold An Old Friend's Hand (includes "Hearts Never Lie," "I'll Be the Girl," and "I Ain't Gonna Eat Out My Heart Anymore"), MCA, 1988.

Also featured on the soundtrack for *Jetsons: The Movie*.

Sources

Advertising Age, June 6, 1988.
Detroit Free Press, December 4, 1987; July 29, 1988.
Life, May, 1988.
Los Angeles Herald Examiner, July 1, 1988.
Los Angeles Times, June 12, 1988.
Orange County Register, July 1, 1988.
People, June 27, 1988; January 23, 1989.
Rolling Stone, April 21, 1988; February 9, 1989.

—*Gary Graff*

Mel Torme

Singer, songwriter

Singer-songwriter Mel Torme, often referred to as "the Velvet Fog," has had a long and varied career. He sang with big bands during the 1940s but became more jazz-oriented in the 1950s; his more recent concert appearances have included a mixture of both jazz and old ballad standards. Torme has played in the best clubs in the United States, including the Copacabana and Marty's in New York City; he is also very popular in the venue of the larger hotels of Las Vegas, Nevada. Multitalented, Torme has acted in many films and appeared often on television; he has also written for the latter medium. As for his musical compositions, they are many and include the holiday classic, "The Christmas Song." He continues to record successfully, and his 1982 album *An Evening With George Shearing and Mel Torme* garnered him a Grammy Award.

Torme was born September 13, 1925, in Chicago, Illinois, to Jewish-Russian immigrant parents. His father was a retail merchant, and his mother worked as a sheet-music demonstrator at a Woolworth's store; she taught Torme all the new songs from an early age. Young Torme also loved to listen to the radio, and was memorizing musical arrangements before kindergarten. He told Chris Albertson in *Stereo Review:* "I had my electric train, little fire engines, and all that stuff, but the radio was my favorite toy, and I loved the bands." His family would also gather on the porch after their Sabbath dinner and sing together. When Torme was four years old, his parents took him to hear one of his favorite radio bands, the Coon-Sanders Original Nighthawk Orchestra. One of the bandleaders spotted the small boy sitting in the first row, singing and tapping his feet to the music, and invited him up to sing with them. The experience turned into Torme's first job as a performer, and he appeared weekly with the Nighthawk Orchestra for a time. At some point during his youth, Torme had his tonsils removed, and strangely enough, they partially grew back—some critics credit a certain fuzziness in his voice to this odd occurrence.

Torme also served as a radio actor during his childhood, giving voice to characters in programs such as "The Romance of Helen Trent," "Jack Armstrong, the All-American Boy," and "Lights Out." Perhaps because of this early fame, he did not fare well with his classmates; he confessed to Whitney Balliet in the *New Yorker* that he "got beaten up regularly." Torme also credits his life-long aversion to smoking to some bullies who forced him to eat tobacco as a child. But he was happier in high school. He played drums in a group that included future entertainer Steve Allen on the piano; the two became good friends.

While still in high school, Torme began to audition for

Full name Melvin Howard Torme; born September 13, 1925, in Chicago, Ill.; son of William (a retail merchant) and Sarah Sopkin (a sheet music demonstrator) Torme; married Candy Toxton (an actress) 1949 (divorced 1955); married Arlene Mills (a model) 1956 (divorced 1966); married Janette Scott (an actress) 1966 (divorced 1977); children: five in total.

Singer, songwriter, piano, drums, ukelele; jazz, big band, ballads; has sung professionally with bands off and on since the age of four; was a child actor in radio shows, including "The Romance of Helen Trent," "Jack Armstrong, the All-American Boy," and "Lights Out"; began writing songs while still in high school; appeared in over twenty films, including *Higher and Higher*, RKO, 1943, *Pardon My Rhythm*, Universal, 1944, *Let's Go Steady*, Columbia, 1945, *Good News*, MGM, 1947, *Words and Music*, MGM, 1948, *Girls Town*, MGM, 1959, *The Big Operator*, MGM, 1959, *The Private Lives of Adam and Eve*, Universal, 1960. Appeared in television programs, including "The Comedian," 1957, and the series "Night Court"; had own television talk show during 1950s, has written and produced for television, served as musical writer and advisor for "The Judy Garland Show," 1963-64. Has also written books, including a novel, an autobiography, and an account of his experiences with Garland.

Awards: Emmy nomination for best supporting actor for "The Comedian," 1957; Grammy Award for best male vocalist in 1983, on *An Evening with George Shearing and Mel Torme*, and another Grammy for best male jazz vocal, 1984.

Addresses: *Agent*—c/o Dale Sheets & Associates, Suite 206, 3518 W. Cahuenga Blvd., Los Angeles, Calif. 90068.

more mature spots with big bands. When he was fifteen, he almost made the cut for the famed Harry James band, but his age would have meant an added expense for the group—by law they would have had to hire a tutor for him. Nevertheless, James decided to record the song that Torme auditioned with—Torme's own composition, "Lament for Love." The song proved so successful that other big bands recorded it, and it was performed on the radio show "Your Hit Parade."

A few years later, in 1942, Torme won a place with the West Coast-based Chico Marx band; he served as rhythm singer and arranged the band's vocal performances. Though the band broke up eleven months after he joined it, Torme was spotted in its farewell appear-

ance by an executive from the RKO motion picture studios, who signed him for his first film role. Torme acted with famed singer Frank Sinatra in the 1943 movie *Higher and Higher*. More film rolls followed, and he appeared in pictures such as *Pardon My Rhythm*, *Let's Go Steady*, *Good News*, and *Words and Music* during the 1940s.

At about the same time as his film career took off, Torme was recording with a backup group called the Mel-Tones and performing in the better clubs, and, as Albertson reported, was saddled with the nickname, "the Velvet Fog." The crooner now feels this was a misnomer, and explained to Albertson that "that whole 'velvet fog' sound, that sort of head-toney, creamy, wispy sound, was—well, I can't say manufactured, because I was singing legitimately, but not as robustly as I could have been." Torme added that later, during the 1950s he "was able to relax and open up, and sing like I really like to sing . . . . My whole range has gained at least an octave, and I just don't sing like I used to. . . . The 'Velvet Fog' . . . simply does not fit."

In addition to a change in his vocal stylings during the 1950s, Torme moved away somewhat from the big band sound in favor of a more purely jazz repertoire. While singing jazz in small clubs, Torme also continued to make his mark on other media. A stint as substitute host on fellow entertainer Perry Como's television show garnered him his own daytime talk show on CBS. Torme acted for television, too—his performance in the 1958 CBS television film *The Comedian* won him an Emmy nomination for best supporting actor. Torme's big-screen films during the 1950s included *Girls Town* and *The Big Operator*. He began the 1960s with the motion picture *The Private Lives of Adam and Eve*.

Despite Torme's long-lived popularity as a performer, he has not been terribly successful in terms of making hit records. His disc of his self-composed classic "The Christmas Song," was overshadowed by singer Nat King Cole's smash-hit version of the same. In fact, Torme only made it into the top forty on the charts with a single once—"Comin' Home, Baby," which he released in 1962. Yet during the 1960s he won more critical claim for his talents, which he put to use as music writer and adviser to "The Judy Garland Show," among other projects. Torme also wrote for television, and was involved with the NBC series "The Virginian" and "Run for Your Life." In 1971 he was the host for ABC's documentary series "It Was a Very Good Year," and during the 1980s he has made several guest appearances on the NBC comedy series "Night Court."

During the 1970s—and well beyond—Torme's musical popularity has experienced a new vitality because of a renewed interest in the jazz genre. He has received

---

two Grammy Awards for the albums he recorded with pianist George Shearing, and he has told interviewers, including Albertson, that he is proudest of the discs he has recorded since 1976, when he released *Mel Torme Live at the Maisonette.* Torme is also justifiably proud of the mixed composition of his fans; he boasted to Albertson: "My audience is filled with extremely young yuppies, not just a mass of snow-white heads."

Selected discography

Mel Torme Live at the Maisonette, Atlantic, 1976.
Mel Torme and Friends, Finesse, c. 1981.
An Evening With George Shearing and Mel Torme, Concord, 1982.
Mel Torme With Rob McConnell and the Boss Brass, Concord, c. 1986.
Mel Torme and George Shearing: A Vintage Year, Concord, 1988.

Has also recorded many albums on various labels, including *Together Again—For the First Time,* with the late drummer Buddy Rich, and *A New Album.*

Writings

It Wasn't All Velvet: An Autobiography, Viking, 1988.

Sources

New Yorker, March 16, 1981.
People, December 1, 1986.
Stereo Review, March 1987; August 1988.

—*Elizabeth Thomas*

Ernest Tubb

Singer, songwriter, guitarist

Few country singers have inspired more affection than Ernest Tubb, the affable "Texas Troubadour." Tubb's career spanned some fifty years and effectively bridged the gap between the first true country recording artists, like Jimmie Rodgers, and the latest generation of stars, like Johnny Cash and Loretta Lynn. So many "firsts" are associated with Tubb that it is easy to miss a few: he was the first country artist to popularize electric guitar accompaniment, the first major purveyor of honky-tonk music, and the first country musician to headline a performance at Carnegie Hall. He is also remembered fondly for the helping hand he gave freely to other aspiring singers, among them Elvis Presley, Jack Greene, and Cal Smith.

Ernest Dale Tubb, the youngest of five children, was born near Crisp, Texas, in 1914. His father was an overseer to a 300-acre cotton farm, so all of the Tubb children spent more time in the fields working than in school. Ernest once estimated that he spent only seventeen months in a formal educational setting, but he made up for the deficit in education by reading constantly in his later years. Tubb's mother was a deeply religious woman who could play the organ and piano; she and Tubb's siblings encouraged his early interest in music and poetry-writing.

Country music became Tubb's passion when he encountered the songs of Jimmie Rodgers in the early 1930s. Rodgers is widely considered the first country superstar, and his landmark "blue yodels" were imitated by a host of admirers. Tubb was one of these admirers. He saved his dimes in order to buy each Rodgers release and painstakingly taught himself to play the guitar in his idol's style. Tubb said that when Rodgers died in 1933, "I thought my world had come to an end." He was wrong about that—his world had not ended, but was only beginning to unfold before him.

Throughout the worst years of the Depression, Tubb worked at any job he could find, from farm laborer to soda jerk. He also managed to pull in a few pennies by singing on the radio and in the rowdy Texas nightclubs where the honky-tonk sound was born. Late in 1935 he found himself in San Antonio, the city where Rodgers had been living before his death. On a hunch Tubb looked in the phone book for Rodgers's name and found a listing for his widow. Tubb phoned Mrs. Rodgers, and she was so impressed with his sincerity she invited him to her home.

Tubb spent an afternoon singing Rodgers's songs— he knew the words to every one—and listening raptly to Mrs. Rodgers's anecdotes. Even though he did not sound a bit like her husband, despite his most earnest efforts, Mrs. Rodgers agreed to help Tubb secure a recording contract. Her efforts resulted in a session for

RCA Records in 1936. Using Jimmie Rodgers's guitar, Tubb made several singles with RCA, including "The Passing of Jimmie Rodgers" and "The Last Thoughts of Jimmie Rodgers." These and several others failed to sell well—RCA did not promote Tubb aggressively—and soon the young artist was back on the road in Texas.

A simple illness probably saved Tubb's career. In 1939 he had his tonsils removed, and thereafter he could not yodel. He was forced to find a new singing style, and it was then that he began the drawling, almost narrative type of singing that would become his trademark. In the wake of the tonsillectomy, he secured a better contract with the new Decca label (also with the help of Mrs. Rodgers) and began to record again in 1940. Decca producer Dave Kapp was more sensitive to Tubb's special talents, and from the first Tubb's Decca singles sold well. Superstardom found the singer the following year when he released "I'm Walking the Floor over You," a spirited piece he had written himself. "I'm Walking the Floor over You" sold a phenomenal 400,000 copies in its first year of release and has since sold millions. On the strength of that song Tubb secured a sponsor, Universal Mills, and an appearance on the Grand Ole Opry in Nashville. His first Opry set was received so enthusiastically that he had to play three encores—he soon became a regular and moved to Nashville permanently.

By the mid-1940s—and for decades thereafter—Tubb exerted a major influence on the country music industry. A veritable string of hits as a solo performer and in duet with Red Foley led to movie appearances and nationwide tours. During these performances Tubb discovered that the acoustic guitars he and his band members used often could not be heard over the din of the crowd. He was not the first country singer to incorporate electric guitars, but he was the most famous to do so, and the dance-hall variety of honky-tonk music was born in his band.

On September 18, 1947, Tubb headlined a country-music show at Carnegie Hall. His opening comment—"My, my, this place sure could hold a lot of hay"—is remembered to this day. Tubb then returned to Nashville and opened his own record store, among the first to offer mail-order sales nationwide. He also began recording his songs in Nashville, thus becoming one of the first five performers to cut work there. Rounding out the busy year of 1947, Tubb founded a radio program, "Midnight Jamboree," that originated in his record shop. "Midnight Jamboree" aired on WSM radio right after the Grand Ole Opry, and it served as a showcase for up-and-coming talent. Among those who received career boosts from this exposure were Elvis Presley, the Everly Brothers, Bobby Helms, and Loretta Lynn.

Tubb always toured to the point beyond exhaustion. Typically his custom-made bus would travel as much as four hundred miles per night between engagements. He appeared in every state in the nation, as well as in Canada, Europe, Korea, Japan, Mexico, and South America. When emphysema threatened to sap his strength, he quit smoking and drinking—and continued touring. Throughout the 1950s and 1960s Tubb was never far from the Top 10 on the country charts. Major hits included "Goodnight Irene" (with Foley), "Hey, Mister Bluebird," "Our Baby's Book," and "Mr. and Mrs. Used-To-Be" (with Lynn). He also enjoyed singing about his home state, scoring hits with "There's a Little Bit of Everything in Texas" and "The Yellow Rose of Texas."

Only two years before his death in 1984, Tubb was still playing between 200 and 300 live engagements per year. In 1982 he was feted on television in a WOR-TV presentation "All-Star Tribute to Ernest Tubb: An American Original." Far more lasting than the television special, however, is the list of current artists who owe some aspect of their styles to Tubb, or those whose careers were enhanced by Tubb's help. Stylistically, Tubb broke ground for the honky-tonk artists like Buck Owens and Dwight Yoakam, as well as for the Texas-based performers like Willie Nelson and Waylon Jennings. He was instrumental in the careers of a staggering number of stars, including Johnny Cash, Hank Snow, Patsy Cline, and Charlie Pride. All of Nashville mourned his passing on September 6, 1984.

Tubb was elected to the Country Music Hall of Fame in 1965. Shortly before his death he told *The Country Music Encyclopedia* that he was never tempted to stray into the mainstream. "Country music over the years has been the most successful type and I neither intend to knock it or to give it up," he said. "There are those who cross over the bridge and mix their music, but I personally have no desire to do this. Country music is good. It is humble, simple, and honest and relaxed. It is a way of life. It is not confined to any segment of the country. We see young faces and we see old faces—and many in-between faces. Therefore, country music must have a general appeal to all ages, to all sections. I like it, the people like it, and I'll stick to it."

Selected discography

Singles

"The Passing of Jimmie Rodgers," RCA, 1936.
"The T.B. Is Whipping Me," RCA, 1937.
"Blue Eyed Elaine," Decca, 1940.
"I'll Never Cry over You," Decca, 1940.
"I'm Walking the Floor over You," Decca, 1941.
"I Wonder Why You Said Goodbye," Decca, 1942.
"Married Man Blues," RCA, 1942.
"The Right Train to Heaven," RCA, 1942.

LPs

The Daddy of 'Em All, Decca, 1959.
The Importance of Being Ernest, Decca, 1959.
Ernest Tubb's Golden Favorites, Decca, 1961.
Ernest Tubb's All Time Hits, Decca, 1961.
Ernest Tubb on Tour, Decca, 1962.
Just Call Me Lonesome, Decca, 1963.
Family Bible, Decca, 1963.

Thanks a Lot, Decca, 1965.
Blue Christmas, MCA.
Midnight Jamboree, MCA.
The Ernest Tubb Story, MCA.
The Ernest Tubb-Loretta Lynn Story, MCA.
Ernest Tubb's Greatest Hits, MCA.
Ernest Tubb's Greatest Hits, Volume 2, MCA.
Ernest Tubb with the Texas Troubadours, Vocalion.
I've Got All the Heartaches I Can Handle, MCA.
Saturday Satan, Sunday Saint, MCA.
Let's Turn Back the Years, MCA.
My Hillbilly Baby, Hillside.
Stand by Me, Vocalion.
(With Willie Nelson, Loretta Lynn, Merle Haggard, and others) *The Legend and the Legacy,* Cachet, 1979.
Honky-Tonk Classics, Rounder, 1982.

Sources

Books

The Best of Country Music, KBO Publishers, 1975.
The Illustrated Encyclopedia of Country Music, Harmony, 1977.
Malone, Bill C., *Country Music U.S.A.,* revised edition, University of Texas Press, 1985.
Malone, Bill C. and Judith McCulloh, *Stars of Country Music,* University of Illinois Press, 1975.
Shelton, Robert and Burt Goldblatt, *The Country Music Story: A Picture History of Country and Western Music,* Bobbs-Merrill, 1966, reprinted, Arlington House, 1971.
Shestack, Melvin, *The Country Music Encyclopedia,* Crowell, 1974.
Stambler, Irwin and Grelun Landon, *The Encyclopedia of Folk, Country, and Western Music,* St. Martin's, 1969.

Periodicals

Country Music, May 1973; April 1974.
Saga, May 1957.

—*Anne Janette Johnson*

UB40

British reggae band

Almost like a pop-music testament to the postulate that the whole is greater than the sum of its parts, the strength of UB40, the enormously successful British reggae band, lies in the strong communal bond that holds its multi-racial membership together. All eight members of the group—brothers Robin and Ali Campbell, who play guitar and sing; singer, trumpeter, and "toaster," or rapper, Astro; saxophonist Brian Travers; keyboardist Michael Virtue; drummer Jimmy Brown; percussionist Norman Hassan, and bassist Earl Falconer— were born and raised in Balsall Heath, a neighborhood in the English Midlands industrial city of Birmingham, an area that has always attracted large numbers of West Indians, Asian Indians, and working-class whites and blacks looking for scarce jobs.

Though times were tough growing up in that neighborhood in the 1960s, Travers told *Time*'s Jay Cocks: "Don't get the idea that we grew up poor, because we didn't. We didn't go hungry and have holes in our shoes or anything." And rather than being torn apart by large-scale unemployment or racial tension, the members of

For the Record. . .

Band members are **Robin Campbell** (guitar, vocals); **Ali Campbell** (guitar, vocals); **Astro** (saxophone, vocals); **Brian Travers** (saxophone); **Michael Virtue** (keyboards); **Jimmy Brown** (drums); **Norman Hassan** (percussion); **Earl Falconer** (bass).

Reggae; group assembled in Birmingham, England, 1977; cut demo tape with producer Bob Lamb; signed with Graduate record label; toured with rock group Pretenders, 1980; single "King" made U.K. Top 30, 1980; parted with Lamb and Graduate to form own record label, Dep International, 1980; toured the United States, 1983; single "Red Red Wine" reached Number 1 on U.S. charts, 1988.

Addresses: *Record company*—Virgin Records, Ltd., 9247 Alden Drive, Beverly Hills, CA 90210.

UB40 came together in those days with the help of music, specifically the charged rhythms of Jamaican reggae and the lyric melodies of Motown that were popular in Balsall Heath. "At the age when you start to form your musical allegiances," Robin Campbell told *Rolling Stone,* "we were hearing reggae. They used to play it at ear-bleeding volume, so you couldn't help but hear it."

Considering that at the time of UB40's inception none of its members could play an instrument, the birth of the group was somewhat curious. Then seventeen, Ali Campbell "got very drunk and upset somebody," brother Robin told *Rolling Stone*'s Parke Puterbaugh, "and he got a flying glass in his face." With the money he received from criminal injuries compensation, Ali went out and bought a guitar and drum set, and the others went out and bought instruments for themselves.

What UB40 lacked in musical talent in those early days, they more than made up for with self-confidence and ambition. Embarking on their "master plan," the group, which they named after the all-too-familiar unemployment benefits application form, had plenty of time to practice in a cellar, where they honed their sound and practiced scribbling their soon-to-be-famous autographs on the walls. To avoid becoming merely a local favorite, the band vowed to play its hometown only once every six weeks, and spread word that in the times between they were on the road touring, when in fact they were usually right back in the cellar practicing. The first producer to show genuine interest in UB40 was Bob Lamb, who played the group's demo tape for several influential DJs and eventually got them signed to the Graduate record label. The band's second single, "King," received extensive airplay, and when Chrissie Hynde, lead singer of the path-breaking group Pretenders, heard UB40 playing in a London pub, she invited them to join her band on its upcoming tour.

The exposure brought on by this popular tour catapulted UB40 into instant stardom. Their subsequent album, *Signing Off,* became the first reggae record to reach the British pop 30, and UB40 has since amassed more than 25 hit singles in the U.K. But in the recording industry, to achieve true stardom and, of course, financial success, the greatest test for a group is whether or not it can conquer America. Strangely, UB40's first foray into the U.S. pop world fell astonishingly flat. "No, no, no, it just doesn't happen this way," *Time*'s Jay Cocks sarcastically wrote of that ill-fated venture. "Smash Brit band, bedecked with hit singles and platinum albums from abroad, storms U.S. shores in 1983. Plays some concerts, manages to squeeze one hit onto the low midrange of the singles charts, then goes back home. Modest hit single, which had reached the Number 1 spot in twelve other countries, expires from widespread Stateside indifference."

The "modest hit single" Cocks refers to was "Red Red Wine," from the LP *Labour of Love,* a compilation of all cover songs taken from favorites the band had over the years of listening to reggae. Ironically, "Red Red Wine" was not, like most of the songs on the album, a classic Jamaican reggae hit; rather, it was penned in 1968 by the legendary Tin Pan Alley songwriter Neil Diamond and first covered by Tony Tribe. "Red Red Wine" was a Number 1 single in Britain and a smash hit worldwide, but U.S. audiences strangely shunned it when UB40's new label, A & M Records, released it in 1983. Meanwhile, in the ensuing years the group released two critically acclaimed albums of original songs, *Rat in the Kitchen* (1986) and *UB40* (1988), which were both, again, well-received in the U.K. and hardly noticed in the U.S.

In fact, UB40's breakthrough in the American market did come finally in 1988, but it had nothing to do with either of these fine albums. Rather, it came with a lot of luck, by way of the whim of Phoenix radio station KZZP which, for some strange reason, put the five-year-old single "Red Red Wine" on its playlist in May of that year. By August, the song was the station's Number 1 requested single, and other album-rock stations around the country began playing the record with such success that A & M decided to re-release it. By October "Red Red Wine" was the Number 1 song on the *Billboard* charts. This belated success left some of the band members admittedly a little confused and ambivalent about the U.S. market, but as Astro told *Rolling Stone,* "Who cares? As long as it's a hit, I'll accept it."

Labour of Love received more belated honors when it was named among *Rolling Stone*'s Top 100 albums of the 1980s. The emphasis in making that record, Robin Campbell told the magazine, was to reestablish reggae as an enjoyable musical form in its own right, rather than merely a vehicle for religious or political messages as it had come to be known since Bob Marley's Rastafarian days. Campbell said that before Marley, reggae was simply a form of Jamaican pop music, meant for dancing and feeling good. "It's African and calypso rhythms fused together with American rhythm and blues. All it's ever been is homemade pop music, and it just gets up my nose when people start talking about reggae as a political or religious music."

But that does not explain the overtly political and social flavor of much of UB40's original music. Indeed, the band often targets the harshness of capitalism and racism and the injustice in South Africa. Perhaps this is why UB40 was extended an invitation to play a short tour in the Soviet Union in 1986, an experience that may have opened the band's eyes a little about life in that country. For instance, though the concerts were sold out everywhere, the fans, under the watchful eyes of special security police, were not allowed to dance to the music; and when the band members spoke directly to the audience about the meaning in a particular song, the Soviet translator often misconstrued their meaning to make it less "controversial." "There'd have to be some pretty strong persuasion to make me come back here," a frustrated Robin Campbell told *Rolling Stone.*

UB40 instead likes to make itself a little commune. The band members all still live in Balsall Heath, albeit in nicer houses, and the democratic make-up of the group has created only one strict rule: "Do what you do easiest." And in 1988 the group got together to realize the ultimate dream of all boyhood chums when they purchased 270 acres of land on an island south of Jamaica. "We thought, 'Why don't we buy a place and build ourselves a bunch of houses and a shop and a bar and just have our own little community?'" Robin told *Rolling Stone.* "Sounds like fun to me."

Selected discography

Signing Off, Graduate, 1980.
Present Arms, Dep International.
Labour of Love, A & M, 1983.
Geffrey Morgan, A & M, 1984.
Rat in the Kitchen, A & M, 1986.
UB40, A & M, 1988.

Sources

Books

Clifford, Mike, *The Illustrated Encyclopedia of Black Music,* Harmony Books, 1982.

Periodicals

Rolling Stone, October 9, 1986; December 4, 1986; December 1, 1988; November 16, 1989.
Time, October 31, 1988.

—David Collins

Muddy Waters

Blues slide guitarist, harmonica player

How many blues artists could boast of an alumni of band members that includes Otis Spann, Little Walter, Junior Wells, Fred Below, Walter Horton, Jimmy Rogers, James Cotton, Leroy Foster, Buddy Guy, Luther Johnson, Willie Dixon, Hubert Sumlin, and Earl Hooker, just to name a few? Muddy Waters gave these and many more their first big break in music while creating a style known now as Chicago blues (guitar, piano, bass, drums, and harmonica).

"Contemporary Chicago blues starts, and in some ways may very well end, with Muddy Waters," wrote Peter Guralnick in *Listener's Guide To The Blues*. From the 1950s until his death in 1983, Waters literally ruled the Windy City with a commanding stage presence that combined both dignity and raw sexual appeal with a fierce and emotional style of slide guitar playing.

Waters was born McKinley Morganfield in Rolling Fork, Mississippi, in 1915 but grew up in Clarksdale, where his grandmother raised him after his mother died in 1918. His fondness for playing in mud earned him his nickname at an early age. Waters started out on harmonica but by age seventeen he was playing the guitar at parties and fish fries, emulating two blues artists who were extremely popular in the south, Son House and Robert Johnson. "His thick heavy tone, the dark coloration of his voice and his firm almost stolid manner were all clearly derived from House," wrote Guralnick in *Feel Like Going Home,* "but the embellishments which he added, the imaginative slide technique and more agile rhythms, were closer to Johnson."

In 1940 Waters moved to St. Louis before playing with Silas Green a year later and returning back to Mississippi. In the early part of the decade he ran a juke house, complete with gambling, moonshine, a jukebox, and live music courtesy of Muddy himself. In the summer of 1941 Alan Lomax came to Stovall, Mississippi, on behalf of the Library of Congress to record various country blues musicians. "He brought his stuff down and recorded me right in my house," Waters recalled in *Rolling Stone,* "and when he played back the first song I sounded just like anybody's records. Man, you don't know how I felt that Saturday afternoon when I heard that voice and it was my own voice. Later on he sent me two copies of the pressing and a check for twenty bucks, and I carried that record up to the corner and put it on the jukebox. Just played it and played it and said, 'I can do it, I can do it.'" Lomax came back again in July of 1942 to record Waters again. Both sessions were eventually released as *Down On Stovall's Plantation* on the Testament label.

In 1943 Waters headed north to Chicago in hopes of becoming a full-time professional. He lived with a relative for a short period while driving a truck and working in a factory by day and playing at night. Big Bill Broonzy was the top cat in Chicago until his death in 1958 and the city was a very competitive market for a newcomer to become established. Broonzy helped Waters out by letting him open for the star in the rowdy clubs. In 1945 Waters's uncle gave him his first electric guitar, which enabled him to be heard above the noisy crowds.

In 1946 Waters recorded some tunes for Mayo Williams at Columbia but they were never released. Later that year he began recording for Aristocrat, a newly-formed label run by two brothers, Leonard and Phil Chess. In 1947 Waters played guitar with Sunnyland Slim on piano on the cuts "Gypsy Woman" and "Little Anna Mae." These were also shelved, but in 1948 Waters's "I Can't Be Satisfied" and "I Feel Like Going Home" became big and his popularity in clubs began to take off. Soon after, Aristocrat changed their name to Chess and Waters's signature tune, "Rollin' Stone," became a smash hit.

The Chess brothers would not allow Waters to use his own musicians (Jimmy Rogers and Blue Smitty) in the studio; instead he was only provided with a backing bass by Big Crawford. However, by 1950 Waters was recording with perhaps the hottest blues group ever:

Little Walter Jacobs on harp; Jimmy Rogers on guitar; Elgin Evans on drums; Otis Spann on piano; Big Crawford on bass; and Waters handling vocals and slide guitar. The band recorded a string of great blues classics during the early 1950's with the help of bassist/songwriter Willie Dixon's pen. "Hoochie Coochie Man" (Number 8 on the R & B charts), "I Just Want To Make Love To You" (Number 4), and "I'm Ready." These three were "the most macho songs in his repertoire," wrote Robert Palmer in *Rolling Stone*. "Muddy would never have composed anything so unsubtle. But they gave him a succession of showstoppers and an image, which were important for a bluesman trying to break out of the grind of local gigs into national prominence."

Waters was at the height of his career and his band steamed like a high-powered locomotive, cruising form club to club as the Headhunters, crushing any other blues band that challenged their musical authority. "By the time he achieved his popular peak, Muddy Waters had become a shouting, declamatory kind of singer who had forsaken his guitar as a kind of anachronism and whose band played with a single pulsating rhythm," wrote Guralnick in his *Listener's Guide*.

Unfortunately, Waters's success as the frontman led others in his group to seek the same recognition. In 1953 Little Walter left when his "Juke" became a hit and in 1955 Rogers quit to form his own band. Waters could never recapture the glory of his pre-1956 years as the pressures of being a leader led him to use various studio musicians for quite a few years following.

He headed to England in 1958 and shocked his overseas audiences with loud, amplified electric guitar and a thunderous beat. When R & B began to die down shortly after, Waters switched back to his older style of country blues. His gig at the Newport Folk Festival in 1960 turned on a whole new generation to Waters's Delta sound. As English rockers like Eric Clapton and the Rolling Stones got hip to the blues, Waters switched back to electric circa 1964. He expressed anger when he realized that members of his own race were turning their backs to the genre while the white kids were showing respect and love for it.

However, for the better part of twenty years (since his last big hit in 1956, "I'm Ready") Waters was put on the back shelf by the Chess label and subjected to all sorts of ridiculous album themes: *Brass And The Blues, Electric Mud,* etc. In 1972 he went back to England to record *The London Muddy Waters Sessions* with four hotshot rockers—Rory Gallagher, Steve Winwood, Rick Grech, and Mitch Mitchell—but their playing wasn't up to his standards. "These boys are top musicians, they can play with me, put the book before 'em and play it, you know," he told Guralnick. "But that ain't what I need to sell my people, it ain't the Muddy Waters sound. An if you change my sound, then you gonna change the whole man."

Waters sound was basically Delta country blues electrified, but his use of microtones, in both his vocals and slide playing, made it extremely difficult to duplicate and follow correctly. "When I plays onstage with my band, I have to get in there with my guitar and try to bring the sound down to me," he said in Rolling Stone. "But no sooner than I quit playing, it goes back to another, different sound. My blues look so simple, so easy to do, but it's not. They say my blues is the hardest blues in the world to play."

Fortunately for Waters and his fans there was one man who understood the feeling he was trying to convey: Johnny Winter, an albino Texan who could play some of the nastiest guitar east or west of the Mississippi. In 1976 Winter convinced his label, Blue Sky, to sign Waters and the beginning of a fruitful partnership was begun. Waters's "comeback" LP, Hard Again, was recorded in just two days and was as close to the original Chicago sound he had created as anyone could ever hope for. Winter produced/played and pushed the master to the limit. Former Waters sideman James Cotton kicked in on harp on the Grammy Award-winning album and a brief but incredible tour followed. "He sounds happy, energetic and out for business," stated Dan Oppenheimer in Rolling Stone. "In short, Muddy Waters is kicking in another mule's stall."

In 1978 Winter recruited Walter Horton and Jimmy Rogers to help out on Waters's I'm Ready LP and another impressive outing was in the can. The roll continued in 1979 with the blistering Muddy "Mississippi" Waters Live. "Muddy was loose for this one," wrote Jas Obrecht in Guitar Player, "and the result is the next best thing to being ringside at one of his foot-thumping, head-nodding, downhome blues shows." King Bee the following year concluded Water's reign at Blue Sky and all four LP's turned out to be his biggest-selling albums ever.

In 1983 Muddy Waters passed away in his sleep. At his funeral, throngs of blues musicians showed up to pay tribute to one of the true originals of the art form. "Muddy was a master of just the right notes," John Hammond, Jr., told Guitar World. "It was profound guitar playing, deep and simple . . . more country blues transposed to the electric guitar, the kind of playing that enhanced the lyrics, gave profundity to the words themselves." Two years after his death, the city that made Muddy Waters (and vice versa) honored their father by changing the name of 43rd Street to Muddy Waters Drive. Following Waters's death, B.B. King told Guitar World, "It's going to be years and years before

most people realize how great he was to American music."

Selected discography

Released on Chess

Muddy Waters at Newport, 1960;reissued, 1987.
Folk Singer, 1964; reissued, 1987.
Muddy Waters, 1964.
Brass and the Blues, 1966.
The Real Folk Blues, 1966; reissued, 1988.
Electric Mud, 1968.
After the Rain, 1969.
Fathers and Sons, 1969.
They Call Me Muddy Waters, c. 1969.
The London Muddy Waters Sessions, 1972; reissued, 1989.
McKinley Morganfield, 1972.
Muddy Waters Live, 1972.
Can't Get No Grindin', 1973.
Unk in Funk, 1974.
Muddy Waters at Woodstock, 1975.
The Best of Muddy Waters (1948-1954), 1987.
Muddy Waters Sings Big Bill Broonzy, 1960; reissued, 1987.
Troubles No More: Singles, 1955-1959, 1989.

Released on Blue Sky

Hard Again, 1977.
I'm Ready, 1978.
Muddy "Mississippi" Waters Live, 1979.
King Bee, 1981.

Released on other labels

Afro-American Blues and Game Songs, Library of Congress, c. 1942.
Down on Stovall's Plantation, Testament, c. 1942.Chicago Blues: The Beginning, Testament, 1971.
Muddy Waters: The Chess Box, Chess/MCA, 1989.

Sources

Books

Christgau, Robert, Christgau's Record Guide, Ticknor & Fields, 1981.
Guralnick, Peter, Feel Like Going Home, Vintage Books, 1981.
Guralnick, Peter, The Listener's Guide to the Blues, Facts on File, 1982.
Harris, Sheldon, Blues Who's Who, Da Capo, 1979.
Kozinn, Allan, Pete Welding, Dan Forte, and Gene Santoro, The Guitar: The History The Music The Players, Quill, 1984.

The Rolling Stone Record Guide, edited by Dave Marsh with
  John Swenson, Random House/Rolling Stone Press, 1979.

Periodicals

Guitar Player, July 1979; July 1983; August 1983.
Guitar World, September 1983; January 1986; March 1989;
  March 1990.
Living Blues, September-October 1989.
Rolling Stone, March 24, 1977; October 5, 1978.

—*Calen D. Stone*

Don Williams

Singer, songwriter, guitarist

Country artist Don Williams is "a reluctant superstar," according to John Morthland in *Country Music*. "The songs that have made him successful," lauded Dick J. Reavis in *Texas Monthly*, "are as strong and warm as morning coffee," but due to Williams's preferences of shunning publicity and keeping his touring to a minimum, he remains what Reavis described as "a mid-level star." Nevertheless the singer-songwriter has released at least twenty albums, scored hits like "Amanda," "Some Broken Hearts Never End," and "I Wouldn't Want to Live If You Didn't Love Me," and was voted Male Vocalist of the Year in 1979 by the Country Music Association of America. In addition to many such honors in the country genre, Morthland claimed in another review that "Williams is one of the uncredited creators of . . . 'New Age' music" with his "spare, acoustic sound."

Williams was born May 27, 1939, in Floydada, Texas. His father was a mechanic, but his mother was musical and taught him how to play the guitar by the time he was twelve. Though he always enjoyed country music, Williams as a young man also liked the sounds of rock and roll stars such as Elvis Presley and Chuck Berry. But he didn't begin to work on performing as a career until after serving in the U.S. Army for two years. While supporting himself with odd jobs in the area of Corpus Christi, Texas, including driving a truck and working in oil fields, Williams and a friend named Lofton Kline started singing in bars as the Strangers Two.

One night the duo played a college dance and found themselves on the same bill with singer Susan Taylor. The three became acquainted, and Taylor joined Williams and Kline to form a folk trio. Calling themselves the Pozo Seco Singers, they released a single, "Time," on an independent label. The song became a hit in their home state, and led them to a recording contract with Columbia Records. By 1966, "Time" had become a national hit. Though the Pozo Seco Singers had only the smallest, local hits afterwards, they stayed together for over five years. Reavis reflected that the group's biggest drawback was that they were "mellow to a fault"; he went on to explain that their sound "lacked the accusatory edge that lifted [folk artists] Bob Dylan and Joan Baez above the ranks." Despite the honor of being asked to sing at President Lyndon Johnson's ranch in 1968, by the dawn of the 1970s Williams and his friends were reduced to singing in rowdy bars. Disgusted with this type of audience, Williams gave up the group in 1971 to open a furniture store with his father-in-law.

But he was not contented with that life, and the following year Williams went to Nashville, Tennessee, seeking work as a songwriter. He was hired both to write and

and began a long tenure in country music's bush leagues.

The Alabama honky tonks where Williams played were so rough that they were called "blood buckets." In that unsavory atmosphere the young singer developed his style as well as his fatal attraction to alcohol. Williams was so unsuccessful in the early years that he quit music during the Second World War and worked as a welder in the Mobile shipyards. After the war he returned to music, determined at least to sell some of the songs he had written.

In 1946, the twenty-three year-old Williams set off for Nashville with his wife Audrey. There they paid an unsolicited call on Fred Rose, Nashville's biggest music writer and publisher. Rose listened to Williams sing and play a half dozen of his songs and signed him to a contract immediately. The years of struggle were finally over for Williams, as Rose took the singer on as a protege and literally directed the course of his entire career. Rose helped Williams to secure a contract with MGM Records, and after Williams's first country hit, "Move It on Over," helped the singer to land a job with the "Louisiana Hayride" radio show in Shreveport.

Fred Rose a...
polish his son...
sold to the luc...
bore fruit with...
"Cold, Cold Hea...
"Cold, Cold Hea...
for Tony Bennett...
Number 1 count...
liams notes that t...
one of the most su...
It was a perfect un...
craftsmanship and...

Williams was the he...
for two years, earnin...
on Over," "I Heard...
"Lovesick Blues." The...
Tin Pan Alley number,...
perform on the Grand...
June 11, 1949, remain...
history. The audience...
encores of "Lovesick B...
order for the show to c...
cized drinking problems...
regular on the Opry.

As an Opry regular, Willia...
He reorganized the Driftin...
Rivers (fiddle), Don Helms...
(lead guitar) and Hillous...
other studio musicians bega...
the bone-wearying cross-c...
appearances. Williams and...
across America and made se...
one to Germany to entertain...
tioned there.

Within a year, Hank Williams wa...
country star in the business. His...
recordings topped $200,000 pe...
Rose he was wise about securin...
his work. Still Williams faced a de...
when he was sober, he could per...
drunk, he could do nothing at all. H...
to keep him alcohol- and drug-...
limited success. Even at the height...
seemed bent on self-destruction.

With Number 1 hits like "Why Don...
"Cold, Cold Heart," and "Long Gone...
Williams won a popular acclaim that...
had previously equaled. Music fans ou...
sphere bought his records and learned...
country fans could not get enough of him...
this first "crossover" artist epitomized...
rural sound. On stage Williams was a...
easygoing performer with a magnetic s...

to try to sell songs to country artists by Jack Music Publishing. After only a short time of having these artists almost buy his songs but reject them because they were afraid that his work was just too different to be popular with country fans, Williams heeded their advice about recording them himself. He signed with JMI Records, which, like Jack Music, belonged to Jack Clement. Though he did perform his own compositions, he did not restrict himself to them. Williams's solo debut album, Don Williams, Volume One, featured the now-classic "Amanda," which also became a hit for Waylon Jennings, and another successful single, "In the Shelter of Your Eyes." Following the release of Don Williams, Volume Two, though, JMI went out of business, and Williams signed with ABC/Dot Records. When the latter company merged with MCA Records in 1978, Williams stayed on, scoring hits with them such as "You're My Best Friend," "Till the Rivers All Run Dry," and "Tulsa Time." The last was voted Single Record of the Year by the Academy of Country Music in 1979.

No matter what company Williams has recorded with during his solo career, however, he has always maintained tight artistic control. As Reavis reported, "he refuse(s) to consider singing any songs about fighting, marital infidelity, or drinking." Apparently it is not so much to take a high moral tone as to be true to his own experiences; Williams told Reavis: "I've never really done those things, they haven't been a part of my life, so I guess I just don't relate to them very well." Instead he prefers love ballads, or songs that tell a story. And according to Morthland, Williams "sifts through 50 to 100 songs for each one of the 15 he records for an album before picking the final 10." Williams also remains in control of his concert appearances. Not only does he limit himself to approximately forty dates a year, but "if he notice(s) people in his audience openly smoking marijuana, he [asks] them to leave," Reavis affirmed. Williams even disbanded his own fan club to protect his privacy and that of his family, and because he simply doesn't believe in them. He told Reavis: "I just don't believe that you've got to know Henry to drive a Ford."

Despite his deliberate distance from the spotlight, Williams continues to satisfy country fans. His 1987 album Traces included songs such as "Old Coyote Town," "Till I Can't Take It Anymore," and "Come From the Heart." Morthland, while faulting the quality of some of the material—Williams no longer writes his own songs—concluded that Traces makes it "clear why" fans "keep coming back for more."

Selected discography

LPs

Don Williams, Volume One (includes "Amanda," "The Shelter of Your Eyes," and "Come Early Morning"), JMI, 1972.
Don Williams, Volume Two, JMI, c. 1973.
Don Williams, Volume Three, ABC/Dot, 1974.
You're My Best Friend, ABC/Dot, 1975.
Don Williams's Greatest Hits, ABC/Dot, 1975.
Harmony, ABC/Dot, c. 1976.
Visions, ABC/Dot, c. 1976.
Country Boy, ABC/Dot, c. 1977.
Traces (includes "Desperately," "Old Coyote Town," "Easy Touch," "Running Out of Reasons to Run," "Till I Can't Take It Anymore," and "Come From the Heart"), Capitol, 1987.
Prime Cuts, Capitol, 1989.

Single releases

In addition to the songs attributed to some of the above albums, Williams has released on ABC/Dot, MCA, and Capitol Records the following hits during the late 1970s and 1980s: "Some Broken Hearts Never End," "Till the Rivers All Run Dry," "Louisiana Saturday Night," "Say It Again," "I Wouldn't Want to Live if You Didn't Love Me," "She Never Knew Me," "The Ties That Bind,"

"Rake and Ramblin' Man," "Tulsa Time," "Lord, I Hope This Day Is Good," and "Then It's Love."

Sources

Country Music, January/February 1988; March/April 1988; May/June 1989.
Texas Monthly, October 1986.

—*Elizabeth Thomas*

nk
iams, Sr.

ongwriter, guitarist

He is known simply as the greatest country singer of all time—the immortal Hank Williams, whose ballads and laments of frustrated love brought a regional music squarely into the mainstream. Williams was one of the best songwriters ever to emerge in the country genre, and his exceptional creative ability was enhanced by a magnetic, if utterly rural, stage presence. In *Country Music U.S.A.,* Bill C. Malone calls Williams "the most dramatic symbol of country music's postwar surge," an artist whose "early death solidified the legend that had already begun during his lifetime."

Most country singers rely upon outside sources for at least some of their songs. Williams was an exception to that rule: his concerts were composed almost exclusively of pieces he wrote himself, now-classic tunes like "Cold, Cold Heart," "I Saw the Light," "Your Cheatin' Heart," and "Why Don't You Love Me?" According to Roger M. Williams in *Stars of Country Music,* the fact that Williams had such a lengthy and varied repertory is one mark of his greatness. The critic adds: "A larger mark is the extraordinary number of truly memorable songs [Williams] turned out. Those songs transcend country music, or any category short of pop. They are part of America's musical heritage, and they elevate the man who wrote them to a very high rank among the nation's songwriters."

For all his greatness, however, Williams had only a brief period of success, marred by the excessive drinking that would kill him before he turned thirty. The greatest part of his short life was spent in near-poverty, playing in the deep South's roughest honky tonks and on small radio stations in Alabama and Louisiana. Hiram King Williams was born September 17, 1923, in tiny Moun[t] Olive, Alabama. His family was very poor, because hi[s] father—a part-time farmer and log train engineer— suffered from poor health. When Williams was seve[n] his father disappeared into a veteran's hospital a[nd] was never seen again. Young Hank was called on [to] help support the family by selling peanuts and news[pa]pers and shining shoes.

Williams was fronting a country band by the tim[e he] turned fourteen. He drew upon numerous source[s for] his musical style, from the gospel sounds he hea[rd in] church (his mother was an organist) to the tunes [of] Acuff and Ernest Tubb. The singer also owed a s[trong] debt to black music; he was taught guitar by a [black] street singer named Tee-Tot (Rufus Payne) who [lived in] his home town. At any rate, Williams was writing [his own] songs and singing them from his earliest teens. [His first] recognition came at an amateur contest in Mo[ntgom]ery, Alabama, where he won first place for a [perform]ance of "WPA Blues," a song he wrote himsel[f. Soon] thereafter he formed his band, the Drifting C[owboys.]

was pure country, strong and steady but with a keening edge that leant pathos to his love ballads. Analyzing the singer's vast popularity, Roger Williams simply concludes that Hank "had the infectious appeal common to all great performers."

This appeal was not enough to assure Williams's continued success. In 1952 he was fired from the Opry for drunkenness, and he returned to the "Louisiana Hayride" for a brief period. His first marriage ended in divorce, and he became somewhat a laughingstock for his wedding to a Louisiana beauty—the ceremony was conducted twice, in public, and admission was charged. By that time Williams was a walking victim of drug abuse—a back ailment from his early years led to the use of painkillers in addition to alcohol. His sudden death of a heart attack on New Year's Eve 1953 still came as a shock to the nation. He died in his sleep en route to a concert in Canton, Ohio. He was twenty-nine.

Death only enhanced Williams's appeal to his legions of fans. A number of Williams singles were released

---

> *Williams, the hard-living, self-destructive rambling bard, mined his own misery for lyrics and gave the world a number of its most memorable country songs.*

---

posthumously, including the classic "Your Cheatin' Heart." To this day Hank Williams remains one of the best-selling country singers, with numerous albums in print in any given year. His songs have been covered countless times by all kinds of singers—especially his famous son, Hank, Jr. Royalties on Hank Williams songs have earned the Williams family millions of dollars in the decades since the performer's death. It is certainly not surprising that he was the very first entertainer elected to the prestigious Country Music Hall of Fame when it opened in 1961.

Grounded as he was in the country tradition, Williams had a seminal influence on the acceptance of country by mainstream audiences. His appeal was basic: he could communicate *sincerely* with listeners. Malone notes that Williams "'lived' the songs he sang—he could communicate his feelings to the listener and make each person feel as if the song were being sung directly and only to him or her." Roger Williams writes:

"Everybody understands what a Hank Williams song means, and almost everybody senses the straightforward, bedrock emotion—joy or anguish or both—from which it springs."

Williams, the hard-living, self-destructive rambling bard, mined his own misery for lyrics and gave the world a number of its most memorable country songs. He explained the popularity of his work this way: "When a hillbilly sings a crazy song, he feels crazy. When he sings, 'I Laid My Mother Away,' he sees her a-laying right there in the coffin. He sings more sincere than most entertainers because the hillbilly was raised rougher than most entertainers. You got to know a lot about hard work. You got to have smelt a lot of mule manure before you can sing like a hillbilly. The people who has been raised something like the way the hillbilly has knows what he is singing about and appreciates it." Williams's genius lay in his ability to bring out the hillbilly in all Americans, rich and poor, rural and urban, simple and sophisticated.

Selected discography

Hank Williams' Greatest Hits, MGM.
The Humor of Hank Williams, MGM.
I'm Blue Inside, MGM.
I Saw the Light, MGM.
Life to Legend, MGM.
Movin' On—Luke the Drifter, MGM.
24 of Hank Williams' Greatest Hits, MGM.
The Very Best of Hank Williams, Volume 1, MGM.
The Very Best of Hank Williams, Volume 2, MGM.
Wait for the Light To Shine, MGM, reissued, Polydor.
Hank Williams on Stage, Volume 1, MGM.
Hank Williams on Stage, Volume 2, MGM.
The Essential Hank Williams, MGM.
Hank Williams, Sr. Live at the Grand Ole Opry, MGM.
Hank Williams Memorial Album, MGM, reprinted, Polydor.
Hank Williams' Greatest Hits, Volume 2, MGM.
Hank Williams' Greatest Hits, Volume 3, MGM.
Home in Heaven, MGM.
Beyond the Sunset, MGM.
Lost Highway, MGM.
Honky Tonkin', MGM.
40 Greatest Hits of Hank Williams, Polydor.
Hey, Good Lookin', Polydor.
I Ain't Got Nuthin' but Time, Polydor.
I Won't Be Home No More, Polydor.
I'm So Lonesome I Could Cry, Polydor.
Let's Turn back the Years, Polydor.
Long Gone Lonesome Blues, Polydor.
Lovesick Blues, Polydor.
Moanin' the Blues, Polydor.

Hank Williams on the Air, Polydor.
Rare Takes & Radio Cuts, Polydor.
Wanderin' Around, Polydor.

Sources

Brown, Charles T., *Music U.S.A.: America's Country & Western Tradition,* Prentice-Hall, 1986.
The Great American Popular Singers, Simon & Schuster, 1974.
The Illustrated Encyclopedia of Country Music, Harmony, 1977.
Malone, Bill C., *Country Music U.S.A.,* revised edition, University of Texas Press, 1985.

Malone, Bill C., and Judith McCulloh, *Stars of Country Music,* University of Illinois Press, 1975.
Rivers, Jerry, *Hank Williams: From Life to Legend,* Heather Enterprises, 1967.
Sandberg, Larry, and Dick Weissman, *The Folk Music Sourcebook,* Knopf, 1976.
Shestack, Melvin, *The Country Music Encyclopedia,* Crowell, 1974.
Stambler, Irwin, and Grelun Landon, *The Encyclopedia of Folk, Country, and Western Music,* St. Martin's, 1969.
Williams, Roger M., *Sing a Sad Song: The Life of Hank Williams,* Doubleday, 1970.

—Anne Janette Johnson

"Rake and Ramblin' Man," "Tulsa Time," "Lord, I Hope This Day Is Good," and "Then It's Love."

Sources

Country Music, January/February 1988; March/April 1988; May/
June 1989.
Texas Monthly, October 1986.

—*Elizabeth Thomas*

Born May 27, 1939, in Floydada, Texas; son of a mechanic; married Joy (Bucher) Williams, 1960; children: Gary and Tim. *Religion:* Church of Christ.

Country vocalist, guitarist, and songwriter; served in the U.S. Army, c. 1957-59; sang with Lofton Kline as the Strangers Two during the early 1960s; also worked odd jobs such as driving a bread truck, collecting bills, and working in the oil fields; sang with Kline and Susan Taylor as the Pozo Seco Singers, 1964-71; co-owned a furniture store, 1971; signed as a songwriter and song salesman for Jack Music Publishing in Nashville, Tenn., 1972; recording artist and concert performer, 1972—. Appeared in film *W.W. and the Dixie Dance Kings.*

Awards: Voted Male Vocalist of the Year by the Country Music Association, 1978; "Tulsa Time" voted Record of the Year by Academy of Country Music, 1979; CMA of Great Britain voted Williams both Male Singer and Performer of the Year, 1975, and voted *You're My Best Friend* Album of the Year, 1975.

Addresses: *Office*—Hallmark Direction, 15 Music Square West, Nashville, TN 37203. *Record company*—Capitol Records, 38 Music Square East, Nashville, TN 37203.

to try to sell songs to country artists by Jack Music Publishing. After only a short time of having these artists *almost* buy his songs but reject them because they were afraid that his work was just too different to be popular with country fans, Williams heeded their advice about recording them himself. He signed with JMI Records, which, like Jack Music, belonged to Jack Clement. Though he did perform his own compositions, he did not restrict himself to them. Williams's solo debut album, *Don Williams, Volume One,* featured the now-classic "Amanda," which also became a hit for Waylon Jennings, and another successful single, "In the Shelter of Your Eyes." Following the release of *Don Williams, Volume Two,* though, JMI went out of business, and Williams signed with ABC/Dot Records. When the latter company merged with MCA Records in 1978, Williams stayed on, scoring hits with them such as "You're My Best Friend," "Till the Rivers All Run Dry," and "Tulsa Time." The last was voted Single Record of the Year by the Academy of Country Music in 1979.

No matter what company Williams has recorded with during his solo career, however, he has always maintained tight artistic control. As Reavis reported, "he refuse(s) to consider singing any songs about fighting, marital infidelity, or drinking." Apparently it is not so much to take a high moral tone as to be true to his own experiences; Williams told Reavis: "I've never really done those things, they haven't been a part of my life, so I guess I just don't relate to them very well." Instead he prefers love ballads, or songs that tell a story. And according to Morthland, Williams "sifts through 50 to 100 songs for each one of the 15 he records for an album before picking the final 10." Williams also remains in control of his concert appearances. Not only does he limit himself to approximately forty dates a year, but "if he notice(s) people in his audience openly smoking marijuana, he [asks] them to leave," Reavis affirmed. Williams even disbanded his own fan club to protect his privacy and that of his family, and because he simply doesn't believe in them. He told Reavis: "I just don't believe that you've got to know Henry to drive a Ford."

Despite his deliberate distance from the spotlight, Williams continues to satisfy country fans. His 1987 album *Traces* included songs such as "Old Coyote Town," "Till I Can't Take It Anymore," and "Come From the Heart." Morthland, while faulting the quality of some of the material—Williams no longer writes his own songs—concluded that *Traces* makes it "clear why" fans "keep coming back for more."

Selected discography

LPs

Don Williams, Volume One (includes "Amanda," "The Shelter of Your Eyes," and "Come Early Morning"), JMI, 1972.
Don Williams, Volume Two, JMI, c. 1973.
Don Williams, Volume Three, ABC/Dot, 1974.
You're My Best Friend, ABC/Dot, 1975.
Don Williams's Greatest Hits, ABC/Dot, 1975.
Harmony, ABC/Dot, c. 1976.
Visions, ABC/Dot, c. 1976.
Country Boy, ABC/Dot, c. 1977.
Traces (includes "Desperately," "Old Coyote Town," "Easy Touch," "Running Out of Reasons to Run," "Till I Can't Take It Anymore," and "Come From the Heart"), Capitol, 1987.
Prime Cuts, Capitol, 1989.

Single releases

In addition to the songs attributed to some of the above albums, Williams has released on ABC/Dot, MCA, and Capitol Records the following hits during the late 1970s and 1980s: "Some Broken Hearts Never End," "Till the Rivers All Run Dry," "Louisiana Saturday Night," "Say It Again," "I Wouldn't Want to Live if You Didn't Love Me," "She Never Knew Me," "The Ties That Bind,"

Full name Hiram King Williams; born September 17, 1923, in Mount Olive, Alabama; died of alcohol-induced heart failure January 1, 1953, in Oak Hill, West Virginia; son of Lonnie (a farmer and log train engineer) and Lilly (a church organist) Williams; married Audrey Sheppard, 1942 (divorced, 1952); married Billie Jones (a model and singer), 1952; children: (first marriage) Hank Jr.; one daughter, Cathy Yvonne Stone, out of wedlock.

Country singer, songwriter, guitar player, 1937-53. Won amateur night contest in Montgomery, Alabama, singing own composition, "WPA Blues," 1937; formed band the Drifting Cowboys, 1937; played and sang with the Drifting Cowboys at honky tonks and on radio station WSFA, Montgomery, 1937-46; signed with Sterling Records, 1946, moved to MGM Records, 1947. Became a regular on radio station KWKH's "Louisiana Hayride," Shreveport, La., 1947; made debut on the Grand Ole Opry, June 11, 1949. Cast member of the Grand Ole Opry, 1949-52.

Awards: Hit singles for MGM include "Why Don't You Love Me?" "Hey Good Lookin'," "Cold, Cold Heart," and "Your Cheatin' Heart." Inducted into the Country Music Hall of Fame as the first member, 1961.

and began a long tenure in country music's bush leagues.

The Alabama honky tonks where Williams played were so rough that they were called "blood buckets." In that unsavory atmosphere the young singer developed his style as well as his fatal attraction to alcohol. Williams was so unsuccessful in the early years that he quit music during the Second World War and worked as a welder in the Mobile shipyards. After the war he returned to music, determined at least to sell some of the songs he had written.

In 1946, the twenty-three year-old Williams set off for Nashville with his wife Audrey. There they paid an unsolicited call on Fred Rose, Nashville's biggest music writer and publisher. Rose listened to Williams sing and play a half dozen of his songs and signed him to a contract immediately. The years of struggle were finally over for Williams, as Rose took the singer on as a protege and literally directed the course of his entire career. Rose helped Williams to secure a contract with MGM Records, and after Williams's first country hit, "Move It on Over," helped the singer to land a job with the "Louisiana Hayride" radio show in Shreveport.

Fred Rose also helped the semi-literate Williams to polish his songs, bearing in mind that they might be sold to the lucrative pop music market. The ambition bore fruit with a number of Williams tunes, especially "Cold, Cold Heart." A mournful song of unrequited love, "Cold, Cold Heart" became the breakthrough pop hit for Tony Bennett, selling over a million copies, and a Number 1 country hit for Williams as well. Roger Williams notes that the Williams-Rose collaboration "was one of the most successful in American musical history. It was a perfect union: Williams's native genius, Rose's craftsmanship and sure sense of the market."

Williams was the headliner on the "Louisiana Hayride" for two years, earning hits with singles such as "Move It on Over," "I Heard You Crying in Your Sleep," and "Lovesick Blues." The success of the latter song, an old Tin Pan Alley number, secured Williams an invitation to perform on the Grand Ole Opry. His debut there, on June 11, 1949, remains a highlight of country music history. The audience brought Williams back for six encores of "Lovesick Blues" and had to be quieted in order for the show to continue. Despite his well-publicized drinking problems, Williams was invited to be a regular on the Opry.

As an Opry regular, Williams had to have his own band. He reorganized the Drifting Cowboys, drafting Jerry Rivers (fiddle), Don Helms (steel guitar), Bob McNett (lead guitar) and Hillous Butrum (bass). These and other studio musicians began to travel with Williams on the bone-wearying cross-country trips to live show appearances. Williams and his band performed all across America and made several visits to Canada and one to Germany to entertain American soldiers stationed there.

Within a year, Hank Williams was the most sought-after country star in the business. His salary from shows and recordings topped $200,000 per year, and thanks to Rose he was wise about securing publishing rights to his work. Still Williams faced a devastating problem—when he was sober, he could perform brilliantly. When drunk, he could do nothing at all. His backup band tried to keep him alcohol- and drug-free, but with only limited success. Even at the height of his fame Williams seemed bent on self-destruction.

With Number 1 hits like "Why Don't You Love Me?" "Cold, Cold Heart," and "Long Gone Lonesome Blues," Williams won a popular acclaim that no country singer had previously equaled. Music fans outside the country sphere bought his records and learned his songs, and country fans could not get enough of him. Oddly enough, this first "crossover" artist epitomized the traditional, rural sound. On stage Williams was a spontaneous, easygoing performer with a magnetic smile. His voice

Hank Williams, Sr.

Singer, songwriter, guitarist

He is known simply as the greatest country singer of all time—the immortal Hank Williams, whose ballads and laments of frustrated love brought a regional music squarely into the mainstream. Williams was one of the best songwriters ever to emerge in the country genre, and his exceptional creative ability was enhanced by a magnetic, if utterly rural, stage presence. In *Country Music U.S.A.*, Bill C. Malone calls Williams "the most dramatic symbol of country music's postwar surge," an artist whose "early death solidified the legend that had already begun during his lifetime."

Most country singers rely upon outside sources for at least some of their songs. Williams was an exception to that rule: his concerts were composed almost exclusively of pieces he wrote himself, now-classic tunes like "Cold, Cold Heart," "I Saw the Light," "Your Cheatin' Heart," and "Why Don't You Love Me?" According to Roger M. Williams in *Stars of Country Music,* the fact that Williams had such a lengthy and varied repertory is one mark of his greatness. The critic adds: "A larger mark is the extraordinary number of truly memorable songs [Williams] turned out. Those songs transcend country music, or any category short of pop. They are part of America's musical heritage, and they elevate the man who wrote them to a very high rank among the nation's songwriters."

For all his greatness, however, Williams had only a brief period of success, marred by the excessive drinking that would kill him before he turned thirty. The greatest part of his short life was spent in near-poverty, playing in the deep South's roughest honky tonks and on small radio stations in Alabama and Louisiana. Hiram King Williams was born September 17, 1923, in tiny Mount Olive, Alabama. His family was very poor, because his father—a part-time farmer and log train engineer—suffered from poor health. When Williams was seven, his father disappeared into a veteran's hospital and was never seen again. Young Hank was called on to help support the family by selling peanuts and newspapers and shining shoes.

Williams was fronting a country band by the time he turned fourteen. He drew upon numerous sources for his musical style, from the gospel sounds he heard in church (his mother was an organist) to the tunes of Roy Acuff and Ernest Tubb. The singer also owed a stylistic debt to black music; he was taught guitar by a local street singer named Tee-Tot (Rufus Payne) who lived in his home town. At any rate, Williams was writing his own songs and singing them from his earliest teens. His first recognition came at an amateur contest in Montgomery, Alabama, where he won first place for a performance of "WPA Blues," a song he wrote himself. Shortly thereafter he formed his band, the Drifting Cowboys,

Hank Williams on the Air, Polydor.
Rare Takes & Radio Cuts, Polydor.
Wanderin' Around, Polydor.

Sources

Brown, Charles T., *Music U.S.A.: America's Country & Western Tradition,* Prentice-Hall, 1986.
The Great American Popular Singers, Simon & Schuster, 1974.
The Illustrated Encyclopedia of Country Music, Harmony, 1977.
Malone, Bill C., *Country Music U.S.A.,* revised edition, University of Texas Press, 1985.

Malone, Bill C., and Judith McCulloh, *Stars of Country Music,* University of Illinois Press, 1975.
Rivers, Jerry, *Hank Williams: From Life to Legend,* Heather Enterprises, 1967.
Sandberg, Larry, and Dick Weissman, *The Folk Music Sourcebook,* Knopf, 1976.
Shestack, Melvin, *The Country Music Encyclopedia,* Crowell, 1974.
Stambler, Irwin, and Grelun Landon, *The Encyclopedia of Folk, Country, and Western Music,* St. Martin's, 1969.
Williams, Roger M., *Sing a Sad Song: The Life of Hank Williams,* Doubleday, 1970.

—*Anne Janette Johnson*

was pure country, strong and steady but with a keening edge that leant pathos to his love ballads. Analyzing the singer's vast popularity, Roger Williams simply concludes that Hank "had the infectious appeal common to all great performers."

This appeal was not enough to assure Williams's continued success. In 1952 he was fired from the Opry for drunkenness, and he returned to the "Louisiana Hayride" for a brief period. His first marriage ended in divorce, and he became somewhat a laughingstock for his wedding to a Louisiana beauty—the ceremony was conducted twice, in public, and admission was charged. By that time Williams was a walking victim of drug abuse—a back ailment from his early years led to the use of painkillers in addition to alcohol. His sudden death of a heart attack on New Year's Eve 1953 still came as a shock to the nation. He died in his sleep en route to a concert in Canton, Ohio. He was twenty-nine.

Death only enhanced Williams's appeal to his legions of fans. A number of Williams singles were released

---

Williams, the hard-living, self-destructive rambling bard, mined his own misery for lyrics and gave the world a number of its most memorable country songs.

---

posthumously, including the classic "Your Cheatin' Heart." To this day Hank Williams remains one of the best-selling country singers, with numerous albums in print in any given year. His songs have been covered countless times by all kinds of singers—especially his famous son, Hank, Jr. Royalties on Hank Williams songs have earned the Williams family millions of dollars in the decades since the performer's death. It is certainly not surprising that he was the very first entertainer elected to the prestigious Country Music Hall of Fame when it opened in 1961.

Grounded as he was in the country tradition, Williams had a seminal influence on the acceptance of country by mainstream audiences. His appeal was basic: he could communicate *sincerely* with listeners. Malone notes that Williams "'lived' the songs he sang—he could communicate his feelings to the listener and make each person feel as if the song were being sung directly and only to him or her." Roger Williams writes:

"Everybody understands what a Hank Williams song means, and almost everybody senses the straightforward, bedrock emotion—joy or anguish or both—from which it springs."

Williams, the hard-living, self-destructive rambling bard, mined his own misery for lyrics and gave the world a number of its most memorable country songs. He explained the popularity of his work this way: "When a hillbilly sings a crazy song, he feels crazy. When he sings, 'I Laid My Mother Away,' he sees her a-laying right there in the coffin. He sings more sincere than most entertainers because the hillbilly was raised rougher than most entertainers. You got to know a lot about hard work. You got to have smelt a lot of mule manure before you can sing like a hillbilly. The people who has been raised something like the way the hillbilly has knows what he is singing about and appreciates it." Williams's genius lay in his ability to bring out the hillbilly in all Americans, rich and poor, rural and urban, simple and sophisticated.

Selected discography

Hank Williams' Greatest Hits, MGM.
The Humor of Hank Williams, MGM.
I'm Blue Inside, MGM.
I Saw the Light, MGM.
Life to Legend, MGM.
Movin' On—Luke the Drifter, MGM.
24 of Hank Williams' Greatest Hits, MGM.
The Very Best of Hank Williams, Volume 1, MGM.
The Very Best of Hank Williams, Volume 2, MGM.
Wait for the Light To Shine, MGM, reissued, Polydor.
Hank Williams on Stage, Volume 1, MGM.
Hank Williams on Stage, Volume 2, MGM.
The Essential Hank Williams, MGM.
Hank Williams, Sr. Live at the Grand Ole Opry, MGM.
Hank Williams Memorial Album, MGM, reprinted, Polydor.
Hank Williams' Greatest Hits, Volume 2, MGM.
Hank Williams' Greatest Hits, Volume 3, MGM.
Home in Heaven, MGM.
Beyond the Sunset, MGM.
Lost Highway, MGM.
Honky Tonkin', MGM.
40 Greatest Hits of Hank Williams, Polydor.
Hey, Good Lookin', Polydor.
I Ain't Got Nuthin' but Time, Polydor.
I Won't Be Home No More, Polydor.
I'm So Lonesome I Could Cry, Polydor.
Let's Turn back the Years, Polydor.
Long Gone Lonesome Blues, Polydor.
Lovesick Blues, Polydor.
Moanin' the Blues, Polydor.

Kazuhito Yamashita

Classical guitarist

Japan's Kazuhito Yamashita "has . . . made a career of annexing orchestral classics to his kingdom of the guitar," according to Jeff Magee in the *Ann Arbor News*. The classical guitarist transcribes symphonies and other classical pieces, usually played by many varied instruments together, so that he and others can play them on the guitar. He has been compared to revolutionary classical guitarist Andres Segovia, and is acclaimed by most serious music critics, though Jim Ferguson of *Guitar Player* admitted that some experts consider Yamashita an eccentric who attempts tasks too large for his ability. In addition to his transcription talents, his actual playing has also won raves from the critics; for instance, reviewer Michael Wright labeled Yamashita's technique with the instrument "brilliant and flawless" in *Audio*.

Yamashita showed his genius early, and entered international competitions while an adolescent. While still in his teens he gained worldwide attention by winning three of them; one in Spain, one in Italy, and another in Paris, France. Afterwards he gave many concerts in his native Japan, and by 1978, when he was about seventeen years old, he was ready to make his first professional European appearance. Music apparently runs in the Yamashita family; his sister Naoko is also a classical guitarist, and has recorded with him.

Yamashita's transcription credits include J. S. Bach's First Sonata for Unaccompanied Violin, Dvorak's "New World" Symphony, Rimsky-Korsakov's "Scheherazade," Stravinsky's "Firebird Suite," and Mussorgsky's "Pictures at an Exhibition." The last was lauded as "almost legendary" by Ferguson, who also had praise for Yamashita's recordings *Guitar Concertos: Vivaldi, Carulli, Giuliani* and *Music of Spain,* though he felt the material on both of these albums was somewhat "tame" for Yamashita. "A musician of his exceptional abilities is best showcased with exceptional material," he concluded. Wright disagreed, saying that *Guitar Concertos* "is stunningly vital." Further, Walter F. Grueninger, reviewing the album in *Consumer's Research Magazine,* declared his amazement at Yamashita's "virtuosity and range of expression" in the work.

As for Yamashita's transcription of Rimsky-Korsakov's "Scheherazade," Tom Mulhern of *Guitar Player* hailed it as "dynamic and expansive." Yamashita chose to record this work with his sister Naoko; together, according to Mulhern, the Yamashitas lived up to the greatest possibilities inherent in the performance of classical guitar duets. The album with "Scheherazade" also included the "Petite Suite" by Claude Debussy, played with "striking grace and precision" in Mulhern's opinion, and four short pieces listed together under the title of "Francaix Divertissement."

Stravinsky's "Firebird Suite" is rendered by Yamashita as a "fascinating . . . work filled with a broad range of textures and timbres," Ferguson claimed in another *Guitar Player* review. The critic also pointed out the skillful way that Yamashita tackled the difficulties of making such a complex work manageable for the guitar. With "Firebird Suite" Yamashita also recorded his famed interpretation of Dvorak's Ninth Symphony—also known as the "New World" Symphony—which Ferguson gleefully proclaimed a "relentless display of 'impossible' guitar work."

Yamashita has performed, among other works, his transcription of J. S. Bach's First Sonata for Unaccompanied Violin in the United States. But besides devoting himself to the older classical composers and being, as Ferguson asserted, the only classical guitarist who produces transcriptions of full symphonic works, Yamashita also "champions new music," according to Magee. One of the modern composers he has promoted is the Japanese composer Toru Takemitsu, whose "Folios I, II, and III" he performed at a 1989 concert in Ann Arbor, Michigan.

Selected transcriptions

Bach's Sonata No. 1 for Unaccompanied Violin.
Dvorak's "New World" Symphony.
Mussorgsky's "Pictures at an Exhibition."
Rimsky-Korsakov's "Scheherazade."
Stravinsky's "Firebird Suite."

Selected discography

Music of Spain, *RCA, c. 1987.*
Guitar Concertos: Vivaldi, Carulli, Giuliani, *RCA, c. 1987.*
(With Naoko Yamashita) Rimsky-Korsakov: Scheherazade/ Debussy: Petite Suite, *RCA, c. 1988.*
Dvorak—Symphony No. 9 ("From the New World")/Stravinsky— The Firebird Suite, *RCA, c. 1989.*

Sources

Ann Arbor News, *November 5, 1989.*
Audio, *January 1988.*
Consumer's Research Magazine, *April 1988.*
Guitar Player, *June 1987; June 1988; July 1989.*

—Elizabeth Thomas

Young M.C.

Rap artist

Young M.C., the winner of the rap Grammy in 1990, is a G-rated musician in an X-rated genre. Most rap artists try to shock their audiences; Marvin Young, the real name of Young M.C., merely tries to entertain them. "There's a lot of impressionable people listening to the music," Young told *Newsweek,* "If I wasn't to take notice of that, I would be shirking responsibility." Profiled in *People* as having only "a flair for language and a love of big beat" in common with his hip-hop peers, Young boasts humorously in his lyrics, "If every rapper were Hawaiian, I'd be Don Ho."

"His lyrics don't reflect a hard, street kind of vibe," DJ-producer Michael Ross told *People.* Ross, who signed Young to his independent label Delicious Vinyl, recognized that Young was capable of writing lyrics which could give rap broad, commercial success. Young told Jeffrey Ressner in *Rolling Stone,* "I was in my dorm room after classes one day, and I didn't have any homework. They called and asked if I could do some lyrics, because they felt I'd be able to write something that would be more conducive to pop radio. I said I'd call them back in a half-hour, and about thirty-five minutes later, I read it back to them." Young's contribution to the writing of the platinum single "Wild Thing" and "Funky Cold Medina" for Tone-Loc, followed by his own platinum LP *Stone Cold Rhymin',* put rap in the mainstream of pop culture.

Young was born in London in 1968 and raised in Hollis, Queens, the home of rap stars Run-D.M.C. and L.L. Cool J. His parents are Jamaicans who moved to New York in 1970, where Young's father is a telephone company executive and his mother is a nurse. Young told Ressner in *Rolling Stone* that he composed his first songs during childhood. "When I was small, I used to write lyrics about fairy tales like 'Little Red Riding Hood,' 'The Three Bears,' 'Old McDonald,' all that stuff."

Recuperating in a hospital when he was twelve, Young discovered that his rhymes could entertain. Young related in *People* that he wrote a poem for the nurses which ended with the lines: "He's fully recovered; he's come right back/Then he saw the bill and had a heart attack."

Influenced by the pioneer rappers Grandmaster Flash and the Furious Five, in addition to the Jamaican artists Yellowman, Young joined some rap groups while in high school, but his career did not spiral until college. Young told *People* that he enrolled at USC, from where he graduated with a degree in economics in 1988, to "have a good job and make decent money." He explained further his decision to pursue the knowledge gained through academics instead of through street-life to Ressner in *Rolling Stone.* "I stayed in school because I wanted to. Now I can sit down, have a meeting with someone in a business-oriented position, and not be totally out of place."

While a college student, Young auditioned a cappella over the phone for Mike Ross, whom he had met previously through a mutual friend. Ross was the DJ-producer who, along with Matt Dike, had begun the independent label Delicious Vinyl. Ross and Dike signed Young in December 1987. Young's debut came early in 1988 when he received good notices in the United States and the United Kingdom for his single "I Let 'Em Know."

In 1989 Young co-penned the lyrics of "Wild Thing" for performer Tone-Loc, a song which not only graced the pop singles chart at Number Two, but also set a new precedent in rap music. Before, rappers and producers had written their own lyrics, eschewing outside writers, but Young's contribution as an outside writer to the lyrics of "Wild Thing" changed the old format. Young then contributed some key lines to "Funky Cold Medina," an acclaimed follow-up single for Tone-Loc.

Young's next successful project also came in 1989, while still a student at USC, with his platinum LP *Stone Cold Rhymin'*. "Bust a Move," a hit single from the album, demonstrates the vocal style and smooth articulation that won Young M.C. this year's rap Grammy.

Young does not opt for a flamboyant lifestyle. Commenting on his small, modest apartment in Hollywood, the rap star told Ressner in *Rolling Stone*, "This place is just somewhere I stay until I can get something more permanent. I'm out of town a whole bunch, so even if I had a house, I wouldn't be able to take care of it."

Promotional trips take up much of Young's time. He also prepares new singles and opens shows for acts on the road that range from Fine Young Cannibals to Boogie Down Productions. "I'm exhausted," Young joked to Ressner, "I've been busy prostituting myself all over Europe."

At home, the twenty-two-year-old Young does not party much as he revealed in *People;* neither does he drink nor smoke, as he states in his lyrics. He visits the club scene occasionally, but most of his time is spent working out rhythms and composing lyrics. Nor has he any serious romantic involvement at present, since he is "too busy."

Since much of *Stone Cold Rhymin'* was written while Marvin Young was still in high school, he foresees a new direction in his future work which will have political overtones. He has already contributed writing to the album *Silent Assassin* by the reggae stars Sly and Robbie, where Young also appears, which reflects this new bent. Confident about adding another dimension to his rap, Young told Ressner in *Rolling Stone,* "That's the kind of direction I want on my subsequent albums. I felt that if I came out singing things like 'Under Arrest' [one of the tracks on *Silent Assassin*] right off the bat, people wouldn't necessarily listen. Now that they know who I am, I'm going to talk about more political issues. It's all well and good that people can identify with school or shy men meeting women, but there are other things that need to be addressed as well."

Selected discography

LPs

Stone Cold Rhymin', (includes "Bust a Move" and "Principal's Office"), Delicious Vinyl, 1989.

Single

"I Let 'em Know."

Contributed to "Wild Thing" and "Funky Cold Medina" for Tone-Loc; and *Silent Assassin* by Sly and Robbie.

Sources

Billboard, December 16, 1989.
Newsweek, March 19, 1990.
People, February 26, 1990.
Rolling Stone, February 22, 1990.

—Marjorie Burgess

Pinchas Zukerman

Violinist, violist, conductor

Violinist, violist, conductor—Pinchas Zukerman could have made an outstanding career with only one of these pursuits, but this multi-faceted artist combines all three. Known for his rich tone, masterful technique, and well thought-out interpretations of works for violin and viola, Zukerman performs with the leading orchestras and chamber ensembles worldwide. As a conductor Zukerman has garnered mixed reviews; yet he is in high demand for guest appearances. Seen often on commercial and public television and known as Pinky to his friends, Zuckerman enjoys an almost superstar status.

Pinchas was born into a musical family on July 16, 1948, in Tel Aviv, Israel. He is the only child of professional violinist Juhda Zukerman and Miriam (Lieberman-Skotchilas) Zukerman, who, concentration-camp survivors from Poland, had emigrated to Israel in 1947. At age five, Pinchas learned to play a recorder given to him by his father. After later trying and disliking the clarinet, he settled on the violin, which his father taught him. At age eight, he began studying with Ilona Feher, the noted Hungarian violinist who was also the early teacher of Shmuel Ashkenasi and Shlomo Mintz (see *Newsmakers* entry), at the Israel conservatory and the Academy of Music in Tel Aviv.

During a visit to Israel in 1961, celebrated cellist Pablo Casals and world famous violinist Isaac Stern heard Zukerman perform. Stern was impressed enough that he guided the course of the young violinist's education, even becoming his legal guardian to do so. With support from the American-Israel Cultural Foundation and scholarships from Juilliard and the Helena Rubinstein Foundation, Zuckerman was able to study violin and, beginning at age fourteen, viola with the famous string teacher Ivan Galamian at the Juilliard School of Music in New York City.

While studying at the Juilliard School, Zukerman also attended the Professional Children's School and the High School of Performing Arts, living with the parents of pianist Eugene Isotomin.

Zukerman, who admits that he was an arrogant child prodigy, found it difficult to adjust to life in New York City—he did not then speak English—and to being one of many musical prodigies. He rebelled against Galamian's insistence that he concentrate on the basics and maintain a rigid practice schedule, and often skipped school and roamed the streets. Finally, Stern took Zukerman to task. "I knew I had something in me, something on the violin that I had to say," Zukerman told David Hawley of the *St. Paul Pioneer Press*, "And I knew that eventually I was going to say it. With the guidance of these people it luckily worked out."

Zukerman ended his formal schooling when on May 16,

For the Record. . .

Born July 16, 1948, in Tel Aviv, Israel; came to United States, 1962; son of Yehuda and Miriam Lieberman Zukerman; married Eugenia Rich, May 26, 1968 (divorced); children: Natalia, Arianna; married Tuesday Weld, 1985. *Education:* Attended Juilliard School of Music, 1965-68.

Concert violinist 1968—. With impresario, Sol Hurok, 1967-76; conductor, soloist English Chamber Orchestra, 1974, Mostly Mozart Festival, N.Y.C., 1975; guest conductor, soloist Los Angeles Philharmonic, Boston Symphony, Philadelphia Orchestra, N.Y. Philharmonic Orchestra; music dir. South Bank Festival, London, 1978-80, St.Paul Chamber Orch., 1980-87; toured with Isaac Stern; mem. trio with Daniel Barenboim and Jacqueline du Pre; recording artist with CBS, EMI, Philips Classics labels.

Awards: Winner International Levintritt Competition, 1967.

Addresses: *Office:* c/o Shirley Kirshbaum & Assocs. 711 West End Ave., New York, NY 10025.

1967, he was co-winner with Kyung Wha Chung of Korea of the Leventritt International Competition. Publicity from this prize and his replacing Stern, who was ill, in a series of concerts set the stage for Zuckerman's solo career. Since then he has performed numerous solo recitals on both violin and viola and chamber music with many other noted artists, including Stern, violinist Itzhak Perlman (see *Musicians* entry), cellist Jacqueline Du Pre, flutist Jean-Pierre Rampal (see *Musicians* entry), and the Guarneri and Cleveland quartets.

Though Zukerman had begun to study conducting while at theJuilliard School, he first became actively interested inconducting in the late 1960s when he played with the English Chamber Orchestra directed by Israeli conductor Daniel Barenboim. Encouraged by members of the orchestra, Zukerman conducted from the concertmaster's chair works by Bach and Vivaldi. Pieces by eighteenth-century composers were often conducted by the lead violin before the advent of the conductor as we now know it. Zuckerman became more and more experienced at leading the group while playing the violin and in 1974 officially made his conducting debut with the English Chamber Orchestra. While he has since then guest conducted most of the major orchestras in the United States, including the New York Philharmonic, Boston Symphony, Los Angeles Philharmonic, and the National Symphony, reviews of his conducting are mixed.

In 1980 Zukerman assumed the directorship of the St. Paul Chamber Orchestra (SPCO), the nation's only full-time professional chamber orchestra. During his seven-year tenure there, Zukerman increased attendence threefold, was instrumental in the building of a permanent home for the orchestra, increased the number of musicians in the ensemble, made eight albums on major labels, and led the orchestra on tours of the United States and South America. He often performed as soloist with the SPCO, conducting from the concertmaster's chair. Zukerman, tired of the administrative duties required of a music director, decided to leave the SPCO after the 1987 season, though he was offered a longer contract.

Since then Zukerman has increased his solo performance schedule and limited his conducting to guest appearances and the principal guest conductorship of the Dallas Symphony Orchestra's International Festival. Zukerman limits his teaching to a few master classes in the summer, usually at music festivals, such as those at Aspen, Colorado, and Tanglewood, Massachusetts.

Zukerman lays claim to an impressive discography numbering more than seventy-five releases, which are widely representative of the violin and viola repertoire. His catalog of recordings for Angel, CBS Masterworks, Deutsche Grammaphon, London Records, Philips Classics, and RCA contains more than a dozen Grammy nominations and two awards: "Best Classical Performance—Instrumental Soloist with Orchestra" for the *Isaac Stern Sixtieth Anniversary Celebration,* which contains Mozart's *Sinfonia Concertante for Violin and Viola,* recorded as a tribute to Zukerman's long-time supporter; "Best Chamber Music Performance" for his Angel/EMI release of Moszkowski's *Suite for Two Violins and Piano,* Shostakovich's *Three Violin Duos,* and Prokofiev's *Sonata for Two Violins.*

After collapsing from exhaustion in March 1981, Zuckerman has been careful to pace himself more conservatively, though he has sacrificed none of the diversity of his efforts. He once told *The Strad,* "The diversity of my career has allowed me to explore all aspects of music, and I feel that my artistic life today is on a level of greater maturity. I hope that when the day comes that my abilities as a soloist begin to deteriorate, I will have the strength of character to retire from the concert stage and continue my contribution to music in other ways."

As a violinist, Zukerman plays a Guarnerius "del Gesu" instrument.

Selected discography

Bach: *Violin Concerto; Brandenberg Concerto No. 3,* CBS.

Complete Forty-Four Violin Duos of Bartok (with Itzhak Perlman, violin), EMI/Angel.

Bartok: *Violin Concerto,* CBS.

Beethoven: *Romances for Violin and Orchestra Nos. 1 and 2,* DG.

Beethoven: *Violin Concerto, Op. 61,* DG.

Berg: *Violin Concerto,* CBS.

Bloch: *Nigun from Baal Shem;* Kabalevsky: *Violin Concerto;* Wienawski: *Violin Concerto No. 2,* CBS.

Bolling: *Suite for Violin and Jazz Piano,* CBS.

Brahms: *Sonata for Violin and Piano; Sonata for Viola and Piano,* DG.

Bruch: *Violin Concerto No. 1;* Lalo: *Symphony Espagnole,* CBS.

Debussy: *Violin Sonata No. 3;* Faure: *Sonata Op. 13 "Berceuse,"* CBS.

Dohnanyi: *Serenade, Op. 10;* Beethoven: *Serenade, Op. 8,* CBS.

Elgar: *Violin Concerto,* CBS.

Greatest Hits: The Violin, CBS.

Haydn: *Violin Concerto No. 1; Symphonia Concertante,* DG.

Issac Stern Sixtieth Anniversary Celebration (contains Bach: *Concerto for Two Violins, Concerto for Three Violins;* Mozart: *Sinfonia Concertante for Violin and Viola* [Isaac Stern violin; Itzhak Perlman, violin]), CBS.

Mendelssohn: *Violin Concerto,* CBS.

Mozart: *Violin Concertos No. 4 and 5,* CBS.

Moszkowski: *Suite for Two Violins and Piano;* Shostakovich: *Three Violin Duos;* Prokofiev: *Sonata for Two Violins, Op. 56* (with Itzhak Perlman, violin and Samuel Sanders, piano), EMI/ Angel.

Music of Fritz Kreisler, CBS.

Sibelius: *Violin Concerto, Op. 47,* DG.

Tchaikovsky/Mendelssohn: *Violin Concertos,* CBS.

Vaughan Williams: *The Lark Ascending,* DG.

Vieuxtemps: *Violin Concerto No. 5;* Wieniawski: *Polonaise, Op. 4;* Saint-Saens: *Introduction and Rondo Capriccioso;* Chausson: *Poeme,* CBS.

Vivaldi: *The Four Seasons,* CBS.

Vivaldi: *Violin Concertos Op. 8* (Nos. 5-8), CBS.

Vivaldi: *Violin Concertos, Op. 8* (Nos. 9-12), CBS.

Sources

Arizona Republic, November 13, 1983.

Chicago Sun-Times, November 15, 1981.

Chicago Tribune, December 22, 1985; February 29, 1989.

Chronicle (San Francisco), February 25, 1981.

Dallas Times-Herald, January 23, 1985; February 27, 1989.

Denver Post, November 16, 1987.

Los Angeles Times, January 10, 1988.

Miami Herald, December 22, 1987.

Minneapolis Star Tribune, January 9, 1986; May 24, 1987.

Musical America, December 1984.

Saint Paul Pioneer Press, January 9, 1986.

Santa Barbara News-Press, October 26, 1986.

Seattle Times, January 23, 1983.

The Strad, October 1987; April 1988.

The Washington Post, April 18, 1987; April 7, 1989.

—Jeanne M. Lesinski

Subject Index

Volume numbers appear in **bold**.

A cappella
McFerrin, Bobby **3**

African
Ladysmith Black Mambazo **1**
Sweet Honey in the Rock **1**

Avant Garde
Anderson, Laurie **1**
B-52s **4**
Canadian Brass **4**
Davis, Chip **4**
Gabriel, Peter **2**
Genesis **4**
Glass, Philip **1**
Monk, Meredith **1**
Pink Floyd **2**
Reed, Lou **1**
Reid, Vernon **2**
The Smiths **3**
Summers, Andy **3**
Talking Heads **1**
10,000 Maniacs **3**
Zappa, Frank **1**

Ballet
Copland, Aaron **2**

Bandleaders
Armstrong, Louis **4**
Basie, Count **2**
Berigan, Bunny **2**
Eckstine, Billy **1**
Ellington, Duke **2**
Goodman, Benny **4**
Jones, Quincy **2**
Santana, Carlos **1**
Severinsen, Doc **1**
Zappa, Frank **1**

Banjo
Clark, Roy **1**
Eldridge, Ben
    See the Seldom Scene **4**
Fleck, Bela
    See New Grass Revival **4**
Hartford, John **1**
Johnson, Courtney
    See New Grass Revival **4**
Lindley, David **2**
Rodgers, Jimmie **3**
Scruggs, Earl **3**
Seeger, Pete **4**
Watson, Doc **2**

Bass
Anton, Alan
    See Cowboy Junkies **4**
Beers, Garry Gary
    See INXS **2**
Bryson, Bill
    See Desert Rose Band **4**
Cates, Ronny
    See Petra **3**
Cetera, Peter
    See Chicago **3**
Clarke, Stanley **3**
Clayton, Adam
    See U2 **2**

Cowan, John
    See New Grass Revival **4**
Dempsey, Michael
    See The Cure **3**
Entwistle, John
    See the Who **3**
Estrada, Roy
    See Little Feat **4**
Evans, Mark
    See AC/DC **4**
Falconer, Earl
    See UB40 **4**
Fossen, Steve
    See Heart **1**
Gaines, Timothy
    See Stryper **2**
Gallup, Simon
    See The Cure **3**
Gentry, Teddy
    See Alabama **1**
Gibb, Maurice
    See the Bee Gees **3**
Gradney, Ken
    See Little Feat **4**
Gray, Tom
    See the Seldom Scene **4**
Griffin, Bob
    See BoDeans **3**
Gustafson, Steve
    See 10,000 Maniacs **3**
Hall, Tony
    See the Neville Brothers **4**
Hamilton, Tom
    See Aerosmith **3**
Hill, Dusty
    See ZZ Top **2**
Hubbard, Preston
    See the Fabulous Thunderbirds **1**
Johnson, Daryl
    See the Neville Brothers **4**
Johnston, Bruce
    See the Beach Boys **1**
Jones, John Paul
    See Led Zeppelin **1**
Lozano, Conrad
    See Los Lobos **2**
Lupo, Pat
    See the Beaver Brown Band **3**
McCartney, Paul **4**
    Also see the Beatles **2**
McKagan, Duff
    See Guns n' Roses **2**
Meisner, Randy
    See the Eagles **3**
Porter, Tiran
    See the Doobie Brothers **3**
Rourke, Andy
    See the Smiths **3**
Rutherford, Mike
    See Genesis **4**
Savage, Rick
    See Def Leppard **3**
Schmit, Timothy B.
    See the Eagles **3**
Shogren, Dave
    See the Doobie Brothers **3**
Simonon, Paul
    See the Clash **4**
Sixx, Nikki
    See Mötley Crüe **1**

Sting **2**
Stone, Curtis
    See Highway 101 **4**
Taylor, Dick
    See the Rolling Stones **3**
Taylor, John
    See Duran Duran **4**
Walker, Ebo
    See New Grass Revival **4**
Waters, Roger
    See Pink Floyd **2**
Williams, Cliff
    See AC/DC **4**
Wilson, Brian
    See the Beach Boys **1**
Wyman, Bill
    See the Rolling Stones **3**

Big Band/Swing
Basie, Count **2**
Bennett, Tony **2**
Berrigan, Bunny **2**
Carter, Benny **3**
Eckstine, Billy **1**
Ellington, Duke **2**
Fitzgerald, Ella **1**
Goodman, Benny **4**
Jackson, Joe **4**
Ronstadt, Linda **2**
Severinsen, Doc **1**
Sinatra, Frank **1**
Torme, Mel **4**
Vaughan, Sarah **2**

Bluegrass
Auldridge, Mike **4**
Flatt, Lester **3**
Hartford, John **1**
Lindley, David **2**
Monroe, Bill **1**
New Grass Revival **4**
O'Connor, Mark **1**
Scruggs, Earl **3**
The Seldom Scene **4**
Watson, Doc **2**

Blues
Berry, Chuck **1**
The Blues Brothers **3**
Charles, Ray **1**
Clapton, Eric **1**
Collins, Albert **4**
Cowboy Junkies **4**
Diddley, Bo **3**
The Fabulous Thunderbirds **1**
Guy, Buddy **4**
Healey, Jeff **4**
Hooker, John Lee **1**
Joplin, Janis **3**
King, Albert **2**
King, B.B. **1**
Led Zeppelin **1**
Little Feat **4**
Los Lobos **2**
Plant, Robert **2**
Raitt, Bonnie **3**
Rich, Charlie **3**
Robertson, Robbie **2**
Robillard, Duke **2**
Smith, Bessie **3**
Snow, Phoebe **4**

Vaughan, Stevie Ray **1**
Waits, Tom **1**
Waters, Muddy **4**
ZZ Top **2**

Cello
Harrell, Lynn **3**
Ma, Yo-Yo **2**

Choreography
Abdul, Paula **3**

Christian Music
Dion **4**
Petra **3**
Oak Ridge Boys **4**
Stryper **2**

Clarinet
Goodman, Benny **4**
Parazaider, Walter
    See Chicago **3**
Classical
Arrau, Claudio **1**
Bernstein, Leonard **2**
Canadian Brass **4**
Clayderman, Richard **1**
Copland, Aaron **2**
Davis, Chip **4**
Galway, James **3**
Goodman, Benny **4**
Harrell, Lynn **3**
Horowitz, Vladimir **1**
Jarrett, Keith **1**
Ma, Yo-Yo **2**
Ott, David **2**
Perlman, Itzhak **2**
Phillips, Harvey **3**
Salerno-Sonnenberg, Nadja **3**
von Karajan, Herbert **1**
Yamashita, Kazuhito **4**
Zukerman, Pinchas **4**

Composers
Anka, Paul **2**
Bacharach, Burt **1**
Bernstein, Leonard **2**
Clarke, Stanley **3**
Cooder, Ry **2**
Copland, Ry **2**
Davis, Chip **4**
Davis, Miles **1**
Ellington, Duke **2**
Glass, Philip **1**
Guaraldi, Vince **3**
Hamlisch, Marvin **1**
Jackson, Joe **4**
Jarre, Jean-Michel **2**
Jarrett, Keith **1**
Jones, Quincy **2**
Jordan, Stanley **1**
Kitaro **1**
Mancini, Henry **1**
Metheny, Pat **2**
Monk, Meredith **1**
Newman, Randy **4**
Ott, David **2**
Robertson, Robbie **2**
Satriani, Joe **4**
Solal, Martial **4**
Sting **2**
Story, Liz **2**
Summers, Andy **3**

Conductors
Bacharach, Burt **1**
Bernstein, Leonard **2**
Copland, Aaron **2**
Domingo, Placido **1**

Jarrett, Keith **1**
Mancini, Henry **1**
von Karajan, Herbert **1**
Zukerman, Pinchas **4**

Country
Acuff, Roy **2**
Alabama **1**
Auldridge, Mike **4**
Berry, Chuck **1**
Buffett, Jimmy **4**
Campbell, Glen **2**
The Carter Family **3**
Cash, Johnny **1**
Cash, Rosanne **2**
Charles, Ray **1**
Clark, Roy **1**
Coe, David Allan **4**
Cooder, Ry **2**
Cowboy Junkies **4**
Denver, John **1**
Desert Rose Band **4**
Dylan, Bob **3**
The Everly Brothers **2**
Flatt, Lester **3**
Ford, Tennessee Ernie **3**
Gayle, Crystal **1**
Griffith, Nanci **3**
Haggard, Merle **2**
Hall, Tom T. **4**
Harris, Emmylou **4**
Hartford, John **1**
Hay, George D. **3**
Healey, Jeff **4**
Highway 101 **4**
Jennings, Waylon **4**
Jones, George **4**
The Judds **2**
Kristofferson, Kris **4**
Lang, K.D. **4**
Lewis, Jerry Lee **2**
Little Feat **4**
Lynn, Loretta **2**
Mandrell, Barbara **4**
Miller, Roger **4**
Milsap, Ronnie **2**
Monroe, Bill **1**
Murray, Anne **4**
Myles, Alannah **4**
Nelson, Willie **1**
Oak Ridge Boys **4**
O'Connor, Mark **1**
Orbison, Roy **2**
Oslin, K.T. **3**
Owens, Buck **2**
Parton, Dolly **2**
Paul, Les **2**
Pearl, Minnie **3**
Presley, Elvis **1**
Pride, Charley **4**
Raitt, Bonnie **3**
Rich, Charlie **3**
Rodgers, Jimmie **3**
Rogers, Kenny **1**
Ronstadt, Linda **2**
Scruggs, Earl **3**
Tubb, Ernest **4**
Tucker, Tanya **3**
Watson, Doc **2**
Williams, Don **4**
Williams, Hank Jr. **1**
Williams, Hank Sr. **4**
Wynette, Tammy **2**
Yoakam, Dwight **1**

Country Jazz
Haggard, Merle **2**
The Judds **2**
Rich, Charlie **3**

Disco
Abdul, Paula **3**
The Bee Gees **3**
Fox, Samantha **3**
Richie, Lionel **2**
Stewart, Rod **2**

Dobro
Auldridge, Mike **4**
Burch, Curtis
    See New Grass Revival **4**
Knopfler, Mark **3**

Drums
See **Percussion**

Dulcimer
Ritchie, Jean **4**

Feminist Music
Near, Holly **1**

Fiddle
See **Violin**

Film Scores
Anka, Paul **2**
Bacharach, Burt **1**
Bernstein, Leonard **2**
Cafferty, John
    See the Beaver Brown Band **3**
Copland, Aaron **2**
Ellington, Duke **2**
Guaraldi, Vince **3**
Hamlisch, Marvin **1**
Harrison, George **2**
Hedges, Michael **3**
Jones, Quincy **2**
Knopfler, Mark **3**
Lennon, John
    See the Beatles **2**
Mancini, Henry **1**
McCartney, Paul
    See the Beatles **2**
Metheny, Pat **2**
Richie, Lionel **2**
Robertson, Robbie **2**
Waits, Tom **1**
Young, Neil **2**

Flamenco
de Lucia, Paco **1**

Flute
Galway, James **3**

Folk
Armatrading, Joan **4**
Baez, Joan **1**
The Carter Family **3**
Chapman, Tracy **4**
Childs, Toni **2**
Cohen, Leonard **3**
Collins, Judy **4**
Crosby, David **3**
Denver, John **1**
Dylan, Bob **3**
Galway, James **3**
Garfunkel, Art **4**
Griffith, Nanci **3**
Guthrie, Woodie **2**
Hartford, John **1**
Indigo Girls **3**
Lightfoot, Gordon **3**
Mitchell, Joni **2**
Morrison, Van **3**
Near, Holly **1**
O'Connor, Sinead **3**
Penn, Michael **4**

Peter, Paul & Mary **4**
Redpath, Jean **1**
Ritchie, Jean, **4**
Rodgers, Jimmie **3**
Rogers, Kenny **1**
Seals & Crofts **3**
Seeger, Pete **4**
Simon, Paul **1**
Snow, Pheobe **4**
Vega, Suzanne **3**
Watson, Doc **2**
Young, Neil **2**

Funk
Abdul, Paula **3**
Brown, Bobby **4**
Brown, James **2**
Jackson, Freddie **3**
Jackson, Janet **3**
James, Rick **2**
Reid, Vernon **2**
Richie, Lionel **2**
Sheila E. **3**

French Horn
Ohanian, David
   See Canadian Brass **4**

Fusion
Clarke, Stanley **3**
Davis, Miles **1**
Jarreau, Al **1**
Metheny, Pat **2**
O'Connor, Mark **1**
Summers, Andy **3**

Gospel
Brown, James **2**
The Carter Family **3**
Charles, Ray **1**
Cleveland, James **1**
Cooke, Sam **1**
Ford, Tennessee Ernie **3**
Dion **4**
Franklin, Aretha **2**
Knight, Gladys **1**
Little Richard **1**
Oak Ridge Boys **4**
Presley, Elvis **1**
Watson, Doc **2**
Williams, Deniece **1**

Guitar
Ackerman, Will **3**
Adams, Bryan **2**
Armatrading, Joan **4**
Auldridge, Mike **4**
  Also see the Seldom Scene **4**
Baez, Joan **1**
Barrere, Paul
   See Little Feat **4**
Barrett, (Roger) Syd
   See Pink Floyd **2**
Baxter, Jeff
   See the Doobie Brothers **3**
Beck, Jeff **4**
Berry, Chuck **1**
Bono
   See U2 **2**
Browne, Jackson **3**
Buck, Robert
   See 10,000 Maniacs **3**
Buffett, Jimmy **4**
Burch, Curtis
   See New Grass Revival **4**
Bush, Sam
   See New Grass Revival **4**
Byrne, David
   See Talking Heads **3**

Cafferty, John
   See the Beaver Brown Band **3**
Campbell, Ali
   See UB40 **4**
Campbell, Glen **2**
Campbell, Robin
   See UB40 **4**
Cash, Johnny **1**
Chapman, Tracy **4**
Clapton, Eric **1**
Clark, Roy **1**
Clark, Steve
   See Def Leppard **3**
Cohen, Leonard **3**
Collin, Phil
   See Def Leppard **3**
Collins, Albert **4**
Collins, Judy **4**
Cooder, Ry **2**
Cook, Jeff
   See Alabama **1**
Costello, Elvis **2**
Cougar, John(ny)
   See Mellencamp, John "Cougar" **2**
Croce, Jim **3**
Crofts, Dash
   See Seals & Crofts **3**
Crosby, David **3**
Dacus, Donnie
   See Chicago **3**
Daniels, Jack
   See Highway 101 **4**
de Lucia, Paco **1**
Denver, John **1**
Diamond, Neil **1**
Diddley, Bo **3**
Dion **4**
Dylan, Bob **3**
The Edge
   See U2 **2**
Etheridge, Melissa **4**
Everly, Don
   See the Everly Brothers **2**
Everly, Phil
   See the Everly Brothers **2**
Farriss, Tim
   See INXS **2**
Felder, Don
   See the Eagles **3**
Fisher, Roger
   See Heart **1**
Flatt, Lester **3**
Flynn, Pat
   See New Grass Revival **4**
Fogelberg, Dan **4**
Fogerty, John **2**
Fox, Oz
   See Stryper **2**
Frampton, Peter **3**
Frey, Glenn **3**
Garcia, Jerry **4**
Gaye, Marvin **4**
George, Lowell
   See Little Feat **4**
Gibb, Barry
   See the Bee Gees **3**
Gibb, Maurice
   See the Bee Gees **3**
Gibbons, Billy
   See ZZ Top **2**
Gilmour, David
   See Pink Floyd **2**
Gramolini, Gary
   See the Beaver Brown Band **3**
Grebenshikov, Boris **3**
Griffith, Nanci **3**
Guthrie, Woodie **2**
Guy, Buddy **4**

Hackett, Steve
   See Genesis **4**
Haggard, Merle **2**
Hall, Tom T. **4**
Harris, Emmylou **4**
Harrison, George **2**
Hartford, John **1**
Hartman, Bob
   See Petra **3**
Healey, Jeff **4**
Hedges, Michael **3**
Hendrix, Jimi **2**
Hidalgo, David
   See Los Lobos **2**
Hillman, Chris **4**
Holly, Buddy **1**
Hooker, John Lee **1**
Jardine, Al
   See the Beach Boys **1**
Jett, Joan **3**
Jennings, Waylon **4**
Johnston, Bruce
   See the Beach Boys **1**
Johnston, Tom
   See the Doobie Brothers **3**
Jones, Brian
   See the Rolling Stones **3**
Jones, George **4**
Jones, Mick
   See the Clash **4**
Jordan, Stanley **1**
Jorgensor, John
   See Desert Rose Band **4**
Kath, Terry
   See Chicago **3**
King, Albert **2**
King, B.B. **1**
Knopfler, Mark **3**
Krieger, Robert
   See the Doors **4**
Kristofferson, Kris **4**
Leadon, Bernie
   See the Eagles **3**
Leese, Howard
   See Heart **1**
Lennon, John
   See the Beatles **2**
Lennon, Julian **2**
Lightfoot, Gordon **1**
Lindley, David **2**
Llanas, Sammy
   See BoDeans **3**
Lozano, Conrad
   See Los Lobos **2**
MacDonald, Barbara
   See Timbuk 3 **3**
MacDonald, Pat
   See Timbuk 3 **3**
Mandrell, Barbara **4**
Maness, J.D.
   See Desert Rose Band **4**
Marley, Bob **3**
Marley, Ziggy **3**
Marr, Johnny
   See the Smiths **3**
Mars, Mick
   See Mötley Crüe **1**
Marx, Richard **3**
McCartney, Paul **4**
   Also see the Beatles **2**
Mellencamp, John "Cougar"
  2
Metheny, Pat **2**
Miller, Roger **4**
Miller, Steve **2**
Mitchell, Joni **2**
Montgomery, Wes **3**
Nelson, Rick **2**
Nelson, Willie **1**

Neville, Art
    See the Neville Brothers **4**
O'Donnell, Roger
    See The Cure **3**
Osmond, Donny **3**
Payne, Bill
    See Little Feat **4**
Pierson, Kate
    See B-52s **4**
Rhodes, Nick
    See Duran Duran **4**
Schneider, Fred III
    See B-52s **4**
Taylor, Andy
    See Duran Duran **4**
Thompson, Porl
    See The Cure **3**
Tolhurst, Laurence
    See The Cure **3**
Virtue, Michael
    See UB40 **4**
Wilson, Brian
    See the Beach Boys **1**
Winwood, Steve **2**
Wonder, Stevie **2**
Wood, Danny
    See New Kids on the Block **3**
Wright, Rick
    See Pink Floyd **2**

Latin Music
Blades, Ruben **2**
Estefan, Gloria **2**
Iglesias, Julio **2**
Jackson, Joe **4**
Los Lobos **2**
Ronstadt, Linda **2**
Santana, Carlos **1**

Mandolin
Bush, Sam
    See New Grass Revival **4**
Crofts, Dash
    See Seals & Crofts **3**
Duffey, John
    See the Seldom Scene **4**
Hartford, John **1**
Lindley, David **2**
Monroe, Bill **1**
Rosas, Cesar **2**
Seals, Jim
    See Seals & Crofts **3**

Minimalism
Glass, Philip **1**

Musical comedy
Pearl, Minnie **3**

Musicals
Andrews, Julie **4**
Bacharach, Burt **1**
Buckley, Betty **1**
Crawford, Michael **4**
Curry, Tim **3**
Davis, Sammy Jr. **4**
Hamlisch, Marvin **1**
Patinkin, Mandy **3**

Music Publishers
Acuff, Roy **2**

New Age
Ackerman, Will **3**
Davis, Chip **4**
Hedges, Michael **3**
Jarre, Jean-Michel **2**
Kitaro **1**
Story, Liz **2**
Summers, Andy **3**

New Wave
B-52s **4**
Talking Heads **1**
Costello, Elvis **2**

Nortena
Los Lobos **2**

Opera
Cotrubas, Ileana **1**
Curry, Tim **3**
Domingo, Placido **1**
Pavarotti, Luciano **1**
Te Kanawa, Kiri **2**
von Karajan, Herbert **1**

Percussion
Adler, Steven
    See Guns n' Roses **2**
Allen, Rick
    See Def Leppard **3**
Augustyniak, Jerry
    See 10,000 Maniacs **3**
Beard, Frank
    See ZZ Top **2**
Best, Pete
    See the Beatles **2**
Bonham, John
    See Led Zeppelin **1**
Brown, Jimmy
    See UB40 **4**
Buck, Mike
    See the Fabulous Thunderbirds **1**
Chimes, Terry
    See the Clash **4**
Christina, Fran
    See the Fabulous Thunderbirds **1**
Clayton, Sam
    See Little Feat **4**
Collins, Phil **2**
    Also see Genesis **4**
Crofts, Dash
    See Seals & Crofts **3**
Davis, Chip **4**
Densmore, John
    See the Doors **4**
De Oliveria, Laudir
    See Chicago **3**
Derosier, Michael
    See Heart **1**
Duncan, Steve
    See Desert Rose Band **4**
Farriss, Jon
    See INXS **2**
Frantz, Chris
    See Talking Heads **1**
Gallup, Simon
    See The Cure **3**
Green, Willie
    See the Neville Brothers **4**
Hartman, John
    See the Doobie Brothers **3**
Hassan, Norman
    See UB40 **4**
Hayward, Richard
    See Little Feat **4**
Headon, Topper
    See the Clash **4**
Henley, Don **3**
Herndon, Mark
    See Alabama **1**
Hoffman, Guy
    See BoDeans **3**
Hossack, Michael
    See the Doobie Brothers **3**
Jones, Kenny
    See the Who **3**
Joyce, Mike
    See the Smiths **3**

Knudsen, Keith
    See the Doobie Brothers **3**
Kramer, Joey
    See Aerosmith **3**
Lee, Tommy
    See Mötley Crüe **1**
Lewis, Otis
    See the Fabulous Thunderbirds **1**
Mason, Nick
    See Pink Floyd **2**
McCracken, Chet
    See the Doobie Brothers **3**
Moon, Keith
    See the Who **3**
Moser, Cactus (Scott)
    See Highway 101 **4**
Mullen, Larry
    See U2 **2**
Neville, Cyril
    See the Neville Brothers **4**
Perez, Louie
    See Los Lobos **2**
Rudd, Phil
    See AC/DC **4**
Seraphine, Daniel
    See Chicago **3**
Sheila E. **3**
Silva, Kenny Jo
    See the Beaver Brown Band
        3
Starr, Ringo
    See the Beatles **2**
Strickland, Keith
    See B-52s **4**
Sweet, Robert
    See Stryper **2**
Taylor, Roger
    See Duran Duran **4**
Timmins, Peter
    See Cowboy Junkies **4**
Watts, Charlie
    See the Rolling Stones **3**
Weaver, Louie
    See Petra **3**
Williams, Boris
    See The Cure **3**
Wilson, Cindy
    See B-52s **4**
Wilson, Dennis
    See the Beach Boys **1**
Wright, Simon
    See AC/DC **4**

Performance Art
Anderson, Laurie **1**

Piano
Arrau, Claudio **1**
Bacharach, Burt **1**
Basie, Count **2**
Browne, Jackson **3**
Bush, Kate **4**
Charles, Ray **1**
Clayderman, Richard **1**
Cleveland, James **1**
Cole, Nat King **3**
Collins, Judy **4**
Collins, Phil **2**
    Also see Genesis **4**
Connick, Harry Jr. **4**
Cotoia, Robert
    See the Beaver Brown Band **3**
Crofts, Dash
    See Seals & Crofts **3**
Domino, Fats
Drew, Dennis
    See 10,000 Maniacs **3**
Ellington, Duke **2**
Frey, Glenn **3**

Gaye, Marvin **4**
Gibb, Maurice
   See the Bee Gees **3**
Glass, Philip **1**
Guaraldi, Vince **3**
Hamlisch, Marvin **1**
Hornsby, Bruce **3**
Horowitz, Vladimir **1**
Jackson, Joe **4**
Jarrett, Keith **1**
Joel, Billy **2**
John, Elton **3**
Lamm, Robert
   See Chicago **3**
Lennon, John
   See the Beatles **2**
Lewis, Jerry Lee **2**
Little Richard **1**
Manilow, Barry **2**
McCartney, Paul **4**
   Also see the Beatles **2**
McDonald, Michael
   See the Doobie Brothers **3**
Milsap, Ronnie **2**
Mitchell, Joni **2**
Newman, Randy **4**
Payne, Bill
   See Little Feat **4**
Rich, Charlie **3**
Sedaka, Neil **4**
Simon, Carly **4**
Solal, Martial **4**
Stevens, Cat **3**
Stewart, Ian
   See the Rolling Stones **3**
Story, Liz **2**
Waits, Tom **1**
Winwood, Steve **2**
Wonder, Stevie **2**
Wright, Rick
   See Pink Floyd **2**

Piccolo
Galway, James **3**

Pop
Abdul, Paula **3**
Adams, Bryan **2**
Aerosmith **3**
Armatrading, Joan **4**
Armstrong, Louis **4**
B-52s **4**
Bacharach, Burt **1**
The Beach Boys **1**
The Beatles **2**
The Beaver Brown Band **3**
The Bee Gees **3**
Bennett, Tony **2**
Berry, Chuck **1**
The Blues Brothers **3**
BoDeans **3**
Bolton, Michael **4**
Bowie, David **1**
Branigan, Laura **2**
Brickell, Edie **3**
Brown, Bobby **4**
Browne, Jackson **3**
Buffett, Jimmy **4**
Campbell, Glen **2**
Carnes, Kim **4**
Cash, Johnny **1**
Chapman, Tracy **4**
Charles, Ray **1**
Cher **1**
Cherry, Neneh **4**
Chicago **3**
Clapton, Eric **1**
Clark, Dick **2**
Clark, Roy **1**

Clayderman, Richard **1**
Cocker, Joe **4**
Cohen, Leonard **3**
Cole, Nat King **3**
Cole, Natalie **1**
Collins, Judy **4**
Collins, Phil **2**
Connick, Harry Jr. **4**
Cooder, Ry **2**
Cooke, Sam **1**
Costello, Elvis **2**
Croce, Jim **3**
Crosby, David **3**
Daltrey, Roger **3**
   Also see The Who **3**
D'Arby, Terence Trent **3**
Darin, Bobby **4**
Davis, Sammy Jr. **4**
Dayne, Taylor **4**
Denver, John **1**
Diamond, Neil **1**
Dion **4**
Domino, Fats **2**
The Doobie Brothers **3**
The Doors **4**
Duran Duran **4**
Dylan, Bob **3**
The Eagles **3**
Easton, Sheena **2**
Estefan, Gloria **2**
The Everly Brothers **2**
Exposé **4**
Ferry, Bryan **1**
Fitzgerald, Ella **1**
Fogelberg, Dan **4**
Ford, Tennessee Ernie **3**
Fox, Samantha **3**
Frampton, Peter **3**
Franklin, Aretha **2**
Frey, Glenn **3**
   Also see the Eagles **3**
Galway, James **3**
Garfunkel, Art **4**
Gaye, Marvin **4**
Gayle, Crystal **1**
Genesis **4**
Gibson, Debbie **1**
Gift, Roland **3**
Goodman, Benny **4**
Grebenshikov, Boris **3**
Griffith, Nanci **3**
Harris, Emmylou **4**
Harrison, George **2**
   Also see the Beatles **2**
Harry, Deborah **4**
Hartford, John **1**
Healey, Jeff **4**
Henley, Don **3**
   Also see the Eagles **3**
Holly, Buddy **1**
Hornsby, Bruce **3**
Idol, Billy **3**
Iglesias, Julio **2**
Indigo Girls **3**
Jackson, Janet **3**
Jackson, Joe **4**
Jackson, Michael **1**
James, Rick **2**
Jarreau, Al **1**
Joel, Billy **2**
John, Elton **3**
Jones, Rickie Lee **4**
Jones, Quincy **2**
Joplin, Janis **3**
Knight, Gladys **1**
Knopfler, Mark **3**
Kristofferson, Kris **4**
Lennon, Julian **2**
Lightfoot, Gordon **3**

Lindley, David **2**
Little Richard **1**
Loggins, Kenny **3**
Madonna **4**
Mancini, Henry **1**
Manilow, Barry **2**
Marley, Bob **3**
Marley, Ziggy **3**
Marx, Richard **3**
Mathis, Johnny **2**
Martin, Dean **1**
McCartney, Paul **4**
   Also see the Beatles **2**
McFerrin, Bobby **3**
Medley, Bill **3**
Miller, Roger **4**
Milli Vanilli **4**
Mitchell, Joni **2**
Morrison, Jim **3**
Morrison, Van **3**
Murray, Anne **4**
Myles, Alannah **4**
Nelson, Willie **1**
The Neville Brothers **4**
New Kids on the Block **3**
Newman, Randy **4**
Newton, Wayne **2**
Nicks, Stevie **2**
Ocean, Billy **4**
O'Connor, Sinead **3**
Osmond, Donny **3**
Page, Jimmy **4**
   Also see Led Zeppelin **1**
Parton, Dolly **2**
Paul, Les **2**
Pavarotti, Luciano **1**
Pendergrass, Teddy **3**
Penn, Michael **4**
Peter, Paul & Mary **4**
Plant, Robert **2**
   Also see Led Zeppelin **1**
Presley, Elvis **1**
Prince **1**
Raitt, Bonnie **3**
Reeves, Martha **4**
Richie, Lionel **2**
Robinson, Smokey **1**
Rogers, Kenny **1**
Rolling Stones **3**
Ronstadt, Linda **2**
Ross, Diana **1**
Roth, David Lee **1**
Sade **2**
Sanborn, David **1**
Seals & Crofts **3**
Sedaka, Neil **4**
Sheila E. **3**
Simon, Carly **4**
Simon, Paul **1**
Sinatra, Frank **1**
Snow, Pheobe **4**
Spector, Phil **4**
Stevens, Cat **3**
Stewart, Rod **2**
Sting **2**
Streisand, Barbra **2**
Taylor, James **2**
The Temptations **3**
Tiffany **4**
Timbuk 3 **3**
Torme, Mel **4**
Townshend, Pete **1**
   Also see The Who **3**
Turner, Tina **1**
Vandross, Luther **2**
Vega, Suzanne **3**
Warnes, Jennifer **3**
Warwick, Dionne **2**
The Who **3**

Lamm, Robert
  See Chicago **3**
Lang, K.D. **4**
Leadon, Bernie
  See the Eagles **3**
LeBon, Simon
  See Duran Duran **4**
Lennon, John
  See the Beatles **2**
Lennon, Julian **2**
Levene, Keith
  See the Clash **4**
Lightfoot, Gordon **3**
Little Richard **1**
Llanas, Sammy
  See BoDeans **3**
Loggins, Kenny **3**
Loughnane, Lee
  See Chicago **3**
Lynn, Loretta **2**
MacDonald, Barbara
  See Timbuk 3 **3**
MacDonald, Pat
  See Timbuk 3 **3**
Madonna **4**
Manilow, Barry **2**
Manzarek, Ray
  See the Doors **4**
Marley, Bob **3**
Marley, Ziggy **3**
Marx, Richard **3**
McCartney, Paul **4**
  Also see the Beatles **2**
McDonald, Michael
  See the Doobie Brothers **3**
Medley, Bill **3**
Miller, Roger **4**
Meisner, Randy
  See the Eagles **3**
Mellencamp, John "Cougar" **2**
Merchant, Natalie
  See 10,000 Maniacs **3**
Miller, Steve **2**
Milsap, Ronnie **2**
Mitchell, Joni **2**
Morrison, Jim **3**
Morrison, Van **3**
Mullen, Larry
  See U2 **2**
Myles, Alannah **4**
Near, Holly **1**
Nelson, Rick **2**
Nelson, Willie **1**
Neville, Art
  See the Neville Brothers **4**
Newman, Randy **4**
Newmann, Kurt
  See BoDeans **3**
Nicks, Stevie **2**
Nugent, Ted **2**
Ocean, Billy **4**
O'Connor, Sinead **3**
Orbison, Roy **2**
Osbourne, Ozzy **3**
Oslin, K.T. **3**
Owens, Buck **2**
Page, Jimmy **4**
  Also see Led Zeppelin **1**
Palmer, Robert **2**
Pankow, James
  See Chicago **3**
Parton, Dolly **2**
Paul, Les **2**
Pedersen, Herb
  See Desert Rose Band **4**
Penn, Michael **4**
Perez, Louie
  See Los Lobos **2**

Perry, Joe
  See Aerosmith **3**
Pierson, Kate
  See B-52s **4**
Plant, Robert **2**
  Also see Led Zeppelin **1**
Pop, Iggy **1**
Presley, Elvis **1**
Prince **1**
Raitt, Bonnie **3**
Ray, Amy
  See Indigo Girls **3**
Reed, Lou **1**
Reid, Vernon **2**
Rhodes, Nick
  See Duran Duran **4**
Rich, Charlie **3**
Richard, Keith
  See the Rolling Stones **3**
Richie, Lionel **2**
Ritchie, Jean **4**
Robertson, Robbie **2**
Robillard, Duke **2**
Robinson, Smokey **1**
Rodgers, Jimmie **3**
Roth, David Lee **1**
Rutherford, Mike
  See Genesis **4**
Sade **2**
Saliers, Emily
  See Indigo Girls **3**
Satriani, Joe **4**
Schmit, Timothy B.
  See the Eagles **3**
Schneider, Fred III
  See B-52s **4**
Scott, Bon (Ronald Belford)
  See AC/DC **4**
Scruggs, Earl **3**
Seals, Jim
  See Seals & Crofts **3**
Sedaka, Neil **4**
Seeger, Pete **4**
Seraphine, Daniel
  See Chicago **3**
Sheila E. **3**
Shocked, Michelle **4**
Simmons, Patrick
  See the Doobie Brothers **3**
Simon, Carly **4**
Simon, Paul **1**
Simonon, Paul
  See the Clash **4**
Smith, Patti **1**
Smith, Robert
  See The Cure **3**
Spector, Phil **4**
Starr, Ringo
  See the Beatles **2**
Stevens, Cat **3**
Stewart, Rod **2**
Sting **2**
Stookey, Paul
  See Peter, Paul & Mary **4**
Streisand, Barbra **2**
Strickland, Keith
  See B-52s **4**
Strummer, Joe
  See the Clash **4**
Summers, Andy **3**
Taylor, Andy
  See Duran Duran **4**
Taylor, James **2**
Taylor, John
  See Duran Duran **4**
Taylor, Mick
  See the Rolling Stones **3**
Timmins, Margo
  See Cowboy Junkies **4**

Timmins, Michael
  See Cowboy Junkies **4**
Tone-Lōc **3**
Torme, Mel **4**
Tosh, Peter **3**
Townshend, Pete **1**
  Also see The Who **3**
Travers, Mary
  See Peter, Paul & Mary **4**
Tubb, Ernest **4**
Tyler, Steve
  See Aerosmith **3**
Vandross, Luther **2**
Vega, Suzanne **3**
Vox, Bono
  See U2 **2**
Waits, Tom **1**
Walsh, Joe
  See the Eagles **3**
Waters, Muddy **4**
Waters, Roger
  See Pink Floyd **2**
Watts, Charlie
  See the Rolling Stones
  3
Williams, Deniece **1**
Williams, Don **4**
Williams, Hank Jr. **1**
Williams, Hank Sr. **4**
Willis, Pete
  See Def Leppard **3**
Wilson, Brian
  See the Beach Boys **1**
Wilson, Cindy
  See B-52s **4**
Wilson, Ricky
  See B-52s **4**
Winwood, Steve **2**
Wonder, Stevie **2**
Wood, Ron
  See the Rolling Stones
  3
Wyman, Bill
  See the Rolling Stones
  3
Wynette, Tammy **2**
Yarrow, Peter
  See Peter, Paul & Mary **4**
Yoakam, Dwight **1**
Young, Angus
  See AC/DC **4**
Young, Malcolm
  See AC/DC **4**
Young, Neil **2**
Zappa, Frank **1**

Soul
The Blues Brothers **3**
Bolton, Michael **4**
Brown, James **2**
Charles, Ray **1**
Cooke, Sam **1**
Franklin, Aretha **2**
Gaye, Marvin **4**
Jackson, Freddie **3**
Knight, Gladys **1**
Little Richard **1**
Medley, Bill **3**
Morrison, Van **3**
The Neville Brothers **4**
Pendergrass, Teddy **3**
Reeves, Martha **4**
Reid, Vernon **2**
Robinson, Smokey **1**
Ross, Diana **2**
The Temptations **3**
Vandross, Luther **2**
Wilson, Jackie **3**
Wonder, Stevie **2**

Musicians Index

Volume numbers appear in **bold.**

Travers, Brian
    See UB40
Travers, Mary
    See Peter, Paul & Mary
Tubb, Ernest **4**
Tucker, Tanya **3**
Turner, Tina **1**
Tyler, Steve
    See Aerosmith
Tyson, Ron
    See the Temptations
UB40 **4**
U2 **2**
Vandross, Luther **2**
Vaughan, Jimmie
    See the Fabulous Thunderbirds
Vaughan, Sarah **2**
Vaughan, Stevie Ray **1**
Vega, Suzanne **3**
Virtue, Michael
    See UB40
Volz, Greg
    See Petra
von Karajan, Herbert **1**
Vox, Bono
    See U2
Wahlberg, Donnie
    See New Kids on the Block
Waits, Tom **1**
Walker, Ebo
    See New Grass Revival
Walsh, Joe
    See the Eagles
Warnes, Jennifer **3**
Warwick, Dionne **2**
Waters, Muddy **4**
Waters, Roger
    See Pink Floyd

Watson, Doc **2**
Watts, Charlie
    See the Rolling Stones
Watts, Eugene
    See Canadian Brass
Weaver, Louie
    See Petra
Weymouth, Tina
    See Talking Heads
Whitford, Brad
    See Aerosmith
The Who **3**
    Also see Daltrey, Roger
    Also see Townshend, Pete
Williams, Andy **2**
Williams, Boris
    See The Cure
Williams, Cliff
    See AC/DC
Williams, Deniece **1**
Williams, Don **4**
Williams, Hank Jr. **1**
Williams, Hank, Sr.
        4
Williams, Otis
    See the Temptations
Williams, Paul
    See the Temptations
Willis, Pete
    See Def Leppard
Wilson, Anne
    See Heart
Wilson, Brian
    See the Beach Boys
Wilson, Carl
    See the Beach Boys
Wilson, Cindy
    See B-52s

Wilson, Dennis
    See the Beach Boys
Wilson, Jackie **3**
Wilson, Kim
    See the Fabulous Thunderbirds
Wilson, Nancy
    See Heart
Wilson, Ricky
    See B-52s
Winwood, Steve **2**
Wonder, Stevie **2**
Wood, Danny
    See New Kids on the Block
Wood, Ron
    See the Rolling Stones
Woodson, Ollie
    See the Temptations
Wright, Rick
    See Pink Floyd
Wright, Simon
    See AC/DC
Wyman, Bill
    See the Rolling Stones
Wynette, Tammy **2**
Yamashita, Kazuhito **4**
Yarrow, Peter
    See Peter, Paul & Mary
Yoakam, Dwight **1**
Young, Angus
    See AC/DC
Young, Malcolm
    See AC/DC
Young M.C. **4**
Young, Neil **2**
Zappa, Frank **1**
Zukerman, Pinchas **4**
ZZ Top **2**